LEGAL INSANITY AND THE BRAIN

This landmark publication offers a unique comparative and interdisciplinary study of criminal insanity and neuroscience. Criminal law theories and ideologies which underpin the regulation of criminal insanity have always been the subject of controversy. The history of criminal insanity is characterised by conceptual and empirical tension between two disciplinary realms: the law and the mind sciences. The authors in this anthology explore in depth the state of the art of legal insanity and the numerous intricate, fascinating, pioneering and sophisticated questions raised by the integration of different criminal law and behaviour theories, diverse disciplines and methodologies, in a genuinely interdisciplinary perspective. This volume will serve as a practical guide for the comparative legal scholar and the judge, as well as stimulating scholarly reading for the neuroscientist, the social scientist and the philosopher with interdisciplinary scientific interests.

Legal Insanity and the Brain

Science, Law and European Courts

With a Foreword by Justice András Sajó,
Vice-President of the European Court of Human Rights

Edited by
Sofia Moratti and Dennis Patterson

•HART•
OXFORD • LONDON • NEW YORK • NEW DELHI • SYDNEY

HART PUBLISHING
Bloomsbury Publishing Plc
Kemp House, Chawley Park, Cumnor Hill, Oxford, OX2 9PH, UK

HART PUBLISHING, the Hart/Stag logo, BLOOMSBURY and the Diana logo are
trademarks of Bloomsbury Publishing Plc
First published in Great Britain 2016

First published in hardback, 2016
Paperback edition, 2019

A catalogue record for this book is available from the British Library.

Library of Congress Cataloging-in-Publication Data

Names: Moratti, Sofia, editor. | Patterson, Dennis (Law teacher) editor.
Title: Legal insanity and the brain : science, law and European courts / With a Foreword by Justice András Sajó,
Vice-President of the European Court of Human Rights ; Edited by Sofia Moratti and Dennis Patterson.
Description: Portland, Oregon : Hart Publishing, 2016. | Includes bibliographical references and index.
Identifers:L CCN 2016019861 (print) | QCN 2016020002 (ebook)| ISBN 9781849467919
(hardback : alk. paper) | ISBN 9781509902330 (Epub)
Subjects: ICSH: insanity (Law)—Europe. | Neurosciences. | Criminal psychology—Europe. | Forensic
psychology—Europe. | Mentally ill offenders—Legal status, laws, etc.—Europe. | Science and law—Europe.
Classifcation:L CC KJC8132 .L44 2016 (print) | QC KJC8132 (ebook) | DD 345.4/04—dc23
LC record available at https://lccn.loc.gov/2016019861

ISBN: HB: 978-1-84946-791-9
PB: 978-1-50992-754-8
ePDF: 978-1-50990-232-3
ePub: 978-1-50990-233-0

Typeset by Compuscript Ltd, Shannon

To find out more about our authors and books visit www.hartpublishing.co.uk. Here you will find
extracts, author information, details of forthcoming events and the option to sign up for our
newsletters.

FOREWORD

JUSTICE ANDRÁS SAJÓ,
VICE-PRESIDENT OF THE EUROPEAN COURT OF HUMAN RIGHTS

More than 10 years ago, the late Lord Tom Bingham wrote a Preface to the 'Law and the Brain' special issue of the *Philosophical Transactions of the Royal Society*. In his welcoming piece, he quoted a metaphor used in that same issue by Good-enough and Prehn:

> [O]ne could develop a useful science of automobiles without ever opening up the hood or bonnet of a car, but it would rely on explanations such as 'the car's desire to move inspires its motive force'. With the engine exposed, a much more complete explanation is possible.[1]

In 2004 it was already clear that the law would be challenged and perhaps helped by neuroscience in a variety of areas, including the criminal law and particularly its principal concept, criminal responsibility. Neuroscience seemed to have the potential to challenge the fundamental assumption of human 'free will', which certain criminal law theories treat as the foundation for holding individuals accountable for criminal conduct. One could argue that frontier research in neuroscience is but the latest pretext to revive the time-honoured criminal law and moral philosophy debate on determinism and human agency. However, the present volume demonstrates that this objection is often unfounded.

The present volume focuses on the defence of insanity in light of state-of-the-art neuroscience. Neuroscience-based forensic evidence is now slowly finding its way into the mainstream courtroom evidentiary arsenal, at least in some countries, although serious issues of reliability persist. This development is constrained not only by the limited reliability of the neuroscientific evidence produced, but also by the costs of gathering it. Neuroscience can be a powerful tool in court. That is undeniable. There is, however, an unfortunate temptation to interpret and use neuroscientific evidence in court in disregard of the character and meaning of the available data produced by scientific research in the cognitive neuroscience of intention and agency. This may be the consequence of the psychological and emotional power of the pictures of the brain on the minds of adjudicators, although

---

[1] (2004) 359 *Philosophical Transactions of the Royal Society B* 1659.

this hypothesis is controversial.[2] Most likely, neuroscientific evidence involving imaging is more effective than traditional, not image-based clinical psychological evidence in persuading jurors that the defendant's disorder did affect his capacity to control his actions. Concerns about the form of neuroscientific evidence presentation in the courtroom should not be confused with questions pertaining to the admission of neuroscientific evidence as such. The regulation of admission of neuroscientific evidence may well be analogous to that of traditional clinical psychological evidence; admission in court remains a matter of legal choice.

It is only in an interaction between law and neuroscience that an adequate procedural approach can be developed, one that takes into consideration the specificities of each particular legal system. For example, the handling of evidence to be submitted to a jury often raises concerns, which do not apply when the case is adjudicated by professional judges. Evidentiary rules, however, cannot be applied within a given procedural context without the proper understanding of the nature, as opposed to the form, of neuroscientific evidence. *Mutatis mutandis*, the same could apply to neuroscience-informed criminal policy in the future.

The authors of the present volume extend their analysis well beyond the impact of neuroscientific evidence in criminal processes. Their analysis concerns the fundamental issue of 'proving' insanity for the purposes of criminal sentencing. In a modest but most appropriate way, most studies in this volume contextualise the issue. The authors describe whether and how, at the present time, neuroscientific evidence to substantiate insanity pleas is accepted in their respective national legal systems. I think this anchoring in national substantive and procedural law is an appropriate methodological choice. It reflects a paradigm that has a long-term relevance, and will remain relevant as evidence based on neuroscience becomes increasingly reliable. If the validity and explanatory power of neuroscience increases and science offers a deterministic explanation of individual behaviour, some fundamental legal choices will have to be made, based on socially shared values and interests. The use of neuroscientific information concerning the mind and behaviour of the individual, and even the level of reliability of acceptable information, are likely to be regulated based on standards of fairness and human rights. If that does not happen, they may be influenced by concerns not related to science, for example the wish for security. In a hypothetical dystopian world, which may serve as a theoretical, conceptual model to assess the potential impact of the legal application of neuroscience, the desire for security (interpreted as total political control) would make the use of biometric identifiers legitimate. Such a system would presuppose the collection of relevant personal data from all citizens; for example, a governmental collection of DNA samples from all citizens. Likewise, a neuroscience-based prediction of social dangerousness applicable to all citizens will only become possible if the social demand to prevent crime and

---

[2] See NJ Schweitzer, MJ Saks, ER Murphy, AL Roskies, W Sinnott-Armstrong and LM Gaudet, 'Neuroimages as Evidence in a *Mens Rea* Defense: No impact' (2011) 17 *Psychology, Public Policy, and Law* 357–93.

antisocial behaviour is powerful enough to overrule fundamental contemporary legal principles and the rule of law.

Also the standards of scientific reliability ultimately depend on social and legal values, and not on the acceptable error rate in the relevant scientific community. A risk-averse society will be ready to accept a higher scientific error rate for purposes of neuroscience-based crime prevention policies. The quantification of the 'acceptable error rate' for policy purposes remains a matter of social choice, and it is to an extent irrespective of the accepted error rate in the relevant scientific or expert community. A security-driven society may conclude that preventive intervention on the basis of brain scans is acceptable, even where the science indicates, for instance, a 1 per cent error rate, meaning that one person in 100 undergoing 'preventive' interventions would in fact have no 'criminal predisposition' at all.[3] These are traditional criminal justice dilemmas, in a new perspective. In his discussion of lie detection in the courtroom, Frederick Schauer has argued that, irrespective of the current poor reliability of lie detectors from a science perspective, a general rule applies: it is not scientific standards that should determine when these methods are ready for legal use, but rather legal standards.[4]

One other long-standing controversy that may receive new vigour from the increasing use of neuroscience in court is the placement of defendants ruled 'criminally insane'. In some criminal justice systems, the 'criminally insane' reside in a mental care institution with other psychiatric patients. In other jurisdictions, they are deprived of personal liberty and reside in a penitentiary. The fundamental human rights and rule of law problem currently is, for how long are they going to remain deprived of their liberty? Further, assuming that the detention, possibly in a mental care institution, results from a conviction, is it appropriate to extend the detention on grounds of insanity, or more precisely, on grounds of the danger to others resulting from the insanity? These are and will most likely remain genuine legal issues, even if our capacity to diagnose mental pathologies and predict behaviour improves thanks to advances in neuroscience.

There are more questions that remain matters of legal discretion, to be decided upon in interaction between neuroscientists (and other scientists), the legal community, and the general public. One such question invests the boundaries between tolerable deviance from socially accepted behavioural standards and criminally relevant behaviour. When does defiance and non-compliance become criminally relevant? And, more germane to the specific problem discussed in the present volume: who is to be considered insane? The latter remains a matter of normative consensus. Brain scientists will be able to detect with increasing certainty when particular aspects of the functioning of the neural system are statistically different from what is understood as statistically normal. At which point is this functional

---

[3] The intervention may be of a medical or even a criminal justice nature, such as preventive detention. This was to an extent the ideology driving the 'social defense' movement in the 1930s.

[4] F Schauer, 'Neuroscience, Lie-detection, and the Law' (2010) 14 *Trends in Cognitive Sciences* 101–03.

difference sufficient to conclude that the person is 'insane'? How large a departure from the 'normal' is needed to establish 'insanity'? This cannot be considered an exclusively scientific question.

This volume reminds its readers that the rapidly changing knowledge emerging from neuroscience offers opportunities and challenges to the criminal law, in particular in the context of insanity assessments. This may have implications on the ongoing rethinking of the concept and defence of insanity. Irrespective of the inclusion of neuroscience-based insanity evidence into individual legal systems (which are not equally disposed to such accommodation), the knowledge produced by neuroscience will continue to be an inspiration in the ongoing reflection on, and related reforms of, criminal responsibility.

SUMMARY CONTENTS

DETAILED CONTENTS

LIST OF CONTRIBUTORS

Editors

Sofia Moratti is Senior Research Fellow at the Department of Law of the European University Institute in Florence, Italy. She graduated in law with distinction from the University of Pavia, Italy. She received a PhD in legal theory from the University of Groningen, the Netherlands. Sofia has published extensively in different languages on a wide array of subjects, including law and neuroscience and neuroethics. She has been a Max Weber Fellow at the EUI, where she taught and organised international, interdisciplinary conferences in law and neuroscience.

Dennis Patterson is Professor of Legal Theory and Legal Philosophy at the European University Institute in Florence, Italy. He is also Professor of Jurisprudence and International Trade Law at Swansea University, School of Law, Wales, UK and Board of Governors Professor of Law and Philosophy at Rutgers University, School of Law, Camden, New Jersey, US. Dennis has been awarded senior research grants from the Fulbright Commission, Humboldt Stiftung and the American Council of Learned Societies. He has been a visiting professor at the universities of Berlin, Vienna, Texas and Georgetown. His most recent books are *Minds, Brains and Law* (2013) and the edited volume *Philosophical Foundations of Law and Neuroscience* (in press), both joint works with Michael Pardo and published by Oxford University Press.

Contributors

Tova Bennet is graduate researcher in criminal law at Lund University, Sweden. Her research focuses on the prerequisites for the attribution of criminal responsibility, and includes a study of court verdicts and forensic psychiatric expert opinions. She has published work on the attribution of criminal responsibility in Sweden, on medical expert opinions in international criminal law and on criminal responsibility and delusions.

Barbara Bottalico is a licensed lawyer in Italy. She graduated in law with distinction from the University of Pavia, Italy. Barbara received a PhD in comparative and European legal studies from the University of Trento, Italy. Barbara has been teaching and carrying out research in law and neuroscience at the European Centre for Law, Science and New Technologies (ECLT) of the University of Pavia and at the Faculty of Law of the University of Milan. She has published numerous works in law and neuroscience. Barbara has held a Max Weber Fellowship at the European University Institute.

Paul Catley is Head of the Open University Law School. The Open University Law School is the largest provider of undergraduate legal education in the United Kingdom with over 6,000 undergraduate law students. Paul is on the Steering Committee of the European Association for Neuroscience and Law and a member of the International Neuroethics Society. He has taught at the International Postgraduate Winter School in Law and Neuroscience at the University of Pavia, Italy since 2012. Paul has published several contributions in law and neuroscience. He is involved in a large project with colleagues in the US, Canada, Singapore and the Netherlands to investigate the use of neuroscientific evidence by defendants in criminal trials between 2005 and 2012 in five jurisdictions. Preliminary findings have been published in the *Journal of Law and the Biosciences*.

Lisa Claydon is Senior Lecturer in Law at the Open University and a Senior Honorary Research Fellow at the University of Manchester, UK. Lisa served on the Royal Society Working Group investigating neuroscience and the law. She is Secretary to the European Association for Neuroscience and Law and a programme committee member of the International Neuroethics Society. In 2014 Lisa was granted funding by the Arts and Humanities Research Council to carry out together with Professor Patrick Haggard, Deputy Director of the Institute of Cognitive Neuroscience at University College London, a research project entitled: *Sense of Agency and Responsibility: Integrating Legal and Neurocognitive Accounts.*

Rafael Encinas de Muñagorri is Professor of Law at the University of Nantes, France, and Director of the French Network of Law, Sciences and Technologies (RDST). He has been a visiting research scholar at the Department of History of Science of Harvard University. His main research interests include expertise and legal evidence, legal responsibility, and law and cognitive sciences. Recently, he has published extensively on the role of expertise in different settings. He is the editor of *Expertise et Gouvernance du Changement Climatique*, published in 2009 by Librairie Générale de Droit et de Jurisprudence (LGDJ).

Katrien Hanoulle holds an MA in law and a degree in criminological sciences from the University of Leuven, Belgium (KU Leuven). She has been a teaching and research assistant at KU Leuven Institute of Criminal Law since 2008. Katrien is currently conducting her doctoral research under the supervision of Frank Verbruggen. She is developing suggestions for legal change, to make the approach to mentally disordered offenders in the Belgian jurisdictions more compliant with fundamental human rights.

Michael Koenigs is Associate Professor in the Department of Psychiatry at the University of Wisconsin-Madison, US. He received a BS in neurobiology from the University of Wisconsin-Madison and a PhD in neuroscience from the University of Iowa. Michael completed a postdoctoral fellowship in cognitive neuroscience at the National Institutes of Health. His research seeks to characterise the brain circuitry underlying emotion, social behaviour and decision making, with a particular focus on antisocial and maladaptive behaviour. Michael uses brain imaging, physiological recording and cognitive testing to study a variety of clinical populations with social and affective deficits. The ultimate goal of his work is to develop more effective methods for diagnosing and treating psychopathology.

Cole Korponay is graduate researcher in the Neuroscience and Public Policy program at the University of Wisconsin-Madison, US, pursuing a PhD in neuroscience and a Masters in public affairs. Cole received a BA in cognitive science from the University of Pennsylvania. The aim of his work is to augment public policy decisions with considerations from emerging research and technology in neuroscience that help us to better understand human behaviour. Specifically, Cole's research has focused on elucidating the neurobiological foundations of psychiatric disorders often associated with criminal behaviour, and on exploring ways in which neuroscience may affect research-guided policy reform within the criminal justice system.

Gerben Meynen works as a psychiatrist at an outpatient clinic for anxiety disorders, GGZ inGeest, in Amsterdam, the Netherlands. He studied medicine at the Free University of Amsterdam (VU) and philosophy and theology at the University of Amsterdam (UvA). Gerben also holds a PhD in philosophy from the University of Nijmegen (RU) as well as one in medicine from VU Amsterdam. He is Assistant Professor at the Department of Philosophy, Faculty of Humanities, VU Amsterdam, and endowed Professor of Forensic Psychiatry at Tilburg Law School. His research interests are the philosophy and ethics of psychiatry, neurolaw, and legal insanity.

Stephen J Morse is Ferdinand Wakeman Hubbell Professor of Law, Professor of Psychology and Law in Psychiatry and Associate Director of the Center for Neuroscience and Society at the University of Pennsylvania, US. He has published numerous interdisciplinary articles and chapters in the fields of criminal law, mental health law and law and neuroscience, and has co-edited collections, including (with A Roskies) *A Primer on Criminal Law and Neuroscience*. He was Co-Director of the MacArthur Foundation Law and Neuroscience Project. He is a Diplomate in Forensic Psychology of the American Board of Professional Psychology; a past president of Division 41 of the American Psychological Association; a recipient of the American Academy of Forensic Psychology's Distinguished Contribution Award; a recipient of the American Psychiatric Association's Isaac Ray Award for distinguished contributions to forensic psychiatry and the psychiatric aspects of jurisprudence; a member of the MacArthur Foundation Research Network on Mental Health and Law; and a trustee of the Bazelon Centre for Mental Health Law.

Susanna Radovic is Associate Professor of Theoretical Philosophy at University of Gothenburg, Sweden. Her research focuses on issues at the intersection between philosophy, psychiatry and law. She has published extensively in different disciplinary areas, including the philosophy of mind, legal philosophy and public health ethics. She directs the Centre for Law, Ethics and Mental Health at the University of Gothenburg.

Claire Saas is Senior Lecturer at the University of Nantes, France. She teaches criminal law, criminal procedure and human rights law. She holds a PhD in law from the University of Paris I Panthéon-Sorbonne, France, and an LLM from the University of Paris I Panthéon-Sorbonne and the University of Cologne, Germany. She has worked at the Max-Planck Institute for Foreign and International Criminal Law in Freiburg, Germany. Her research interests include criminal procedure, dangerousness, sex offences, and migration law and policy, in France, Germany and at the European level.

Amedeo Santosuosso is a judge in Italy. He is President of the First Chamber of the Court of Appeals of Milan. Amedeo is also Adjunct Professor of Law, Science and New Technologies at the Faculty of Law of the University of Pavia, and Scientific Director of the European Centre for Law, Science and New Technologies (ECLT) at the same institution. He is the President of the European Association for Neuroscience and Law (EANL). He is author of several publications on the impact of technology and science on legal studies and practice. His research interests include biolaw, law and neuroscience, law and artificial intelligence.

Frank Verbruggen is Professor at the Institute of Criminal Law of KU Leuven, Belgium, where he teaches criminal law, the law of criminal sanctions, European criminal law and international criminal law. Frank is also a guest professor of (Belgian) criminal law and procedure at the University of Hasselt, Belgium. Frank has studied the impact of the fight against organised crime and terrorism on criminal law and procedure. His current research focuses on pan-European principles legitimising and limiting mutual recognition in criminal matters, the enforcement of criminal sanctions and the legal aspects of the fight against cybercrime. He also is a lawyer at the Leuven Bar, as *of counsel* with Lovius.

TABLE OF CASES

TABLE OF LEGISLATION

TABLE OF CODES, GUIDELINES AND PROFESSIONAL STANDARDS

TABLE OF INTERNATIONAL INSTRUMENTS

1

Introduction

SOFIA MORATTI AND DENNIS PATTERSON

This volume is a comparative, interdisciplinary study of criminal insanity and neuroscience. The criminal policy theories and ideologies underlying the legal regulation of criminal insanity and its judicial operationalisation have always been a subject of controversy, historically and across jurisdictions. The history of criminal insanity is characterised by constant conceptual and empirical tension between two disciplinary realms: the law and the mind sciences (the latter encompass traditional and recently developed psychiatries, psychologies and behavioural sciences of diverse theoretical orientation, and neuroscience). The law and the mind sciences are two domains of knowledge characterised by different practical and theoretical objectives and priorities. They use different specialised languages and are embodied in distinct professional groups with often divergent and partially irreconcilable interests and aims. This contrast emerges with striking potency in the province of criminal insanity. In criminal processes, competency assessments are performed by forensic mental health professionals, appointed by the judge or prosecutor or hired by the defendant. The forensic mental health expert witness is a trained psychologist, psychiatrist, neuroscientist or behavioural expert who answers legal questions by means of mental health diagnostic and prognostic tools, methods and techniques. Expert witnesses must fit their mental health sciences conceptual framework into legal categories, and give definite, conclusive answers, overlooking the nuances and fine distinctions they ordinarily employ in their profession outside of the judicial setting. In every country, this discrepancy gives rise to an array of difficulties in insanity assessments in individual cases.

The tension between the methods and goals of the law and those of the mind sciences often becomes apparent also in the intra-professional and public debate that accompanies the process of legal regulation, and in the disagreements and contentions that recurrently emerge in court insanity assessments, occasionally amplified when pertaining to high-profile cases reported in the media. Legal insanity is a highly politicised area of criminal justice, and the public perception of insanity pleas plays a critical role in the debate and in the process of regulation.

The advent of the brain sciences in the past two decades has revived long-standing criminal law and policy debates and controversies that had never been quite settled. Brain science, or neuroscience, is the study of the physical and bio-chemical structure and functioning of the living human brain, primarily by means of brain imaging tools. One of the traditional fundamental controversies in legal philosophy and criminal law theory concerns the constraints of human agency. Renowned studies in contemporary neuroscience offer empirical and scientific support to determinism. Prominent contributors have argued that this undermines the conceptual foundations of the criminal law and it calls for a comprehensive revision of the penal sanctions system and radically new criminal policies. However, this argument is fallacious. Criminal punishment does not necessarily presuppose human agency. The interpretation of punishment as retribution based on moral desert is rooted in long-established, centuries-old philosophical and intellectual traditions. Several examples could be made here. The most striking exemplification is the *Inferno* in Dante Alighieri's *Divina Commedia*, a metaphorical journey through a Christian hell where the damned souls are confined into one of nine concentric circles, depending on their sins in life. The souls are punished in accordance with the *contrapasso* principle. The word means 'to suffer the opposite'. In Dante's hell, fortune-tellers and false prophets have their heads twisted around on their bodies backwards for eternity, so they can never see ahead of them and must walk in reverse. Corrupt politicians lie in a lake of boiling pitch, symbolising the viscid and opaque nature of their deeds. For many centuries, this frame of mind was dominant also in criminal punishment theory. Penal sanctioning remained conceived of and interpreted as vengeance, nemesis, retribution for immoral behaviour, especially after the gradual disappearance of corporal punishment and torture from Western criminal justice systems. It was not until the late nineteenth century that the pillars of earlier criminal law theory—punishment as desert-based retribution and human agency—were questioned by a group of positivist criminal law scholars. They argued for biological determinism and against agency. They postulated that the primary responsibility of the criminal justice system is to protect society from dangerous individuals and groups. To determine whether an offender is a menace to others was seen as more important than to assess his mental capacity and criminal culpability. The tension between earlier criminal punishment theories, positivist conceptions, and successive criminological and sociological theories of deviance led to multiple criminal justice reforms in many European countries during the past century. The current regulation of sanctions in the criminal jurisdictions of Europe is the result of an encounter and a compromise between contrasting criminal justice ideologies. Punishment for unlawful behaviour and preventive measures based on dangerousness coexist, generating a degree of ambiguity. This emerges with particular clarity in the province of criminal insanity, and it can create paradoxical situations. In some criminal jurisdictions that do not provide for the life imprisonment of convicts, preventive measures for individuals acquitted on grounds of insanity but classed as 'socially dangerous' may consist of internment for an indeterminate amount of time. In theory, imprisonment and internment should take place in distinct types of facilities, offering different treatment; but the two do not significantly differ in practice in some criminal justice systems. The simultaneous presence of criminal justice and mental health concerns in the operationalisation of legal insanity impacts on the management of the culprit after acquittal in several ways. There is a long-standing controversy internationally on whether offenders declared 'legally insane' should be treated primarily as criminals, or as psychiatric patients. In some countries, offenders acquitted on grounds of legal insanity leave the criminal justice system. They are hospitalised in regular mental health care facilities, along with other individuals suffering from psychiatric pathologies. Different attempts to syncretise and harmonise medical treatment and detention have been made, mainly consisting of the systematic provision of psychiatric care to offenders in forensic-psychiatric custody facilities.

One other long-standing fundamental controversy in the criminal insanity debate invests the very definition of legal insanity. In most jurisdictions, criminal insanity comprises a cognitive and a volitional component. The 'cognitive' element means that the agent is considered legally insane when his discernment, understanding, and reasoning ability are found to be compromised. The 'volitional' component refers to the ability to control one's own behaviour. Some jurisdictions depart from this binary legal insanity assessment model; others do not define 'insanity' in statutory law at all. In most countries, the current statutory and case law definitions of insanity are under criticism, following the development of neuroscience and the recent evolution of psychiatry and the mind sciences in general. Many insanity tests are believed to be obsolete, rudimentary and inconsistent with state-of-the-art science, but reforming poses substantial conceptual and practical difficulties.

The authors in this volume explore in depth the state of the art of legal insanity and the numerous intricate, fascinating, pioneering and sophisticated questions raised by the integration of different criminal law and behaviour theories and diverse disciplines and methodologies in a genuinely interdisciplinary perspective.

Cognitive neuroscientists Cole Korponay and Michael Koenigs offer an accurate and accessible overview of brain science concepts and methods, and discuss findings on the neurobiology of moral judgement, impulse control, psychopathy, and psychosis that bear most directly on the definition and assessment of legal insanity. They conclude that, at the present time, brain imaging has important technological and methodological limitations, and knowledge in the field of neuroscience is still limited. It is not yet possible to conclusively infer that particular brain abnormalities played a decisive role in the emergence of criminal behaviour in individual cases. They suggest that neuroscience can best be employed as complementary and secondary to the traditional forms of behavioural evidence currently in use to assess legal insanity. However, the two neuroscientists emphasise that brain science can, already at this stage of its development, affect legal insanity in two ways. It can lead to an informed revision of the legal definition of insanity, currently too limited in scope to encompass the full range of neurobiological impairments and accompanying behavioural deficits that can lead to criminal behaviour. Neuroscience may also be able to aid in the sentencing phase of trials, by increasing the accuracy of dangerousness and recidivism assessments, and by determining a defendant's amenability to treatment.

The engaging contribution by Katrien Hanoulle and Frank Verbruggen opens with a description of the Belgian criminal law provisions relevant to mentally disordered offenders, including very recent, yet to be implemented reforms. The authors focus on the insanity defence and on the preventive measure of internment, and particularly on controversy pertaining to the interpretation of legal provisions and the role of forensic mental health expert witnesses in Belgian criminal processes. The authors present examples of the use of neuroscientific evidence in Belgian criminal proceedings and conclude that, so far, neuroscience has had a very limited impact on the Belgian criminal justice system. They discuss issues that could arise if neuroscientific evidence was admitted in Belgian criminal courts with a higher frequency than is the case at present, and feasible solutions within the current Belgian scientific evidence normative framework. In Belgium, there is no specific legal regulation of the obtainment, admission and assessment of neuroscientific evidence.

In their elegant contribution, Rafael Encinas de Muñagorri and Claire Saas discuss the 2011 French Bioethics Law, which explicitly regulates the use of brain scans in court, against the backdrop of the French legal and criminal justice system. The authors present the regulation of legal insanity in France and the French schools of criminal law theory and criminology in a historical perspective. They submit that the recent evolution of French insanity law reflects a subtle restatement of the issue of criminal responsibility, and a growing concern for dangerousness. The authors discuss the role of forensic mental health expert witnesses in criminal processes and present two recent well-known cases in which neuroscience was used to substantiate legal insanity pleas. They analyse in depth the procedural constraints and judicial discretion in neuroscientific evidence assessments in French courts. The authors discuss the role of the criminal justice system vis-à-vis that of the health care system after sentencing, the difficulties in coordinating the two in a context of decreasing psychiatric institutionalisation, and the growing difficulty in maintaining the distinction between dangerousness in a psychiatric and in a criminological sense. Finally, they review a very recent reform proposal and examine the position of French legal practitioners on the use of neuroscientific evidence in criminal processes.

In their informative chapter, Barbara Bottalico and Amedeo Santosuosso present the regulation of criminal responsibility and legal insanity in Italy and the rules on (neuro)scientific evidence admission in criminal trials. They discuss recent Italian cases in which neuroscience played a crucial role in the assessment of competency and criminal responsibility. They examine the historically difficult relationship between law and psychiatry in the domain of legal insanity in Italy, and consider whether the introduction of a neuroscientific explanation of criminal behaviour can bring significant changes into current evidentiary practice. The authors describe the effects of a verdict of 'not guilty by reason of insanity' in the post-sentencing phase, and review the situation of criminal psychiatric institutions in Italy, currently in the process of being replaced by community care-oriented facilities. The goal of the reform is to offer personalised treatment in a suitable care-oriented setting, while current criminal psychiatric institutions are in practice detention establishments, providing little or no medical care. The conclusion of the authors is that neuroscience will not lead to significant revisions of the regulation of legal insanity, but it may affect assessments of responsibility. Neuroscientific technology may complement traditional psychiatry in individual mental illness assessments. In particular, it may contribute to determining the impact of mental illness on decision-making capacity. Neuroscience may enable court experts to offer more fine-graded, informed and individualised competency assessments and to devise more personalised forms of punishment, consistently with the goals of the recent reform of criminal psychiatric facilities in Italy.

Gerben Meynen offers a highly interdisciplinary account of the regulation of insanity in Dutch law and the impact of neuroscience on criminal responsibility and legal insanity assessments in the Netherlands. In Dutch law, there is no legal standard specifying under what conditions a mental disorder can substantiate an insanity plea. In other legal systems, the criteria are usually set down in statutory law or have emerged from case law. The author discusses the consequences of this situation, particularly for the work of forensic mental health practitioners appointed to perform court assessments. One other peculiarity of Dutch criminal insanity law is that it lists as many as five grades or levels of criminal responsibility. Most jurisdictions rely on the dichotomy 'sane' versus 'insane', others also provide a 'diminished capacity' mitigating factor; but very few jurisdictions include more than three levels of criminal responsibility in their statutory law. The author discusses the practical consequences of this regulation for courtroom competency evaluations and reviews reform proposals that have been advanced recently. Currently, neuroscience and 'neurolaw' are topics of great interest among Dutch legal scholars and forensic mental health practitioners. The author gives a clear, comprehensive description of the current debate and examines how neuroscience information may contribute to insanity assessments in individual cases. He further discusses the possible criminal responsibility implications of the use of medications affecting brain functioning and of Deep Brain Stimulation (DBS), used as medical treatment for a few conditions, but known to affect behaviour and decision-making capacity in some patients. Finally, the author examines a number of limitations intrinsic to current neuroscientific techniques and their consequences for courtroom use, and highlights a few issues in law and neuroscience research relevant to small civil law countries such as the Netherlands.

The thought-provoking chapter by Tova Bennet and Susanna Radovic begins with a detailed account of the very exceptional regulation of legal insanity in Sweden. There is no insanity clause in Swedish law. Offenders cannot be acquitted on grounds of legal insanity. Following a major legal reform in the 1960s, all defendants of age are imputable. All defendants undergo the same type of intent assessment. If intent legal requirements are fulfilled, the defendant is convicted. However, if the crime is found to have been committed under the influence of a 'severe mental disorder', the offender cannot be sentenced to imprisonment but rather to compulsory psychiatric care. The Swedish system is almost unique in this respect. Only Greenland, and the States of Montana, Idaho, Utah and Kansas have a similar regulation of legal responsibility. The authors present the political, legal, scholarly and scientific debate preceding and following the controversial 1960s' reform. They examine several post-reform governmental reports that suggested a reintroduction of an insanity clause in Swedish criminal law, focusing on the two most recent proposals of 2002 and 2012. Finally, they discuss an empirical study they have recently conducted, consisting of a review of forensic-psychiatric court assessments of individual defendants. The results of the study shed light on Swedish court practice and provide an important stepping stone in the current imputability reform debate. The authors conclude in favour of a reintroduction of an insanity clause in Swedish law, for purposes of legal certainty, justice and fairness, and to solve some of the theoretical and practical conundrums that systematically emerge under the current regulation.

Lisa Claydon and Paul Catley discuss how the relationship between medical science and the law has defined and shaped the insanity defence in the United Kingdom. Their analysis is insightful. The authors explore how the M'Naghten legal insanity rules have reached a point where they are viewed as unnecessarily complex and far removed from a modern medical perspective of mental disorder. They trace the difficult politico-legal environment in which the insanity defence has developed. In 2012–13, the Law Commission for England and Wales undertook a thorough review of the defences of insanity and automatism. The Commission was critical of the current insanity clause, which attributes an 'inaccurate, unfair and stigmatising' label and 'does not fairly identify those who ought not to be held criminally responsible as a result of their mental condition, and so some of those vulnerable people remain in the penal system'. The Commission identified several issues that explain the underuse of the insanity defence in the UK, mainly the distinction between 'sane' and 'insane' automatism, highly problematic conceptually and practically, and the very nature of the M'Naghten rules and how they are applied. In reviewing the law and how it should be reformed, the Commission also briefly touched upon the possible implications of growing scientific understanding of the brain for the reformed defence. The authors review the proposals put forward by the Commission and consider whether the Commission has actually achieved in its conclusions and proposals the objective that it set out:

> [T]hat criminal responsibility should be correctly ascribed. Doing so, through operation of the law, reflects society's judgment and attribution of blame. It is not just a matter

of accurately communicating by means of a verdict what conclusion a court has reached about a person's culpability (what is described as 'fair labelling'), though that is important too.

In his compelling contribution, American scholar Stephen Morse argues that the insanity defence is morally necessary. As long as society takes people seriously as potential moral agents, some form of considering the influence of afflictions of the mind on practical reasoning will be necessary for criminal justice to operate fairly. Morse contends that the primary arguments for the abolition of the insanity defence, including alternatives, fail conceptually and to do justice. His argument rests on a conception of justice that is not tied to any particular constitutional order. Next, he analyses the legal insanity criteria, with special attention to whether an independent control test, in addition to a cognitive test, is conceptually coherent and practically workable. The discussion then shifts to neuroscience. Morse contends that, at the present time, neuroscience cannot make any contribution to adjudication of individual cases and to criminal law policy. He concludes that, in principle, neuroscience does not pose any fundamental challenge to the validity of the doctrine of legal insanity. The findings of neuroscience will not entail either its abolition or even extensive revision in the short and mid term. Morse expresses cautious hope for the long term. Future neuroscience and other sciences might help make decisions about responsibility more accurate and fair by guiding the evaluation of empirical claims.

This volume will serve as a practical guide for the comparative legal scholar and the judge, as well as stimulating scholarly reading for the neuroscientist, the social scientist and the philosopher with interdisciplinary scientific interests.

2

The Neurobiology of Antisocial and Amoral Behaviour: Insights from Brain Science and Implications for Law

COLE KORPONAY AND MICHAEL KOENIGS

I. Introduction

Advances in modern brain science are poised to make a major impact on the criminal justice system in the coming years. The growing interest in the nascent field of 'neurolaw' is driven largely by the increasing sophistication with which neuroscientific methods have been able to elucidate the biological substrates of human faculties such as empathy, honesty, moral judgement and impulse control (as well as deficits thereof). One of the most profound challenges will be to reconcile the growing understanding of the neurobiological underpinnings of social and moral function with legal conceptions of responsibility for action. In particular, much speculation has surrounded the potential role of neuroscience in supplementing evaluations of legal insanity, and in shedding new light on definitions of legal insanity. How do current definitions of insanity hold up in the face of new knowledge about how dysfunction in particular neural circuits may contribute to criminal behaviour? Can brain-imaging scans be used as evidence to purport the insanity defence? Navigating these complex issues will require a collaborative effort among experts in law, neuroscience, philosophy and public policy. The purpose of this chapter is to highlight the concepts, methods and findings from the field of neuroscience that bear most directly on these issues. To this end, the chapter will consist of two major parts. The first section will provide a lay summary of relevant background information on neuroscience. This section will include a description of how the brain transmits signals at the molecular level, as well as how the brain is organised at the macroscopic level. Key terminology regarding brain anatomy will be defined. This section will also describe the medical imaging technologies that allow scientists to 'see' the brain in action and measure the structural and functional characteristics that underlie variation in human behaviour. This section will conclude with a discussion of the inherent limitations of these imaging techniques vis-à-vis their applicability to legal determinations of responsibility for action. The second part of the chapter will then review selected findings from neuroscientific research that may be most relevant to criminal liability assessments. Specifically, this section will reference data on the neurobiology underlying moral judgment, impulse control, psychopathy and psychosis. This section will conclude with a discussion of ways in which neuroscientific data may make the most immediate impact in the criminal justice system.

II. Neuroscience Background

The Structure of Neurons

The brain is essentially a computer whose hardware is cells rather than silicon. Its fundamental processing unit is called a neuron, of which the brain has about 100 billion. Computationally, most neurons may be thought of as having two states: a resting 'off' state and an active 'on', or 'firing', state. Toggling between these two states is the mechanism by which the brain initiates, sustains and inactivates all of the various processes and behaviours that it controls. How does the brain achieve its remarkable complexity from such a simple on-off system? It does so by interweaving millions, and sometimes billions, of these neurons into networks that integrate individual outputs and generate nuanced and highly sophisticated patterns of activity.

Neurons are connected to one another via long, branch-like terminals that extend off the neuron's cell body, or 'soma'. Each neuron's soma projects a huge number of these connective branches, allowing a single neuron to communicate with sometimes thousands of others. The connective branches that extend from the soma of one neuron and send information to another neuron that is subsequent in the processing stream are called 'axons'. The branches that receive information from a neuron antecedent in the processing stream are called 'dendrites'. In all, the brain contains about 100 trillion neuronal connections, allowing for an unfathomable degree of complexity.

A key physical distinction between a neuron's soma and its connective branches—one which is exploited by neuroimaging technology and which will be elaborated upon later—is the presence or absence of a white, fatty substance called myelin. Myelin coats the exterior of neurons' connective branches, serving as an insulator that allows for a more faithful transfer of information between neurons. Thus, the myelin-containing connective branches of neurons are referred to as the 'white matter' of the brain, whereas the neuronal somas, which lack myelin, are referred to as the 'grey matter'. Grey matter may be thought of as the computational processing centres, and white matter as the cables that link the different centres.

The actual point of contact between two neurons occurs between the axon of the antecedent neuron and the dendrite of the subsequent neuron, which are separated in space by a few tens of nanometres at a junction called a 'synapse'. In reference to their position at the synapse, the antecedent neuron and its axons are referred to as 'presynaptic', whereas the subsequent neuron and its dendrites are 'postsynaptic'. In sum, the molecular structure of the brain sets the stage for a system of information flow—from the soma of the presynaptic neuron to its axons, through the synapse and to the dendrites of the postsynaptic neuron, on to its soma, and so on.

But what is this 'information' that is communicated between neurons? How exactly is it communicated, and, most importantly, how does it drive our behaviour?

Communication Between Neurons

The informational currency of neurons is electricity, in the form of charged particles called ions. Through pores in the outer layer ('membrane') of the neuron, ions that carry an electrical charge such as potassium (K^{+1}) and sodium (Na^{+1}) can enter or leave the neuron and change the overall magnitude of charge inside it. What is important for driving neuronal activity is not necessarily the absolute amount of charge inside the neuron, but the relative difference between the amount of charge inside the neuron and the amount of charge outside the neuron (in a space referred to as the 'extracellular fluid'). This difference in relative charge is called the 'electrical potential', and it is measured in reference to the inside of the neuron. For instance, if the inside of a neuron contained two sodium ions (a total of two positive charges), and the extracellular fluid outside the neuron contained four sodium ions (a total of four positive charges), then the electrical potential of the neuron would be $(+2_{inside}) - (+4_{outside}) = -2$. The meaning of this number, -2, is that the inside of the neuron is electrically negative *relative* to the extracellular fluid, despite having a positive absolute charge of $+2$.

With the concept of electrical potential in mind we can begin to understand what the 'on' and 'off' states of a neuron are and how information about these states is communicated between neurons. The 'on' and 'off' states of a neuron each correspond to different values of electrical potential. For a typical neuron in the brain that is 'off', or in what is referred to as its 'resting state', its electrical potential is maintained at around -70 millivolts (mv). A neuron that has been turned 'on', via a rapid transfer of positive ions into the cell through 'ion channels', typically reaches an electrical potential of around $+40$ mv. The fast rise in positive voltage that turns a neuron on is referred to as an 'action potential', during which time the neuron is said to 'fire'.

A neuron that is firing is capable of propagating its positive electrical potential to a neuron that it is connected to (via the axon-synapse-dendrite pathway discussed earlier), thereby raising the electrical potential of that neuron from its 'off' potential to its 'on' potential, too. However, there is an intermediary step that occurs at the synapse between the neurons. Since the presynaptic neuron and postsynaptic neuron are separated by this small gap in space, the axons of the presynaptic neuron must send a chemical signal across the synapse to inform the postsynaptic neuron about its electrical state. These communicative chemicals are called 'neurotransmitters' and they are only sent across the synapse when the presynaptic neuron is on and firing action potentials. When the neurotransmitters reach the dendrites of the postsynaptic neuron, they open the ion channels in the membrane to let in positive ions that raise the neuron's electrical potential to its 'on' state.

This type of interaction, where one neuron turns on another neuron, is referred to as an 'excitatory' connection. However, many neuronal connections in the brain are 'inhibitory' connections, in which a neuron turns off another neuron that was previously on, or prevents a neuron that is off from turning on. Inhibitory connections are just as vital to driving behaviour as excitatory connections.

Through a mechanism that is still mysterious to neuroscientists, the electrical activity of neurons somehow translates into what we perceive as our thoughts and emotions, and serves as the substrate through which we deliberate our decisions. Every conversation we have with ourselves is underlain by a network of neurons turning on and off and propagating electric potentials. In an abstract sense, this interplay of thoughts and feelings eventually conglomerates into a decision state, and through a process we more thoroughly understand, neurons in the brain propagate their electrical information to our body's musculoskeletal system to generate behavioural outputs.

When neuroscientists speak of 'damage' or 'lesions' or 'abnormalities' in the brain, ultimately what this corresponds to is some disruption to the molecular system of neurons discussed here. This can consist of a paucity of grey matter in some area of the brain, leaving a computational centre with an insufficient amount of neurons to accomplish its job; a lack of myelin-coated connective branches that hampers communication between different computational centres; or issues with neurotransmitters or the channels that interfere with the flow of ions and the firing of action potentials. While these types of molecular abnormalities can be observed in animals via highly invasive techniques, it is not safe or practical to employ these techniques in living humans. However, molecular-level abnormalities often leave macro-scale signatures that are detectable via safe, non-invasive imaging techniques. Before discussing the details and capabilities of these imaging techniques it is helpful to become familiarised with and oriented within the macro-scale structure of the brain, for this is the level at which neuroimaging will provide its data.

Macroscopic Organisation of the Brain

The brain is organised into modules of neuronal networks specialised for certain functions. One coarse functional-anatomical division in the brain is between its cortical and subcortical layers. The subcortical layer of the brain, which resides across the bottom (inferior) and midline (medial) regions of the brain, contains evolutionarily ancient neuronal modules (nuclei) that regulate basic aspects of behaviour and homeostasis. Humans share many of these subcortical structures with virtually all mammalian and even some non-mammalian ancestors, such as reptiles. For example, one neuronal module in this subcortical layer is the hypothalamus, which controls such functions as feeding behaviour and body temperature regulation. The cortical layer of the brain (often referred to as 'cerebral cortex'), on the other hand, is an evolutionarily recent structure that is most fully formed in primates and humans. The cerebral cortex comprises the characteristic bumps ('gyri') and grooves ('sulci') that are readily apparent on visual inspection of a whole, intact brain. Occupying the top (superior) and outer (lateral) portions of the brain, this convoluted layer of tissue physically surrounds the white matter and subcortical nuclei and underlies the complex functions that enable us to be intelligent and highly conscious life forms. In addition to this cortical-subcortical segmentation of the brain, there is also a left-right segmentation in which each side is referred to as a 'hemisphere'. At the gross anatomical level, the left and right hemispheres of the brain look like mirror images, though at the molecular level they are quite different in some areas. Each hemisphere contains four cerebral lobes, distinguished primarily by anatomical location (but also by function): the frontal lobe at the front (rostral) end of the brain, occipital lobe at the back (caudal) end, temporal lobe at the lower side (lateral inferior) end, and parietal lobe, located behind the frontal lobe and above the occipital lobe. In very broad terms, the occipital lobe primarily mediates basic aspects of vision. The parietal lobe mediates perception of motion, space, touch, as well as some aspects of attention and cognitive control. The temporal lobe mediates visual object recognition, memory, audition, receptive language, and social/semantic knowledge. The frontal lobe coordinates movement, expressive language, planning, cognitive control, emotion regulation and decision making.

It is within this macro-scale framework that neuroscientists have identified areas associated with asocial and criminal behaviour when defective. Before we can examine these findings, assess their validity and gauge their relevance to insanity assessments, though, we should critique how neuroscientists come to these conclusions in the first place. How do neuroscientists analyse the brain to determine which ones appear healthy and which ones appear disordered? Furthermore, what is the capacity of these technologies when applied to the courtroom for insanity assessments?

Neuroimaging

Neuroscientists have an array of technologies at their disposal that allow them to evaluate the structure and function of the brain. These technologies, which may be collectively termed as 'neuroimaging', allow for a non-invasive, *in vivo* study of the human brain. In other words, neuroscientists need not perform surgery or wait until an individual's death to explore his or her brain. Today, looking at someone's brain is as simple—logistically speaking—as asking them to lie down in a scanner for 15 minutes. The technology behind these imaging machines is not as simple, but it works on principles that are easy enough to grasp at a general level. An understanding of how neuroimaging works will provide context for how to interpret the findings that result from them, and will allow the reader to think critically about the technology's capabilities for courtroom insanity assessments.

There exist two complementary classes of neuroimaging technologies: those that assess the structural health of the brain, and those that assess the functional health of the brain. Structure and function are complementary because structure underlies function, but independent evaluations of these metrics can allow for tests of consistency and corroboration. For example, if a structural abnormality is observed in some brain region, an independent evaluation of that region's functional capacity can provide information about whether the structural abnormality is meaningful. The two types of structural neuroimaging technologies are magnetic resonance imaging (MRI) and diffusion tensor imaging (DTI). The primary functional neuroimaging technology is functional magnetic resonance imaging (fMRI), which may be subdivided into resting-state fMRI and task-based fMRI. The following sections will discuss the specifics of each type of imaging method and the kinds of information each provides.

Structural Neuroimaging

Magnetic Resonance Imaging

As the name suggests, MRI uses magnetic energy to peer inside the skull and create images of the brain—similar in concept to how an X-ray machine uses the energy in X-rays to reconstitute images of the bones under our flesh. MRI is able to generate images based on the magnetic properties of the atoms that constitute our brain tissue. Different combinations and arrangements of atoms in the brain form the building blocks for the different components of neurons (dendrites, somas, axons). Recalling from the section on the structural biology of neurons, a key physical distinction between the soma (grey matter) of neurons and their dendrites and axons (white matter) is the presence of myelin in the latter and the absence of myelin in the former. MRI uses the different atomic makeup of grey matter and white matter to differentiate them by magnetic properties.

An MRI machine first releases pulses of magnetic energy tuned to specific frequencies into the brain. The atoms in the brain absorb this energy, become energised, and then release the energy with a magnitude characteristic to the type of atom. This released energy is then measured by the scanner and converted into an image of the brain. Since the amount of energy absorbed and released is different for grey matter and white matter, they show up as different intensities (darker and lighter, respectively) in the resulting image.

MRI can yield multiple structural measures of the brain: the total grey matter volume in the brain; the grey matter volume and density of individual cortical and subcortical brain regions; the cortical thickness of individual brain regions in cerebral cortex; the total white matter volume in the brain and in specific regions; and the degree of folding or 'gyrification' of the cerebral cortex. These structural morphometric properties are some of the metrics that may be used to evaluate the health of a brain.

Diffusion Tensor Imaging

Whereas MRI looks at structural morphometry in the brain, DTI looks at structural connectivity. DTI employs a similar use of magnetic energy as MRI, but geared in such a way as to provide more focused information about the white matter pathways that crisscross the brain. The scanner collects energy released specifically by magnetically energised atoms that are part of water molecules passing ('diffusing') through white matter tissue. Exploited here is the fact that the way the atoms release this energy depends on the relationship between the orientations of the diffusion gradient, dictated by the scanner, and of the white matter tracts in the brain. By manipulating the diffusion gradient and collecting subsequent information about the released energy from the atoms, the DTI scanner can calculate a series of properties about individual white matter pathways that speak to their health and structural integrity. In simple terms, the diffusion, or movement, of water in the brain is dictated by the physical structures in the brain. Water will preferentially move along (rather than across) the bundles of tightly packed myelinated axons that comprise white matter pathways. Because the diffusion depends on the number of axons in the pathway, how tightly they are packed, and how intact the myelin sheaths are, DTI is able to provide a coarse measure of the structural integrity of the white matter pathways in the brain. Defects in white matter pathway integrity can affect the ability of different regions of the brain to communicate with one another, and thus provides another metric to evaluate the health of a brain.

Functional Neuroimaging

Functional magnetic resonance imaging (fMRI) also works off the basic principle of using magnetic energy to energise atoms in the brain, collecting their pattern of energy release, and reconstituting this information into an image. However, fMRI seeks to gain an understanding of the dynamic patterns of activity in the brain, as opposed to more static structural features. To do this, fMRI exploits the magnetic properties of blood that nourishes the neurons of the brain. Blood exists in two primary forms in the body, including in the brain—oxygenated blood that has arrived fresh from the lungs and heart to provide the oxygen necessary to drive activity within a cell, and deoxygenated blood whose oxygen has been spent. Neurons that are active in some process and which are firing action potentials require increased levels of oxygenated blood to sustain their activity. Thus, the level of oxygen in the blood around a group of neurons can be used as a proxy for the activity level of the neurons. The key fact that allows fMRI to provide information about blood oxygen levels is that oxygenated blood and deoxygenated blood have different magnetic properties. The quantitative measure of oxygen level provided by fMRI is referred to as the 'blood-oxygenation-level-dependent' (BOLD) signal; the higher the BOLD signal in an area of neurons, the more active they are presumed to be compared to other areas.

There are two subtypes of fMRI that provide different information about the activity in an individual's brain. The first subtype is task-based fMRI, in which the subject is asked to carry out some task or objective while they are in the scanner. For example, subjects may be shown pictures of faces and asked to describe what emotion best characterises each face (anger, surprise, happiness etc). Since this type of task is known to rely on processing in a part of the brain called the 'amygdala', researchers can look to correlate task performance (the number of correctly characterised faces) with the degree of amygdala activity as given by the BOLD signal. If the experiment reveals that subjects with lower than average BOLD signal in the amygdala tended to score worse on the task, this may indicate that these subjects have a general deficit in emotional processing which is related to faulty functioning of their amygdala.

The other subtype of fMRI is resting-state fMRI. Here, a subject lies in the scanner without performing any task (the brain is still very much active even when it is not engaged in some exogenously cued task). Complementary to the information about structural connectivity provided by DTI, resting-state fMRI provides information about functional connectivity. In other words, it tells us about how different areas of the brain are communicating with each other at baseline levels of activity, and more specifically, how neuronal activity (measured by the BOLD signal) in one area of the brain correlates with neuronal activity in other areas of the brain.

Neuroimaging in the Courtroom: Limitations

While neuroimaging is a powerful investigative tool to learn about the human brain, it is limited in the scope of what information it can provide and what conclusions it can offer. Furthermore, the prospect of using neuroimaging for insanity assessments in a legal setting invites a host of cautions beyond those typically encountered in its use for academic purposes. This section will help to ground the expectations of what neuroimaging can realistically provide for assisting in insanity assessments.

Correlation Does Not Imply Causation

An essential point to understand is that an image of the brain has no inherent meaning in itself. A chain of inferences is necessary to make sense of the results of a brain scan, and this limits our ability to draw definitive conclusions in several ways. First, the types of neuroimaging techniques discussed here provide information only about correlation, *not* causation. For instance, if a defendant is shown via MRI to have some structural abnormality in his brain, there is no basis to conclude with certainty that this defect was the *cause* for his behaviour. This is the same for functional data as well. If fMRI is used to show that a defendant's poor performance on a task is related to reduced BOLD signal in some brain region, all we can say is that reduced activity in that brain region is correlated with poor performance on the task, not that the BOLD signal deficiency caused the poor performance.

Brains Change Over Time

A second logical issue results from the fact that brains change over time, both as a natural consequence of aging and in response to influences in the environment. This means that we can never say with certainty that the structure and functioning of a defendant's brain as it is imaged during trial is the same as it was at the time of the crime. Indeed, the defendant's brain may experience changes as a result of having been involved in the crime and going through the trial process itself, introducing new aspects to his brain that would not have been present at the time of the crime. This makes it essentially impossible to replicate the brain state of the defendant that was present during the crime.

Comparing a Group to an Individual Introduces
Statistical Ambiguity

Third, statistical analyses of brain imaging data for the purposes of the courtroom are not as robust as the analyses conducted in the research setting. In clinical research, data may be compared between two sizable groups of subjects, where an *average* value of the metric of interest for each group, rather than individual values, are used as the basis for statistical comparison. This kind of design is strategic because averages taken from many individuals are more representative of true population values than values taken from single individuals. The more subjects in a group, the more representative the average value is of the true population average represented by the group, and conversely, the fewer subjects in a group the less representative the average value will be of the true population value. This is because a population as a whole typically has a considerable degree of variability within it. While most people in a population will have a value close to the average, plenty will have slightly more extreme values. The implication of this concept when comparing two groups is this: even if two groups, representing two distinct populations, have different averages for some value of interest, it is possible for some individuals from one population to have values that overlap with the values of some individuals from the other population. In research, the ability to use two large groups mitigates this issue because it enables the comparison of averages, which may not overlap between two different populations even if some segment of the individuals do. However, in the courtroom, instead of comparing two large groups, it may be more likely that one large group would be compared to a single individual. This arrangement could lead to challenges interpreting the results.

Consider this hypothetical scenario. The one large group provides an average value for some brain metric from the non-criminal, neurologically and psychiatrically healthy population, and the goal is to determine whether the defendant's metric differs sufficiently from this average metric to warrant labelling as a disease or defect. Even if the defendant truly belongs to a separate, unhealthy population, as an individual, the value of his metric may overlap with the most extreme values for the non-criminal population. If this were the case, would there be sufficient statistical evidence to conclude that the defendant's brain is fundamentally different in some way from the non-criminal population? What threshold would be applied to determine disease or defect? Would there have to be zero overlap between the individual's metric and the metrics of the entire non-criminal population? Would some other statistical threshold be applied (eg, greater than two standard deviations from the population mean)?

Neuroimaging Technology and Methodology
Carries Inherent Error Rates

A fourth caveat involves the inherent error rate of brain imaging methodology and technology. The Daubert standard requires judges to consider the known or potential error rate of a technique when determining the validity of scientific testimony. In brain imaging, there are two potential sources of error to consider—one from the technology itself and one from the data analysis process. Sources of measurement errors, or 'noise', arising from the scanning technology can include technical factors such as scan parameters and electrical component quality, in addition to subject-related factors such as head motion during scans. For example, even a few millimetres of head motion during an fMRI scan can produce significant changes in the measured levels of BOLD activity. On the data analysis side, errors can arise because the statistical tests used to determine if there are significant differences between groups allow for some possibility that the obtained results are due to random chance. As a result, there is always the possibility that a finding is due to chance rather than being representative of a true relationship. Researchers try to minimise the possibility of making incorrect conclusions attributable to randomness by selecting a strict numerical threshold of what constitutes true 'significant difference'. This threshold, called 'alpha', defines the probability that a researcher will detect a significant difference that is due to chance rather than a true difference. In brain imaging research, the standard alpha that is used is 5 per cent. This means that brain-imaging findings that are considered representative of true differences between groups may carry up to a 5 per cent chance of being falsely deduced from random variation.

Neuroimaging Yields a Coarse Measure of Brain
Structure and Function

The last caveat is one regarding the state of progress of neuroimaging technology
and of our knowledge of the brain. As described above, neuroimaging techniques
like fMRI and DTI generate brain images and metrics *indirectly* from features of
brain physiology (eg blood oxygenation or water diffusion). Hence, these images
may signal underlying brain health, but they carry inherent spatial and temporal
resolutions that do not correspond to actual neuronal activity. At this point, the
spatial resolution of MRI is limited to patches of brain, referred to as 'voxels', of
a few millimetres in size. A few millimetres of brain space may contain several
million neurons and tens of billions of synapses. Thus, it is not only possible, but
also likely, that current neuroimaging techniques fail to pick up finer-grained
abnormalities that can contribute to aberrant behaviour. As neuroimaging
technology continues to improve, along with clearer ideas regarding how and why
neural health may be compromised, we will no doubt see more precise applications
of brain imaging to diagnose neurological and psychiatric illness.

Summary

To summarise the takeaway from this section, contemporary neuroimaging techniques carry a number of inherent limitations that may preclude its imminent
use in courtroom determinations of insanity. Nonetheless, through its use in several decades' worth of controlled, peer-reviewed, and replicated scientific studies,
neuroimaging has contributed a wealth of knowledge to the field of neuroscience
about how certain brain characteristics appear related to abnormal behaviours
that are associated with criminality. The following sections will outline the current
state of knowledge about the kinds of brain characteristics that may be relevant for
an individual's capacity to regulate his behaviour.

III. Neuroscience Data Relevant to Legal Insanity

In the United States, the 46 states that permit an insanity defence are about equally
divided between two legal definitions of insanity. One group of states uses some
variation of the M'Naghten Rule, which requires that in order for a defendant to be
ruled insane, he must either have an inability to understand right from wrong or
have a general inability to understand what he has done. The other group of states
uses some variation of the Model Penal Code (MPC) test. The MPC encompasses
the criteria of the M'Naghten Rule, but also allows a defendant to be ruled insane
if he is 'unable to conform his conduct to the requirements of the law'. To cast

these definitions in more neuropsychological terms, about half of states limit a ruling of insanity to defendants who have a diminished understanding of morality or reality in general; the other half of states also appear to be concerned with the defendant's capacity to control his impulses.

The conceptions of insanity encapsulated in the M'Naghten Rule, the MPC and many other legal systems around the world were established before the era of modern brain science. Since then, the field has begun to make important inroads into understanding the neurobiology of criminal behaviour, with the potential for new knowledge to prompt reconsideration of how insanity is legally defined.

The Neurobiology of Criminal Behaviour and Insanity

First and foremost, neuroscience reveals that there is no one centre in the brain that dictates whether an individual will be a law-abiding citizen or a criminal offender. Behaving in a law-abiding manner requires that several different areas of the brain underlying different aspects of behaviour function properly together; criminality may arise through impairment in one or more neuropsychological domains. To begin to understand what these brain regions and behaviours are and how they fit together, we will first make some assumptions regarding the neuropsychological capacities necessary for socially responsible behaviour. First, law-abiding individuals need an intact moral processing system that can distinguish and place emotional (or at least motivational) value on notions of 'right' and 'wrong'. Second, they need an intact behavioural inhibition system that can prevent illegal urges or inclinations from being acted out. Third, they need a lucid consciousness grounded in an accurate understanding of reality to facilitate rational decision making. Brain abnormalities in areas underlying any of these three capacities have the potential to drive criminal behaviour. Indeed, the neuroscience literature provides evidence for three classes of brain circuitry dysfunction that correspond to the above framework:

1. abnormalities in brain regions that mediate moral cognition, which impair the ability for morally guided, pro-social decision-making;
2. abnormalities in brain regions that mediate behavioural inhibition or reward sensitivity, which facilitates impulsive behaviour;
3. abnormalities that give rise to psychosis or low IQ, which diminish or delude the understanding of reality.

The following sections will explore the neuroimaging evidence for these three types of impairments and how each can contribute to criminal behaviour.

Neurobiology of Abnormal Morality and Emotion Processing

Our ability to make socially appropriate decisions is guided, in part, by an interplay between our sense of morality and our emotions. Neuroscience has been yielding mounting evidence for a network in the brain that underlies our sense of right and wrong.[1] Interestingly, this network combines brain regions responsible for executive function and logical reasoning with brain regions that mediate and regulate our emotions. This combination provides a clue that behaving in accordance with normative morality is not simply a matter of being cognisant of the difference between right and wrong at a semantic or intellectual level. Indeed, research has shown that intact emotional processing is a vital component of moral and pro-social behaviour, functioning to infuse the notions of right and wrong with their respective positive and negative emotional valances. Right and wrong by themselves are abstract notions. The emotions attached to them, however, act as strong influences to pursue 'right' behaviours (and experience positive emotions like happiness, pride and compassion) and avoid 'wrong' behaviours (to evade negative emotions like guilt, embarrassment and shame). This section will explore the types of neurological deficits that compromise an individual's ability for moral and emotional processing, potentially leading to asocial and criminal behaviour.

Knowledge that a particular area of the brain regulates our social behaviour first came from the famous case of Phineas Gage. Gage was an American railroad worker in the 1840s who one day on the job suffered the misfortune of having an iron rod blown through his face and out the top of his head. Remarkably, he survived, but something about him changed as a result of the brain injury. He became 'fitful, irreverent, indulging at times in the grossest profanities which was not previously his custom, manifesting but little deference for his fellows ... His mind was radically changed, so decidedly that his friends and acquaintances said he was "no longer Gage".[2] It seemed that the part of Gage's brain pierced by the rod was critical for proper social functioning. Later analyses of Gage's skull revealed that the rod must have impacted his brain in the region of the prefrontal cortex, the most rostral region of the frontal lobe.

A more modern case study in the age of neuroimaging corroborated the findings from Phineas Gage and cast them in more detailed relief.[3] At the age of 35, patient EVR had portions of his frontal lobes removed in order to treat a brain tumour. More specifically, the areas removed consisted of a part of the frontal lobe known as ventromedial prefrontal cortex (vmPFC). Before the surgery, patient EVR was a respected accountant with a stable marriage and high intelligence. After the surgery EVR retained his superior intelligence (insofar as standard IQ tests are

---

[1] MF Mendez, 'The Neurobiology of Moral Behavior: Review and Neuropsychiatric Implications (2009) 14 *CNS Spectrums* 608; L Pascual, P Rodrigues and D Gallardo-Pujol, 'How Does Morality Work in the Brain? A Functional and Structural Perspective of Moral Behavior' (2013) 7 *Frontiers in Integrative Neuroscience* 56; M Fumagalli and A Priori, 'Functional and Clinical Neuroanatomy of Morality' (2012) 135 *Brain* 2006.

[2] JM Harlow, 'Recovery from the Passage of an Iron Bar through the Head' (1868) 2 *Publications of the Massachusetts Medical Society* 327.

[3] PJ Eslinger and AR Damasio, 'Severe Disturbance of Higher Cognition after Bilateral Frontal Lobe Ablation Patient EVR' (1985) 35 *Neurology* 1731.

concerned), but began to exhibit a profound lack of guilt or empathy. His social life and interpersonal relationships collapsed. He went bankrupt, divorced his wife and married a prostitute, and became estranged from his family and friends. This case, and other similar cases, fuelled the 'somatic marker hypothesis', which postulated that responsible social conduct and decision making depends critically on patent emotional capacities (and the underlying neural substrates), rather than simply declarative knowledge or cold, rational logic.[4]

It has since been established that the vmPFC is of central importance in supporting normative morality and pro-social decision making. This has been demonstrated through a host of studies that employ moral dilemma tasks and compare the performance of vmPFC-damaged subjects (as confirmed by structural MRI) to healthy subjects. In one such study,[5] researchers made use of a paradigm known as the 'trolley paradox'. Two types of scenarios are presented to subjects in this task. In the first, a hypothetical trolley is said to be approaching a fork in the tracks where, on one side of the fork, five workers are on the tracks, and on the other side of the fork a single worker is on the tracks. The default direction of the trolley is to head towards the five workers, but the subject can choose to pull a switch that redirects the train to the other side of the fork to cause the death of only one worker instead of five. In the second scenario, the subject has to consider whether he would push another individual off a bridge and down onto the tracks below in order to stop the trolley and save the five workers. The 'paradox' is that, experimentally, normal subjects tend to endorse pulling the switch in the first scenario, but not pushing the stranger in the second scenario, even though the net result is the same (death of one individual instead of five). While both scenarios require subjects to pit utilitarian reasoning (maximising aggregate welfare) against an aversive alternative (causing someone's death), the two scenarios are fundamentally different in that the second involves 'personal harm' (pushing a stranger off a bridge) and is therefore presumably more emotionally salient than the first task, which only involves 'impersonal harm' (pulling a switch for the track). The researchers compared the performance of vmPFC-damaged subjects on the two scenarios with both non-brain damaged subjects and subjects who had other kinds of brain damage but an intact vmPFC. First, they found no significant difference between the performance of the vmPFC-damaged subjects and the other subjects on the impersonal task; all groups made a similar percentage of utilitarian responses. However, on the personal harm task, the vmPFC-damaged subjects exhibited markedly different behaviour than the control groups, endorsing the utilitarian personal harm at much higher rates. Thus, vmPFC damage appears to

---

[4] AR Damasio, BJ Everitt and D Bishop, 'The Somatic Marker Hypothesis and the Possible Functions of the Prefrontal Cortex [and Discussion]' (1996) 351 *Philosophical Transactions of the Royal Society B: Biological Sciences* 1413.

[5] M Koenigs, L Young, R Adolphs, D Tranel, F Cushman, M Hauser and A Damasio, 'Damage to the Prefrontal Cortex Increases Utilitarian Moral Judgements' (2007) 446 *Nature* 908.

disrupt the processing that attaches emotional valence to moral considerations. Without this, vmPFC-damaged individuals have an easier time endorsing the utilitarian option under emotionally salient conditions, with a diminished degree of emotional conflict that is normally experienced by vmPFC-intact individuals. The pattern of results from the trolley scenarios illustrates an important point. While the abnormal performance of vmPFC-damaged subjects on the second scenario points to the essential role of the vmPFC in the emotion-processing component of moral decision making, the normal performance of these subjects on the first scenario suggests that they still retain basic rational abilities. Nonetheless, the lack of an emotional valence encapsulating these norms makes it more difficult for these individuals to be driven to act in accordance with them.

The critical role of vmPFC in governing moral behaviour is further evidenced by patients with certain variants of frontotemporal dementia (FTD). FTD is a neurodegenerative illness that predominantly affects the prefrontal and anterior temporal cortices. When the progressive deterioration of brain tissue is focused on the medial frontal regions, including vmPFC, the patient may evince gross disruptions of social and moral behaviour. In addition to affective personality changes such as flattened affect and lack of empathy, FTD patients may develop criminal behaviour such as sexual assault and shoplifting. Importantly, these patients can commit such behaviours (clearly attributable to their brain atrophy) while still retaining declarative knowledge that their behaviour is immoral and illegal.[6] These cases demonstrate a key point in regard to the relevance of neuroscience for defining legal culpability: the ability to conform to laws and social norms is dependent on the patent function of particular neural circuits that do not subserve declarative knowledge of right and wrong.

vmPFC Dysfunction in Psychopathy

Whereas the studies discussed in the preceding section examined individuals who acquired vmPFC damage later in life, the ability of the vmPFC to function properly is also a consideration for some neurodevelopmental disorders—most notably, psychopathy. Psychopathy is a personality disorder defined by a constellation of antisocial and affective behavioural traits. In the media, psychopathy is often inappropriately conflated with psychosis and mass murder. While psychopathy is an enormously important disorder for us to understand within the context of criminal justice and the insanity defence—psychopathic offenders are thought to constitute 15–25 per cent of the adult prison population[7]—the definition of the disorder is more nuanced. In a seminal description, Cleckley

---

[6] MF Mendez, 'The Unique Predisposition to Criminal Violations in Frontotemporal Dementia' (2010) 38 *Journal of the American Academy of Psychiatry and the Law Online* 318.

[7] RD Hare, *The Hare Psychopathy Checklist—Revised* (Toronto, Multi-Health Systems Inc, 1991).

writes in *The Mask of Sanity*:[8] 'the psychopath has a basic inadequacy of feeling and realization that prevents him from normally experiencing the major emotions and from reacting adequately to the chief goals of human life'. More specifically, psychopathy manifests itself through traits such as lack of empathy, pathological lying, grandiose sense of self-worth, impulsivity, lack of realistic long-term goals, and irresponsibility. The presence of these traits in offender populations is typically measured with the Psychopathy Checklist-Revised (PCL-R), where 20 traits are rated 0, 1 or 2.[9] Scores of 30 and above are considered to indicate psychopathy. In addition to comprising an outsize proportion of arrested criminals, psychopathic offenders are also three times more likely to reoffend and four times more likely to reoffend violently within one year of release, as compared to non-psychopathic offenders.[10] It has been hypothesised that psychopathic personality and behaviour is due, in part, to a dysfunctional vmPFC. The following section will examine the evidence for this notion.

One line of evidence implicating a compromised vmPFC in psychopathy is the similar performance of psychopathic criminals to adult-onset vmPFC-damaged subjects in moral dilemma tasks in the laboratory. In one study,[11] psychopathic inmates were compared with non-psychopathic inmates on the trolley paradox task. The psychopathic inmates were further subdivided into two groups, to test for differences between low-anxious (primary) psychopathic offenders and high-anxious (secondary) psychopathic offenders. Just like the vmPFC-damaged subjects in the earlier study, the primary psychopathic offenders endorsed significantly more utilitarian actions on the personal harm scenario than the non-psychopathic offenders (secondary psychopathic offenders did not differ from the non-psychopathic offenders), consistent with a deficit in emotional processing due to a faulty vmPFC.

A subsequent line of research has sought to examine whether neuroimaging would more directly reveal a faulty vmPFC in criminal offenders classified with psychopathy. With the help of a mobile MRI machine operated by Dr Kent Kiehl and the Mind Research Network, the past few years have seen the largest and most rigorous neuroimaging studies ever conducted on psychopathic inmates. The first finding relating to the vmPFC of psychopathic offenders is in the realm of structural connectivity. One of the essential white matter connections from the vmPFC is to the amygdala, a subcortical structure in the medial temporal lobe that is central to the regulation of emotional behaviours such as fear, anxiety and

---

[8] H Cleckley, *The Mask of Sanity; An Attempt to Reinterpret the So-called Psychopathic Personality* (St Louis, MO, CV Mosby, 1941).

[9] RD Hare and CS Neumann, 'The PCL-R Assessment of Psychopathy' (2006) *Handbook of Psychopathy* 58.

[10] JF Hemphill, RD Hare and S Wong, 'Psychopathy and Recidivism: A Review' (1998) 3 *Legal and Criminological Psychology* 139.

[11] M Koenigs, M Kruepke, J Zeier and JP Newman, 'Utilitarian Moral Judgment in Psychopathy' (2012) 7 *Social, Cognitive, and Affective Neuroscience* 708.

aggression. Motzkin et al[12] used DTI to investigate the structural integrity of this vmPFC-amygdala white matter connection, called the Uncinate Fasciculus (UF), in psychopathic prisoners. They found that virtually the only white matter tract in the whole brain that differed between the psychopathic inmates and a control group of non-psychopathic inmates was the UF, with psychopathic offenders having significantly reduced integrity. This finding has been replicated in multiple independent studies.[13] The research group then looked to corroborate this structural finding with functional data, using resting-state fMRI to examine functional connectivity between the vmPFC and amygdala. Again, they found that the psychopathic group had significantly reduced functional connectivity between these two structures compared to the non-psychopathic group.

Another study[14] linked deficient neural activity in these areas to deficits in morality processing in psychopathic criminals. Using task-based fMRI, the researchers showed a group of psychopathic criminals and a group of non-psychopathic criminals pictures of scenarios that did or did not involve moral transgressions, and asked the subjects to rate the severity of moral violation in each scenario. First, they found that, within non-psychopathic criminals, there was greater activity in vmPFC in response to the moral violations relative to the non-moral images. By contrast, the psychopathic criminals exhibited no such discrimination between moral and non-moral pictures with respect to their vmPFC activity. Second, they found that BOLD signal in the amygdalae of psychopathic criminals showed less of a positive association to moral violation severity compared to non-psychopathic criminals. Overall, these results suggest reduced functionality of both the vmPFC and amygdala in psychopathic criminals while processing moral violations.

As the previous two studies suggest, the vmPFC is not the only structure in the brain thought to underlie psychopathy. For one, the amygdala appears to function in tandem with the vmPFC in order to regulate normal emotion processing and social behaviour. Studies have revealed both structural and functional abnormalities in the amygdalae of psychopathic offenders. Yang et al[15] used structural MRI to show that psychopathic individuals had a 17.1 per cent reduction in volume of the left amygdala and 18.9 per cent volume reduction in the right amygdala compared to non-psychopathic individuals, and that the degree of volume reduction correlated with the severity of psychopathy as assessed by the

[12] J Motzkin, JP Newman, K Kiehl and M Koenigs, 'Reduced Prefrontal Connectivity in Psychopathy' (2011) 31 *Journal of Neuroscience* 17348.

[13] MC Craig, M Catani, Q Deeley, R Latham, E Daly, R Kanaan et al, 'Altered Connections on the Road to Psychopathy' (2009) 14 *Molecular Psychiatry* 946; SS Hoppenbrouwers, A Nazeri, DR de Jesus, T Stirpe, D Felsky, DJ Schutter et al, 'White Matter Deficits in Psychopathic Offenders and Correlation with Factor Structure' (2013) 8 *PloS one* e72375.

[14] CL Harenski, KA Harenski, MS Shane and KA Kiehl, 'Aberrant Neural Processing of Moral Violations in Criminal Psychopaths' (2010) 119 *Journal of Abnormal Psychology* 863.

[15] Y Yang, A Raine, P Colletti, AW Toga and KL Narr, 'Morphological Alterations in the Prefrontal Cortex and the Amygdala in Unsuccessful Psychopaths' (2010) 119 *Journal of Abnormal Psychology* 546.

PCL-R. Glenn et al[16] demonstrated using fMRI a reduction in amygdala activity in subjects with higher psychopathy scores during an emotional moral decision-making task.

A host of other brain abnormalities have been implicated in psychopathy as well. These include structural findings such as cortical thinning,[17] reduced volume of the posterior hippocampus,[18] abnormal shape of the hippocampus,[19] and increased volume of the striatum,[20] as well as functional findings, such as reduced activity levels in the anterior and posterior cingulate cortex,[21] hippocampal and parahippocampal gyri,[22] insula,[23] and ventral striatum.[24] With such a disparate array of findings, likely attributable to a combination of differences in experimental methodology and psychopathy classification schemes among different labs,[25] at this point there is no unequivocal neuroimaging marker for psychopathy. Moreover, it is not yet clear how neuroimaging measures could be used to attribute psychopathic behaviour to a particular neural defect for the purpose of assessing insanity.

It is worth returning to the point that psychopathic offenders and other individuals with vmPFC dysfunction who behave amorally appear to retain demonstrable semantic knowledge of moral and social norms—of 'right' versus 'wrong'. As it stands currently, most legal systems dictate that one of the grounds for guilt in a criminal trial is knowledge that one has transgressed normative morality—in essence, recognition that what one has done is 'wrong'. In doing so, the law assumes that semantic or declarative knowledge of society's rules should be sufficient capacity not to transgress them. But what modern neuroscience has revealed is that the capacity to act in accordance with moral norms requires

---

[16] AL Glenn, A Raine and RA Schug, 'The Neural Correlates of Moral Decision-making in Psychopathy' (2009) 14 *Molecular Psychiatry* 5.

[17] M Ly, JC Motzkin, CL Philippi, GR Kirk, JP Newman, KA Kiehl and M Koenigs, 'Cortical Thinning in Psychopathy' (2012) 169 *American Journal of Psychiatry* 743.

[18] MP Laakso, O Vaurio, E Koivisto, L Savolainen, M Eronen, HJ Aronen, P Hakola, E Repo, H Soininen and J Tiihonen, 'Psychopathy and the Posterior Hippocampus' (2001) 118 *Behavioural Brain Research* 187.

[19] M Boccardi, R Ganzola, R Rossi, F Sabattoli, MP Laakso, E Repo-Tiihonen et al, 'Abnormal Hippocampal Shape in Offenders with Psychopathy' (2010) 31 *Human Brain Mapping* 438.

[20] AL Glenn, A Raine, PS Yaralian and Y Yang, 'Increased Volume of the Striatum in Psychopathic Individuals' (2010) 67 *Biological Psychiatry* 52.

[21] JK Rilling, AL Glenn, MR Jairam, G Pagnoni, DR Goldsmith, HA Elfenbein et al, 'Neural Correlates of Social Cooperation and Non-cooperation as a Function of Psychopathy' (2007) 61 *Biological Psychiatry* 1260.

[22] KA Kiehl, AM Smith, RD Hare, A Mendrek, BB Forster, J Brink et al, 'Limbic Abnormalities in Affective Processing by Criminal Psychopaths as revealed by Functional Magnetic Resonance Imaging' (2001) 50 *Biological Psychiatry* 677.

[23] N Birbaumer, R Veit, M Lotze, M Erb, C Hermann, W Grodd et al. 'Deficient Fear Conditioning in Psychopathy: A Functional Magnetic Resonance Imaging Study' (2005) 62 *Archives of General Psychiatry* 799.

[24] Kiehl et al (n 22).

[25] M Koenigs, A Baskin-Sommers, J Zeier, and JP Newman, 'Investigating the Neural Correlates of Psychopathy: A Critical Review' (2011) 16 *Molecular Psychiatry* 792.

much more from the brain than simple recognition of right and wrong at an intellectual level. If moral behaviour is envisioned as being directed by a compass, moral knowledge simply fills in the demarcations of north, south, east and west (right and wrong). But without the addition of a 'magnetising force' to provide orientation, these directional demarcations are all but meaningless. In the brain (and mind), the magnetising force that drives moral behaviour is emotion. If psychopathic individuals and vmPFC-damaged individuals lack the proper neural infrastructure to generate the negative emotions of guilt, remorse, embarrassment and shame that would otherwise provide negative affirmation and motivation to not behave amorally, can we really say that they have the same capacity to behave morally as everyone else just because they have moral knowledge? With this in mind, it may be worth considering within the legal community whether this standard for guilt accurately reflects the current neuropsychological understanding of moral and amoral behaviour.

Neurobiology of Abnormal Impulsivity and Reward Sensitivity

Any normal, healthy individual may occasionally feel an urge to carry out an illegal act, like punching an overbearing boss or running a red light. Yet, the law requires that we exercise control over these urges when they affect the rights and welfare of others. Much of the capacity to tranquilise our urges stems from our ability to prioritise long-term, delayed positive outcomes over short-term, immediate pleasure or benefit. For instance, punching one's boss in the face might provide an instant of great subjective pleasure, but the long-term consequences of such an action vastly outweigh its immediate benefits. The ability to wilfully suspend such gratification contributes crucially to maintaining pro-social, law-abiding behaviour. It is conceivable that failure to inhibit antisocial urges could be due to weak restraint or inhibition, excessive drive and motivation, or some combination of the two. In this section we consider the neural circuitry underlying these psychological processes.

Relevant Brain Regions and Circuits

The brain's inhibition and reward circuit consists of several key cortical and subcortical nodes. Here we will discuss three such regions that have been studied extensively in humans and rodents. One is a section of prefrontal cortex discussed extensively in the preceding section—the vmPFC and neighbouring orbitofrontal cortex (OFC). Another is an adjacent region called the dorsal anterior cingulate cortex (dACC). The other is a subcortical structure called the ventral striatum.

Ventral Striatum

The ventral striatum is involved with a sub-network of structures, including the ventral tegmental area and nucleus accumbens (NAc), which process reward expectancy and whose activation triggers the subjective feeling of pleasure. Activation of this reward circuit is a powerful motivator of behaviour, as was first demonstrated in mice by Olds and Milner in 1954.[26] The researchers placed electrodes at sites along the reward circuit of the mice that, when activated, stimulated the reward circuit. Via levers within their cage, the mice controlled activation of the electrodes. The researchers observed that the mice repeatedly pushed the lever to stimulate their reward circuit, which showed that their behaviour could be strongly influenced by activation of the reward circuit. Amazingly, the mice would seek this electrical stimulation with as much (or more) vigour than naturally pleasurable rewards such as food. In addition, the mice were willing to undergo noxious punishment (a painful foot shock) in order to access the stimulation. Decades of subsequent research have highlighted the ventral striatum as a key subcortical node within the reward circuit. Studies on rodents with damage to the NAc region of the ventral striatum reveal that they have difficulty withholding impulses, preferring immediate rewards even though they are small over larger rewards that are delayed.[27] In a value-based discrimination-learning task, rats with a normally functioning NAc are able to increase their responses to an odour that is paired with a positive outcome (appetitive sucrose solution) and withhold their response to an odour paired with a negative outcome (aversive quinine solution). By contrast, rats with NAc damage do not learn to withhold their responses to the odour predicting the negative outcome.[28]

As neuroimaging studies have confirmed homologous reward circuit areas in rodents and humans,[29] there appears to be potential relevance of this research for understanding the neurobiology of criminal behaviour. For instance, virtually all substances of abuse act upon the ventral striatum region of the reward circuit.[30] In addition, the antisocial and impulsive traits of psychopathy have been linked to hypersensitivity of this area.[31] If alteration of this circuit *causes* a disruption in processing reward and punishment (as the rodent data indicate), then

[26] J Olds and P Milner, 'Positive Reinforcement Produced by Electrical Stimulation of Septal Area and Other Regions of Rat Brain' (1954) 47 *Journal of Comparative and Physiological Psychology* 419.

[27] RN Cardinal and NJ Howes, 'Effects of Lesions of the Nucleus Accumbens Core on Choice between Small Certain Rewards and Large Uncertain Rewards in Rats' (2005) 6(37) *BioMed Central Neuroscience* 1; RN Cardinal, DR Pennicott, CL Sugathapala, TW Robbins and BJ Everitt, 'Impulsive Choice Induced in Rats by Lesions of the Nucleus Accumbens Core' (2001) 292 *Science* 2499.

[28] G Schoenbaum and B Setlow, 'Lesions of Nucleus Accumbens Disrupt Learning About Aversive Outcomes' (2003) 23 *Journal of Neuroscience* 9833.

[29] B Knutson and JC Cooper, 'Functional Magnetic Resonance Imaging of Reward Prediction' (2005) 18 *Current Opinion in Neurology* 411; B Knutson, CM Adams, GW Fong and D Hommer, 'Anticipation of Increasing Monetary Reward Selectively Recruits Nucleus Accumbens' (2001) 21 *Journal of Neuroscience* 159; JP O'Doherty, R Deichmann, HD Critchley and RJ Dolan, 'Neural Responses During Anticipation of a Primary Taste Reward' (2002) 33 *Neuron* 815; J Yacubian, J Gläscher, K Schroeder, T Sommer, DF Braus and C Büchel, 'Dissociable Systems for Gain- and Loss-related Value Predictions and Errors of Prediction in the Human Brain' (2006) 26 *Journal of Neuroscience* 9530.

[30] BJ Everitt and TW Robbins, 'Neural Systems of Reinforcement for Drug Addiction: From Actions to Habits to Compulsion' (2005) 8 *Nature Neuroscience* 1481.

[31] JW Buckholtz, MT Treadway, RL Cowan, ND Woodward, SD Benning, R Li et al, 'Mesolimbic Dopamine Reward System Hypersensitivity in Individuals with Psychopathic Traits' (2010) 13 *Nature Neuroscience* 419.

offenders with ventral striatal dysfunction may not process and respond to reward and punishment like most people. In other words, these individuals may not learn from the negative consequences of their actions to avoid them in the future. Whether neuroimaging data will provide a useful measure for predicting recidivism and guiding sentencing is an issue we will revisit later in the chapter.

vmPFC/OFC

In addition to the moral processing capacities outlined previously in the chapter, there is compelling evidence that vmPFC/OFC also plays a critical role in processing more basic elements of risk, uncertainty, reward and punishment. Several decades of studies on patients with brain injuries have demonstrated the necessity of a properly functioning vmPFC/OFC for these types of processing. Without them, decision-making can become short-sighted and impulsive. Indeed, one of the most conspicuous behavioural changes in Phineas Gage was that he became 'impatient of restraint or advice when it conflict[ed] with his desires'.[32] Similar impairments in vmPFC/OFC-damaged individuals have been consistently demonstrated through laboratory paradigms such as the Iowa Gambling Task (IGT). In the IGT, subjects play cards from four decks that vary with respect to the amount and relative frequency of monetary loss or gain. Through trial and error, subjects must learn to adapt their card choices to enact advantageous selections in their subsequent turns. Bechara et al[33] first reported the performance of vmPFC/OFC-damaged individuals on this task, observing that they would base their card choices on the risky prospect of large, immediate payouts rather than more modest but consistent payouts that were more advantageous in the long run. This 'myopia for the future', as the researchers called it, resulted from an impaired ability to process risk and reward due to a damaged vmPFC/OFC. Since this initial finding, impairments in the IGT and related gambling tasks as a function of vmPFC/OFC damage have been replicated several times.[34] In a related line of work, the vmPFC/OFC has also been shown to be crucial to temporal discounting—the ability to inhibit prepotent responses to immediate, small rewards in favour of delayed, larger rewards. Although human vmPFC/OFC lesion studies of temporal discounting

---

[32] Harlow (n 2).

[33] A Bechara, AR Damasio, H Damasio and SW Anderson, 'Insensitivity to Future Consequences Following Damage to Human Prefrontal Cortex' (1994) 50 *Cognition* 7.

[34] LK Fellows and MJ Farah, 'Ventromedial Frontal Cortex Mediates Affective Shifting in Humans: Evidence from a Reversal Learning Paradigm' (2003) 126 *Brain* 1830; M Hsu, M Bhatt, R Adolphs, D Tranel, and CF Camerer, 'Neural Systems Responding to Degrees of Uncertainty in Human Decision-making' (2005) 310 *Science* 1680; L Naccache, S Dehaene, L Cohen, MO Habert, E Guichart, E Gomez, D Galanaud et al, 'Effortless Control: Executive Attention and Conscious Feeling of Mental Effort Are Dissociable' (2005) 43 *Neuropsychologia* 1318; SM Waters-Wood, L Xiao, NL Denburg, M Hernandez and A Bechara, 'Failure to Learn from Repeated Mistakes: Persistent Decision-making Impairment as Measured by the Iowa Gambling Task in Patients with Ventromedial Prefrontal Cortex Lesions' (2012) 18 *Journal of the International Neuropsychological Society* 927.

have yielded mixed results,[35] work in rodents suggests that the vmPFC/OFC may be crucial for temporal discounting.[36]

Dorsal Anterior Cingulate Cortex

The dACC is thought to serve as a point of contact between brain regions that process negative feedback and punishment and brain regions that direct the motor and behavioural output dependent on this processing. As such, the dACC is essential in facilitating behavioural inhibition and control, by way of appropriately modulating motor output when it receives input suggesting that the generation of a certain behaviour may result in negative consequences.[37] More specifically, human fMRI studies have consistently shown that dACC activity is sensitive to errors and negative feedback in ongoing task performance. It is believed that this dACC signal is thus critical for abating and correcting maladaptive behaviour.

In fact, the first US criminal court case to admit fMRI evidence involved scan data showing reduced BOLD activity in areas of the brain associated with behavioural inhibition, including dACC.[38] In 2009, the defendant Brian Dugan faced the death penalty for multiple rape-murders. Dugan scored 38 out of 40 on the Psychopathy Checklist-Revised (PCL-R), indicating a severely high level of psychopathy. The defence argued that the fMRI results showed that Dugan lacked the proper brain functionality to control his violent impulses, but the prosecution countered by listing several of the limitations of brain imaging technology for purposes of the courtroom (discussed earlier in this chapter). Specifically, the prosecution used the 'brains change over time' argument to assert that there was no way to know that Dugan's brain functioned the same way as measured now by the fMRI machine as it did 26 years earlier at the time of the murders. They also invoked the 'comparing a group to an individual introduces statistical ambiguity' argument. To unpack this to the jury, the prosecution used an analogy with professional basketball players, pointing out that while the average player might be six foot five, the majority of individuals in the general population who are six foot five are not professional basketball players. Likewise, while it may be true that the brains of most murderers show abnormalities in the behavioural control and

---

[35] LK Fellows and MJ Farah, 'Dissociable Elements of Human Foresight: a Role for the Ventromedial Frontal Lobes in Framing the Future, but Not in Discounting Future Rewards' (2005) 43 *Neuropsychologia* 1214; M Sellitto, E Ciaramelli and G di Pellegrino, 'Myopic Discounting of Future Rewards after Medial Orbitofrontal Damage in Humans' (2010) 30 *Journal of Neuroscience* 16429.

[36] Cardinal et al (n 27); S Kheramin, S Body, MY Ho, DN Velázquez-Martinez, CM Bradshaw, E Szabadi et al, 'Effects of Orbital Prefrontal Cortex Dopamine Depletion on Inter-temporal Choice: A Quantitative Analysis' (2004) 175 *Psychopharmacology* 206; S Mobini, S Body, MY Ho, CM Bradshaw, E Szabadi, JF Deakin et al, 'Effects of Lesions of the Orbitofrontal Cortex on Sensitivity to Delayed and Probabilistic Reinforcement' (2002) 160 *Psychopharmacology* 290.

[37] AJ Shackman, TV Salomons, HA Slagter, AS Fox, JJ Winter and RJ Davidson, 'The Integration of Negative Affect, Pain and Cognitive Control in the Cingulate Cortex' (2011) 12 *Nature Reviews Neuroscience* 154.

[38] V Hughes, 'Science in Court: Head Case' (2010) 464 *Nature* 340.

reward circuit, not everyone with such abnormalities is a murderer. Ultimately, the jury unanimously voted to sentence Dugan to the death penalty.

Dugan's case highlights again the difficulty of using neuroimaging to make definitive judgements about a defendant's degree of insanity and about the causal relationships between a brain abnormality and a crime. Nonetheless, the neuroscientific evidence implicating faulty inhibition and reward sensitivity networks in poor behavioural control and impulsivity suggests that these kinds of impairments may be relevant factors in assessments of legal insanity.

Neurobiology of Low Intelligence and Psychosis

This category of brain and behavioural deficits is the one that legal definitions of insanity have traditionally emphasised. Most generally, these are instances of individuals with either abnormally low IQs due to cognitive deficits or individuals with florid psychosis. In both instances, such individuals lack an understanding of reality as most people know it, and may be unable to comprehend the legal or moral significance of their actions.

Low IQ

While a host of studies exist that examine correlations between IQ and various brain metrics in the healthy population, relatively few have investigated brain deficits associated with abnormally low IQ. At least one study[39] has identified reductions in white matter tract integrity along several important pathways in low IQ individuals compared to controls. These include the corpus callosum, which connects the left and right hemispheres of the brain, as well as the UF, which connects structures in the temporal lobe like the hippocampus and amygdala to the frontal lobes. Other studies that have examined cases of low IQ as a symptom of disorders like Fragile X Syndrome, Rett Syndrome and autism have also identified reduced integrity of the corpus callosum, in addition to a range of other abnormalities.[40] Additionally, a large study of patients with neurological damage found that general intelligence declined most sharply with damage involving areas of lateral frontal and parietal cortex, as well as substantial regions of white matter tracts.[41] Despite this collection of results, the relatively limited data and lack of replication in this area of research suggests that, at present, neuroimaging evidence may provide little supplementary value to cases where defendant's claim issues of low IQ.

---

[39] C Yu, J Li, Y Liu, W Qin, Y Li, N Shu et al, 'White Matter Tract Integrity and Intelligence in Patients with Mental Retardation and Healthy Adults' (2008) 40 *Neuroimage* 1533.

[40] AL Alexander, JE Lee, M Lazar, R Boudos, MB DuBray, TR Oakes et al, 'Diffusion Tensor Imaging of the Corpus Callosum in Autism' (2007) 34 *Neuroimage* 61.

[41] J Gläscher, D Rudrauf, R Colom, LK Paul, D Tranel, H Damasio and R Adolphs, 'Distributed Neural System for General Intelligence Revealed by Lesion Mapping' (2010) 107 *Proceedings of the National Academy of Sciences* 4705.

Psychosis

Psychosis refers to a loss of contact with reality, either via hallucinations—seeing or hearing things that are not really there—or delusions—false, often anxiety-fuelled beliefs about the actions or intentions of others or about the state of the world. Psychosis is a prominent symptom of psychiatric illnesses such as schizophrenia and some types of bipolar disorder, and tends to occur in discrete episodes. It may be during these psychotic episodes that sufferers of psychiatric illness are prone, in some cases, to commit crimes. While use of the insanity defence often requires proof of insanity during the crime itself, neuroimaging does not have the ability to provide proof of a past psychotic episode, for such episodes do not leave any sort of recognisable timestamp or trace that they occurred on the brain. Thus, the most relevant neuroimaging data in these cases would be structural or functional abnormalities that are generally associated with psychosis.

Although neuroscientists have identified a host of abnormalities in individuals with psychiatric illnesses that involve psychosis, it has proven difficult to pin down definitive markers of psychosis that consistently span all such individuals. One challenge is the wide variation in the manifestation of these disorders. A further complication is that individuals at different stages of the disorder (first-episode versus chronic) may display different degrees of abnormalities due to progression of the illness over time. Underscoring the variability in imaging findings related to psychosis is a meta-analysis conducted by Honea et al.[42] The researchers found that among 15 studies encompassing 390 schizophrenic patients, a total of 50 different brain abnormalities had been reported across the schizophrenic subjects. Nine of the 50 findings were reported in only single studies, while the two most common findings—grey matter volume reductions in the left superior temporal gyrus and in the left medial temporal lobe—were reported in only about half of the studies. Another finding revealed by a separate meta-analysis encompassing 58 studies and 1,588 schizophrenic patients was that schizophrenic individuals had an abnormally high volume of the lateral ventricles compared to controls.[43]

The variation in brain abnormalities in individuals with psychosis has important ramifications for the courtroom. First, since many of the findings are based on differences in large group averages, it is possible that an individual scanned for a trial may not show significant differences from a batch of controls even if he truly suffers from psychosis. Even if a significant brain abnormality were detected, it would be difficult for the defence to argue that it is a definitive marker of psychosis proneness. That said, scans that reveal some of the more common abnormalities,

---

[42] R Honea, TJ Crow, D Passingham and CE Mackay, 'Regional Deficits in Brain Volume in Schizophrenia: A Meta-analysis of Voxel-based Morphometry Studies' (2005) 162 *American Journal of Psychiatry* 2233.

[43] IC Wright, S Rabe-Hesketh, PW Woodruff, AS David, RM Murray and ET Bullmore, 'Meta-analysis of Regional Brain Volumes in Schizophrenia' (2000) 157 *American Journal of Psychiatry* 16.

such as reductions in temporal lobe volumes or enlargements of the lateral ventricles, could help to corroborate psychological evaluations of psychosis in the defendant.

What Value Can Neuroscience Realistically Add?

As discussed throughout this chapter, neuroimaging is far from providing the sort of definitive scientific testimony that, say, DNA sequencing and matching provides. At this point in time, a neuroscientist cannot look at a neuroimaging scan and definitively conclude whether an individual qualifies as legally insane, nor can he definitively conclude that a particular abnormality contributed to a crime. This is due to both the technological and methodological limitations of neuroimaging as well as the burgeoning, but still limited, knowledge in the field of neuroscience at present. As a result, neuroimaging data at this time may function best as suggestive evidence that is complementary and secondary to the traditional forms of behavioural evidence currently in use to assess insanity. For example, if a defendant's behavioural profile is indicative of excessive impulsivity, neuroimaging data that reveals abnormalities in brain regions relevant to impulsivity can help corroborate the veracity of the behavioural profile. Furthermore, the current state of technology and knowledge in neuroscience can contribute to the legal system and the legal understanding of insanity in other ways.

First, the field's accumulation of knowledge about the neurobiology of criminal behaviour may prompt the legal community to consider a second look at how insanity is legally defined. In light of the three distinct types of neurological and behavioural deficits identified and discussed here, current definitions may be too limited in scope to encompass the full range of neurobiological impairments and accompanying behavioural deficits that can lead to criminal behaviour. In addition to this potential expansion of the definition, the content that exists in current definitions may need to be revised in consideration of new knowledge about how morality works in neuropsychological terms.

Second, neuroscience may be able to aid in the sentencing phase of trials. The bulk of this chapter has been concerned with the guilt phase of trials, and how neuroscience could (or could not) be used to identify instances of insanity and shed light on the culpability of individuals. But determining guilt and ensuring justice is only one part of the function of the legal system. A second is to increase the well-being and safety of society, and neuroscience can be informative here in several ways. First, neuroimaging data can add information to assessments that calculate a convicted defendant's likelihood of recidivating. Currently, risk assessment tools are based largely on biographical factors such as demographic information, past offences, gang affiliation, substance abuse and personality characteristics. Analyses based on these factors are useful, but not perfect. Neuroimaging data has shown the potential to increase the accuracy of these assessments. For example, a study by Aharoni et al[44] demonstrated that among a population of offenders who participated in an inhibitory control task, those with relatively low levels of activity in the dACC during the task as measured by fMRI were twice as likely to be rearrested compared to offenders with higher levels of activity in this region. This type of information might guide a court to issue a longer prison sentence for individuals with brain characteristics that predict reoffending. Another way in which neuroscience could potentially aid in the sentencing process is determining a defendant's amenability to treatment. It is a realistic possibility that neuroimaging data will in the future help psychiatrists determine whether and which treatment would be most likely to be effective to ameliorate the patient's symptoms. This sort of neurally aided diagnosis could influence the decision about whether the defendant and society would be better served placing the defendant in prison or in a mental health treatment facility. For example, while there is no known cure for psychiatric disorders like schizophrenia, there are several FDA-approved drugs that exist which can help manage symptoms and reduce the incidence of psychotic episodes, as well as cognitive-behavioural therapies aimed at accomplishing the same goals. Thus, if a convicted defendant is thought to have a disorder such as schizophrenia, and the neuroimaging data indicates he is likely to respond to certain kinds of treatment, sentencing him to a mental health facility may be the best option to decrease the likelihood of his engaging in criminal behaviour again, by giving him access to the treatments he needs to adjust his behaviour.

Psychopathic offenders represent an intriguing case in which neuroscience may drive into conflict the dual goals of ensuring fair justice and increasing societal well-being. On one hand, neuroscientific data may suggest that psychopathic offenders have reduced culpability due to brain abnormalities that render them less able to generate emotion that guides moral behaviour or control impulses for immediate rewards. On the basis of ensuring fair justice, this reduced culpability may warrant shortened prison time or deferment to a mental health treatment facility. On the other hand, neuroscientific data may also provide evidence that psychopathic offenders have a high likelihood of recidivating partly due to neurobiological deficits that render them less able to learn from punishment or feel remorse. On the basis of protecting society, then, shortened prison sentences for such individuals may not be the best option. Furthermore, since there is not yet any established treatment for psychopathy, deferment to a mental health facility that has little to nothing to offer such individuals seems like a poor option too. At some point, legal experts may wish to leverage the knowledge from neuroscience to consider the best course of action in such situations to satisfy the goals of the legal system.

---

[44] E Aharoni, GM Vincent, CL Harenski, VD Calhoun, W Sinnott-Armstrong, MS Gazzaniga and KA Kiehl, 'Neuroprediction of Future Rearrest' (2013) 110 *Proceedings of the National Academy of Sciences* 6223.

Cautions

The application of neuroscience to criminal behaviour may result in some unintended consequences that deserve consideration. The first concerns the outsized weight that people tend to give to psychological explanations that are based on neuroscience. In a seminal paper titled 'The Seductive Allure of Neuroscience Explanations',[45] researchers demonstrated that individuals who were non-experts in neuroscience were more likely to rate explanations of a given phenomenon as satisfying if the explanation contained grounding in neuroscience—*even if the neuroscience information was completely irrelevant to the phenomenon*. In the context of the courtroom, this puts judges and jurors in a vulnerable position when presented with neuroimaging data. Even though this chapter has argued that neuroimaging data is currently best used as secondary, complementary evidence, the inherent allure of neuroscience explanations may make jurors liable to overvalue or be misled by defence arguments couched in neuroimaging data. Evidence of the potential for neuroimaging evidence to influence the rulings of judges has already surfaced. In a study by Aspinwall et al,[46] 181 US state trial court judges were presented with a hypothetical but realistic case involving an offender who is convicted of aggravated battery from severely beating a restaurant manager during a robbery. Half of the judges were also presented with evidence for a biomechanism to explain the defendant's impulsive behaviour, which included a genetic profile relating to neurotransmitter function as well as fMRI data showing atypical amygdala activity. When this neuroscience evidence was presented by the defence, judges were twice as likely to cite mitigating factors that warranted shorter sentences for the offender, compared to instances when judges were not presented with this evidence or when the evidence was presented by the prosecution.

The other potential impact of applying neuroscience to explain, and sometimes pardon, criminal behaviour may occur outside the courtroom. Neuroscience-based explanations of behaviour tend to peel back the feeling that people have free will, in favour of the idea that our actions are predetermined by the causal mechanisms programmed into our biology. The degree to which people believe in free will has been shown to influence behaviour, particularly due to the fact that free will encourages a sense of personal responsibility and control. An oft-cited study by Vohs and Schooler[47] showed that among two groups of students

[45] DS Weisberg, FC Keil, J Goodstein, E Rawson and JR Gray, 'The Seductive Allure of Neuroscience Explanations' (2008) 20 *Journal of Cognitive Neuroscience* 470.

[46] LG Aspinwall, TR Brown and J Tabery, 'The Double-edged Sword: Does Biomechanism Increase or Decrease Judges' Sentencing of Psychopaths?' (2012) 337 *Science* 846.

[47] KD Vohs and JW Schooler, 'The Value of Believing in Free Will Encouraging a Belief in Determinism Increases Cheating' (2008) 19 *Psychological Science* 49.

who took a maths test, the group that read a passage prior to taking the test about how our biology and the environment shape our behaviour (supporting a deterministic outlook) was more likely to cheat in the test. Will enshrining the idea in our legal system that the brain drives behaviour in a way that is out of our control prompt more law breaking by individuals who feel a lack of responsibility for their actions?

IV. Conclusion

Although neuroscientific research is yielding increasingly sophisticated and convincing evidence that amoral and criminal behaviour can be linked to faulty brain circuitry, there does not yet appear to be sufficient knowledge to support definitive judgements about what kind and degree of brain abnormalities qualify one for the insanity defence. Nonetheless, there are a number of foreseeable circumstances in which neuroscience and neuroimaging technology could potentially have a significant impact in the courtroom.

Bibliography

Aharoni, E, Vincent, GM, Harenski, CL, Calhoun, VD, Sinnott-Armstrong, W, Gazzaniga, MS and Kiehl, KA, 'Neuroprediction of Future Rearrest' (2013) 110 *Proceedings of the National Academy of Sciences* 6223.

Alexander, AL, Lee, JE, Lazar, M, Boudos, R, DuBray, MB, Oakes, TR et al, 'Diffusion Tensor Imaging of the Corpus Callosum in Autism' (2007) 34 *Neuroimage* 61.

Aspinwall, LG, Brown, TR and Tabery, J, 'The Double-edged Sword: Does Biomechanism Increase or Decrease Judges' Sentencing of Psychopaths?' (2012) 337 *Science* 846.

Bechara, A, Damasio, AR, Damasio, H and Anderson, SW, 'Insensitivity to Future Consequences Following Damage to Human Prefrontal Cortex' (1994) 50 *Cognition* 7.

Birbaumer, N, Veit, R, Lotze, M, Erb, M, Hermann, C, Grodd, W et al, 'Deficient Fear Conditioning in Psychopathy: A Functional Magnetic Resonance Imaging Study' (2005) 62 *Archives of General Psychiatry* 799.

Boccardi, M, Ganzola, R, Rossi, R, Sabattoli, F, Laakso, MP, Repo-Tiihonen, E et al, 'Abnormal Hippocampal Shape in Offenders with Psychopathy' (2010) 31 *Human Brain Mapping* 438.

Buckholtz, JW, Treadway, MT, Cowan, RL, Woodward, ND, Benning, SD, Li, R et al, 'Mesolimbic Dopamine Reward System Hypersensitivity in Individuals with Psychopathic Traits' (2010) 13 *Nature Neuroscience* 419.

Cardinal, RN and Howes, NJ, 'Effects of Lesions of the Nucleus Accumbens Core on Choice between Small Certain Rewards and Large Uncertain Rewards in Rats' (2005) 6(37) *BioMed Central Neuroscience* 1.

Cardinal, RN, Pennicott, DR, Sugathapala, CL, Robbins, TW and Everitt, BJ, 'Impulsive Choice Induced in Rats by Lesions of the Nucleus Accumbens Core' (2001) 292 *Science* 2499.

Cleckley, H, *The Mask of Sanity; An Attempt to Reinterpret the So-called Psychopathic Personality* (St Louis, MO, CV Mosby, 1941).

Craig, MC, Catani, M, Deeley, Q, Latham, R, Daly, E, Kanaan, R et al, 'Altered Connections on the Road to Psychopathy' (2009) 14 *Molecular Psychiatry* 946.

Damasio, AR, Everitt, BJ and Bishop, D, 'The Somatic Marker Hypothesis and the Possible Functions of the Prefrontal Cortex [and Discussion]' (1996) 351 *Philosophical Transactions of the Royal Society B: Biological Sciences* 1413.

Eslinger, PJ and Damasio, AR, 'Severe Disturbance of Higher Cognition after Bilateral Frontal Lobe Ablation Patient EVR' (1985) 35 *Neurology* 1731.

Everitt, BJ and Robbins, TW, 'Neural Systems of Reinforcement for Drug Addiction: From Actions to Habits to Compulsion' (2005) 8 *Nature Neuroscience* 1481.

Fellows, LK and Farah, MJ, 'Dissociable Elements of Human Foresight: A Role for the Ventromedial Frontal Lobes in Framing the Future, but Not in Discounting Future Rewards' (2005) 43 *Neuropsychologia* 1214.

Fellows, LK and Farah, MJ, 'Ventromedial Frontal Cortex Mediates Affective Shifting in Humans: Evidence from a Reversal Learning Paradigm' (2003) 126 *Brain* 1830.

Fumagalli, M and Priori, A, 'Functional and Clinical Neuroanatomy of Morality' (2012) 135 *Brain* 2006.

Gläscher, J, Rudrauf, D, Colom, R, Paul, LK, Tranel, D, Damasio, H and Adolphs, R, 'Distributed Neural System for General Intelligence Revealed by Lesion Mapping' (2010) 107 *Proceedings of the National Academy of Sciences* 4705.

Glenn, AL, Raine, A and Schug, RA, 'The Neural Correlates of Moral Decision-making in Psychopathy' (2009) 14 *Molecular Psychiatry* 5.

Glenn, AL, Raine, A, Yaralian, PS and Yang, Y, 'Increased Volume of the Striatum in Psychopathic Individuals' (2010) 67 *Biological Psychiatry* 52.

Hare, RD, *The Hare Psychopathy Checklist—Revised* (Toronto, Multi-Health Systems Inc, 1991).

Hare, RD and Neumann, CS, 'The PCL-R Assessment of Psychopathy' (2006) *Handbook of Psychopathy* 58.

Harenski, CL, Harenski, KA, Shane, MS and Kiehl, KA, 'Aberrant Neural Processing of Moral Violations in Criminal Psychopaths' (2010) 119 *Journal of Abnormal Psychology* 863.

Harlow, JM, 'Recovery from the Passage of an Iron Bar through the Head' (1868) 2 *Publications of the Massachusetts Medical Society* 327.

Hemphill, JF, Hare, RD and Wong, S, 'Psychopathy and Recidivism: A Review' (1998) 3 *Legal and criminological Psychology* 139.

Honea, R, Crow, TJ, Passingham, D and Mackay, CE, 'Regional Deficits in Brain Volume in Schizophrenia: A Meta-analysis of Voxel-based Morphometry Studies' (2005) 162 *American Journal of Psychiatry* 2233.

Hoppenbrouwers, SS, Nazeri, A, Jesus, DR de, Stirpe, T, Felsky, D, Schutter, DJ et al, 'White Matter Deficits in Psychopathic Offenders and Correlation with Factor Structure' (2013) 8 *PloS one* e72375.

Hsu, M, Bhatt, M, Adolphs, R, Tranel, D, and Camerer, CF, 'Neural Systems Responding to Degrees of Uncertainty in Human Decision-making' (2005) 310 *Science* 1680.

Hughes, V, 'Science in Court: Head Case' (2010) 464 *Nature* 340.

Kheramin, S, Body, S, Ho, MY, Velázquez-Martinez, DN, Bradshaw, CM, Szabadi, E, et al, 'Effects of Orbital Prefrontal Cortex Dopamine Depletion on Inter-temporal Choice: A Quantitative Analysis' (2004) 175 *Psychopharmacology* 206.

Kiehl, KA, Smith, AM, Hare, RD, Mendrek, A, Forster, BB, Brink, J et al, 'Limbic Abnormalities in Affective Processing by Criminal Psychopaths as Revealed by Functional Magnetic Resonance Imaging' (2001) 50 *Biological Psychiatry* 677.

Knutson, B, Adams, CM, Fong, GW and Hommer, D, 'Anticipation of Increasing Monetary Reward Selectively Recruits Nucleus Accumbens' (2001) 21 *Journal of Neuroscience* 159.

Knutson, B and Cooper, JC, 'Functional Magnetic Resonance Imaging of Reward Prediction' (2005) 18 *Current Opinion in Neurology* 411.

Koenigs, M, Baskin-Sommers, A, Zeier, J and Newman, JP, 'Investigating the Neural Correlates of Psychopathy: A Critical Review' (2011) 16 *Molecular Psychiatry* 792.

Koenigs, M, Kruepke, M, Zeier, J and Newman, JP, 'Utilitarian Moral Judgment in Psychopathy' (2012) 7 *Social, Cognitive, and Affective Neuroscience* 708.

Koenigs, M, Young, L, Adolphs, R, Tranel, D, Cushman, F, Hauser, M and Damasio, A, 'Damage to the Prefrontal Cortex Increases Utilitarian Moral Judgements' (2007) 446 *Nature* 908.

Laakso, MP, Vaurio, O, Koivisto, E, Savolainen, L, Eronen, M, Aronen, HJ, Hakola, P, Repo, E, Soininen, H and Tiihonen, J, 'Psychopathy and the Posterior Hippocampus' (2001) 118 *Behavioural Brain Research* 187.

Ly, M, Motzkin, JC, Philippi, CL, Kirk, GR, Newman, JP, Kiehl, KA and Koenigs, M, 'Cortical Thinning in Psychopathy' (2012) 169 *American journal of Psychiatry* 743.

Mendez, MF, 'The Neurobiology of Moral Behaviour: Review and Neuropsychiatric Implications' (2009) 14 *CNS Spectrums* 608.

Mendez, MF, 'The Unique Predisposition to Criminal Violations in Frontotemporal Dementia' (2010) 38 *Journal of the American Academy of Psychiatry and the Law Online* 318.

Mobini, S, Body, S, Ho, MY, Bradshaw, CM, Szabadi, E, Deakin, JF et al, 'Effects of Lesions of the Orbitofrontal Cortex on Sensitivity to Delayed and Probabilistic Reinforcement' (2002) 160 *Psychopharmacology* 290.

Motzkin, J, Newman, JP, Kiehl, K and Koenigs, M, 'Reduced Prefrontal Connectivity in Psychopathy' (2011) 31 *Journal of Neuroscience* 17348.

Naccache, L, Dehaene, S, Cohen, L, Habert, MO, Guichart, E, Gomez, E, Galanaud, D et al, 'Effortless Control: Executive Attention and Conscious Feeling of Mental Effort are Dissociable' (2005) 43 *Neuropsychologia* 1318.

O'Doherty, JP, Deichmann, R, Critchley, HD and Dolan, RJ, 'Neural Responses During Anticipation of a Primary Taste Reward' (2002) 33 *Neuron* 815.

Olds, J and Milner, P, 'Positive Reinforcement Produced by Electrical Stimulation of Septal Area and Other Regions of Rat Brain' (1954) 47 *Journal of Comparative and Physiological Psychology* 419.

Pascual, L, Rodrigues, P and Gallardo-Pujol, D, 'How Does Morality Work in the Brain? A Functional and Structural Perspective of Moral Behaviour' (2013) 7 *Frontiers in Integrative Neuroscience* 65.

Rilling, JK, Glenn, AL, Jairam, MR, Pagnoni, G, Goldsmith, DR, Elfenbein, HA et al, 'Neural Correlates of Social Cooperation and Non-cooperation as a Function of Psychopathy' (2007) 61 *Biological Psychiatry* 1260.

Schoenbaum, G and Setlow, B, 'Lesions of Nucleus Accumbens Disrupt Learning about Aversive Outcomes' (2003) 23 *Journal of Neuroscience* 9833.

Sellitto, M, Ciaramelli, E and Pellegrino, G di, 'Myopic Discounting of Future Rewards after Medial Orbitofrontal Damage in Humans' (2010) 30 *Journal of Neuroscience* 16429.

Shackman, AJ, Salomons, TV, Slagter, HA, Fox, AS, Winter, JJ and Davidson, RJ, 'The Integration of Negative Affect, Pain and Cognitive Control in the Cingulate Cortex' (2011) 12 *Nature Reviews Neuroscience* 154.

Vohs, KD and Schooler, JW, 'The value of believing in free will encouraging a belief in determinism increases cheating' (2008) 19 *Psychological Science* 49–54.

Waters-Wood, SM, Xiao, L, Denburg, NL, Hernandez, M and Bechara, A, 'Failure to Learn from Repeated Mistakes: Persistent Decision-making Impairment as Measured by the Iowa Gambling Task in Patients with Ventromedial Prefrontal Cortex Lesions' (2012) 18 *Journal of the International Neuropsychological Society* 927.

Weisberg, DS, Keil, FC, Goodstein, J, Rawson, E and Gray, JR, 'The Seductive Allure of Neuroscience Explanations' (2008) 20 *Journal of Cognitive Neuroscience* 470.

Wright, IC, Rabe-Hesketh, S, Woodruff, PW, David, AS, Murray, RM and Bullmore, ET, 'Meta-analysis of Regional Brain Volumes in Schizophrenia' (2000) 157 *American Journal of Psychiatry* 16.

Yacubian, J, Gläscher, J, Schroeder, K, Sommer, T, Braus, DF and Büchel, C, 'Dissociable Systems for Gain- and Loss-related Value Predictions and Errors of Prediction in the Human Brain' (2006) 26 *Journal of Neuroscience* 9530.

Yang, Y, Raine, A, Colletti, P, Toga, AW and Narr, KL, 'Morphological Alterations in the Prefrontal Cortex and the Amygdala in Unsuccessful Psychopaths' (2010) 119 *Journal of Abnormal Psychology* 546.

Yu, C, Li, J, Liu, Y, Qin, W, Li, Y, Shu, N et al, 'White Matter Tract Integrity and Intelligence in Patients with Mental Retardation and Healthy Adults' (2008) 40 *Neuroimage* 1533.

3

'Neuroscepticism' in the Courtroom: The Limited Role of Neuroscientific Evidence in Belgian Criminal Proceedings

KATRIEN HANOULLE AND FRANK VERBRUGGEN*

I. Introduction

When investigators or judges in a criminal case face a mentally disordered offender, Belgian law offers them two different options: the insanity defence[1] and internment, a preventive measure. Albeit conceptually and legally distinct, the two are often similar in practice. The defence of insanity is based on the mental state of the offender at the time when he committed the crime, while internment is based on his mental state and dangerousness at the time of the judicial decision. This difference is a consequence of the fact that the insanity clause and internment were conceived in distinct historical periods and reflect different legal philosophies.

In this type of case, neuroscientific evidence, including evidence based on brain imaging techniques, is hardly ever presented. Some believe that neuroscience will enter Belgian courtrooms more regularly in the (possibly near) future. Belgium currently has no clear legal framework on how neuroscientific evidence should be obtained, presented and evaluated in criminal processes. The drafting of such a framework raises fundamental questions, as well as problems of a practical nature, which we will elaborate upon in the present chapter. The chapter describes Belgian criminal law regarding (potentially) mentally disordered offenders, including legal changes that will be implemented shortly. Our emphasis will be on the interpretation of the provisions in question and on the regulation and role of forensic

---

* The research outlined in this chapter was conducted by Katrien Hanoulle, under the supervision of and with the cooperation of Frank Verbruggen.
[1] In the Belgian mainly inquisitorial criminal justice system, insanity is not a 'defence' on the procedural level. Rather, it excludes the culpability of the defendant on the substantive level. It is therefore referred to as an 'excuse'. However, for purposes of consistency with the rest of this volume, the phrase 'insanity defence' will be used throughout this chapter.

mental health expert advice. We will present examples of the use of neuroscientific evidence in Belgian criminal proceedings, then proceed to argue that for the time being neuroscience will have only a limited impact on the Belgian criminal justice system. Lastly, we will discuss issues that could arise if and when neuroscientific evidence is presented and admitted in Belgian criminal courts with a higher frequency than is the case at present. Neuroscientific evidence is a novelty in Belgian criminal law practice, and the solution to most evidentiary issues that could emerge remains unclear.

II. Insanity Defence

The insanity clause can be found in article 71 of the Belgian Criminal Code of 1867, along with the defence of *force majeure* or duress. The provision reads as follows:

> There is no offence, when the defendant or the suspect was in a state of insanity at the time of the act, or when he was constrained by a force that he could not have resisted.[2]

The clause is based on article 64 of the Napoleonic Criminal Code of 1810, which is the paragon of classical continental criminal law, inspired by the principles of the Enlightenment. Policy makers of the late eighteenth century introduced two fundamental principles into the criminal law. The first is that to create a society founded on humanity, equality, reason and freedom, government intervention should be limited and performed in a non-discretionary, non-discriminatory manner.[3] Hence the criminal law should be based upon an objective criterion— the presence of a criminal act—and strict legal rules.[4] Furthermore, Enlightenment thinkers argued that the criminal law should conceive of the offender as a *homo œconomicus*, a self-interested and rational free agent, who weighs up the pros and cons of his own behaviour, aiming at personal gain.[5] A non-arbitrary and foreseeable statutory sanction can serve as a general deterrent if it outweighs the advantages that the potential perpetrator could derive from committing the crime;

---

[2] Our translation. The original text of the provision in Dutch and French reads as follows:

> Er is geen misdrijf, wanneer de beschuldigde of de beklaagde op het ogenblik van het feit in staat van krankzinnigheid was of wanneer hij gedwongen werd door een macht die hij niet heeft kunnen weerstaan.

> Il n'y pas d'infraction lorsque l'accusé ou le prévenu était en état de démence au moment du fait, ou lorsqu'il a été contraint par une force à laquelle il n'a pu resister.

[3] R Focqué and AC 't Hart, *Instrumentaliteit en rechtsbescherming. Grondslagen van een strafrechtelijke waardendiscussie* (Antwerp, Kluwer Rechtswetenschappen, 1990) 42.

[4] MS Dupont-Bouchat, *La Belgique criminelle. Droit, justice, société (XIVe–XXe siècles)* (Louvain-la-Neuve, Bruylant-Academia, 2006) 153.

[5] C Debuyst, 'Les savoirs diffus et préscientifiques sur les situations-problèmes au XVIIIe siècle' in C Debuyst, F Digneffe, JM Labadie and AP Pires (eds), *Histoire des savoirs sur le crime et la peine* (Brussels, Larcier, 2008) pt 1, 90.

moreover, the experience of punishment can dissuade the individual offender from committing new crimes.[6] In addition, the criminal law serves a retributive cause and it protects society by reacting in a repressive manner when its foundations have been threatened by a criminal act.[7]

The deterrent and retributive functions of criminal law presuppose that the potential offender possesses the intellectual capacity to reason and act freely.[8] If one lacks it, one cannot be held criminally responsible. Therefore, the legislator of 1810 foresaw a legal excuse for offenders who commit a crime while insane or pushed by *force majeure*.

Belgium became independent in 1830. After applying the French Code for some decades, it enacted its own Criminal Code in 1867. The regulation of criminal insanity remained the same. The Belgian Code states that there is no offence when the accused at the time of the act found himself in a state of insanity *(krankzinnigheid/démence)* or was compelled to act by irresistible force *(force majeure* or duress). Insanity was defined as 'disturbance of the intellectual capacities that deprive the person of the consciousness of the morality of his acts'.[9] The wording of the provision is imprecise in that it states that 'there is no offence'. The insanity defence is an excuse exempting the individual from punishment, but the act itself remains an offence. The unlawfulness of the act remains intact. This allows, for instance, the prosecution and conviction of aiders or abettors.

III. Internment Measure

Legal History Background

The institution of internment *(internering/internement)* was introduced following the criminal justice theories conceived in the late nineteenth century by 'social defence'-inspired criminal law schools. At that time, many Western European societies were facing issues of social upheaval, poverty and criminality. Strikes, large demonstrations and street riots to obtain social rights were seen as a threat by the establishment.[10] 'Social defence' criminal justice theories were an attempt

---

[6] C Beccaria, *Over misdaden en straffen* (Antwerp, Standaard, 1971) 307; P Lascoumes, 'Beccaria et l'ordre public moderne' in M Porret (ed), *Beccaria et la culture juridique des Lumières* (Geneva, Librairie Droz, 1997) 114; R Martinage, *Histoire du droit pénal en Europe* (Paris, Presses Universitaires de France, 1998) 54.

[7] A Mooij, 'Toerekeningsvatbaarheid en de vraag naar het kwaad' in BF Keulen, G Knigge and HD Wolswijk (eds), *Pet af: liber amicorum DH de Jong* (Nijmegen, Wolf Legal Publishers, 2007) 337.

[8] Debuyst (n 5) 81–83; PAF Gérard, *Le Code Pénal Expliqué* (Brussels, 1867) 90.

[9] J Nypels, *Le code pénal belge interprété* (Brussels, Bruylant-Christophe, 1867) 225.

[10] F Digneffe, 'Problèmes sociaux et représentation du crime et du criminel' in C Debuyst, F Digneffe, JM Labadie and AP Pires (eds), *Histoire des savoirs* (Brussels, Larcier, 2008) pt 1, 149; R Harris, *Murders and Madness. Medicine, Law, and Society in the Fin de* Siècle (Oxford, Clarendon Press, 1989) 80; F Tulkens, 'Généalogie de la défense sociale en Belgique (1880–1914)' in M Foucault (ed), *Généalogie de la défense sociale en Belgique* (Brussels, Story-Scientia, 1988) 7.

to face the emerging social issues. The central argument was that the function of the justice system and of the government in general is protecting society against destabilising forces, including crime. 'Social defence' scholars argued that the sky-high recidivism rates of the time proved the failure of earlier 'classical' approaches to criminal justice.[11] They contended that new 'scientific' research on criminality was going to provide a foundation for a new approach, one that would take into account the characteristics of individual offenders.

It was argued that the typical offender does not quite conform to the *homo œconomicus* ideal. Human beings are far from possessing the rationality, morality and willpower that the 'classical' approach attributed to them. The ideals of general and individual deterrence and behavioural change through punishment were a far cry from reality. Instead of a *homo œconomicus*, the typical reoffender was found to be more of a *homo criminalis*,[12] a term coined by Cesare Lombroso. However, Belgian social defence laws were inspired by sociological rather than biological theories of the causes of crime. According to 'sociological' theories, crime was the result of social circumstances such as poverty combined with character traits labelled as 'biological' such as impulsiveness, insensitivity and irrationality.[13] Adolphe Prins illustrated this view in his influential work *La défense sociale* and derived his own offender classification model.[14] The primary goal of Prins' endeavour was practical. He assumed that individuals ordinarily possess free will and argued against the need for further research on the question.[15] Prins designed a two-track criminal justice model, leaving the established sanctions system intact but flanking it with a new array of preventive measures for particularly dangerous criminals. His model distinguished between 'normal' people who rarely commit crimes, typical offenders who were called 'deficient criminals' (*delinquents défectueux*) and insane offenders. The protection of society is best achieved by administering specific sanctions for each type of perpetrator, responding to individual characteristics and needs. Prins argued that the 'classical' approach to criminal justice should apply only to the average person, who can be assumed to adhere to the *homo œconomicus* ideal. Other offenders require a new type of measure, particularly recidivists who seem not to respond to punishment 'because of their insensitivity, impulsiveness and lack of reason'.[16] They cannot be held (fully) responsible for their behaviour and at the same time

---

[11] M Ancel, *Social Defence. A Modern Approach to Criminal Problems* (London, Routledge & Kegan Paul, 1965) 44.

[12] For instance, E Ferri, *La sociologie criminelle* (Paris, Félix Alcan, 1914); R Garofalo, *La criminologie: étude sur la nature du crime et la théorie de la pénalité* (Paris, Félix Alcan, 1888); C Lombroso, *Criminal Man* (Durham, NC, Duke University Press, 2006).

[13] C Debuyst, 'L'école française dite "du milieu social"' Debuyst, Digneffe, Labadie and Pires (eds) (n 10) 346; A Prins, *La défense sociale et les transformations du droit pénal* (Geneva, Editions Médicine et Hygiène, 1986) 111.

[14] C Christiaensen, 'Adolphe Prins. 1845–1919' in C Fijnaut (ed), *Gestalten uit het verleden* (Deurne, Kluwer, 1993) 117.

[15] Prins (n 13) 38, 43–44 and 120.

[16] ibid 111.

their proclivity to crime makes them dangerous, which calls for the intervention of the 'social defence'-oriented criminal justice system. The same is true for insane offenders.[17]

Society Protection Act

Parliamentary Debate

The principle that dangerousness can and should be a ground for criminal justice interventions eventually found acceptance in the Belgian Parliament. The work of Prins, among others, added to the awareness among criminal justice operators that the available legal tools were not adequate for some types of offenders.

In the nineteenth century, Belgian criminal law allowed for only two types of sanctions: imprisonment and fines.[18] Offenders with mental issues were either punished—the mental disorder was then considered a mitigating circumstance— or acquitted on the basis of the insanity clause. The defence was applicable solely to offenders who were found to be entirely deprived of their senses, to the exclusion of diminished mental capacity. However, it emerged from criminal justice practice and from the social defence literature that many offenders could be regarded neither as fully responsible nor as criminally insane. Punishing them did not lead to behavioural change, and they could pose a threat to society if released, because Belgian criminal law at the time did not foresee any preventive measure following insanity acquittals.[19] In practice, the public prosecutor often requested involuntary placement from the civil judge.[20] Criminals found to be insane or to have diminished responsibility were placed in regular psychiatric institutions that lacked the safety conditions of a prison and were not suitable for this type of patient.[21]

The need to adopt a new approach to insane offenders and offenders with diminished responsibility led to the passing of the Act of 9 April 1930 on the 'protection of society against abnormal individuals and recidivists' (*Wet tot bescherming van de maatschappij tegen de abnormalen en de gewoontemisdadigers/ Loi de défense sociale à l'égard des anormaux et des délinquants d'habitude*). The 1930 legislator introduced the psychiatric observation of offenders and their possible internment. The controversial Act was enacted after nearly four decades

[17] ibid 129.

[18] The law also foresaw the death penalty and penal servitude, which were commuted into imprisonment. Additional sanctions were deposition, deprivation of rights and publication of judicial decisions, which were considered to be very degrading in the nineteenth century.

[19] J Goethals, *Abnormaal en delinkwent. De geschiedenis en het actueel functioneren van de wet tot bescherming van de maatschappij* (Antwerp, Kluwer, 1991) 5–7.

[20] Involuntary placement is a civil (and not criminal) protective measure. It can be imposed upon a mentally ill individual who is a threat to his or her own safety or to the safety of others.

[21] Goethals (n 19) 8–11; M van de Kerchove, 'Le juge et le psychiatre. Evolution de leurs pouvoirs respectifs' in P Gerard, F Ost and M van de Kerchove (eds), *Fonction de juger et pouvoir judiciaire* (Brussels, Facultés universitaires Saint-Louis, 1983) 330.

of discussion in Parliament. There were several points of vehement disagreement; some of a practical nature, such as whether the internment should take place in special institutions or in dedicated prison wards; others more fundamental, including the right to detain people based on their 'being abnormal' and the risks of abuse. Throughout the entire discussion in Parliament, the most striking discord was between lawyers and so-called *médécins-legistes* ('forensic medical doctors'), who disagreed on the formulation of the internment conditions and the role of psychiatrists, as detailed below.[22]

The Act of 9 April 1930 was later replaced by the Act of 1 July 1964 on the 'protection of society against abnormal individuals, recidivists and offenders who committed particular types of sex offences' (*Wet tot bescherming van de maatschappij tegen abnormalen, gewoontemisdadigers en pledgers van bepaalde seksuele strafbare feiten/Loi de défense sociale à l'égard des anormaux, des délinquants d'habitude et des auteurs des certains délits sexuels*). The 1964 law introduced only minor changes to the earlier regulation. It is still in force but will soon be replaced. It sets out two criminal law measures for mentally disordered offenders: psychiatric observation (*inobservatiestelling/mise en observation*) and internment.

Forensic Psychiatric Observation

The goal of forensic psychiatric observation is evaluating the mental state of the accused. Forensic psychiatric observation can be ordered during the pre-trial investigation by the investigating judge (*onderzoeksrechter/juge d'instruction*) or the chambers supervising judicial investigation (*onderzoeksgerecht/juridiction d'instruction*). The trial judge also has the authority to order forensic psychiatric observation at a later stage, during the trial. Forensic psychiatric observation takes place in a psychiatric prison ward and can therefore only be ordered when the conditions for pre-trial custody (*voorlopige hechtenis/détention preventive*) are fulfilled. In addition to these conditions, there must be reasons to presume that the accused finds himself in one of the mental states that are legal grounds for internment. It is therefore always illegal to order forensic psychiatric observation with the goal of establishing that the accused is *not* in such a mental state, even if the accused requests it.[23] Psychiatric observation as regulated in the Society Protection Act can only be ordered with a view to internment, and not for other purposes.

The law prescribes that psychiatric observation take place in a psychiatric prison ward. There is no dedicated specialised centre. Belgian prisons have a shortage of medical personnel and the regular prison staff are not trained for psychiatric observation and evaluation: therefore, the measure is hardly ever applied.[24] However,

---

[22] Goethals (n 19) 10.

[23] Indictment Chamber Antwerp 23 September 1980, *RW* 1983–84, 1482.

[24] C de Kogel, MH Nagtegaal, E Neven en G Vervaeke, *Gewelds- en zedendelinquenten met een psychische stoornis. Wetgeving in Engeland, Duitsland, Canada, Zweden en België* (The Hague, Boom Juridische Uitgevers, 2006) 237.

internment can legally be ordered without prior psychiatric observation. Judges and public prosecutors usually turn to other means of psychiatric examination.

Internment Measure

Internment cannot be classified as a type of punishment, but rather as a preventive measure aimed at protecting society and treating the mentally disordered offender.[25] Articles 1 and 7 of the Act lay down the conditions for internment.[26] The perpetrator must have committed an offence described in statutory law as a felony or misdemeanour. He must be found to be in a state of insanity, serious mental disorder or deficiency that renders him unable to control his actions. The Court of Cassation (*Hof van Cassatie/Court de Cassation*)[27] added one further condition: the offender must be dangerous to society.[28]

Because internment is a protective measure aimed at treatment, it is based on the mental state and dangerousness of the offender at the time of the judicial decision rather than at the time of the offence. It is not linked to the insanity defence provided for in article 71 of the Criminal Code. Perpetrators found to be of sound mind when committing the offence can in principle be interned if they have developed a mental disorder during the investigations. Moreover, the Court of Cassation has confirmed the 'supremacy of internment over the insanity defence'. When the conditions for internment are met, the judge does not have

---

[25] Cass 23 March 1946, *Pas* 1946, I, 116.

[26] Article 7 reads as follows (our translation):

> The investigating courts, unless the case concerns a political or press felony or offence, and the trial courts may order the internment of a suspect who has committed an actqualified as felony or misdemeanour and finds himself in one of the conditions for which at article 1.

The relevant part of art 1 reads (our translation) '... either in a state of insanity, in a severe state of mental disturbance or deficiency that renders him unfit to control his actions ...'.

The original text of art 7 reads as follows:

> De onderzoeksgerechten, tenzij het een politieke misdaad, een politiek wanbedrijf of een pers-delict betreft, en de vonnisgerechten kunnen de internering gelasten van een verdachte die een feit, misdaad of wanbedrijf genoemd, heeft gepleegd en zich in één van de in artikel 1 bepaalde staten bevindt.

> Les juridictions d'instruction, à moins qu'il ne s'agisse d'un crime ou d'un délit politiques ou de presse, et les juridictions de jugement peuvent ordonner l'internement de l'inculpé qui a commis un fait qualifié crime ou délit et qui est dans un des états prévus à l'article premier.

The original text of art 1 reads as follows:

> ... hetzij in een staat van krankzinnigheid, hetzij in een ernstige staat van geestesstoornis of van zwakzinnigheid die hem ongeschikt maakt tot het controleren van zijn daden ...

> ... soit en état de démence, soit dans un état grave de déséquilibre mental ou de débilité mentale le rendant incapable du contrôle de ses actions ....

[27] This is the highest ordinary court. Belgium also has a separate Constitutional Court.

[28] Cass 26 February 1934, *Pas* 1934, I, 180.

to assess whether the insanity defence applies.[29] The insanity defence is therefore rarely decisive.[30] Most of the offenders pronounced insane at the time of the crime are found to be in that same state at the time of the investigation or the trial, and are consequently interned. However, in judicial practice the mental state at the time of the offence is always examined because it can offer a wider understanding and indication of the mental state and dangerousness of the perpetrator at the time of the trial.

Procedural Aspects

There are three types of internment procedures.

Internment can be imposed by the trial court, consisting either of a police tribunal (*politierechtbank/tribunal de police*), a court for misdemeanours (*correctionele rechtbank/tribunal correctional*) or an assize court (*hof van assisen/court d'assises*). Internment for political or press offences, including misdemeanours, can only be imposed by the assize court. 'Political offences' are attacks against either the political institutions or the political rights of citizens. A 'press offence' consists of the actual publication of a punishable opinion. The Belgian legislator chose to give lay juries the authority to judge this type of offence, arguing that professional judges can be seen as part of the establishment and as such potentially prone to interfere with political liberties and freedom of speech and particularly if given the power to impose the label of 'mentally disordered' on defendants and to issue open-ended internment orders. Political and press offences aside, most offences are tried before the court for misdemeanours, which also issues the majority of the orders for internment in the Belgian criminal justice system. Belgian assize courts have only issued three internment orders since 2005.[31]

Internment can also be imposed by the chambers supervising judicial investigation, with the exception of political or press offences. The investigating court (*onderzoeksgerecht/juridiction d'instruction*) is only involved in criminal proceedings after the public prosecutor has ordered that the investigating judge take charge of the investigation. The investigating court functions as a filter between the investigation phase and the trial phase. It has the authority to refer the suspect to the trial court, if there are sufficient indications that he has committed the offence; otherwise, it can dismiss the charges and release the suspect. When it is clear that the suspect has committed the offence, the investigating court can impose internment upon request of the suspect or of the public prosecutor.

Belgian law also provides for a third and particularly controversial internment procedure: the internment of a convicted detainee, provided for at article 21 of the Act. It applies to detainees convicted for a felony or misdemeanour if during their detention period they are found to be in a state of insanity, serious mental

---

[29] Cass 25 March 1946, *Pas* 1946, I, 117.
[30] Article 71 is mostly used for the excuse of *force majeure* and duress.
[31] www.dsb-spc.be.

disorder or mental deficiency that renders them unfit to control their actions. The detainee can be interned by a decision of the Minister of Justice. A dedicated body, the Commission for the Protection of Society (*commissie tot bescherming van de maatschappij/commission de défense sociale*) has the authority to decide on the implementation of the internment and its duration. Detainee internment can only be ordered if the Commission renders unanimous favourable advice. If the mental condition improves before the conclusion of the term of imprisonment, the convict is sent back to prison. If the improvement does not happen, the decision of the Minister becomes effective for an indeterminate period of time.[32] The Constitutional Court ruled that this particular type of open-ended internment does not violate the Belgian Constitution because the measure is preventive and not punitive.[33]

The judge decides with sovereign authority whether the internment conditions are met. Belgian criminal proceedings are inquisitorial and the presumption of innocence applies. Therefore, as a rule the burden of proof is on the public prosecutor, while the accused is not obliged to cooperate or to try to prove his innocence. However, when the insanity defence is raised, the burden of proof is split between the defence and the prosecutor. First, the accused has to argue that the defence can credibly apply in his case.[34] If this threshold is reached, the prosecutor has to prove that the conditions for a successful insanity defence are not fulfilled; if they are, the judge must order release. The victim can offer evidence as well if formally participating in the proceedings to obtain damages as a 'civil party' (*burgerlijke partij/partie civile*).

Belgian criminal law, as opposed to civil and commercial law, acknowledges the free evidence principle. Statutory exceptions aside, evidence can be produced by all means. There are legal provisions in place to safeguard reliability when

---

[32] The original text of art 21 reads as follows:

> De wegens een misdaad of wanbedrijf veroordeelde personen die, tijdens hun hechtenis, in staat van krankzinnigheid of in een ernstige staat van zwakzinnigheid worden bevonden, die hen ongeschikt maakt tot het controleren van hun daden, kunnen geïnterneerd worden krachtens een beslissing van de minister van Justitie, genomen op eensluidend advies van de commissie tot bescherming van de maatschappij. ... Indien de geestestoestand van de veroordeelde vóór het verstrijken van de straftijd voldoende is verbeterd zodat zijn internering niet meer nodig is, stelt de commissie dat vast en gelast de minister van Justitie de terugkeer van de veroordeelde naar de strafinrichting waar hij voordien in hechtenis was.

> Les condamnés pour crimes et délits qui, au cours de leur détention, sont reconnus en état de démence ou dans un état grave de déséquilibre mental ou de débilité mentale les rendant incapables du contrôle de leurs actions, peuvent être internés en vertu d'une décision du Ministre de la Justice rendue sur avis conforme de la commission de défense sociale. ... Si, avant l'expiration de la durée prévue pour la peine, l'état mental du condamné est suffisamment amélioré pour ne plus nécessiter son internement, la commission le constate et le Ministre de la Justice ordonne le retour du condamné au centre pénitentiaire où il se trouvait antérieurement détenu.

[33] Constitutional Court 10 February 2011, no 23/2011.
[34] Cass 24 March 1994, *Arr Cass* 1999, 424.

obtaining evidence from the human body, including DNA tests and alcohol and drug tests. Neuroimaging techniques are hardly ever used as evidence in Belgian criminal processes. This type of evidence is not (yet) specifically regulated by statute. However, it has to comply with the few general rules on evidence in criminal proceedings, mostly concerning the exclusion of illegally obtained evidence. 'Illegally obtained' refers to evidence acquired in breach of legal rules, by means of an offence, through violation of human dignity, the right to a defence or the right to privacy. This type of evidence must be excluded when the law so orders, if its reliability is impaired or its use violates the right to a fair trial. Neuroscientific evidence could in principle violate the rights to privacy and fair trial, if compelled. As a general rule, it is forbidden to compel a medical or mental health examination. Given the lack of special regulations for neuroscientific tests, these can only be carried out after informed consent has been obtained.[35] No mandatory exclusion rule operates for compelled neuroscientific tests presented as evidence in criminal trials; rather, proof is required that the test results are unreliable or that their use violates the right to a fair trial.

Moreover, some types of evidence, such as the results of a polygraph test, can never be decisive but only auxiliary to other incriminating proof. Apart from these restrictions, the decision on how much weight to attach to evidence presented is made by the judge. There is no 'beyond reasonable doubt' or comparable evidence standard in Belgian criminal law. The judge has to be persuaded to a degree he can decide by his 'inner conviction' (*innerlijke overtuiging/intime conviction*). He can also come to the conclusion that the expert report does not contain sufficiently persuasive or precise data or is based on insufficient, wrong, uncontrolled or uncontrollable data.[36] The influence of scientific examinations thus depends partly upon the judge's belief as to its evidential value. Judges may be rather sceptical of new neuroimaging techniques. There are very few examples of the use of neuroscientific evidence in Belgian criminal proceedings with respect to a potentially mentally disordered offender. The issue is not discussed in legal literature, apart from the essentially philosophical debate on cognitive neuroscience, human agency and the criminal law. Nevertheless, a few commentators foresee an increase of the use of neuroscience-based evidence in criminal trials, and believe neuroscience may help to overcome some of the limitations of current psychiatric expert witness practice.[37]

The Society Protection Act and the Code of Criminal Procedure do not contain provisions regulating forensic psychiatric expert advice. During the parliamentary discussions of the Society Protection Act, disagreement emerged as to whether

---

[35] Cass 7 March 1975, *Arr Cass* 1975, 764; Cass 17 December 1998, *Arr Cass* 1999, 197; C Desmet, 'Het menselijk lichaam als bewijsmiddel in strafzaken' (2006–07) *T Gez* 89–90.

[36] A Christiaens and F Hutsebaut, 'Het deskundigenverslag—Bewijswaarde—Honoraria' in D De Buyst, P Kortleven, T Lysens and C Ronse (eds), *Bestendig handboek deskundigenonderzoek* (Mechelen, Kluwer, 2009) 350.

[37] R Boone, 'Schuld onder de schedel' (2013) 270 *Juristenkrant* 6–7; J Decoker, 'Zijn we klaar voor het neurorecht' (2012) 246 *Juristenkrant* 12–13.

forensic psychiatric expert assessment should be made compulsory in internment procedures. Proponents stressed that the judge would face difficulties when judging not purely legal elements, while opponents were concerned about the potential influence of psychiatrists on criminal proceedings. The Act dates from a time when psychiatry was in its infancy and still had to prove itself as reliable science. Many members of the Belgian Parliament still associated psychiatry with the 'criminal anthropology' of Cesare Lombroso. They did not appreciate the added value of psychiatric expertise and feared possible misuse of psychiatric labels to marginalise and stigmatise particular individuals and groups.[38]

The discussion was eventually settled and the opponents prevailed. The Act did not, and still does not, regulate forensic psychiatric expert advice, apart from the observation and the general provision that the judge is 'allowed' (and not required) to 'hear' expert witnesses.[39] In default of a specific regulation in the Society Protection Act, general criminal procedural law should apply, but the Belgian Code of Criminal Procedure does not regulate forensic expert opinion either. However, it is by now generally accepted in court practice that the public prosecutor, the investigating judge, the investigating court and the trial judge all have the authority to appoint experts. The Belgian Court of Cassation defines an expert as

> someone who because of his expert knowledge, without being the judge's delegate, is appointed by the judge to render technical advice, independently and impartially, to allow the judge to fulfil his task. He drafts a report with his findings and conclusions, after having sworn to report honourably and conscientiously, accurately and honestly.[40]

The defendant can also appoint an expert whose work he will have to pay for. Alternatively, the defendant can request the judge to appoint a new expert.

A forensic psychiatric expert is in practice almost always involved in internment decisions,[41] consistently with the case law of the European Court of Human Rights (ECtHR) on lawful and unlawful deprivation of liberty of a person unsound of mind.[42] In recent decades, medical expertise has become increasingly more important in

---

[38] Goethals (n 19) 37; T Collignon and R van der Made, *La loi Belge de Défense sociale à l'égard des anormaux et des délinquants d'habitude* (Brussels, Larcier, 1943) 7.

[39] In the Belgian criminal justice system, court experts are not witnesses. Witnesses testify for the prosecution or for the defence. Experts are in a different situation. They are technical consultants to the judge and are under an obligation to report impartially and independently, irrespective of whether they were appointed by the prosecution or by the court. When appointed by the defence, they are not labelled as experts but as technical advisors. However, for purposes of consistency with the rest of this volume, the phrase 'expert witness' is used throughout this chapter.

[40] Cass 15 February 2006, AR P.05.1583.F.

[41] de Kogel, Nagtegaal, Neven and Vervaeke (n 24) 238; Observatoire international des prisons— section belge, Notice 2013 de l'état du système carcéral belge.

[42] *Winterwerp v the Netherlands* (1979) Series A no 33, para 39:

> [t]he individual concerned should not be deprived of his liberty unless he has been reliably shown to be of 'unsound mind'. The very nature of what has to be established before the competent national authority—that is, a true mental disorder—calls for objective medical expertise. Further, the mental disorder must be of a kind or degree warranting compulsory confinement. What is more, the validity of continued confinement depends upon the persistence of such a disorder.

criminal proceedings. Since criminal cases often involve complex non-legal issues, including the mental state of the defendant, it is now widely accepted that the judge, whose expertise is primarily legal and not medical, needs advice from mental health practitioners.[43]

There are no legal provisions regulating access to the role of forensic expert witness and no legal requirements of scientific, academic or professional training or experience.[44] The judge is free to choose the person he finds most suitable for the task. However, for internment procedures the judge is only allowed to appoint a licensed physician, because the law characterises psychiatric examination and advice as 'medical acts'.[45] The physician does not necessarily have to be a psychiatrist, although in practice most mental health examinations in internment proceedings are carried out by psychiatrists. Most offices of the public prosecutorial service keep unofficial lists of frequently appointed experts, who do not hold any type of formal accreditation. Rather, they are professionals willing to offer their services for criminal trials. There are no clear rules on how to be included in or struck off the unofficial list. This may jeopardise the objectivity and impartiality of potential forensic experts. In the hope of future appointments, appointed experts may try to guess and follow the preferences of the prosecutor or judge who appointed them. Cartuyvels et al found that most judges admit they prefer to appoint a psychiatrist they have worked with before, so they know which elements in the case the expert is more likely to focus on. Especially investigating judges were found to be supportive of this informal appointment practice and opposed to the introduction of a binding list of accredited psychiatrists, which they perceive as a potential threat to their role of leadership in the criminal investigation.[46]

Most orders for forensic psychiatric advice in internment procedures are worded as follows. The psychiatrist has to advise as to whether the accused found himself at the time of the offence and 'at present' (meaning at the time of the investigation, trial or detention) in a state of insanity, or a serious state of mental deficiency or mental retardation which renders him unfit to control his actions; and whether the accused is dangerous to himself or society.[47] These questions almost perfectly overlap with the legal internment conditions.

---

[43] Y Cartuvels, B Champetier and A Wyvekens, *Soigner ou punir? Un regard critique sur la défense sociale en Belgique* (Brussels, Publications des Facultés universitaires Saint-Louis, 2010) 44; P Traest, 'Enkele bedenkingen bij een wettelijke regeling van het deskundigenonderzoek in strafzaken' in F Deruyck and M Rozie (eds), *Het strafrecht bedreven. Liber amicorum Alain De Nauw* (Bruges, Die Keure, 2011) 809.

[44] F Hutsebaut, 'Deskundigenonderzoek in strafzaken en het probleem van de tegenspraak naar Belgisch recht' in F Hutsebaut and JM Reyntjes, *Deskundigen en tegenspraak in het Belgische en Nederlandse strafrecht* (Nijmegen, Wolf Legal Publishers, 2011) 33.

[45] Article 2 RD no 78 of 10 November 1976, concerning the practice of the health professions.

[46] Cartuyvels, Champetier and Wyvekens (n 43) 100.

[47] A Christiaens and F Hutsebaut, 'Het optreden van de gerechtsdeskundige in de verschillende stadia van het onderzoek' in De Buyst, Kortleven, Lysens and Ronse (eds) (n 36) 78.

Conditions

Actus Reus: *Felony or Misdemeanour*

Internment is a criminal law measure and can be imposed only if the prospective internee has been convicted for a criminal act; more specifically, an act described as a felony (*misdaad/crime*) or misdemeanour (*wanbedrijf/délit*) in the criminal law, including crimes against property and unintentional offences. Only minor offences such as vandalism are excluded. Official records from the Criminal Policy Service show that the most common crimes committed by internees are intentional assault and battery, followed by threats and theft.[48]

Mens Rea: *Mental State*

The Act describes three types of mental states that are a legal ground for internment. The definitions and classification used in the Act stem from nineteenth-century psychiatry and their meaning for current mental health nosography is unclear. In court practice, this represents a not negligible problem for forensic psychiatric experts.

The first of the three states, 'insanity', is identical to the ground for excuse laid down in article 71 of the Belgian Criminal Code. There is no statutory definition of 'insanity' in Belgium. Therefore, a general rule in Belgian law applies. The rule states that legal terms should be interpreted according to their meaning in ordinary language and not according to the specific meaning they may assume in particular technical domains (including the medical domain). According to its ordinary meaning, the word 'insanity' refers to a mental disorder that causes complete lack of control over actions and undermines intellectual capacities. The cause and nature of the disorder are irrelevant; it can be congenital or acquired through disease or accident. Intoxication is included, when its nature and the medical nosography permit it to be diagnosed as a mental illness; or when it has caused a mental illness.[49] In practice, any psychiatrist requested to give forensic expert advice finds himself in an impasse: although appointed based on his medical expertise, he has a legal obligation to refrain from interpreting the term 'insane' in accordance with its 'technical', 'medical' meaning. In current psychiatric science, the term 'insanity' does not have a meaning anymore; however, it used to have one. Forensic psychiatrists have therefore developed their own literature, attempting to define which disorders count as 'insanity' for purposes of the insanity defence. According to their literature, only dementia, manic or delirious melancholic depressions, severe psychotic disintegration of the mind and complete intellectual incapacity can substantiate a claim of legal insanity.[50] Most judges have little knowledge of

---

[48] www.dsb-spc.be.

[49] L Dupont, *Beginselen van strafrecht* (Louvain, Acco, 2005) 159–60.

[50] J Casselman, 'Internering: huidige situatie' in J Casselman, P Cosyns, D De Doncker et al (eds), *Internering* (Louvain, Garant, 1997) 41.

psychiatric disorders and rely on the interpretation by the forensic expert. In practice, most offenders who are interned or acquitted on grounds of insanity suffer from either psychosis or dementia.[51]

The second of the three states listed in the Act is 'serious mental disorder' (*ernstige staat van geestesstoornis/état grave de déséquilibre mental*). It refers to all types of mental illness that undermine insight and self-control, while the offender remains aware of the criminal nature of his acts.[52] The medical approach prevails in case law. This does not mean that any type of clinical mental disorder qualifies as 'mental disorder' according to the Society Protection Act. In contemporary psychiatry, 'mental disorder' comprises both mental illnesses and mental disabilities, whereas the term in the Act only includes illnesses. The provision does not exclude any particular illness. However, in the first decade after the Act entered into force, internment was never ordered for perpetrators diagnosed with personality disorders, substance dependency or 'perversions'.[53] Internment practice has since evolved, along with advances in psychiatric science; offenders suffering from paraphilia, personality disorders or substance abuse are no longer systematically excluded.[54]

The Act requires that the mental disorder be 'serious'. Seriousness should not be confused with dangerousness, which will be discussed below. 'Seriousness' refers to the impact of the disorder on the life of the offender. There are no (legal) guidelines on the interpretation of this criterion, nor does the seriousness of a disorder technically form part of psychiatric diagnoses. According to current psychiatry, mental disorders should not be regarded as definite entities; rather, they belong on a continuum, with possible transitions between different disorders, and between disorders, more serious disorders and 'normality'.[55] The vagueness of the 'seriousness' criterion along with the fact that it lacks a scientific foundation leads to uncertainty in its operationalisation.[56]

The third type of mental state that can lead to an internment decision is 'a serious state of mental deficiency' (*ernstige staat van zwakzinnigheid/état grave de débilité mentale*) that is not defined in the law. In psychiatric practice, the assessment of

[51] P Cosyns, C D'Hont, D Janssens, E Maes and R Verellen, 'Geïnterneerden in België. De cijfers' (2007) 28 *Panopticon* 46, 54–55; M Vandenbroucke, 'De nieuwe interneringswet: enkele kanttekeningen' (2007) 114 *Fatik* 21, 22.

[52] Dupont (n 49) 160; J Matthijs, 'La loi de défense sociale à l'égard des anormaux. Evolutions des conceptions' (1965) 5 *JT*, 166.

[53] Goethals (n 19) 145–46.

[54] P Cosyns, 'Psychiatrisch deskundigenonderzoek in strafzaken' in J Casselman and P Cosyns (eds), *Gerechtelijke psychiatrie* (Louvain, Garant, 1995) 48; S De Vuysere, 'Wetgevende thema's inzake internering' in D Van Daele and I Van Welzenis (eds), *Actuele thema's uit het strafrecht en de criminologie* (Louvain, Universitaire Pers Leuven, 2004) 65; A Van der Auwera, J Dheedene and K Seynnaeve, 'Geïnterneerde personen in Vlaanderen en in België' in J Casselman, R De Rycke and H Heimans (eds), *Internering. Nieuwe interneringswet en organisatie van de zorg* (Bruges, die Keure, 2015) 119–20.

[55] PR Adriaens and A De Block 'Alle gekheid op een stokje. Over de wortels van het psychiatrisch essentialisme' (2011) *Tijdschrift voor Filosofie* 7, 12; AS David, 'Why We Need More Debate on Whether Psychotic Symptoms Lie on a Continuum with Normality' (2010) 40 *Psychological Medicine* 1935.

[56] Cosyns (n 54) 48.

cognitive disability is one of the few diagnostic activities that involve the concept of 'seriousness' or severity. However, 'severely retarded' individuals are not the target group of the Society Protection Act. The medical criterion for the inclusion in this category is an IQ below 40.[57] This is very restrictive; the corresponding category in the Act is far more inclusive. The forensic mental health expert is not expected to assess the seriousness of the mental deficiency in terms of an IQ cut-off score, but rather to focus primarily on social malfunctioning and aberrant, aggressive or irresponsible behaviour.[58]

'Unfit to Control'

By reason of the mental disorder, the perpetrator must be unfit (*ongeschikt/ incapable*) to control his actions. No clarification is provided in the Act of the meaning of this phrase. There is great discord in practice on how to interpret it.

The focus of the Act is on control, as opposed to intellectual or cognitive capabilities, knowledge or insight of the criminal nature of the behaviour. It should be noted that lack of control does not equate with lack of criminal intent.[59] Acting with intent means to willingly and knowingly commit an offence, as opposed to acting by accident. Individuals who lack control over their actions because of a disorder can still have the criminal intent required in the criminal law for the attribution of an offence, even when the intent was affected by the disorder.[60] For instance, one might be aware that murder is illegal and at the same time suffer from psychotic delusions, feel threatened by a particular person, and intentionally kill that person to defend oneself from the imaginary threat. The agent in this case acts with full criminal intent, but lacks control over his own actions.

There are no other guidelines on the interpretation of 'control'. The notion can encompass several meanings, including the ability to ponder alternatives; decisiveness; and the capacity to inhibit reactions, perform actions, resist impulses and plan. Forensic psychiatric expert witnesses are requested to render advice without guidance from the criminal law. Jurists tend to believe that psychiatry is the science of the mind that will pre-eminently offer an insight on the mental condition of the offender; however, the concept of control in the strict sense forms part of only a few psychiatric diagnoses. Some disorders are known to be characterised by very poor self-control: the patient is unable to resist impulses. Lack of self-control can vary in degree and severity, from trivial habits like nail biting to behaviour leading to serious consequences, including substance abuse and sexual

---

[57] For instance: people with Down syndrome have an average IQ score of 50.

[58] Casselman (n 50) 41; Cosyns (n 54) 49.

[59] Dupont (n 49) 112.

[60] A De Nauw, 'De niet-toerekeningsvatbaarheid sluit niet noodzakelijkerwijze het opzet uit' in F Deruyck, M De Swaef, J Rozie, M Rozie, P Traest and R Verstraeten (eds), *De wet voorbij. Liber amicorum Luc Huybrechts* (Antwerp, Intersentia, 2010) 65–76; K Hanoulle and F Verbruggen, 'Ivorentorenmentaliteit in de kerkers? Het problematische begrip toerekeningsvatbaarheid' in F Deruyck and M Rozie (eds), *Het strafrecht bedreven. Liber amicorum Alain De Nauw* (Bruges, Die Keure, 2011) 319–20.

disorders driving the patient to harm others. Psychiatric nosography also lists 'impulse control disorders', characterised by inability to resist urges to behave in ways harmful to oneself or others. Examples here are pathological gambling, kleptomania, pyromania and intermittent explosive disorder.[61] Some people can also show a disturbance in their perceived will power and may experience delusions of control and hear imperative voices.[62] For all other mental disorders, the psychiatrist does not deal with the question of control. However, the control disorders listed above are rarely found within the interned population, with the exception of psychotic disorders possibly accompanied by delusions and substance abuse. In sum, forensic mental health practitioners have developed a meaning of the notion of 'control' specific to the criminal process, with wide divergences in its interpretation. The public prosecutor and the judge also have the authority to give their own interpretation of the notion of 'control' in the individual case. There is no consistent case law.

Internment is often imposed on offenders found to suffer from antisocial personality disorder. The disorder consists of a behavioural pattern of contempt for and violation of the rights of others, with symptoms such as extreme impulsiveness and irritableness, aggressiveness and reckless indifference for personal safety; these symptoms can be interpreted as 'lack of control'. What is more, in courtroom practice cognitive and intellectual capabilities are also included in the concept of control.[63]

The Act states that the offender, because of the disorder, has to be 'unfit to control his actions'. Belgian law does not regulate diminished responsibility. The perpetrator is either 'fit' or 'unfit' to control his actions; no third option is available to the judge and the forensic mental health practitioner. This does not mean that an offender should have *entirely* lost control in order to be interned. 'Diminished responsibility' offenders can be interned if diminished responsibility is described in terms of 'unfitness to control'. The Act does formally distinguish between 'insane' and 'seriously disordered or deficient' offenders, but it subjects both groups to exactly the same sanction.

In each individual case, the forensic psychiatric expert has to render advice, and the judge has to decide on whether the perpetrator's capacity of self-control was impaired to a degree sufficient to substantiate the 'unfit to control' label. This distinction makes sense from a legal viewpoint since the criminal law requires clear-cut categories. However, psychiatrists have argued that it is too simplistic an approach to the understanding of human behaviour. As illustrated above, contemporary psychiatry has abandoned its traditional nosography, today considered rudimentary and obsolete. Modern psychiatry characterises mental disorders as

---

[61] PMG Emmelkamp, CAL Hoogduin and W Vandereycken, *Handboek psychopathologie 1* (Houten, Bohn Stafleu van Loghum, 2008) 421–37.

[62] MW Hengeveld, 'De psycho(patho)logie van het wilsleven' in G Meynen and TI Oei (eds), *Toerekeningsvatbaarheid. Over vrije wil, wetenschap en recht* (Nijmegen, Wolf Legal Publishers, 2011) 9.

[63] C Dillen, 'Zinvolheid van nieuwe richtlijnen en initiatieven rond interneren. Het standpunt van een psychiatrisch-forensisch deskundige' (2001) 15 *Orde van de dag* 43, 45.

dimensional or prototypical. The disorder coincides with one particular point on a conceptual continuum, ranging from the ideal of perfect mental health to a theoretical, conjectured 'total' psychopathology encompassing all possible and imaginable mental illness symptoms. Mental disorders vary in severity and there are no sharply defined boundaries between mental health and mental illness.[64] All internment conditions raise intricate interpretative issues for forensic mental health experts; in particular the 'control' requirement has proven extraordinarily difficult to interpret.[65] Ley stated that the forensic psychiatric expert is 'forced to lie' since he cannot advise on the 'unscientific and unanswerable' question of control.[66]

'Dangerous to Society'

The last condition for lawfully imposing internment is that the offender be 'dangerous to society'. There is no express statutory definition of this requirement. Rather, it emerged from the case law of the Court of Cassation.[67] In a 1934 ruling, the reasoning of the Court was twofold. The Act states that when the statutory requirements for lawful internment are fulfilled, the judge can impose internment but is not under an obligation to do so. According to the Court, the judge must consider whether the measure would meet 'a public need' and the 'public need' is met if the offender is dangerous to society. The Court of Cassation further supported its conclusion by making reference to the 1930 Act, which stated that the release of interned offenders depended upon the improvement of their mental condition and their not representing a threat to society.

From a legal point of view, representing 'a threat to society' refers to the risk of reoffending.[68] The mere presence of a mental disorder does not automatically entail that the perpetrator can be considered socially dangerous for criminal law purposes. In a 1977 ruling, the Court of Cassation stressed that internment orders should always include an explanation of the reason for considering the offender dangerous to society.[69] The forensic psychiatrist who serves as an expert witness must render advice on 'dangerousness' without 'dangerousness' assessments forming part of his regular diagnostic practice. Psychiatrists stress that dangerousness is not an unalterable personality trait; rather, it is context dependent.[70]

---

[64] Emmelkamp, Hoogduin and Vandereycken (n 61) 16; R Slovenko, *Psychiatry and Criminal Culpability* (New York, John Wiley & Sons, 1995) 54.

[65] H Ankersäter, P Höglund, S Radovic and C Svennerlind, 'Mental Disorder is a Cause of Crime: The Cornerstone of Forensic Psychiatry' (2009) 32 *International Journal of Law and Psychiatry* 342, 345.

[66] J Ley, 'Le psychiatre et les interventions medico-psychologiques et sociales dans l'administration de la justice pénale' (1967–68) 2 *Révue de droit pénal* 145, 146.

[67] Cass 26 February 1934, *Pas* 1934, I, 180.

[68] Collignon and van der Made (n 38) 127.

[69] Cass 20 September 1977, *Arr Cass* 1978, 90–91.

[70] EM Coles and HOF Veiel, 'Expert Testimony and Pseudoscience: How Mental Health Professionals Are Taking Over the Courtroom' (2001) 24 *International Journal of Law and Psychiatry* 607, 612; D Ruschena, 'Determining Dangerousness: Whatever Happened to the Rules of Evidence?' (2003) 10 *Psychiatry, Psychology and Law* 122, 127; PJ Taylor, 'Mental Disorder and Crime' (2004) 14 *Criminal Behaviour and Mental Health* 31, 34–35.

Legal Reform

Internment Act of 21 April 2007

On 21 April 2007 a new Act on internment of persons with a mental disorder was enacted (*Wet betreffende de internering van personen met een geestesstoornis/ Loi relative à l'internement des personnes atteintes d'un trouble mental*). The Act was based on the work of a parliamentary commission that investigated statutory law and criminal justice practice.[71] The commission criticised the obsolete and incomplete formulation of the internment conditions in the law and the lack of legal regulation of forensic mental health expert advice. In the views of the commission, requesting an expert report should be made compulsory in internment proceedings. The commission objected to the poor quality of most expert reports and stressed that forensic experts are poorly paid and consequently not motivated to conduct a thorough examination. Criticism was addressed to the lack of specialised training and specific accreditation for forensic mental health expert witnesses. The commission stressed the necessity and urgency of a legal reform of the internment procedure for convicted detainees. The work of the various 'Commissions for the protection of society' was criticised, and emphasis was put on the unacceptable frailty of the legal position of the internee.

The commission concluded with a discussion of the main practical difficulty posed by internment: the alarming lack of appropriate psychiatric treatment for internees.[72] In principle, internment is aimed at protecting society *and* treating the internee; in practice, many internees do not receive the treatment they need for long periods of time. There is scarcity of beds in forensic wards of mental health clinics. While on the waiting list for an appropriate mental health facility, mentally ill offenders reside in psychiatric prison wards that are, at the present time, unsuitable for any type of psychiatric treatment. This is especially problematic considering that open-ended internment lasts for an indeterminate amount of time, until the mental condition of the internee has improved. In the 1998 *Aerts* case, the ECtHR first censured Belgium for the practice of keeping internees in prison without appropriate psychiatric treatment, arguing that it amounts to unlawful detention of a person of unsound mind.[73] Many similar ECtHR rulings followed,[74]

---

[71] Final report of the Commission Internment for the revision of the Society Protection Act of 1 July 1964 (Brussels, Ministry of Justice, 1999).

[72] Annual Report of the Central Supervisory Council of the Prison System (2010); Report to the Belgian Government on the visit to Belgium by the European Committee for the Prevention of Torture and Inhuman or Degrading Treatment and Punishment (2012); Observatoire international des prisons—section belge, Notice 2013 de l'état du système carcéral belge; UN Committee against Torture Concluding observations on the third periodic report on Belgium (2014).

[73] *Aerts v Belgium* ECHR 1998-V 1939.

[74] *De Donder and De Clippel v Belgium* App no 8595/06 (ECtHR, 6 December 2011); *LB v Belgium* App no 22831/08 (ECtHR, 2 October 2012); *Claes v Belgium* App no 43418/09 (ECtHR, 10 January 2013); *Dufoort v Belgium* App no 43653/09 (ECtHR, 10 January 2013); *Swennen v Belgium* App no 53448/10 (ECtHR, 10 January 2013); *Caryn v Belgium* 43687/09 (ECtHR, 9 January 2014);

including two recent pronouncements censoring Belgium for inhumane handling of very vulnerable internees who had been kept in prison for many years while deprived of adequate psychiatric care.[75]

The Belgian Parliament discussed a new law but did not have the time to do so thoroughly. Public pressure on the Belgian government and legislator became overwhelming after a released internee abducted, raped and murdered two little girls in 2006. The Parliament then drafted and sought to pass a new internment Bill in great haste, which had a negative impact on the quality of the Act.[76] The Act attracted considerable criticism, never entered into force and was eventually replaced by a new Act in 2014.

Act of 5 May 2014

The regulation of internment was eventually reformed in 2014 with the Internment Act (*Wet betreffende de internering van personen/Loi relative à l'internement des personnes*). The new law contains fewer procedural rules and formalities than the 2007 Act. It aims to find flexible solutions for the specific situations of individual internees. It focuses on treatment and, unlike the 2007 Act, it is not dominated solely by concerns with the protection of society. After some amendments and the issuance of royal decrees of implementation, the new law is expected to enter into force on 1 October 2016. A few significant reforms will be discussed below.

Conditions for Internment

Following the new Act, the legal conditions for internment have changed. However, the nature of internment remains unchanged: it is a protective measure and therefore the mental health and dangerousness of the internee are assessed at the time of the judicial decision as opposed to the time of the crime.

Article 9 of the new Act circumscribes the domain of application of the new Act. Internment can lawfully be ordered only if the perpetrator committed an offence described in the criminal law as a felony or misdemeanour. The offence must carry a statutory term of imprisonment. A recent bill reforming the 2014 Act, proposes to restrict the internment to offences that affect or threaten the physical or psychological integrity. The offender must suffer from a mental disorder that

---

Gelaude v Belgium App no 43733/09 (EctHR, 9 January 2014); *Lankester v Belgium* App no 22283/10 (ECtHR, 9 January 2014); *Moreels v Belgium* App no 43717/09 (ECtHR, 9 January 2014); *Oukili v Belgium* App no 43663/09 (ECtHR, 9 January 2014); *Plaisir v Belgium* App no 28785/09 (ECtHR, 9 January 2014); *Van Meroye v Belgium* App no 330/09 (ECtHR, 9 January 2014); *Smits et al v Belgium* App nos 49484/11, 5703/11, 4710/12, 49863/12, 70761/12 (ECtHR, 3 February 2015); *Vander Velde and Soussi v Belgium and the Netherlands* App nos 49861/12, 49870/12 (ECtHR, 3 February 2015).

[75] *Claes v Belgium* App no 43418/09 (ECtHR, 10 January 2013); *Lankester v Belgium* App no 22283/10 (ECtHR, 9 January 2014).

[76] J Goethals and F Verbruggen, 'Van kommercommissie naar kwelrechtbank? De vernieuwing van de internering (en de TBS)' in C Bevernage, M Boes, S Bonne et al, *Recht in beweging* (Antwerp-Apeldoorn, Maklu, 2008) 364 and 371.

destroys or seriously impairs his ability to judge or to control his actions. The Act uses the phrase 'mental disorder' (*geestesstoornis/trouble mental*), a concept that covers both mental illnesses and disabilities and is recognised by the World Health Organisation and the American Psychiatric Association.[77]

The Act states that not only poor control, but also impaired judgement is a ground for internment. 'Judgement' comprises intellectual faculties and cognition. The commission that prepared the 2007 Act affirmed that an impairment of judgement is 'serious' if it radically undermines reintegration into society. The new Act defined 'dangerousness' as the risk of reoffending because of the mental disorder, possibly in association with other risk factors. 'Dangerousness' is not a personality trait and it cannot be automatically inferred from the very fact that the offender has a particular disorder; rather, it results from the interaction of a multitude of stable and variable factors.

As under the former regulation, the 2014 Internment Act provides no specific sanction or combination of sanctions for diminished responsibility. However, on 11 October 2014 the coalition agreement of the federal Belgian government announced the appointment of a multidisciplinary commission entrusted with the drafting of a new legal reform aimed at introducing different grades of criminal responsibility in Belgian statutory law. In March 2015 the new Minister of Justice presented his own general justice system reform project, which includes only some of the legal changes announced in the coalition agreement. The ministerial project contains a chapter on internment, but it does not include the levels of criminal responsibility. The Minister committed instead to implementing the Internment Act of

---

[77] The original text of art 9, para 1 reads as follows:

> De onderzoeksgerechten, tenzij het gaat om misdaden of wanbedrijven die worden beschouwd als politieke misdrijven of als drukpersmisdrijven, en de vonnisgerechten kunnen de internering bevelen van een persoon:
>
> (a) die een als misdaad of wanbedrijf omschreven feit heeft gepleegd waarop een gevangenisstraf is gesteld; en
> (b) die op het ogenblik van de beoordeling aan een geestesstoornis lijdt die zijn oordeelsvermogen of de controle over zijn daden tenietdoet of ernstig aantast, en
> (c) ten aanzien van wie het gevaar bestaat dat hij tengevolge van zijn geestesstoornis desgevallend in samenhang met andere risicofactoren opnieuw misdrijven zal plegen.
>
> Les juridictions d'instruction, sauf s'il s'agit d'un crime ou d'un délit considéré comme un délit politique ou comme un délit de presse, et les juridictions de jugement peuvent ordonner l'internement d'une personne:
>
> (a) qui a commis un fait qualifié crime ou délit punissable d'une peine d'emprisonnement; et
> (b) qui, est atteinte d'un trouble mental qui abolit ou altère gravement sa capacité de discernement ou de contrôle de ses actes, et
> (c) pour laquelle le danger existe qu'elle commette de nouvelles infractions en raison de son trouble mental, éventuellement combiné avec d'autres facteurs de risques.

5 May 2014 and made no mention of the proposal for a new regulation of the levels of criminal responsibility put forward in the coalition agreement. It is therefore unclear whether different grades of responsibility will be introduced in Belgian criminal law. We believe that, if introduced, they should be accompanied by the establishment of a specific sanction or combination of sanctions for diminished responsibility, which is not provided for in the 2014 Internment Act.

Internment Procedure

Forensic Psychiatric Expert Testimony

Under the 2014 Act, judges are under a legal obligation to seek forensic psychiatric expert advice before issuing an internment order. In the new Act it is stated that a model form will be issued with a list of questions for the expert witness. Individual magistrates will retain the authority to ask additional questions.

The forensic mental health expert witness will be asked to state his opinion on whether, at the time of the offence and at the time of the psychiatric examination, the offender suffered from a mental disorder destroying or seriously impairing his judgement or control. However, the internment decision depends solely upon the mental condition at the time of the judicial pronouncement.

The forensic expert witness must investigate the existence of a possible causal link between the disorder and the alleged offence, without extending his inquiry to the question of whether the alleged offence was actually committed, and by the defendant. The existence of a causal link between disorder and offence is not a legal requirement for the internment decision. The expert is also asked to advise as to whether, and if so how, the person could be treated, guided and cared for with a view to reintegration into society. A positive answer to this question is not a legal requirement for internment either.

Under the 2014 Act, only doctors who are specifically accredited as forensic psychiatrists can be appointed as expert witnesses in internment proceedings. The forensic psychiatrist also has to be qualified and registered to be an expert witness in legal proceedings. The discussion in Parliament also touched on the topic of psychological expertise. The parliamentarians concluded that psychologists cannot perform the role of mental health expert witnesses in criminal processes. It was argued that to examine potential patients and to diagnose mental disorders are strictly medical acts. However, the input of a behavioural expert other than a psychiatrist is valuable and the law allows the leading expert witnesses, who must be a doctor, to conduct his examination with the assistance of other behavioural scientists, possibly in a panel of experts.

The Act also regulates the psychiatric observation of suspects in pre-trial custody. To ensure that this measure can be effective, both the coalition agreement of the federal government and the justice system reform project of the Minister of Justice committed to the establishment of a specialised centre for the observation and diagnosis of offenders.

Sentencing Judge

The tasks of the Commission for the Protection of Society are taken over by the sentencing tribunal (*strafuitvoeringsrechtbank/court d'application des peines*), more specifically by the Special Chamber for the Protection of Society (*kamer voor de bescherming van de maatschappij/chambre de la protection sociale*).

The chamber may also decide to intern a convicted detainee. This becomes a judicial decision, rather than the administrative decision it used to be.

Insanity Defence

The 2014 Act contains amendments to several legal provisions, including article 71 of the Criminal Code regulating the insanity defence. The insanity clause is rephrased with the same wording as the Internment Act: there is no offence when the accused at the time of the act suffered from a mental disorder that destroyed or seriously impaired his ability to judge or to control his actions, or when he was constrained by *force majeure*.[78]

Theoretically, the new phrasing gives the insanity clause a broader scope of application than was formerly the case since 'insanity' used to refer only to destroyed intellectual capacities. Under the new provision, perpetrators can successfully plead insanity on grounds of diminished responsibility as well. However, the practical impact of this legal change must be put into perspective. Most offenders who are judged criminally insane at the time of their offence are still in that same condition when being tried and are consequently interned. In most cases, the insanity defence will not be decisive. In addition, defendants with diminished responsibility were in practice excused also under the old phrasing of the provision: in a few judicial rulings, the scope of the insanity clause was interpreted extensively.[79] Nevertheless, the recent bill reforming the 2014 Act proposes to restrict the defence to an accused that suffered from a mental disorder that *destroyed* his ability to judge or to control his actions.

---

[78] The original text of Art 71 reads as follows:

> Er is geen misdrijf wanneer de beschuldigde of de beklaagde op het tijdstip van de feiten leed aan een geestesstoornis die zijn oordeelsvermogen of de controle over zijn daden heeft tenietgedaan of ernstig heeft aangetast, of wanneer hij werd gedwongen door een macht die hij niet heeft kunnen weerstaan.

> Il n'y a pas d'infraction lorsque l'accusé ou le prévenu était atteint, au moment des faits, d'un trouble mental qui a aboli ou gravement altéré sa capacité de discernement ou le contrôle de ses actes ou lorsqu'il a été contraint par une force a laquelle il n'a pu résister.

[79] Cass 20 September 1977, *Arr Cass* 1978, 90; Cass 12 February 2008, P.01.1185.N; Court of Appeal Antwerp 21 February 1995, *AJT* 1995–96, 109; Indictment Chamber Antwerp 1 June 1995, *Limburgs Rechtsleven* 1997, 25; Court of Appeal Antwerp 1 February 2006, *Nullum Crimen* 2007, 75; Corr Brussels 25 October 1994, *RDPC* 1995, 197; Corr Eupen 22 april 2009, *JLMB* 2011, 282 (short version).

IV. Neuroscientific Evidence

The use of neuroscientific evidence to corroborate insanity pleas in Belgian criminal proceedings is very sporadic and its role in the Belgian criminal justice system is a marginal one. Neuroscientific evidence does not play a role in internment proceedings either. Some believe this will change in the future.[80] This type of evidence may in theory be partially immune to the type of criticism currently aimed at forensic psychiatric examinations. The lack of legal certainty that characterises internment proceedings is partly attributed to the shortcomings of classical psychiatric methods of investigation. Traditional psychiatry is currently under criticism for producing unreliable diagnoses. Different psychiatrists often seem to disagree on the diagnosis and the interpretation of legal conditions for internment and make diverging predictions of dangerousness. This is attributed to the supposedly unscientific character of psychiatry as a branch of knowledge.[81]

Neuroscience is believed to offer techniques of medical investigation that can detect mental disorders with a degree of objectivity that is precluded in traditional psychiatry as a behavioural science. Psychiatrists analyse symptoms and attempt to make inferences on possible disorders. Neuroscience, and neuroimaging in particular, is believed to directly detect the brain mechanisms that generate the symptoms.[82] Some believe that neuroscience offers insight into brain structure and functioning and could be of help in the detection of malingering, ie the attempt to simulate psychiatric symptoms. Psychiatric diagnoses depend largely upon information provided by the examinee; this can be problematic when the examinee is a suspect or defendant in a criminal process.[83] These issues have emerged in Belgian criminal justice practice, but the courts and the legal profession have so far not attempted to tackle them through the use of neuroimaging techniques in the courtroom.

Limited Use of Neuroscience in the Courtroom

Use of Neuroscience to Substantiate Force Majeure: Two Recent Cases

Acute conditions like a seizure or stroke may cause traffic accidents. The offender may then plead irresistible force or *force majeure* and present neuroscientific

---

[80] Boone (n 37) 6–7; Decoker (n 37) 12–13.

[81] Cartuyvels, Champetier and Wyvekens (n 43) 46–48; Coles and Veiel (n 70) 607–25; T Rogers, 'Diagnostic Validity and Psychiatric Expert Testimony' (2004) 27 *International Journal of Law and Psychiatry* 281; N Vincent, 'Strafrechtelijke verantwoordelijkheid en de neurowetenschappen' (2013) 39 *Justitiële Verkenningen* 65, 72–73.

[82] Vincent (n 81) 74.

[83] G Meynen, 'Neurolaw: de relevantie voor de forensische psychiatrie' (2014) 56 *Tijdschrift voor psychiatrie* 597, 600.

evidence. In 2006 a truck driver who had caused a fatal crash put forward a poly-somnografic report proving that he suffered from sleep apnoea that caused him to briefly lose consciousness.[84] The court accepted the evidence, but this did not lead to automatic application of *force majeure*. A person who is aware, or ought to be aware, that he suffers from a medical condition that can lead to dangerous (albeit involuntary) behaviour must exert due caution in his behaviour; only in that case can he be regarded as having acted under irresistible force.[85] In 2011 a driver caused an accident while suffering a seizure caused by a brain tumour.[86] The man had undergone an MRI scan a few days prior to the accident. He had not yet been informed of the results of the scan. However, he knew that he had suffered from brain tumours and epilepsy in the past and had noticed relapse symptoms, prompting him to seek medical attention and to undergo the diagnostic brain scan. The court argued that the driver could not plead *force majeure*.

Use of Neuroscience in Internment Decisions and to Corroborate the Insanity Defence

We found only one Belgian criminal case in which neuroscientific evidence entered the courtroom to support an internment request. The case was judged by the Assize Court of Ghent in 2013.[87] In January 2009 a 20-year old man murdered a 72-year old woman in her home. He had never met her before. He randomly chose her house after he had planned to stab someone. One week later, the man stabbed numerous staff members and children in a day-care centre, killing one carer and two babies and severely injuring several others. Although the victims were chosen randomly, there was reliable evidence that the man had been meticulously planning his crimes for months.

When the police arrested him shortly after the day-care centre homicides, the man did not speak or move. He was believed to be psychotic. However, it was later discovered he had simulated the symptoms of psychosis. During his first interviews he refused to cooperate and denied that he had committed the murders. A few weeks later he confessed, claiming his acts had been carried out in obedience to auditory hallucinations, more specifically of imperative voices. Later the man admitted that this was a lie. However, the prison staff reported that he often displayed bizarre behaviour, which gave them the impression that he was indeed psychotic. The prison psychiatrist prescribed him medications against psychosis.

---

[84] Corr Dendermonde 7 februari 2006, *Verkeer, Aansprakelijkheid, Verzekering* 2006, 583–89.

[85] See also: Cass 10 april 1979, *Arr Cass* 1978–79, 951; Court of Appeal Brussels 19 May 1994, *T Verz* 1995, 256; Corr Ieper 16 November 2000, *TAVW* 2002, 57; Corr Mechelen 13 February 2002, *TAWV* 2002, 350; Corr Nijvel 3 May 2006, *RGAR* 2008, no 14423.

[86] Police tribunal Ghent 14 September 2011, *T Verz* 2012, 380.

[87] The analysis of the case is based upon an in-depth study of the file and observation notes made in the courtroom during eight of the 22 days of the trial, by Katrien Hanoulle. A choice was made to only follow the trial on particular days, specifically when the responsibility of the accused was discussed. This study was approved by the Public Prosecutorial Service of Ghent.

During the investigation and the trial there was extensive discussion of whether his psychosis symptoms were genuine or simulated. The man also gave contradictory reasons for his inexplicable crimes; it was not clear whether and when he spoke the truth. Throughout the trial it was nonetheless assumed and not questioned that the man did suffer from a mental disorder. However, there was no consensus as to whether he should be punished or interned. It was clear from the beginning that the victims wanted him to be punished, a desire they often expressed through the media. The homicides had been performed with exceptional cruelty. This case attracted immense media attention and shocked Belgian society, which strongly sympathised with the victims. The criminal justice system and the judges and expert witnesses directly involved in this particular case were under considerable pressure to inflict exemplary punishment.

The investigating judge had appointed a panel of five forensic psychiatric expert witnesses. They concluded that the defendant suffered from schizotypal personality disorder with narcissistic and antisocial traits; however, they added that it did not amount to 'serious mental disorder' in the sense that the law attributes to this phrase. They stated that the man did have control over his actions. The panel attenuated its statements by concluding that the accused could be considered as having diminished responsibility, but not diminished to a degree that would justify an internment decision. Two forensic psychiatric expert witnesses appointed by the defence concluded that the defendant was schizophrenic, insane and unfit to control his actions.[88] He had been planning his crimes and acted in an organised fashion; however, the expert for the defence pointed out, this does not entail that the man had control over his actions. Psychotic offenders can retain the ability to plan and carry out criminal actions in an organised manner, even when their actions are based upon pathological mental content. The panel responded to this advice by reaffirming its earlier findings. However, in its second report, the panel acknowledged that the accused did suffer from a 'serious mental disorder'. The panel also disclosed that its members did not agree on whether the man had control over his actions; the conclusion that the man did have control over his actions was reached by a majority vote. No dissenting opinions were included and no information was released on how many experts disagreed with the majority conclusion and on what grounds.

The discussion in the trial revolved around the question of the possible psychotic or personality disorder of the offender, as if only psychotic offenders could be interned. As we have seen, that is not the case.

The man often simulated psychotic symptoms. At the same time, there were indications he was indeed afflicted with actual psychotic symptoms. The defence claimed legal insanity and presented the results of a Single-Photon Emission Computed Tomography (SPECT) scan in court to corroborate

---

[88] Also, two psychologists drew up a report, mostly in line with the advice of the two psychiatrists.

the plea.[89] The scan revealed very serious abnormalities in certain brain areas. The expert witness argued that the abnormalities could not have been caused by medication or by the fact that the accused resided in a high-security prison ward. The thalamus and the secondary association cortex were found to be defective, which, the expert witnesses contended, was an indication of deranged perception and empathy. There were no defects in the frontal area, which presides over reasoning, planning and impulse control. The forensic mental health expert witness concluded that the accused suffered from a disturbance of perception: he could reason normally, but based on the wrong information. The expert avoided issuing a diagnosis, but did not exclude that the defendant could indeed suffer from auditory hallucinations, as the findings of the SPECT scan were compatible with this hypothesis. He concluded that the brain image was indicative of a psychiatric disorder, more severe than a mere personality disorder. An MRI brain scan was performed as well, but did not lead to results that the defence found useful. The brain structure of the defendant was found to be 'normal'. The expert witness for the defence argued that this finding was 'not irreconcilable' with the results of the SPECT scan. Different neuroimaging techniques measure different aspects of the structure and the functioning of the human brain, they argued.

The victims' solicitors and the public prosecutor disputed the evidentiary value of the SPECT scan, denouncing the perils of the rise of neuro-determinism, a theory of the mind based on the claim that human behaviour is determined by brain states. They maintained that the accused was not psychotic but rather had a personality disorder. The jury was not convinced either and issued a verdict of life imprisonment, holding the defendant fully criminally responsible. The verdict of the jury was based on the advice of the panel of forensic expert witnesses appointed by the investigative judge and on a few crucial elements, which, the jury argued, implied full competency: the meticulous planning of the crime, the man's emotional aloofness on the crime scene and in the courtroom, and his behaviour during the trial.

The case described was a fine example of the shortcomings inherent in current internment conditions and procedure in Belgium. There is too much room for subjective interpretation, which leads to lengthy discussions in the courtroom and fosters the illusion that disagreements can be settled by involving more forensic expert witnesses in the assessment.

Future Developments

At the present time, Belgian criminal courts are rarely presented with neuroscientific evidence of the mental state of the defendant. It is uncertain whether this will

---

[89] SPECT offers an image of the blood flow in the brain and therefore of the energy level in specific brain areas. It is mostly used to detect dementia, epilepsy, brain trauma and occasionally for psychiatric evaluation.

change in the (near) future. Neuroscientific results have weak evidential value in general, and in particular in relation to legal issues. What is more, if neuroscience is used as a means of evidence in criminal proceedings, several legal, ethical and practical questions will arise, detailed below.

Limited Reliability of Neuroscientific Evidence

Relatively new neuroimaging techniques have considerable potential. However, at present it is essentially not possible to use neuroimaging to reliably determine the mental condition of an individual. It is still very problematic to establish a link between brain abnormalities and mental disorders in individual cases, as studies only present correlations between particular brain abnormalities and particular disorders on a group level.[90] Brain abnormalities do not necessarily adversely affect brain functioning. Most executive functions do not depend on the structure and functioning of one specific brain region, but rather result from the activation of neural networks, encompassing multiple interacting regions. In particular, structural brain abnormalities should be interpreted very cautiously.[91] The few Belgian psychiatrists who have publicly taken a stance on the use of neuroimaging as evidence in criminal processes are not keen on attributing too much weight to it, knowing the current state of the art of neuroscience.[92]

Taking into account its currently limited probative value, should neuroscientific evidence still be used in court, and if so, how?

A first option would be to employ neuroimaging evidence exclusively in the context of lie detection and not for insanity and dangerousness assessments; and to utilise neuroimaging only as secondary evidence. As explained, Belgian law permits the use of polygraph results as a means of evidence only when auxiliary to other incriminating evidence. This rule could be extended to neuroimaging. Current state-of-the-art neuroimaging techniques cannot directly detect dishonesty. Like the classic polygraph test, EEG and fMRI scans can only track reactions, or the lack thereof, associated with lying.[93] This rather weak type of evidence should never be decisive.

---

[90] K de Kogel, 'Neurorecht' (2014) 56 *Tijdschrift voor Criminologie* 108, 111–12; SJ Leistedt, 'Le cerveau à la barre: une expérience nord-américaine' (2014) 94 *Revue de droit pénal et de criminologie* 1238, 1251–52; L Klaming and BJ Koops, 'Neuroscientific Evidence and Criminal Responsibility in the Netherlands' in TM Spranger (ed), *International Neurolaw. A Comparative Analysis* (Berlin, Springer, 2012) 229; S Morse, 'Avoiding Irrational Neurolaw Exuberance: A Plea for Neuromodesty' (2011) 3 *Law, Innovation and Technology* 209, 220; S Schleim, 'Brains in Context in the Neurolaw Debate: The Examples of Free Will and "Dangerous" Brains' (2012) 35 *International Journal of Law and Psychiatry* 104.

[91] W Glannon, 'The Limitations and Potential of Neuroimaging in the Criminal Law' (2014) 18 *Journal of Ethics* 153, 155; AL Glenn and A Raine, 'Neurocriminology: Implications for the Punishment, Prediction and Prevention of Criminal Behaviour' (2014) 15 *Nature Reviews* 54, 57.

[92] For instance the psychiatrists who gave their advice in the above discussed case; Boone (n 37) 7; I Jeandarme, 'Men geeft ons meer expertise dan we hebben' (2013) 270 *Juristenkrant* 8, 9.

[93] I Kerr, M Binnie and C Aoki, 'Tessling My Brain: The Future of Lie Detection and Brain Privacy in the Criminal Justice System' (2008) 50 *Canadian Journal of Criminology and Criminal Justice* 367, 373–75; GJC Lokhorst, 'Hersenen en recht. Geen koninklijke weg' (2008) 34 *Justitiële Verkenningen* 67, 68–69.

A second option is to allow the use of neuroscientific evidence only if beneficial to the defence. In the context of the insanity defence, the judge could use neuroscientific evidence that supports a verdict of acquittal based on criminal insanity. However, in the case of internment, it is not always clear which decision would be beneficial to the defence. Internment is theoretically a protective measure aimed at psychiatric treatment. Nevertheless, not every accused with a mental disorder desires to be interned. Unlike incarceration that is exclusively inflicted on offenders judged competent, internment is of indeterminate duration. In practice, this often leads to a longer detention or supervision period than one would be subjected to if judged competent and incarcerated. In addition, many internees are forced to reside in prison, awaiting transfer to a facility that can provide adequate treatment. In some instances, the admission of the neuroscientific test is requested by the defence. However, that is not in itself an indication that the defendant considers the test beneficial to his cause. The admission request may be an initiative of the defendant's counsel and not of the defendant himself.

More fundamentally, neuroscientific findings seem to have no direct probative value relevant to the assessment of internment conditions. As illustrated above, neuroscientific findings do not comply with the formulation and interpretation of the legal conditions. Neuroscience can detect abnormalities and dysfunctions in the structure or functioning of the brain, but cannot offer conclusive answers to the question of whether a particular individual is disordered or not. In that sense, neuroimaging is not more reliable than forensic psychiatric expert advice. So long as the law requires proof of a mental disorder, neuroscientific evidence cannot stand alone without a psychiatric examination with traditional methods.

The regulation of internment proceedings in the new Act exclusively mentions 'psychiatric examinations'. Neuroscientific evidence in internment proceedings, if presented and admitted, will be secondary to psychiatric evidence and only serve to foster psychiatric examination findings. We welcome this development. However, from the new regulation it is not clear whether brain scans should be performed on request of the expert witness, usually a psychiatrist, as part of the examination, or rather ordered by the judge as a separate examination. Many psychiatrists have little familiarity with brain imaging techniques and do not have the skills to perform brain scans themselves.[94] It could in principle be argued that psychiatrists are not competent to request and evaluate brain scans. However, as we have seen, the law regulating internment requires evidence that the person suffers from a mental disorder. This means that the focus will probably remain on traditional mental health assessment methods, well known to psychiatrists. Findings from brain scans currently have a weak probative value. In our view, it is preferable to admit brain scans in court exclusively in addition to traditional psychiatric assessments. Moreover, brain scan findings and implications for the mental state of the offender should ideally be interpreted and illustrated for the court by a neuroscientist rather than a psychiatrist.

---

[94] Meynen (n 83) 601.

This leads to the most fundamental shortcoming of brain imaging if used as evidence of mental state. The criminal law does not sanction deviant individuals; rather, it sanctions deviant, harmful and dangerous behaviour. Even the behavioural sciences, including psychiatry, cannot give the definite and unambiguous answers that the law requires, because legal questions are ultimately of normative rather than scientific nature. The interpretation of key legal requirements for internment, including fitness to control one's actions and sound judgement, can be unclear, to the detriment of legal certainty. However, we do not believe in attempting to clarify them by adopting a mechanistic or deterministic stance. Functional and structural brain anomalies do not necessarily have implications for self-control, proclivity to break the law, and generally for the ability to follow socially accepted behavioural standards.[95] In its present state, neuroscience cannot yet provide a causal explanation for behaviour. The legal-normative approach should therefore prevail when facing interpretation problems regarding the internment conditions. The criminal justice system should refrain from the illusion that adding a higher number of (scientific) experts, or increasingly diverse types of expertise, will in itself solve complex issues whose nature is essentially legal and normative.

The above said, neuroscience is a rapidly developing field of investigation. Increasingly sophisticated detection methods may become available, offering better diagnostic tools that reliably link brain abnormalities to particular disorders. This may lead to a highly problematic situation, in which only disorders detectable with neuroscientific tools will be considered relevant to the criminal law. However, for the present time 'neuroscepticism' prevails in the Belgian criminal justice system and in the specialised literature.

Neuroscientific Evidence in the Belgian Criminal Justice System: Current Practice

If neuroscience were to make its way into Belgian criminal proceedings, some issues would arise on how to perform neuroscientific examinations; we shall illustrate three such problems, which have no clear solution at present and are in need of further research.

Expert witnesses in Belgian criminal trials are underpaid, and payment is typically delayed. Like many other European countries, Belgium is cutting its public expenditure.[96] It is very unlikely that more costly examinations will be introduced as a part of expert assessments in criminal proceedings, especially if they are not yet accepted scientific practice and the reliability of their results is doubtful, as is the case for neuroscientific tests. In principle, the defendant has the right to present brain imaging evidence too, provided he bears the high financial cost of

---

[95] Glannon (n 91) 154–55; Glenn and Raine (n 91) 58; Morse (n 90) 217–18.
[96] According to the federal Budget of 2015, the Department of Justice has to save 124 million euro.

obtaining it. However, we believe that the costs are and will remain an extremely strong disincentive. The use of brain science on the initiative of the defence will most probably remain a rare occurrence.

All of the above does not mean that neuroscience has no role at all in Belgian criminal justice. Most likely, its use in criminal courts will increase regardless of its current weak predictive value, but exclusively as a risk assessment tool. Belgian society is very keen on prevention of recidivism for particular groups of offenders, particularly sex offenders. In the past decades, the Belgian criminal legislator has focused on sex offences and offenders by developing specific legislation.[97] For instance, criminal proceedings regarding sexual offences against minors have a special statute of limitations. The statute of limitations is known in civil law systems as the 'prescription period' and it sets the deadline to validly initiate legal proceedings after the crime. For sexual offences against minors, the prescription period is exceptionally long. Sex offenders also have to meet more criteria than other offenders to qualify for probation or conditional release. Particular care is put into detecting and treating paraphilia and protecting society from sex offenders, increasingly seen as individuals with an aberrant personality structure predisposing them to recidivism. Belgian society would very much support the use of neuroscience as a predictor of sexually deviant behaviour and possibly as part of the treatment of this type of offender. We believe strong social support may influence the practical functioning of the criminal justice system and make Belgian courts more likely to resort to brain imaging as a means of evidence in sex offences.

If neuroimaging were used more regularly for purposes of risk assessment, one crucial issue would have to be clarified, as it is not yet regulated: the consent requirement. Under which circumstances, if at all, can this type of examination be compelled? Historically, the Belgian criminal justice system has shown a strong reluctance to compel physical examinations and medical treatment, partly influenced by the stance of the medical world on the issue. A blood sample can be taken only with the person's consent; in default of consent, other means of evidence have to be sought.[98] DNA tests can be compelled, but only under very narrow circumstances.[99] A similar regulation is to be expected for neuroimaging.

Finally, it is essential to observe that the legal rules governing evidence in general will apply to evidence based on brain imaging too. The judge, or assize jury, adjudicate according to their 'inner conviction' and have the authority to exclude evidence they deem not sufficiently persuasive. A judge or jury that is not convinced of the probative value of neuroscientific evidence can easily exclude it.

---

[97] S De Decker, 'Seks verandert alles? Het bijzondere regime bij de uitvoering van strafrechtelijke sancties' in A Masset (ed), *De vervolging en behandeling van daders van seksuele misdrijven* (Brussels, La Charte, 2009) 115–59.

[98] Desmet (n 35) 95–96.

[99] A Bailleux, 'Grootschalig DNA-onderzoek: heiligt de efficiënte strafprocedure de opoffering van grondrechten van het individu?' (2013) 8 *Nullum Crimen* 269, 274–76.

Foreign studies of the impact of brain imaging-type evidence on jurors show mixed results. Some research groups have found that brain imaging evidence influences the jury even when not scientifically solid, other researchers have found the opposite.[100] On the whole, the prevailing attitude to neuroscientific evidence in the Belgian criminal justice system is one of scepticism. However, there may be exceptions in individual cases. There is controversy as to the interpretation of internment conditions, which in practice means that jurors are allowed considerable freedom of interpretation, often used to handpick the interpretation that is most fitting to the desired outcome. In practice, a decision for or against internment is de facto made before committing to a particular interpretation of the internment conditions. It should be noted that the measure of internment is often viewed by the jury as unjustly lenient. Jurors tend to think that internment means that the culpable offender will not be punished for the harm and suffering he caused. This emerges especially in cases of extremely serious crimes that attract public attention, as in the assize case described above, with the victims and society strongly pressing for punishment. We believe that evidence that is likely to lead to the desired outcome (conviction or internment) will be accepted more easily, even if it results from not yet reliable brain imaging techniques.

V. Conclusion

In Belgian criminal courts, neuroscientific evidence is hardly ever brought forward to corroborate the insanity defence or to prove mental disorder and dangerousness in internment proceedings. We could find very few examples. Some believe this type of evidence will play a more important role in the future, but this is by no means certain yet. In the light of the present state of the art of neuroscience, brain imaging should preferably be used together with methodologically more established psychiatric evidence. If the Belgian legislator regulates on the use of brain imaging in court, crucial choices will have to be made, particularly on the lawfulness of compelling neuroscientific tests. The criminal law has a normative rather than a scientific nature: including additional scientific means of evidence will not, and should not, bring about fundamental changes in legal proceedings lest we are making normative judgements disguised as scientific facts.

---

[100] Glannon (n 91) 157; DA Kraus and DH Lee, 'Deliberating on Dangerousness and Death: Jurors' Ability to Differentiate between Expert Actuarial and Clinical Predictions of Dangerousness' (2003) 26 *International Journal of Law and Psychiatry* 113.

Bibliography

Adriaens, PR and Block, A de, 'Alle gekheid op een stokje. Over de wortels van het psychiatrisch essentialisme' (2011) *Tijdschrift voor Filosofie* 7.

Ancel, M, *Social Defence. A Modern Approach to Criminal Problems* (London, Routledge & Kegan Paul, 1965).

Ankersäter, H, Höglund, P, Radovic, S and Svennerlind, C, 'Mental Disorder is a Cause of Crime: The Cornerstone of Forensic Psychiatry' (2009) 32 *International Journal of Law and Psychiatry* 342.

Auwera, A van der, Dheedene, J and Seynnaeve, K, 'Geïnterneerde personen in Vlaanderen en in België' in Casselman, J, De Rycke, R and Heimans, H (eds), *Internering. Nieuwe interneringswet en organisatie van de zorg* (Bruges, die Keure, 2015).

Bailleux, A, 'Grootschalig DNA-onderzoek: heiligt de efficiënte strafprocedure de opoffering van grondrechten van het individu?' (2013) 8 *Nullum Crimen* 269.

Beccaria, C, *Over misdaden en straffen* (Antwerp, Standaard, 1971).

Boone, R, 'Schuld onder de schedel' (2013) 270 *Juristenkrant* 6.

Cartuyvels, Y, Champetier, B and Wyvekens, A, *Soigner ou punir? Un regard critique sur la défense sociale en Belgique* (Brussels, Publications des Facultés universitaires Saint-Louis, 2010).

Casselman, J, 'Internering: huidige situatie' in Casselman, J, Cosyns, P, De Doncker, D et al (eds), *Internering* (Louvain, Garant, 1997).

Christiaens, A and Hutsebaut, F, 'Het deskundigenverslag—Bewijswaarde— Honoraria' in De Buyst, D, Kortleven, P, Lysens, T and Ronse, C (eds), *Bestendig handboek deskundigenonderzoek* (Mechelen, Kluwer, 2009).

Christiaens, A and Hutsebaut, F, 'Het optreden van de gerechtsdeskundige in de verschillende stadia van het onderzoek' in De Buyst, D, Kortleven, P, Lysens, T and Ronse, C (eds), *Bestendig handboek deskundigenonderzoek* (Mechelen, Kluwer, 2009).

Christiaensen, C, 'Adolphe Prins. 1845–1919' in Fijnaut, C (ed), *Gestalten uit het verleden* (Deurne, Kluwer, 1993).

Coles, EM and Veiel, HOF, 'Expert Testimony and Pseudoscience: How Mental Health Professionals Are Taking Over the Courtroom' (2001) 24 *International Journal of Law and Psychiatry* 607.

Collignon, T and van der Made, R, *La loi Belge de Défense sociale à l'égard des anormaux et des délinquants d'habitude* (Brussels, Larcier, 1943).

Cosyns, P, 'Psychiatrisch deskundigenonderzoek in strafzaken' in Casselman, J and Cosyns, P (eds), *Gerechtelijke psychiatrie* (Louvain, Garant, 1995).

Cosyns, P, D'Hont, C, Janssens, D, Maes, E and Verellen, R, 'Geïnterneerden in België. De cijfers' (2007) 28 *Panopticon* 46.

David, AS, 'Why We Need More Debate on Whether Psychotic Symptoms Lie on a Continuum with Normality' (2010) 40 *Psychological Medicine* 1935.

Debuyst, C, 'L'école française dite "du milieu social"' in Debuyst, C, Digneffe, Labadie, JM and Pires, AP (eds), *Histoire des savoirs sur le crime et la peine* (Brussels, Larcier, 2008) pt 2.

Debuyst, C, 'Les savoirs diffus et préscientifiques sur les situations-problèmes au XVIIIe siècle' in Debuyst, C, Digneffe, F, Labadie, JM and Pires, AP (eds), *Histoire des savoirs sur le crime et la peine* (Brussels, Larcier, 2008) pt 1.

Decker, S de, 'Seks verandert alles? Het bijzondere regime bij de uitvoering van strafrechtelijke sancties' in Masset, A (ed), *De vervolging en behandeling van daders van seksuele misdrijven* (Brussels, La Charte, 2009).

Decoker, J, 'Zijn we klaar voor het neurorecht' (2012) 246 *Juristenkrant* 12.

Desmet, C, 'Het menselijk lichaam als bewijsmiddel in strafzaken' (2006–07) *T Gez* 86.

Digneffe, F, 'Problèmes sociaux et représentation du crime et du criminel' in Debuyst, C, Digneffe, F, Labadie, JM and Pires, AP (eds), *Histoire des savoirs sur le crime et la peine* (Brussels, Larcier, 2008) pt 1.

Dillen, C, 'Zinvolheid van nieuwe richtlijnen en initiatieven rond interner-ing. Het standpunt van een psychiatrisch-forensisch deskundige' (2001) 15 *De orde van de dag* 43.

Dupont, L, *Beginselen van strafrecht* (Louvain, Acco, 2005).

Dupont-Bouchat, MS, *La Belgique criminelle. Droit, justice, société (XIVe–XXe siècles)* (Louvain-la-Neuve, Bruylant-Academia, 2006).

Emmelkamp, PMG, Hoogduin, CAL and Vandereycken, W, *Handboek psychopathologie 1* (Houten, Bohn Stafleu van Loghum, 2008).

Ferri, E, *La sociologie criminelle* (Paris, Félix Alcan, 1914).

Focqué, R and Hart, AC 't, *Instrumentaliteit en rechtsbescherming. Grondslagen van een strafrechtelijke waardendiscussie* (Antwerp, Kluwer Rechtswetenschappen, 1990).

Garofalo, R, *La criminologie: étude sur la nature du crime et la théorie de la pénalité* (Paris, Félix Alcan, 1888).

Gérard, PAF, *Le Code Pénal expliqué* (Brussels, 1867).

Glannon, W, 'The Limitations and Potential of Neuroimaging in the Criminal Law' 18 (2014) *J Ethics* 153.

Glenn, AL and Raine, A, 'Neurocriminology: Implications for the Punishment, Prediction and Prevention of Criminal Behaviour' (2014) 15 *Nature Reviews* 54.

Goethals, J, *Abnormaal en delinkwent. De geschiedenis en het actueel functioneren van de wet tot bescherming van de maatschappij* (Antwerp, Kluwer, 1991).

Goethals, J and Verbruggen, F, 'Van kommercommissie naar kwelrechtbank? De vernieuwing van de internering (en de TBS)' in Bevernage, C, Boes, M, Bonne, S et al, *Recht in beweging* (Antwerp-Apeldoorn, Maklu, 2008).

Hanoulle, K and Verbruggen, F, 'Ivorentorenmentaliteit in de kerkers? Het problematische begrip toerekeningsvatbaarheid' in Deruyck, F and Rozie, M (eds), *Het strafrecht bedreven. Liber amicorum Alain De Nauw* (Bruges, Die Keure, 2011).

Harris, R, *Murders and Madness. Medicine, Law, and Society in the* Fin de Siècle (Oxford, Clarendon Press, 1989).

Hengeveld, MW, 'De psycho(patho)logie van het wilsleven' in Meynen, G and Oei, TI (eds), *Toerekeningsvatbaarheid. Over vrije wil, wetenschap en recht* (Nijmegen, Wolf Legal Publishers, 2011).

Hutsebaut, F, 'Deskundigenonderzoek in strafzaken en het probleem van de tegenspraak naar Belgisch recht' in Hutsebaut, F and Reyntjes, JM, *Deskundig-enonderzoek en tegenspraak in het Belgische en Nederlandse strafrecht* (Nijmegen, Wolf Legal Publishers, 2011).

Jeandarme, I, 'Men geeft ons meer expertise dan we hebben' (2013) 270 *Juristenkrant* 8.

Kerchove, M van de, 'Le juge et le psychiatre. Evolution de leurs pouvoirs respectifs' in Gerard, P, Ost, F and Kerchove, M van de (eds), *Fonction de juger et pouvoir judiciaire* (Brussels, Facultés universitaires Saint-Louis, 1983).

Kerr, I, Binnie, M and Aoki, A, 'Tessling My Brain: The Future of Lie Detection and Brain Privacy in the Criminal Justice System' (2008) 50 *Canadian Journal of Criminology and Criminal Justice* 367.

Klaming, L and Koops, BJ, 'Neuroscientific Evidence and Criminal Responsibility in the Netherlands' in Spranger, TM (ed), *International Neurolaw. A Comparative Analysis* (Berlin, Springer, 2012).

Kogel, C de, 'Neurorecht' (2014) 56 *Tijdschrift voor criminologie* 108.

Kogel, C de, Nagtegaal, MH, Neven, E and Vervaeke, G, *Gewelds- en zedendelin-quenten met een psychische stoornis. Wetgeving in Engeland, Duitsland, Canada, Zweden en België* (The Hague, Boom Juridische Uitgevers, 2006).

Kraus, DA and Lee, DH, 'Deliberating on Dangerousness and Death: Jurors' Ability to Differentiate between Expert Actuarial and Clinical Predictions of Dangerousness' (2003) 26 *International Journal of Law and Psychiatry* 113.

Lascoumes, P, 'Beccaria et l'ordre public moderne' in Porret, M (ed), *Beccaria et la culture juridique des Lumières* (Geneva, Librairie Droz, 1997).

Leistedt, SJ, 'Le cerveau à la barre: une experience nord-américaine' (2014) 94 *Révue de droit penal et de criminologie* 1238.

Ley, J, 'Le psychiatre et les interventions medico-psychologiques et sociales dans l'administration de la justice pénale' (1967-68) 2 *Révue de droit penal et de criminologie* 145.

Lokhorst, GJC, 'Hersenen en recht. Geen koninklijke weg' (2008) 34 *Justitiële Verkenningen* 67.

Lombroso, C, *Criminal Man* (Durham, NC, Duke University Press, 2006).

Martinage, R, *Histoire du droit pénal en Europe* (Paris, Presses Universitaires de France, 1998).

Matthijs, J, 'La loi de défense sociale à l'égard des anormaux. Evolutions des conceptions' (1965) 5 *JT* 483.

Meynen, G, 'Neurolaw: de relevantie voor de forensische psychiatrie' (2014) 56 *Tijdschrift voor psychiatrie* 597.

Mooij, A, 'Toerekeningsvatbaarheid en de vraag naar het kwaad' in Keulen, BF, Knigge, G and Wolswijk, HD (eds), *Pet af: liber amicorum DH de Jong* (Nijmegen, Wolf Legal Publishers, 2007).

Morse, S, 'Avoiding Irrational Neurolaw Exuberance: A Plea for Neuromodesty' (2011) 3 *Law, Innovation and Technology* 209.

Nauw, A de, 'De niet-toerekeningsvatbaarheid sluit niet noodzakelijkerwijze het opzet uit' in Deruyck, F, Swaef, M de, Rozie, J, Traest, P and Verstraeten, R (eds), *De wet voorbij. Liber amicorum Luc Huybrechts* (Antwerp, Intersentia, 2010).

Nypels, J, *Le code pénal belge interprété* (Brussels, Bruylant-Christophe, 1867).

Prins, A, *La défense sociale et les transformations du droit pénal* (Geneva, Editions Médicine et Hygiène, 1986).

Rogers, T, 'Diagnostic Validity and Psychiatric Expert Testimony' (2004) 27 *International Journal of Law and Psychiatry* 281.

Ruschena, D, 'Determining Dangerousness: Whatever Happened to the Rules of Evidence?' (2003) 10 *Psychiatry, Psychology and Law* 122.

Schleim, S, 'Brains in Context in the Neurolaw Debate: The Examples of Free Will and 'Dangerous' Brains' (2012) 35 *International Journal of Law and Psychiatry* 104.

Slovenko, R, *Psychiatry and Criminal Responsibility* (New York, John Wiley & Sons, 1995).

Taylor, PJ, 'Mental Disorder and Crime' (2004) 14 *Criminal Behaviour and Mental Health* 31.

Traest, P, 'Enkele bedenkingen bij een wettelijke regeling van het deskundigenonderzoek in strafzaken' in Deruyck, F and Rozie, M (eds), *Het strafrecht bedreven. Liber amicorum Alain De Nauw* (Bruges, Die Keure, 2011).

Tulkens, F, 'Généalogie de la défense sociale en Belgique (1880–1914)' in Foucault, M (ed), *Généalogie de la défense sociale en Belgique* (Brussels, Story-Scientia, 1988).

Vandenbroucke, M, 'De nieuwe interneringswet: enkele kanttekeningen' (2007) 114 *Fatik* 21.

Vincent, N, 'Strafrechtelijke verantwoordelijkheid en de neurowetenschappen' (2013) 39 *Justitiële Verkenningen* 65.

Vuysere, S de, 'Wetgevende thema's inzake internering' in Daele, D van and Welzenis, I van (eds), *Actuele thema's uit het strafrecht en de criminologie* (Louvain, Universitaire Pers Leuven, 2004).

4

France. Is the Evidence
Too Cerebral to Be Cartesian?

RAFAEL ENCINAS DE MUÑAGORRI AND CLAIRE SAAS*

I. Introduction

The criminal law sets standards for evaluating individual responsibility, criminal capacity and dangerousness.[1] Several terms are relevant in this regard: 'mad' (*fou*), 'deranged' (*aliéné*), 'demented' (*dément*), 'insane' (*insensé*), and 'person suffering from a psychological or neuropsychological disorder that has deprived the individual of judgement or control over his or her actions' (*personne atteinte d'un trouble psychique ou neuropsychique ayant altéré son discernement ou entravé le contrôle de ses actes*). How are these terms defined? How have these definitions shifted, and what role do such terms play in evaluating criminal responsibility? How do experts and judges assess mental state, and what are the arguments and outlook for taking neuroscience into account in the assessment process? This chapter will address these questions in the context of French law.

Three Approaches to Definitions and Standards

Defining mental states in criminal law is part of a more general problem of naming objects, of categorising them by assigning them a name or linking them to a concept.[2] A problem frequently arises when a legal meaning must be given to a term that is specific to another field, including medicine or technology. This

---

* Translation from French by Naomi Norberg.

[1] See generally, V Rachet-Darfeuille, *L'état mental de la personne: étude juridique* (PhD dissertation, University of Paris I, 2001). See also, from the perspective of criminal law more specifically, C Saas, *L'ajournement du prononcé de la peine—Césure et recomposition du procès pénal* (Paris, Dalloz, 2004); A Coche, *La détermination de la dangerosité des délinquants en droit pénal, étude de droit français* (Aix-Marseille, Presses Universitaires d'Aix-Marseille, 2005).

[2] MS Pardo and D Patterson, *Minds, Brain and Law. The Conceptual Foundations of Law and Neuroscience* (Oxford, Oxford University Press, 2013) 5, 140.

problem lies at the heart of the criminal responsibility standard. When the law establishes standards such as 'demented state'[3] or 'existence of a psychological or neuropsychological disorder',[4] it uses concepts that are likely to be given different meanings by specialists (psychiatrists or psychologists) who have different theoretical and professional approaches. What is the relationship between legal meaning and scientific and technical meaning? At the risk of oversimplifying, we set out three general approaches.

The first approach, which may be called monist, is based on the idea that concepts have only one, single definition. This approach has the apparent advantage of simplicity, but this simplicity is deceptive. First of all, it assumes that concepts have 'true' definitions that only need to be discovered. As a corollary, it leads to favouring one definition over others. Moreover, it is somewhat rigid, because once a definition has been agreed on and used in practice, it becomes difficult to change it, even when our knowledge of the subject matter evolves. When the concept to be defined has its roots in the lexicon of a different discipline, as is the case with mental states, this approach leads lawyers to passive acceptance of extra-legal definitions.

The second approach is dualist and aims to maintain a separation between a term's legal definition and the definition it has in other domains. Although judges and code drafters may draw on other definitions, it is important for them to control how words that may have legal implications are defined. This approach often causes misunderstanding and fairly heated discussions between lawyers and professionals in the other fields concerned. In the examples above, a court of law would find a 'demented state' or the existence of 'a psychological or neuropsychological disorder' within the meaning of the Penal Code. This would not fail to invite criticism from specialists and professionals in the field of mental health, who would claim that the court was trying to replace them by defining technical terms without having the requisite knowledge or professional authority.

The third approach takes into account the fact that words can have several definitions and aims to reduce semantic fragmentation. A synthesis may be sought of the various extra-legal definitions of the term, or the legal definition may result from a subtler game in which lawyers claim not to be medical specialists and medical specialists claim not to be dictating the legal meaning. The judges' familiarity with the experts' knowledge on the one hand, and the experts' knowledge of the legal stakes of the definition on the other hand, lead to a cooperatively constructed, coproduced concept that will serve as a standard for resolving the case at hand. It was this type of interaction between lawyers and mental illness specialists that produced the definitions of 'demented' and 'suffering from a psychological or neuropsychological disorder that has deprived the individual of judgement or control over his or her actions'.

---

[3] Penal Code of 1810 (repealed), Art 64.
[4] Penal Code Art 122-1.

Who Sets the Legal Standards for Insanity?

Legislators, judges and court experts set the mental state standards for criminal responsibility. These warrant special attention from a comparative-law perspective, as each legal system has its own institutional and procedural specificities.

The legislator makes the law. France has a bicameral Parliament, consisting of a national assembly and a senate. As provided for in Article 34 of the French Constitution, the Parliament is responsible for drafting and passing criminal laws, and may initiate this process by submitting legislative proposals. However, the Cabinet also plays an important role in the legislative process by submitting legislative proposals. Bills and draft statutes are prepared by legislators in the offices of the ministries concerned on the basis of a series of reports, hearings and consultations. This process makes it possible to adopt new laws and update old ones. For example, the shift in 1994 that led to abandoning the concept of *démence* in favour of 'psychological or neuropsychological disorder that has deprived the individual of judgement or control over his or her actions' is the result of a legislative evolution that changed the standard for evaluating criminal responsibility in individual cases.[5] Civil law also has standards that involve mental states. The signatory of a legal act must be of sound mind (*sain d'esprit*)[6] for the act to be valid, mental disorder (*trouble mental*)[7] being a ground for invalidation. However, no such standard applies to tort liability.[8]

Judges rule on specific cases submitted to them, and in criminal matters they must apply statutory law according to the principle of strict interpretation. Although the French system maintains its historical attachment to statutes, the French judge is no longer 'the mouth of the law' (*bouche de la loi*). Rather, he interprets legal standards to apply them to individual cases. Judges determine whether an individual was, at the time of the events, suffering from a psychological or neuropsychological disorder that deprived him or her of judgement or control over his or her actions.[9] According to the criminal chamber of the Court of Cassation, this is a question of fact to be resolved by the lower courts in their discretion, not a question of law, unlike constraint, which is also mentioned by the statute in the context of criminal responsibility.

But how does one prove that a person had a particular mental state at a particular time? What are the criteria for establishing this fact? What knowledge, methods and means are employed? Before answering these questions, we must first review a few points of French rules of evidence. In criminal trials all methods of proof are admissible. In French law this is known as the principle of 'free evidence'

---

[5] See II below.
[6] Civil Code Art 414-1.
[7] ibid.
[8] Civil Code Art 474-3.
[9] Penal Code Art 122-1.

(*preuve libre*). The Code of Criminal Procedure does not set out general rules governing probative value. With exceptions, all evidence has (all other things being equal) the same probative value. One single probative standard (*intime conviction*) applies to both misdemeanours[10] and felonies,[11] and it is comparable to the 'beyond reasonable doubt' standard. Neuroscientific knowledge or technologies may therefore be submitted to the court as evidence. There are no evidence-related legal obstacles to their being used; the only guide is the compass of reasonable doubt, but it is hard to trust this to find true North.

Although the parties are free to produce any kind of evidence, the gathering of evidence is governed by the principles of legality, fairness and necessity (*légalité, loyauté, nécessité*). The Code of Criminal Procedure refers in several articles to necessity.[12] The search for evidence may not infringe upon freedom or fundamental rights, such as the right to physical integrity[13] or the right to privacy,[14] which includes the protection of sensitive personal data. These requirements also apply to the use of neuroscientific technologies for evidentiary purposes.

The characteristic features of French criminal procedure with regard to evidence and the opinions of court-appointed experts warrant a few comments here, beyond the rightly criticised, simplistic contrasting of adversarial and inquisitorial systems.[15] Whether during police custody, judicial investigation, or trial, investigating magistrates play a predominant role in searching for evidence. This statement is important primarily for what it does *not* say. By tradition as much as due to material difficulties, the defendant and his or her attorney concentrate on having the prosecution's evidence set aside on procedural grounds. They are generally not able to offer exculpatory evidence and rarely have the means to offer evidence based on recent technologies. Opinions from court experts (*experts judiciaires*) are one of the best illustrations of the inequality between the prosecution and the defence with regard to evidence, as well as of the judge's predominant role. Expert opinions are not considered evidence under French law. Rather, they are seen as the outcome of an investigative measure ordered by a judge. Only the judge has the authority to request an expert's opinion. The prosecution may produce items provided by the forensic team of the police department and defence attorneys may produce studies and analyses as evidence. However, as such, these are not considered expert opinions from a procedural standpoint. A defence attorney may challenge the expert's opinion using the arguments of specialists or may submit a request for a different expert, but the judge needs to agree and issue an order for a new expert analysis. In conclusion, court experts can only be appointed

---

[10] Code of Criminal Procedure, Art 427.
[11] Code of Criminal Procedure, Art 304.
[12] Code of Criminal Procedure, Introductory Article, para III(3).
[13] European Convention for the Protection of Human Rights and Fundamental Freedoms, Art 3.
[14] European Convention for the Protection of Human Rights and Fundamental Freedoms, Art 8.
[15] J Jackson, 'Taking Comparative Evidence Seriously' in P Robert and M Redmayne (eds), *Innovations in Evidence and Proof* (Oxford, Hart Publishing, 2007) 291, 304.

by judges and play an important role in determining the methods used to establish a suspect's mental state. The French legislature has made it clear that they may use brain imaging techniques.

Brain Imaging and Expert Testimony in the 2011 Bioethics Law

To our knowledge, the French law of 16 July 2011 is the first law in the world to explicitly regulate the use of brain scans. The result is a new chapter, entitled 'On the use of cerebral imaging techniques' in the Civil Code's section on individuals and their civil rights. It contains only one article:[16] 'brain imaging techniques can only be used for medical purposes, scientific research, or in the context of judicial expert opinions'. Contrary to what insurance companies, employers and marketing companies might have wished, no assessments or studies can be conducted and no statistics may be gathered for other purposes. The French legislator intended to ensure that brain imaging would not be used in discriminatory fashion or a manner that infringes upon individual liberties. The law's *ratio legis* is therefore close to that underlying the provisions governing the use of DNA-based identification techniques.[17]

However, allowing brain scans in the context of expert opinions is a paradox. In early 2008 the minutes of the public hearing of the Parliamentary office on scientific and technical choices showed hesitation regarding the regulation of this issue.[18] Concerns about 'the potential impact of neuroscience and brain imaging techniques on justice' were also mentioned in the report issued in late 2008 evaluating the application of 2004 bioethics law.[19] Then, in a 2012 Report on new technologies of brain exploration and therapy, the same Parliamentary office recommended 'clarifying, and possibly abolishing, the possibility to use brain imaging in court'.[20]

While noting the intention to prohibit the use of brain imaging other than for medical purposes, a 2010 Parliamentary report indicated that the prohibition 'could be subject to exceptions, in order to authorise certain uses of brain imaging techniques in the courts, for example to evaluate physical harm in the

[16] Civil Code Art 16-14.
[17] M Gaumont-Prat, 'La loi du 7 juillet 2011 relative à la bioéthique et l'encadrement des neurosciences' (2011) 231 *Les petites affiches* 10.
[18] A Claeys and JS Vialatte, Office parlementaire des choix scientifiques et technologiques, *Exploration du cerveau, neurosciences: avancées scientifiques, enjeux éthiques* [Minutes of the public hearing] (Paris, Assemblée Nationale—Sénat, 26 March 2008).
[19] A Claeys and JS Vialatte, Office parlementaire des choix scientifiques et technologiques, *Rapport sur l'évaluation de l'application de la loi n°2004-800 du 6 août 2004 relative à la bioéthique* (Paris, Assemblée Nationale—Sénat, November 2008) part five.
[20] A Claeys and JS Vialatte, Office parlementaire des choix scientifiques et technologiques, *L'impact et les enjeux des nouvelles technologies d'exploration et de thérapie du cerveau* (Paris, Assemblée Nationale—Sénat, 13 March 2012) 146.

context of a tort lawsuit'.[21] Assembly member Jean Léonetti suggested in a 2011 Report on a new legislative proposal that he had introduced that the use of brain imaging could also be justified 'to evaluate a perpetrator's liability, on the basis of Penal Code Article 122-1',[22] which concerns criminal responsibility. He proposed amending Article 16-14(2) of the Civil Code, introducing the possibility to use brain imaging 'in legal proceedings to evaluate harm, as well as to establish the existence of a psychological or neuropsychological disorder within the meaning of Penal Code Article 122-1'. The government proposed an amendment[23] phrased more generally, providing that brain imaging can be used 'in the context of court-ordered expert opinions', including criminal matters, as mentioned in the Bill's policy explanations. This wording was inserted into the final text.

It is always difficult to reconstruct the process leading up to the enactment of a statute and the political debates and social tensions at work. The most that can be said in this case is that the exception providing for use of brain imaging in the context of expert testimony was far from achieving consensus. Unsurprisingly, this text was adopted while the right was in power, led by President Nicolas Sarkozy. The changes French law has undergone in this area reflect a subtle restatement of the issue of criminal responsibility.

II. Insanity as the Sole Ground of Exemption from Criminal Responsibility

The traditional philosophical foundation of the French criminal justice system is the postulate of free will, advanced by the Classical School.[24] From the late eighteenth to the nineteenth century, it was believed that all human beings have free will and control over their actions. Precisely because human beings can formulate desires and choose to act on them or not, they can incur criminal liability for committing an offence. Criminal liability is therefore the counterpart of free will. As Gabriel Tarde famously put it, 'liability is founded on the freedom of the will'.[25]

---

[21] A Clayes and J Léonetti, *Rapport d'information fait au nom de la mission d'information sur la révision des lois de bioéthique* (Paris, Assemblée Nationale, 2010) Partie VI, Chapitre 9, proposition 76.

[22] J Léonetti, Rapport fait au nom de la commission spéciale chargée d'examiner le projet de loi relatif à la bioéthique (Paris, Assemblée Nationale, 26 janvier 2011) amendement AS 229.

[23] Amendement N°219 présenté par le Gouvernement (Assemblée Nationale, 10 February 2011, Bioéthique n° 3111), Art 24 *bis*.

[24] For a precise discussion of the historical aspects, see J Danet and C Saas, 'Le fou et sa "dangerosité", un risque spécifique pour la justice pénale' (2007) 4 *Revue de science criminelle et de droit pénal comparé* 779.

[25] JL Senon, 'Troubles psychiques et réponses pénales', *Champ pénal/Penal field* [online], 34th Congrès français de criminologie, Responsabilité/Irresponsabilité Pénale, published online 15 September 2005, accessed 24 October 2014: http://champpenal.revues.org/77; DOI: 10.4000/champpenal.77 (citing G Tarde, *La philosophie pénale*).

Since a mental disorder can deprive a person of free will and ability to control their actions, the law should reflect this fact by not holding them criminally responsible.

The 'Partially Insane': A Major Omission from the Penal Code of 1810

The 1810 Penal Code made a clear a distinction between two categories of individuals. Individuals believed to have free will incurred criminal liability if they committed an offence and were assumed to be responsive to criminal punishment. Individuals who were completely deprived of free will due to the effects of a mental disorder were considered not responsible. Article 64 of the Penal Code of 1810 provided that 'there is no misdemeanour or felony when the suspect was suffering from a mental disorder at the time of the action, or when he or she was constrained by irresistible force'. The law of 30 June 1838, called the 'law on the insane', set out the framework for interaction between the penal and medical systems, with the 'criminally insane' being subject to internment measures rather than criminal punishment. This scheme soon became obsolete and incompatible with new criminal justice theories and advances in medical knowledge in the area of mental health.

The postulate of free will dear to Enlightenment philosophers was called into question in the nineteenth century by new schools of thought. For example, the Italian positivist school, led by Lombroso, Garofalo and Ferri, embraced a determinist explanation of human action. A human being biologically or socially determined to become a criminal constitutes a threat to society. To respond to this dangerousness, preventive measures must be taken to neutralise, eliminate or re-educate the individual concerned. Criminal liability, the corollary of the freedom to want and to act, was supplanted by social dangerousness originating from individual determining factors. Protecting society from individuals who are socially or biologically determined to commit offences is the moral and legal foundation for imposing criminal measures.

Meanwhile, advances in medical knowledge opened up new perspectives. The early works by so-called 'alienists' (*aliénistes*) creating a clear-cut division between the 'insane' and the 'not insane' were followed by others showing that individuals did not always fit into one of the two existing categories. A third category was created: the 'partially insane' (*demi-fou*). The binary insane/not insane distinction was replaced with a three-part, insane/not insane/partially insane (*fou/non-fou/demi-fou*) distinction. The category of 'partially insane' was further subdivided, depending on the effects of the illness. Not all partially insane individuals were necessarily the same, in terms of their control over their desires and actions. The French criminal justice system created in 1810 thus fairly quickly fell behind medical knowledge and out of step with the prevailing schools of thought. It was nonetheless not revised on this point until 1994, when the entire code was revised.

Adaptation of Legal and Medical Practices

The criminal chamber of the Court of Cassation did not wait until 1994 to take medical and cultural advances into account. In an 1885 case, the Court argued that impaired judgement can justify moderating punishment:

> [T]here is no violation of Article 64 of the Penal Code in a judgment finding a suspect guilty while also finding, to justify moderating the sentence, that he does not enjoy the usual amount of judgment characteristic to full judgement of things, and that he has a certain lack of equilibrium that, while it does not negate liability, nonetheless allows for considering it to be limited.[26]

Article 64 of the Penal Code of 1810 did not regulate impaired judgement and French judges are bound by the principle of strict construction of criminal statutes. Nevertheless, it was a judicial decision that brought legal change by introducing the concept of limited criminal liability.

A few psychiatrists suggested a new approach based on their practices. For example, in a summary of his practices as an expert witness, Gilbert Ballet has asserted that:

> When an individual subjected to medical assessment was of sound mind at the time he accomplished the act of which he is accused, he must be declared liable; if he was insane, he must be declared not responsible and sent to an insane asylum if he is dangerous. If he is not insane but is not in possession of all of his intellectual faculties ... the court should enter a finding of reduced liability.[27]

On 20 December 1905 the Cabinet wrought the desired changes in this area through the so-called Chaumié circular. Joseph Chaumié, then Minister of Justice, sent general instructions to the prosecutors' offices on how the criminal justice system should handle the 'partially insane'. They were to be considered mentally ill and could be regarded as 'mentally abnormal' (*anormaux mentaux*), but they would nevertheless be considered criminally responsible. To incorporate the advances in the knowledge of psychological mechanisms into legal practices and refine their legal effects, the Chaumié circular recommends that certain changes be made in requests for expert opinions and expert practices. The investigating magistrate will ask if the suspect was suffering from dementia at the time of the events and also 'if the psychiatric and biological assessment reveals any mental or physical anomalies likely to attenuate [the suspect's] liability to a certain extent'. The Chaumié circular was a milestone in the evolution of the treatment of individuals suffering from mental illness in the French criminal justice system. The circular did not go so far as to assert that the impairment of mental faculties means

---

[26] Bulletin des arrêts de la Court of Cassation rendus en matière criminelle (1885–1887), tome 90, no 170, p 285.

[27] C Jonas, JL Senon, M Voyer and A Delbreil, *Méthodologie de l'expertise en psychiatrie* (Paris, Dunod, 2013) 47.

an individual is only partially liable and shall therefore be sentenced to only partial or reduced punishment. It merely hinted at partial liability and did not discuss the relation between type of mental affliction and extent to which judgement has been impaired. However, since the 1850s, psychiatric experts had been analysing cases of offenders who were found guilty and often sent to prison, but should have been regarded as insane according to medical standards.

In the first half of the twentieth century, various 'social defence' (*défense sociale*) schools, including the pragmatistic *Saldana* School in Spain and the *Terza Scuola* in Italy, disseminated certain ideas of the Italian positivist school. Many legal systems underwent reforms in the 1930s, inspired by the 'social defence' idea that criminal law's primary objective must be to defend society against criminals. A certain number of so-called 'social defence' laws were adopted in Europe, especially in Germany, Belgium and Switzerland, targeting multi-recidivists and the 'mentally abnormal'.[28] Measures were instituted entailing potentially lifelong internment of certain categories of individuals considered particularly dangerous: preventive detention (*rétention de sûreté*) was born.

In the latter half of the twentieth century, the 'new French school of social defence' (*école de la défense sociale nouvelle*) also began questioning the postulate of free will. Individuals are assumed to have criminal capacity, the ability to be subjected to and benefit from punishment. Regardless of their criminal capacity, dangerous individuals must be subject to preventive measures, possibly focused on psychiatric treatment, for an indefinite amount of time if necessary. The preventive measure may in theory be ordered before any offence has been committed. The 'mentally abnormal' and multi-recidivists are once again among those assumed to be socially dangerous. In 1959, criminologist Georges Levasseur and judge Marc Ancel, leaders of the 'new French school of social defence', proposed a reform to modify the regulation of criminal responsibility by adding special rules for offenders found to be dangerous and insane. The proposal was abandoned due to the political circumstances, as the war in Algeria required the full attention of the government and the legislature.

The 1994 Revision of the Penal Code and Its Ambiguity

It was only in 1994 that Article 64 was replaced with a new provision, Article 122-1 of the new Penal Code. The new article provides for two grounds of exemption from criminal responsibility. The first is almost the same as former Article 64: 'A person is not criminally liable if, at the time of the events, he or she suffers from a psychological or neuropsychological disorder that has deprived him or her

---

[28] J Danet and C Saas, 'De l'usage des notions de "délinquants anormaux" et "délinquants d'habitude" dans les législations allemande, belge, française et suisse', *Champ pénal/Penal field* (on line) (2010) VII, champpenal.revues.org/7955.

of judgement or control over his or her actions' (Article 122-1(1)). The second paragraph in the new provision regulates diminished responsibility:

> A person who, at the time of the events, was suffering from a psychological or neuro-psychological disorder that impaired his or her judgement or prevented him or her from controlling his or her actions may be punished, but the court will take these circumstances into account when determining the sentence and will decide on its implementation (new Penal Code Article 122-1(2)).

The revisers of the Penal Code remained vague. They did not define the degree to which judgement or control over one's acts must be impaired in order to benefit from a reduced sentence. The extent to which punishment may be reduced is also unclear. Criminal law scholars have only recently commented on the resulting ambiguity.[29] It has long been claimed that offenders with 'impaired judgement' were sentenced to particularly harsh punishments and that the prevailing logic when determining their sentences was: 'partially insane, twice the punishment' (*demi-fou, double peine*). According to judges, forensic mental health experts and lawyers, a finding of 'impaired judgement' at the hearing leads to subjecting offenders falling within the scope of Penal Code Article 122-1(2) to a harsher punishment. It is even claimed that offenders with 'impaired judgement' receive harsher punishments than criminally liable offenders. No statistics support this assertion, however. The criminal chamber of the Court of Cassation has left it to the lower courts to apply Penal Code Article 122-1(2) and determine sentences. Sentencing an individual to a harsher punishment without taking into account his or her impaired judgement is therefore not per se contrary to this article, the Court of Cassation argued:

> [T]he courts ... also have full discretion to draw the necessary conclusions as to the length and type of such punishment [and] of the existence of a psychological or neuropsychological disorder that, without depriving the perpetrator of them entirely, impaired his or her judgement or diminished his or her control over his or her actions.[30]

The discretion criminal courts enjoy when it comes to sentencing is settled case law, even in cases when Penal Code Article 122-1(2) applies. According to the criminal chamber of the Court of Cassation, Article 122-1(2) may not under any circumstances be considered legal grounds for reducing a sentence.[31] Judges are not compelled to subject offenders falling within the scope of Penal Code Article 122-1(2) to a reduced punishment. Even where Penal Code Article 122-1(2) applied, the harshest sentence could still be imposed. The law of 15 August 2014, which we discuss below in Section IV, overturns this court discretion rule that had emerged from case law.

---

[29] See Section IV below.
[30] Crim. 29 January 2014, no 12-85603.
[31] Crim. 5 September 1995, Bull. crim. no 270; Crim. 20 October 1999, Bull. crim. no 228.

Without entering into the technical details, we must also underscore that Penal Code Article 122-1 constitutes a subjective ground of exculpation from criminal responsibility, which is still sometimes referred to as a ground for non-imputability (*cause de non-imputabilité*). This interesting term refers to the notion that a particular quality of the perpetrator, including being a minor, acting under constraint, or suffering from a psychological or neuropsychological disorder, prevents the offence from being intellectually attributed to that individual. Acts that may be qualified as criminal were committed, but responsibility for them cannot be attributed to the individual who committed them without being able to control his or her own actions.

Until 2008, under the influence of both the old Penal Code and Article 122-1(1) of the new Penal Code, the public healthcare system took charge of individuals declared not criminally responsible. However, this arrangement underwent a rapid change, as the number of individuals found not criminally responsible decreased during the 1990s and 2000s.[32] Offenders protected under Article 122-1(2) began to enter the penal system, with the question of harsher punishment still unanswered. And finally, individuals who did not qualify for protection under either Article 122-1(1) or 122-1(2) were subjected to a classic sentence that increasingly included treatment. The law of 17 June 1998 introduced social and legal monitoring into French criminal law. This criminal, 'medico-health' punishment reflects an overlapping of approaches. Criminally liable individuals may be subjected not only to criminal punishment, but also to measures primarily aimed at treating offenders who are both mentally ill and likely to reoffend, therefore socially dangerous.

The 2008 Reform: How Dangerousness Replaced Responsibility

The law of 25 February 2008 draws on deterministic theories of the Italian positivist school[33] and caused French criminal law to shift focus, from responsibility

---

[32] The statistical data is not clear. Dismissals on the basis of Art 122-1(1) decreased from 287 in 2000 to 196 in 2006 and 140 in 2002, then increased to 159 in 2012. In the space of 10 years, they were cut in half. Yet this decrease in absolute value does not correspond to a decrease in proportion, which continues to be more or less 15%. JL Senon and C Manzanera, 'L'expertise psychiatrique pénale: les données d'un débat' (2006) 2 *Actualité juridique Droit pénal* 66, 67 (indicating that the number of cases involving criminally irresponsible individuals has stabilised at roughly 300 per year (0.50 of all cases), while case closures based on mental illness increased slightly (6,089 in 2003). G Barbier, Ch Demontès, JR Lecerf, JP Michel, *Rapport d'information fait au nom de la Commission des affaires sociales et de la Commission des lois par le groupe de travail sur la prise en charge des personnes atteintes de troubles mentaux ayant commis des infractions* (Paris, Sénat—Commission des affaires sociales, 2010) 30.

[33] M Van de Kerchove, 'Culpabilité et dangerosité—Réflexion sur la clôture des théories relatives à la criminalité', in C Debuyst and F Tulkens (eds), *Dangerosité et justice pénale* (Issy-les-Moulineaux, Masson, 1981) 291, 296.

and free will to social dangerousness. Borrowing a certain number of elements from the Bill proposed by Levasseur and Ancel and in line with European texts adopted in the 1930s and revised in the 1990s and early 2000s, the 2008 law clearly targeted a particular segment of the criminal population[34] by legalising lifelong internment, or preventive detention, for felons considered potentially dangerous. In addition to this *ante delictum* preventive measure of indefinite duration, the 2008 law created an exceptional procedure called the 'declaration of lack of criminal responsibility based on mental illness'. This allows a judge or court to establish that an individual suffering from a mental illness who committed an offence is not liable. A preventive measure may nonetheless be ordered for social defence purposes and included in the offender's criminal record, thus leaving a trace for many years.

The penal system's radical break with Article 64, which prohibited the mentally ill from being tried or subjected to legal (as opposed to medical) measures of prevention, therefore dates from 2008 rather than 1994. A further modification was made by a law of 15 August 2014, which rewrites Penal Code Article 122-1(1). We discuss this revision in detail in Section IV below.

Although they disagree on many points, French forensic mental health practitioners tend to agree that a distinction should be made between mental illnesses and personality disturbances. Only illnesses may be considered grounds for precluding or attenuating criminal responsibility; psychopathic personality disturbances should have no effect on criminal liability.[35] According to leading psychiatrist Jean-Louis Senon, the psychological and neuropsychological disorders considered to deprive individuals of judgement are essentially schizophrenia and bipolar disorders. Individuals likely to be characterised as sociopaths in the United States would not be protected under French Penal Code Article 122-1.

III. The Role of Court Experts

To evaluate mental state, one must call on an expert, or more precisely, as mentioned above, an expert appointed by a magistrate. The expert is a forensic mental health professional. From a procedural standpoint, the expert analysis of the mental state of the defendant at the time of the events may take place during police custody, investigation or trial.

What criteria and techniques do experts use to determine the existence of 'a psychological or neuropsychological disorder' within the meaning of the law?

---

[34] C Saas, 'Exceptional Laws in Europe, with Emphasis on "Enemies"' in M Caianiello and ML Corrado (eds), *Preventing Danger—New Paradigms in Criminal Justice* (Durham, NC, Carolina Academic Press, 2013) 33–59.

[35] See, *contra*, RE Kendell, 'The Distinction between Personality Disorder and Mental Illness' (2002) 180 *British Journal of Psychiatry* 110.

As illustrated above, this concept replaced 'mental disorder' and is now gradu-ated depending on whether the disorder deprives the perpetrator of judgement or control over his or her actions or simply alters them. Two cases decided the same year by the appellate courts of Toulouse[36] and Montpellier[37] will help to answer the question.

Two Court Cases

On 12 April 2008 police were informed that a male individual (YS) was throwing cinderblocks, pieces of cement, and rocks from a bridge onto vehicles travelling on the Toulouse ring road/express lane. When apprehended, the man acknowl-edged the facts as well as the theft of a chequebook. During police investigation while he was in custody, the offender underwent an expert psychiatric assessment conducted by Dr F, who concluded that:

> Mr YS is suffering from the consequences of cranial trauma and a coma, which might explain an impairment of his capacity for judgement and deficit disorders ... compli-cated by symptoms of psychosis (quirks, difficulties with interaction, etc.). The events do not seem to be in a direct causal relationship with a delirious or hallucinatory preoccupa-tion. The fact that he is not critical of the events gives rise to a fear of social dangerous-ness (perhaps underpinned by the neuropsychological impairment). He would respond to criminal punishment. He must undergo additional treatment and assessments before we are able to make cautious predictions as to the future! An impairment of judgement and control must be present, and needs to be better evaluated: it is not possible to declare incapacity within the meaning of Article 122-1.

The Toulouse criminal court for misdemeanours (*tribunal correctionnel*) ordered a new expert psychiatric assessment of YS. The doctor noted that YS refused to participate in the assessment and was unable to file any conclusions. The court sentenced YS to 30 months' imprisonment. The defendant appealed and agreed to undergo a new psychiatric assessment, ordered by the Court of Appeal on 20 August 2008. In their report, the experts, D and T, describe the offender as follows.

> [A]n unbalanced personality, probably aggravated by the neurological consequences of a serious cranial trauma, in particular a probable frontal syndrome. He also shows traits of immaturity, atypical disorders of the psychotic line, but our assessment has not revealed any pathological mental production ... The clinically unresolved issue was the magni-tude of the intellectual and cognitive deficits, our feeling is that they are related at least to an average or even profound debility ...
>
> THE MRI OF THE BRAIN. Despite its poor quality due to the patient's movements ... it reveals a very significant overall atrophy of the brain, correlated in a certain way with the results of the psychometric analysis ...While the psychiatric assessment strictly

---

[36] Toulouse Court of Appeal, Chamber of criminal appeals 3, 23 September 2008, no 08/00708.
[37] Montpellier Court of Appeal, Criminal chamber 3, 10 December 2009, no 09/00997.

speaking does not make it possible to form a sufficient conviction especially as to a psychotic organization of the personality, it demonstrates a profound intellectual deficit on an already deprived intellectual level, which is also explained by the individual's traumatic antecedents, that caused a major (... consequential) frontal syndrome. This is supported by the neuropsychological evaluation, which corroborates the clinical assessment and leads us to believe that while not totally deprived of judgement, the subject had no control over his actions, explaining the lack of any real self-criticism and in fact of any genuine awareness of the gravity of the acts committed. This extreme lack of behavioural inhibition constitutes the core of a dangerousness that is unfortunately fairly difficult to predict, because it is apparently very impulsive and gratuitous, which may however eventually be contained by appropriate psychotropic treatment. It therefore seems to us that judicialisation is not likely to provide an effective response and that the individual must instead receive long-term specialised treatment to overcome his lack of impulse control. In his current state, YS did not seem to us to be capable of understanding criminal punishment, which therefore does not seem to us to be a response that would be effective in preventing possible recidivism. YS may show signs of dangerousness related to impulsiveness and lack of reflection and self-criticism as a consequence of his frontal syndrome...

CONCLUSION ... The individual shows a profound intellectual deficit and in particular a major frontal syndrome causing unforeseeable behavioural disinhibition. The offenses of which he is accused seem to us to be related to the anomalies thus revealed. The individual therefore seems to us to have been suffering from a psychological disorder at the time of the events that, if it did not totally deprive him of judgement, at least very strongly impaired it, and may have eliminated his ability to control his actions within the meaning of Penal Code Article 122-1. In our opinion, the individual suffers from mental disorders that require treatment and compromise the safety of others, and [he may] therefore be subject to preventive measures, in accordance with the law of 25 February 2008.

When it ruled on criminal liability, the Court found that the first expert report (which found the defendant criminally liable) 'was conducted under emergency circumstances', the expert himself having pointed to the limits of the assessment conducted during police custody in jail. 'However, the experts D and T were able to deepen their investigation and carry out an MRI test. They clearly stated that YS had absolutely no control over his actions at the time of the events'. The Court of Appeal '[could] only uphold' the conclusions of these experts and found the man not criminally responsible, on the basis of Article 122-1.

The second case involves Bernard T, prosecuted for fraud and forgery in the context of buying and selling public works materials, occasionally passing himself off as an employee of companies for which he never worked. On 11 March 2009 he received a suspended sentence of one year in prison and was placed on three years' probation with a specific obligation to compensate the victims. The Court of Appeal appointed Dr Pierre P to conduct a psychological and neuropsychological expert assessment during a preliminary hearing and presented the assessment in the following terms:

The expert filed his report on 13 June 2007, concluding that in 2000 and early 2001, Mr Bernard T suffered from degenerative behavioural disorders with professional and personal difficulties [and] emotional instability that little by little led to the discovery of a malignant frontal tumour, a glioblastoma, an old tumour of the lowest grade possibly becoming cancerous, the first signs of which were not apparent for a long time. According to the expert, the frontal lobe deficits caused by this lesion and the surgery that followed it, completed by radiotherapy and chemotherapy, caused difficulties with conceptualisation, emotional instability, disinhibition with poor emotions and action control, [and] difficulties in clearly perceiving reality, which facilitated the occurrence of the events of which he is accused. According to the expert, Mr Bernard T is aware of the reprehensible nature of these acts but is not likely to tolerate criminal punishment, given the state of his health and the fact that punishment would have very little effect on his future behaviour. His state of health requires regular surveillance and treatment, medical-social care, and measures to protect justice, and warrants his being declared fully disabled and unable to undertake paid work. According to the expert, at the time of the events, Mr Bernard T's judgement was impaired and his ability to control his actions was diminished due to the neuropsychological lesions caused by his lesion [*sic*], ... the condition is not curable and requires regular surveillance and follow-up, recidivism and growth of the tumour remaining possible.

The Court then commissioned a follow-up assessment by the same expert during a second preliminary hearing on 2 July 2007:

Mr Bernard T would not respond to criminal punishment, the behavioural disorders began in 2000, the intervention and radiotherapy occurred in 2001, before the event, during which his cognitive abilities were impaired and, within the meaning of Penal Code Article 122-1, his judgement and control over his actions were not eliminated.

The Court asked Dr Jean-Dominique G to conduct a new expert psychiatric assessment of Bernard T:

The expert filed his report on 8 September 2008, indicating that Mr Bernard T showed a deficient state marked by bradypsychia, ideational perseveration, apathy, indifference, attention and memory problems, occasional fixation amnesia associated with character disorders that may cause him to forget or to have a distortion of the recent past, he may forget instructions or reorganize all his memories. The expert indicates that these disorders appeared after, and seem to be a problem directly related to, the surgery he underwent to ablate a left frontal glioblastoma in 2001 (major surgery) and that the latest cranial-brain MRI conducted in 2006 showed significant elements of degenerative leucopathy related, in particular, to the radiotherapy. The expert concluded by specifying that Mr Bernard T's frontal syndrome falls within the scope of the post-surgery and post-radiotherapy pathology, the offense of which he is accused probably being correlated to such anomalies; the expert indicates that: the man is not dangerous according to the psychiatric meaning of the term, he would not respond to criminal punishment, he does not seem to be curable or capable of rehabilitation, at the time of the events he was suffering from a psychological or neuropsychological disorder that had deprived him of judgement or control over his actions according to the meaning of Penal Code Article 122-1, he did not act under the influence of a force or constraint that he could not resist according to the meaning of Penal Code Article 122-2.

Faced with two differing expert reports, the Court of Appeal chose to disregard the conclusions of the second forensic mental health practitioner because, unlike the first, he had failed to adequately substantiate his findings, 'limiting himself to a peremptory, two-line assertion'. The Court held Mr Bernard T criminally liable.

Procedural Constraints and Judicial Discretion in Assessing Neuroscientific Evidence

The cases presented above provide an opportunity to highlight several aspects of criminal responsibility evaluations in the French criminal justice system. The decision to appoint an expert during the police investigation, particularly during police custody, is made by a magistrate, who may be a prosecutor representing the public prosecutor's office. During the investigation and trial phases, the judge appoints one or more expert witness, either on her own initiative or at the request of the public prosecutor or the parties.[38] It is possible to add a further expert, in addition to the appointed expert(s), and to modify the content of the list of questions submitted to the expert(s). However, this is all subject to authorisation by the judge, who has the final say.[39]

A suspect and her lawyer may in principle produce conclusions and analyses, also based on neuroscientific studies. However, these are considered mere elements to put in the case file, and are not given the procedural, symbolic status of 'expert opinions'. In addition, other than for some types of offences specific to the business world, the defence rarely proffers evidence based on new technologies. For cultural, institutional and financial reasons, the defence concentrates on trying to have the prosecution's evidence of guilt set aside on procedural grounds, rather than on producing its own exculpatory evidence using scientific or technological tools.

Investigating magistrates quasi-systematically appoint experts when there is an issue of criminal capacity. In cases involving sexual offences, expert appointment is mandatory.[40] It is a legal requirement that expert opinions include guidance on treatment in criminal rulings like preventive detention, socio-judicial monitoring or judicial surveillance of dangerous individuals.

Subject to exceptions that must be accounted for, in criminal matters magistrates have an obligation to choose experts from the official list kept by the appellate court of their jurisdiction. The Court of Cassation chooses from its own, national list.[41] To be registered in these lists, experts must meet the applicable criteria of expertise, experience and ethics. Membership is organised by specialty, according to a system of nomenclature set out in an order issued by the

---

[38] Code of Criminal Procedure, Art 156.
[39] Code of Criminal Procedure, Art 161-1.
[40] Code of Criminal Procedure, Art 706-47-1.
[41] Code of Criminal Procedure, Art 157.

Ministry of Justice.[42] 'Psychiatry' (F.2) is distinct from 'psychology' (F.7) and 'radiology' (F.4.1), the latter including neuroimaging. These specialties fall within the broader field of 'health' (F), which is distinct from 'legal, forensic, and criminal science medicine' (G). That said, magistrates are free to appoint any expert(s) on the list, regardless of specialty. Empirically-based sociological studies[43] have shown that the more often an expert is appointed, the more that expert is likely to be re-appointed in the future. Magistrates tend to choose the same experts repeatedly and to assume they will be easier to work with.

Once appointed, the expert works within the scope of an assignment set by the magistrate and must answer the questions posed by the magistrate. For example, in the second case discussed above, the Court asked the expert for a further opinion to have him expressly state that 'in the sense of Penal Code Article 122-1, he [the defendant] was not deprived of judgement or control over his actions'. Concise, express statements represent judges' idea of a good expert opinion: one that helps to reach a solution and is delivered on time. One of the sensitive issues is the remuneration of expert witnesses. In criminal matters, compensation is set by the government, in theory on a fixed-fee basis.[44] The mediocrity of the material and institutional conditions for psychiatric expert opinions resulted in a lack of experts. Since psychiatrists no longer want to play this role, the government sought to promote the appointment of young, inexperienced psychiatrists as court-appointed experts.

While the expert's report is very important to the judge's decision, the judge is not legally bound to follow the expert's recommendations. If there are diverging expert opinions, she may follow the one she deems most appropriate and most convincing. In the Toulouse case discussed above, the judge indisputably granted supreme importance to the MRI-based expert report. In the Montpellier case, the judge favoured instead the first expert report over the second, based on an MRI but deemed 'peremptory'. Since there are no rules regarding the admissibility of expert opinions or their probative value, it is not possible to predict whether the results of a particular medical procedure will even be used as evidence, let alone be considered persuasive. The probative value to be assigned to expert opinions and other evidence is within the discretion of the lower courts, as recently restated by the criminal chamber of the Court of Cassation in a case in which five psychiatrists appointed by the investigating magistrate as experts disagreed on the nature of the defendant's psychological and neuropsychological disorders.[45]

---

[42] The nomenclature is subdivided into branches, categories and specialties. Ministerial order of 10 June 2005 on the nomenclature set out in Art 1 of Decree no 2005-1463 of 23 December 2004.

[43] C Protais, 'Experts et expertises psychiatriques: la question de l'indépendance' in J Pelisse, and C Protais et al (eds), *Des chiffres, des maux et des lettres. Une sociologie de l'expertise judiciaire en économie, psychiatrie et traduction* (Paris, Armand Colin, 2012) 73, 74 (indicating a concentration of more than 80% in Paris and Angers).

[44] Code of Criminal Procedure, Art R 106.

[45] Crim. 21 March 2012, Bull. crim. no 77, no 12-80.178 (our translation): 'the investigating chamber, after having noted that there were sufficient accusations that the suspect committed the alleged

The few elements discussed here highlight a paradox in the French system of evidence and expert opinions in criminal law. On the one hand, the law places no limitations on the type of scientific investigations admissible as evidence and, at least in theory, the most sophisticated techniques may be used. However, expert opinions in fact constitute the decisive evidence and are controlled by the judge. Freedom with regard to evidence is not combined with a free use of expert opinions. When criminal responsibility is at stake, under what conditions can or could experts use new technologies, in particular neuroscientific tools? Answering this question requires taking a closer look at the community of experts specialised in mental illnesses.

Diverse Experts and Approaches

The problems raised by evaluating mental disorders in a legal context are hardly new. A historical study indicates that the issue first arose in France between 1832 and 1838,[46] when extenuating circumstances and the insanity defence became part of the criminal law. Mental health expert evaluations were not yet psychiatric, as this word did not appear in the French dictionary until 1846.[47] However, there were already heated debates not only between experts and magistrates, but also within the experts' community. The experts wanted magistrates to accept their knowledge as authoritative. To be taken seriously, a mental expert evaluation must be perceived as objective, scientific. The challenge is even greater because the mental health experts were developing their own professional and scientific knowledge in this domain of expertise, as they conducted the evaluations. This is how psychiatric expert evaluations became 'legal medicine', or 'forensic science' in today's terminology. The list of mental disorders grew, with each addition receiving a name and a description. In early 1870, pre-eminent forensic medical scientist Ambroise Tardieu and the majority of experts added to medical nosography various new sub-types of insanity, including conditions then designated as 'common madness' and 'maniacal madness', or 'monomania'. Prominent psychiatrist Bénédict Morel introduced the term 'degenerate', referring to a person whose defects are inheritable.[48] In the early twentieth century, studies of the brain and central nervous system led to formulating new hypotheses. Consciousness results from a combination of neurons and when the structure of a cell in

acts and after analysing the psychiatric expert reports as well as the statements of the experts, found that it was not certain that judgement at the time of the events was lacking, that [Criminal Code] Art L. 122-1(1) therefore cannot be applied, and that [the case] should be remanded to the felony criminal court; whereas the investigating chamber has presented its findings, which are within its discretion, in a manner sufficient to support its decision'.

[46] F Chauvaud, *Les experts du crime. La médecine légale en France au XIXème siècle* (Paris, Aubier—Collection historique, 2000) 113.

[47] ibid, 111.

[48] ibid, 133.

the central nervous system is modified or impaired, 'the individual's personality may change ... and thereby reduce liability or cause it to disappear'.[49] Even today, although judges do not always follow the experts' advice, they must rely on experts' opinions to decide whether there is in fact a mental disorder. Experts and judges thus work in tandem.

As a corollary, discussions among experts have led to refining knowledge and streamlining methods. This process seems inherent to constituting the field of forensics: establishing scientific knowledge for legal purposes. The most ambitious plans seek to harmonise forensic science standards and methods at the international level, particularly in the criminal law.[50] It appears that such efforts may lead to neuroscience being taken into account. But if the French situation is any example, we will not reach that point soon. The mental expert field is divided and compartmentalised, even if one looks only at psychiatrists. On the institutional level, experts approved by and listed with the courts come from different backgrounds. A study based on a small survey showed that two-thirds of psychiatric experts work in the public sector (hospitals or public consultation centres) and 20 per cent in the private sector, and roughly 10 per cent are university professors.[51] Psychiatric experts therefore do not form a community. There are professional or local associations, but these do not represent practitioners in the way a psychiatric experts' guild could.[52] In addition, psychiatrists' theoretical orientations are divergent if not antagonistic. Let us think of biological psychiatry, psychoanalysis, cognitive-behavioural techniques and systemic approaches.[53] The context of the expert evaluation therefore leads to a certain amount of eclecticism. A psychiatric expert professionally affiliated with a hospital stated in the above-mentioned survey:

> There are very few mentally ill individuals among the people we see. We therefore have to cobble things together ... We have to re-create a neo-language, neo-practices, we have to reinvent concepts, and rethink a certain number of them ... all in the service of justice.[54]

Lastly, psychiatric experts see their role differently depending on their professional and ideological positions, some of which are still authoritative, including the 1970s anti-psychiatry movement lead by Michel Foucault, among others. The movement criticised psychiatric experts' 'collaboration' with the criminal justice system.[55] There are also more than simple nuances between psychiatrists who limit

---

[49] ibid, 135, n 22, citing P Devernois, *Les aliénés et l'expertise médico-légale* (Toulouse, Dirion, 1905) 28.
[50] JF Niboer and WJJM Sprangers (eds), Harmonisation in Forensic Expertise. An Inquiry into the Desirability of and Opportunities for International Standards (Amsterdam, Thela Thesis, 2000).
[51] Protais, 'Experts et expertises psychiatriques' (n 43) 78.
[52] ibid, 106.
[53] ibid, 85.
[54] ibid, 85.
[55] M Foucault, *Les anormaux. Cours du collège de France, 1974–1975* (Paris, Gallimard-Seuil, 1999) 32, 38.

themselves to their professional expertise when acting as experts, and those who venture beyond it to play as full a role as possible in the legal proceeding.[56] More importantly, there is no unanimity among experts with regard to the appropriate criminal fate of individuals suffering from mental disorders. Part of the psychiatric profession supports the attribution of criminal responsibility and criminal sentencing and incarceration, combined with treatment. The rest believe offenders with mental conditions should never be subjected to criminal punishment, and find internment in mental health facilities preferable.

The disagreements among experts-psychiatrists and the ambiguous relationship between justice and psychiatry are well known to the French legislator who, in summer 2014, incorporated the gradations of mental disorders into positive law while reinforcing treatment ordered by the criminal courts.

IV. Penal and Medical Responses, Calibrated According to the Nature of the Mental Disorder

It has long been known in France that there are many individuals suffering from mental disorders in prison.[57] Their number has increased, as the courts are increasingly finding offenders who suffer from mental disorders criminally liable. But the prison environment, to speak euphemistically, is not suited to treatment. The drop in the number of beds available in the psychiatric sector makes it impossible to adequately care for mentally ill patients full time. Coordinating the penal and medical systems is particularly complex in a context of diminishing psychiatric hospitalisation.[58]

In addition, it is increasingly difficult to maintain the distinction between dangerousness in a psychiatric and in a criminological sense. 'Psychiatric' dangerousness is the manifestation of symptoms related to the direct expression of the mental illness. 'Criminological' dangerousness is the probability that an individual will commit an offence, determined according to environmental and situational factors likely to foster action. There is a risk of confusing the psychiatric patient with the offender.

Since the introduction of so-called 'health-medical penalties', medical treatment has been imposed on offenders with increasing frequency in the French criminal justice system. At first, dangerousness was presented as a new criterion replacing

---

[56] Protais, 'Experts et expertises psychiatriques' (n 43) 97 (contrasting a restrictive model and a broad model).

[57] Other Western countries have made the same observation. See the meta-analysis directed by S Fazel and J Danesh, 'Serious Mental Disorder in 23,000 Prisoners: A Systematic Review of 62 Surveys' (2002) 359 *The Lancet* 545.

[58] See also JF Burgelin, Santé, justice et dangerosité: pour une meilleure prévention de la récidive, commission Santé-Justice (Paris, Ministère de la Justice, 2005).

criminal liability, when offenders could not incur criminal liability because of their mental state. Later, dangerousness started to be taken into account in sentencing, also for criminally liable offenders. Dangerousness and criminal liability are different criteria, but may both be applied in the same case. The same offender can be sentenced to both penalties and medical treatment, thus combining criminal sentences with medical care.

Further Senatorial Proposals to Reform the Insanity Defence

In 2010 the Senate again took up the issue of revising Penal Code Article 122-1.[59] In an informational report,[60] parliamentarians stressed that the courts were not ordering reduced sentences for offenders found to suffer from 'a psychological or neuropsychological disorder' that had 'impaired' their 'judgement or control'. The report contains three main criticisms of the criminal justice system: punishment has no meaning for individuals whose judgement is impaired; prison is not an appropriate place for the kind of treatment this type of offender needs; and criminal sentences are harsher than those of individuals whose judgement is found to be intact. The Senate suggested fostering continuity between treatment dispensed in prison and outside. It insisted on the need to rewrite Penal Code Article 122-1(2), to expressly include the defence of reduced criminal liability in the law and to introduce reduced punishment for offenders whose judgement or control over their actions is impaired. The recognition of the principle of effectively reduced punishment would be combined with reinforced treatment measures. The individuals concerned would receive treatment from a health care facility while in prison, as well as after release. The final proposal is a description of the institutions that should take charge of individuals whose mental state prohibits incarceration but whose dangerousness requires them to be kept in psychiatric units specifically equipped for socially dangerous, mentally ill individuals.

On the basis of this very detailed informational report, senators Barbier, Demontès, and Lecerf submitted Bill no 649 to modify the wording of Penal Code Article 122-1 in an attempt to remedy its current defects. The proposed law sets the punishment incurred by a person found to suffer from 'a disorder that has impaired his or her judgement' to two-thirds of the standard punishment for each offence. Offenders found partially responsible can, however, be sentenced to preventive measures. Offenders found not criminally responsible can instead be sentenced only to a number of particular, exhaustively enumerated preventive

---

[59] P Goujon and C Gautier on behalf of the commission of laws, Les délinquants dangereux atteints de troubles psychiatriques: comment concilier la protection de la société et une meilleure prise en charge médicale? Rapport d'information no. 420 (Paris, Assembl Nationale—Sénat, 2005).

[60] Barbier et al (n 32).

measures and not to criminal sentences. The idea behind this proposal was to reflect in legal terms the fine gradations of an individual's cognitive understanding (judgement, knowing right from wrong or, more objectively, legal from illegal) and volition (the ability to make decisions and control one's actions). The Senate wanted the criminal courts to be bound by a statutorily established decrease in punishment in cases involving impairment of judgement or control over one's actions. Not all problems would be avoided however, as experts may have divergent opinions on the same case, as recently happened in a case of double parricide.[61] Although the Senate adopted the legislative proposal on its first reading on 25 January 2011, in the end the Bill was not passed.

The Content of the Reform

Article 122-1(2) was amended years later, through a different draft law that did not originally concern the insanity defence. The matter was the subject of numerous discussions. The Ministry of Justice, which had submitted the draft law, did not fully agree with the authors of the proposed revision. Nevertheless, the new regulation of the insanity defence was eventually incorporated into 'law no 2014-896 of 15 August 2014 on the individualisation of punishments and the improvement of the effectiveness of criminal penalties'.[62] Article 122-1(2) now reads:

> A person who, at the time of the events, was suffering from a psychological or neuropsychological disorder that impaired his or her judgement or diminished his or her control over his or her actions, shall be punishable. However, the court shall take this disorder into account when determining the sentence and deciding on the type and severity of punishment. The penalties for offences punishable by incarceration shall be reduced by one-third, and to 30 years in the case of felonies punishable by a sentence of life imprisonment. In the case of a misdemeanour, the court may decide not to reduce the sentence, provided it issues a decision supported by specific grounds. When, following a medical opinion, the court determines that the nature of the mental disorder so requires, it shall ensure that the sentence enables the individual to receive adequate treatment.[63]

The law thus expressly establishes the principle of reduced sentences in cases of impaired judgement, making the implicit explicit. However, sentences will not systematically be reduced by one-third. In cases involving misdemeanours, criminal courts may impose the standard sentence if they specify the grounds for doing so in the decision. In felony cases, the decision to set aside Article 122-1(2) must be made by a qualified majority of the judges, as is the case for any decision unfavourable to the defendant.[64]

---

[61] Juvenile criminal Court of Southern Corsica, '*Andy case*', 17 November 2012.

[62] JH Robert, 'Punir dehors—Commentaire de la loi no 2014-896 du 15 août 2014' (September 2014), *Droit pénal*, étude 16.

[63] Penal Code Art 122-1(2).

[64] A qualified majority requires 6 votes of 9 at first instance, and 8 votes of 12 on appeal.

Introducing new statutory grounds for sentence mitigation also affects criminal procedure. Misdemeanour courts (*tribunaux correctionnels*) and felony courts (*cours d'assises*) are composed differently, and different procedural rules apply. In particular, felony courts deliberate on the existence of legal grounds for reducing the sentence.[65] Presiding judges in felony cases will now have to raise the more specific issue of whether there are grounds to reduce the sentence on the basis of Penal Code Article 122-1(2).[66]

If a felony court finds the defendant guilty and criminally responsible, it has an obligation to discuss the issue of impaired judgement. Even after a finding of impaired judgement, the court may decide against the one-third sentence reduction, provided a qualified majority of the judges is opposed to its application in the particular case.[67]

The Pursuit of a Balance Between Treatment and Punishment

For both misdemeanours and felonies, after being given a medical opinion, courts are required to ensure that 'the convict receives adequate treatment'. However, it is difficult to imagine how trial judges who issue their ruling after one single hearing, often with very limited time, can satisfy such a requirement. The judge responsible for monitoring sentence application (sentencing judge, or *juge de l'application des peines*), who follows up on convicts throughout their sentences, seems better situated and equipped for the task.[68]

The introduction of new statutory grounds of sentence reductions would necessitate, at least in theory, reinforcement of the criminal justice and healthcare mechanisms for the care of individuals considered not criminally responsible, or partially responsible. According to Code of Criminal Procedure Article 706-136-1, if the convict has not been required to undergo socio-judicial monitoring, which in theory entails compulsory treatment, the sentencing judge may compel treatment upon release. The treatment period is up to five years in misdemeanour cases and up to 10 years in cases of felonies or misdemeanours punishable by 10 years in prison.

Several provisions further reinforce the mechanisms for having the healthcare system take charge of individuals found to have impaired judgement. Sentencing judges may withdraw sentence-reduction credits if, while incarcerated, the

---

[65] Code of Criminal Procedure, Art 356.
[66] Code of Criminal Procedure, Art 361-1.
[67] Code of Criminal Procedure, Art 362.
[68] M Herzog-Evans, 'Is the French *Juge de l'application des peines* a Problem-solving Court?', in M Herzog-Evans (ed), *Offender Release and Supervision: The Role of Courts and the Use of Discretion* (Nijmegen, Wolf Legal Publishers, 2015).

convict refuses to comply with his or her treatment obligations.[69] Moreover, 'no additional sentence reduction may be granted to a person convicted in the circumstances referred to in the first sentence of Penal Code Article 122-1(2) who refuses the proposed treatment'.[70] Finally, lack of compliance with treatment obligations constitutes a misdemeanour punishable by two years in prison and a fine of 30,000 euros.[71] The treatment mechanism has very clearly been strengthened with regard to both the duration of the preventive measures and the consequences of non-compliance with treatment obligations. A medical opinion is required every time, and far from separating the work of the courts from that of doctors, the law of 15 August 2014 strengthens the ties between the two worlds, thereby potentially blurring the lines between therapeutic and purely repressive measures.

Legislative reform was stretched out over a long time period to take into consideration input from practitioners, including magistrates and psychiatric experts, as well as advances in medical and scientific knowledge. Now that French lawmakers have finally revised the law to reflect the knowledge gained from expert evaluation practices that began in the latter half of the nineteenth century, the time is ripe to turn to the issue of using neuroimaging techniques, at least as a 'decisional aid'.

V. What is the Outlook for the Role of Neuroscience Technologies in French Criminal Trials?

Debates on the use of neuroscience to evaluate mental disorders are taking place in various professional communities. We briefly summarise the perspectives of researchers, experts and lawyers below.

What Can Neuroscience Say About a Suspect's Mental State?

French researchers are at the cutting edge of neuroscience research. The researcher best known to the public is undoubtedly neuroscientist Jean-Pierre Changeux. In his 1983 book *L'homme neuronal*,[72] Changeux argues for a 'strong approach' that explains human beings on the basis of the brain and propounds a neuronal theory of thought. Since then, neuroscience has developed in close

---

[69] See the new wording of Code of Criminal Procedure Art 721(3) (our translation): 'Following a medical opinion, withdrawal may also be ordered when the person sentenced in the circumstances referred to in the first sentence of Penal Code Article 122-1(2) refuses the proposed treatment'.

[70] Code of Criminal Procedure, Art 721-1.

[71] Code of Criminal Procedure, Art 706-139.

[72] JP Changeux, *L'homme neuronal* (Paris, Fayard, 1983).

association with cognitive science, also through interdisciplinary programmes.[73] Nonetheless, applied research rarely touches on the field of law or criminal justice. Only a few neuroscientists, such as Serge Stoléru, wish to build a bridge between research (for example, on the brain, sexual aggression and paedophilia) and its eventual use for legal purposes.[74] So far, the French government has not done much to foster a link between science and forensic medicine, also because many researchers have strong reservations. Prominent neurobiologist Catherine Vidal took a stand against using neuroscience technologies for evidentiary purposes.[75] Neurologist and neuroscientist Hervé Chneiweiss expressed similar reservations several times while collaborating with the legislature prior to the revision of the Bioethics Law:

> The increasing demand for security pushes governments to search for biological indicators of dangerousness in individuals. The issue is therefore yet again to determine the actual predictive value of the test under consideration, rather than validating social prejudice in a pseudoscientific way. The justice system always seeks to establish the facts, hence the idea that the brain's circuitry carries an intrinsic neuropsychological truth.[76]

The fear expressed is also that using neuroimaging or similar technologies in court will harm the reputation of, and reduce the financing for, neuroscience research. '[O]ne of the major dangers of incorporating this demand for security into the law is that our research will become the subject of distrust'.[77]

The criminal justice system has long been preoccupied with finding the perfect evidence, ideally by directly accessing the thoughts of other human beings. The new technological tools that register individual brain activity create the illusion that we can have direct access to cognition. Neuroscientists Arnaud Aubert and Elodie Coudret stated that 'it is impossible for us to share the mental experience of those around us and we must rely on the individuals themselves and on indirect sources of information: language, behaviour, attitudes'.[78] The two neuroscientists caution against 'localisationism'. With this term, they refer to a modern form of Gall's phrenology, a now obsolete theory of cognition that associated particular brain areas with particular functions. Brain mapping may also cause a return to biological determinism. Postulating correspondence between a particular type of lesion in a particular brain area, and a particular level of volition or consciousness, could lead to categorising all individuals who have that type of lesion as also

---

[73] B Chamak, 'Dynamique d'un mouvement scientifique et intellectuel aux contours flous: les sciences cognitives (United States, France)' (2011) 25 *Revue d'histoire des sciences humaines* 13.

[74] V Fonteille, F Cazala, V Moulier, S Stoleru, 'Corrélats cérébraux de la pédophilie: apports de la neurologie et de la neuro-imagerie' (2012) 38 *Encéphale* 496.

[75] C Vidal, 'Vers une neurojustice?' (2011) 4 *Ravages* 17.

[76] H Chneiweiss quoted in Claeys and Vialatte (n 19) part five-III-A-2.

[77] H Chneiweiss, 'Les neurosciences et le Droit: un dialogue difficile mais nécessaire ou comment identifier des causalités sans sombrer dans le déterminisme' (2013) 44 *La lettre des neurosciences* 28.

[78] A Aubert and E Coudret, 'Prédictibilité du comportement: neuro-sciences et neuro-mythes' (2012) 2 *AJ Pénal* 80.

having impaired control. Several psychiatric experts disagree with that categorisation and stress that individual assessments are always necessary.

Most experts appointed by the courts to evaluate the degree of individual mental disorder or dangerousness are psychiatrists. A small survey conducted through interviews confirmed that forensic mental health practitioners rarely use neuroscientific technologies.[79] The experts often reminded the interviewer that even if neuroimaging were reliable and conducted under optimum conditions, it would constitute only one element among others:

> Additional exams are rarely essential. In fact, in the current state of the science, a diagnosis of schizophrenia or bipolar disorder is solely clinical, and is based on the patient's history and the evolution of his disorders. Neuroimaging is used only exceptionally, in particular when a differential neurological diagnosis must be made: subdural hematomas, brain tumours, or complex forms of epilepsy. … Neuroimaging is therefore indicated in limited cases and always follows an extremely thorough clinical assessment. State-of-the-art medicine offers no clinical schema of the destruction of judgement, and we are even less able to hypothesize a correlation between a problem with judgement and functional imaging.[80]

When he was interviewed in July 2014, Jean-Louis Senon stated that he had used an MRI exam in only one out of 100 expert evaluations, simply to confirm the diagnosis in a situation where atypical symptoms were present. He expressed grave reservations with regard to attaching judicial relevance to apparent brain abnormalities that emerge from brain imaging. Brain lesions may cause 'hypofrontality', diminished brain activity in the frontal cortex. 'Hypofrontality' can in turn lead to impaired self-control. However, the connection between 'hypofrontality', self-control, behaviour and criminal responsibility is far from established. Senon provocatively stated that about one-third of the French population would show signs of diminished brain activity in the frontal cortex, if subjected to an MRI!

That said, an MRI could in theory be included in the case file, even when not conducted by a forensic mental health expert for legal purposes. It could still have a certain amount of influence on the severity of the sentence ordered by the judges and the jury in felony cases, as prominent psychiatrist Jean-Pierre Olié observed, recalling a case in which he acted as an expert advisor to one of the parties.[81] In other words, while neuroscience technologies exercise a certain amount of influence, this influence often stems more from the very presence of medical elements in the file than from the participation of expert witnesses in the proceeding.

---

[79] R Encinas de Muñagorri, 'Les techniques d'imagerie cérébrale dans le cadre d'expertises judiciaires' (2014) 113 *Experts* 8.

[80] JL Senon and M Voyer, 'Du concept de responsabilité et d'irresponsabilité en droit pénal français, comme fondement de l'expertise psychiatrique pénale', in O Oullier (ed), *Le cerveau et la loi: analyse de l'émergence du neurodroit* (Paris, Centre d'analyse stratégique, 2012) 78.

[81] Encinas de Muñagorri (n 79) 10.

The legal system thus makes indirect use of medical exams. Unlike the United States, however, France does not have companies that commercially develop neuroscience-based technologies for courtroom use, including lie detectors, often cited as a paradigmatic example of the inappropriate use of neuroscience in legal proceedings. As illustrated above, Article 16-14 of the French Civil Code prohibits the use of neuroimaging for purposes other than medical diagnostics, scientific research or expert reports in court. While this provision concerns only neuro-imaging, it will probably serve as a guide for regulating the use of neuroscientific technology that may become available in the future in general. However, the quantity and assortment of such technology are likely to be relatively limited in the French context.

What Do French Lawyers Think About Using Neuroscience in Criminal Trials?

French legal commentators have only recently begun thinking about the relationship between neuroscience and law,[82] first in the context of the French centre for strategic analysis in the late 2000s,[83] then in publications by legal professionals and scholars.[84] Their researches address the topic of neurolaw in general, while highlighting the importance of criminal law. The possible role of neuroscience (essentially, of neuroimaging techniques) in criminal processes is analysed from the angle of the two mental state standards discussed above. Neuroscience could in principle be of use in criminal responsibility assessments of mentally ill offenders, and in individual dangerousness evaluations.

The tone of these studies reflects reservations, or at least a certain amount of scepticism, with regard to the role neuroscience should play in criminal

---

[82] C Rödinger, 'The Obtainment and Use of Neuroscientific Knowledge in France' in TM Spranger (ed), *International Neurolaw. A Comparative Analysis* (Springer, 2012) 137; S Canselier, 'Neurosciences' in *Dictionnaire permanent santé, bioéthique et biotechnologies* (Montrougte, Editions législatives, 2013) 53.

[83] O Oullier and S Sauneron (eds), *Actes du séminaire 'Perspectives scientifiques et légales sur l'utilisation des sciences du cerveau dans le cadre de procédures judiciaire'* (Paris, Centre d'analyse stratégique, 10 December 2009) and O Oullier (ed), *Le cerveau et la loi: analyse de l'émergence du neurodroit* (Paris, Centre d'analyse stratégique, 2012).

[84] C Byk, 'Responsabilité et dangerosité à l'aune des neurosciences' (2010) 133 *Revue pénitentiaire et de droit pénal*, 325 and C Byk, 'Les neurosciences: une contribution à l'identité individuelle ou au contrôle social?' (2012) 5 *Revue de droit sanitaire et social*, 800; P Larrieu, 'La réception des neurosciences par le droit' (2011) 5 *AJ Pénal*, 231 and P Larrieu, 'Le droit à l'ère des neurosciences' (2012) 115 *Médecine & Droit* 106; G Casile-Hugues, 'La responsabilité pénale à la lumière des neurosciences' (2012) 1 *Revue pénitentiaire et de droit pénal* 9; MC Sordino, 'Le procès pénal confronté aux neurosciences: science sans conscience …?' (2014) 2 *AJ Pénal* 58. See also MC Sordino, 'Enjeux éthique des neurosciences et protection des données personnelles' (2011) 106 *Médecine & Droit* 47 and P Larrieu, B Roullet and C Gavaghan (eds), 'Neurolex sed … dura lex? L'impact des neurosciences sur les disciplines juridiques et les autres sciences humaines: études comparées' (2013) *Comparative Law Journal of the Pacific—Revue Juridique Polynésienne*. Special Issue X.

procedure. Besides the issue of evidence and scientific expertise reliability, the main arguments concern the compatibility of a more liberal use of neuroscientific evidence with current French criminal procedure. As is often the case in French doctrinal analyses, the authors adopt the moral standpoint of legitimacy, rather than the scientific angle of truth.[85] In French criminal law, the criminal proof has been progressively 'judicialised'. It has gradually come to be a question of law rather than a matter of fact. The focus is on whether the evidence was obtained lawfully and in accordance with applicable procedural rules, rather than on the ability of the evidence to prove whether particular claims are true or false. The focus has gradually shifted from substantive to procedural criminal law. French law and legal scholarship do not directly address the question of the probative value of neuroscientific evidence, and lawyers are often ill-equipped to challenge medical knowledge directly. These facts may explain why French law and the French legal profession have turned their attention to the procedural requirements for evidence admission and validity.

However, the procedural requirements turn the discussion back to substantive law. The expert evidence based on technology, including neuroimaging, must be obtained in compliance with fundamental rights established in French law and in the case law of French courts and the European Court of Human Rights: the right to human dignity, defence rights, the right to a fair trial, and the privilege against self-incrimination. The requirement of compliance with fundamental human rights is well justified. The neuroscience in court debate is comparable to the biological evidence controversy. Let us think of the use of DNA for identification purposes.[86] In accordance with Article 16-14 of the French Civil Code, neuroimaging can only be used in a forensic assessment if the individual concerned consents to its use. This raises serious difficulties when the assessment concerns precisely the impairment or destruction of judgement.[87] The procedural framework regulating the use of neuroscience is not limited to requiring consent from the subject of an expert assessment in the context of a legal proceeding. The law includes an express regulation of the technical and human circumstances in which neuroimaging can lawfully be conducted for medical purposes. However, the law expressly defers to the medical definition of 'best practice'[88] and particularly to the standard set by the French National Health Authority (*Haute Autorité de Santé*).

---

[85] X Lagarde, 'Vérité et légitimité en droit de la preuve' (1996) 23 *Droits* 31.

[86] G François, La réception de la preuve biologique: étude comparative de droit civil et droit pénal (PhD dissertation, Paris I, 2004).

[87] Sordino, 'Le procès pénal confronté aux neurosciences' (n 84) 58.

[88] Public Health Code Art L 1134-1: 'A decree from the minister in charge of health sets out the rules of best practices applicable to prescribing and conducting brain imaging assessments for medical purposes. These rules take into account the recommendations of the National Health Authority'. A reply to a ministerial question (OJ, 11 June 2013, 6172) states that 'These rules may constitute a source for acceptable practices in this area [court-ordered expert opinions] and guide magistrates who may use this type of opinion'.

In a 2011 statement issued before the 16 July 2011 law, the Health Authority expressed scepticism on the use of functional neuroimaging in the context of legal proceedings, because given 'the current state of knowledge, [brain imaging] is not a tool for diagnosing or providing a prognosis of the risk of violence in a patient suffering from mental disorders'. The Health Authority nonetheless found that we should 'not deprive ourselves of any additional assessments, in the face of any atypical symptomatology that might be the clinical expression of a neurological disorder or other somatic illness'.[89] It was necessary to take an extremely cautious position. To our knowledge, that position has not changed.

More fundamentally, the very purpose of neuroscientific evidence is the source of a certain uneasiness because it concerns the mental state of an individual. Its closeness to legal concepts (purpose, intent) is perceived as a threat. Other evidentiary procedures including narco-analysis and testifying under hypnosis have been discarded in French case law on the grounds that they undermine the rights of the defendant.[90] As one author has remarked, 'the reason probably lies in the fact that this form of questioning neutralizes volition and one may therefore legitimately wonder about the extent to which it is compatible with the oath the person swore'.[91] Similarly, the aim of using neuroscience technologies to analyse mental state is precisely to gain access to an individual's psychological attitude, regardless of his or her volition.

This observation warrants analysis from the perspective of determining criminal responsibility and dangerousness. A number of neuroscientific experiments call into question the very idea of free will and, it has been argued, shake the very foundations of the criminal law. Let us think of Libet's experiments on neural antecedents to voluntary actions, apparently demonstrating that activation in the brain chronologically precedes awareness of the intention to act. It has been argued that Libet's studies demonstrate that initiating an action or gesture is not a manifestation of free will; only blocking an action is. It has been argued that the foundations of the legal architecture of criminal responsibility based on the free will assumption may be undermined by these results.[92]

Without going that far, taking the temporal dimension into account also seems to be of interest to lawyers. A defendant can be excused under Penal Code Article 122-1 only if evidence is given that he or she is suffering from a psychological or neuro-psychological disorder that explains his or her behaviour at a particular time. The mental state must be evaluated as of the time of the

---

[89] Haute Autorité de Santé, Dangerosité psychiatrique: étude et évaluation des facteurs de risque de violence hétéro-agressive chez les personnes ayant des troubles schizophréniques ou des troubles de l'humeur (Paris, Haute Autorité de Santé, 2011) 45–47.

[90] Court of Cassation, Criminal chamber, 12 December 2000, Bulletin criminel, no 369; (2001) Recueil Dalloz 1340, note D Mayer and JF Chassain.

[91] C Byk, 'Responsabilité et dangerosité à l'aune des neurosciences' (n 84) 330.

[92] L Nadel and W Sinott-Armstrong (eds), Conscious Will and Responsibility: A Tribute to Benjamin Libet (Oxford, Oxford University Press, 2010).

commission of the crime. However, the brain is in a constant state of activity. This makes neuroscientific evidence different from other types of scientific evidence. Let us think of DNA, the substance of which changes little or not at all over time. Brain activity is measured *post hoc* and the measurement will not necessarily reflect what occurred in the brain when the acts were committed. The presence of an abnormality at time t+1 does not necessarily mean that there was an abnormality at time t. Even if this were the case, neuroscience technologies can reconstruct only a fairly hypothetical mental state.[93] It must be added, however, that this criticism may also apply to all other forms of expert opinion.

The assessment of dangerousness causes even greater concern. Dangerousness is not evaluated *post hoc*, but at the time when the penal decision is being made. Dangerousness often has to be reassessed several times. In French statutory and case law, there are few standards for evaluating dangerousness. A joint report published in 2012 by the French Academy of Medicine and the National Council of Court-Appointed Experts Guilds defined the new role given to experts by the law.[94] Experts are no longer to establish a diagnosis, but a prognosis. This role goes beyond that of the psychiatric expert, as it requires interdisciplinary work. And yet the report mentions that:

> New technologies, in particular neuroimaging, reveal neuronal dysfunctions that are factors of vulnerability to, or are concomitant with, mental disorders. For example, lack of empathy with another's suffering may be visualised with the help of functional imaging, and may help to understand the violently destructive conduct of which certain individuals, in particular the mentally ill, are capable.[95]

Neuroscience may reinforce the illusion that it is possible to predict individual propensity to commit a criminal offence, based on anatomical or functional cerebral lesions and their location in the brain. This outlook worries lawyers in particular. It may result in attempts to infer a prognosis of dangerousness from the very presence of a brain lesion correlated with violent behaviour in the literature. This amounts to confusing the actual individual risk of reoffending with a hypothetical, theoretical increased risk of antisocial behaviour. This fallacious line of thought may be reinforced by the patina of 'objective' truth carried by MRI-detected brain lesions. A 'neurological' concept of dangerousness may develop and either supplant the psychiatric or criminological concept of dangerousness, or reinforce psychiatric or criminological assessments of dangerousness. An assessment of dangerousness does not establish the existence of a causal relationship between an individual physical, situational or psychological characteristic and the commission of an offence. However, the 'intense fascination' with neuroimaging could transform a simple risk factor into a perceived causal relationship.

---

[93] Haute Autorité de Santé (n 89) 45–47.

[94] J Hureau, JP Olié, JC Archambault, *Evaluation de la dangerosité psychiatrique et criminologique/ Assessment of psychiatric and criminal danger* (Paris, Académie Nationale de Médecine and Conseil National des compagnies d'experts en justice, 2012).

[95] ibid, 9.

Scattered across a multiplicity of legal texts, the concept of dangerousness constitutes an open, indefinite legal standard. Neurological dangerousness could well find a place in this context, with the danger of stigmatising individuals as intrinsically 'abnormal' and systematically keeping them interned for an indefinite amount of time. With Judge Christian Byk of the Court of Appeal of Paris, we may wonder whether 'the individuals convicted by the courts for certain types of deviant behaviour will become a target population for new neuroscientific applications, at the expense of real debate in our society about this double-edged tool?'[96]

The pessimistic view of Judge Byk coexists with another, more optimistic outlook, a belief that individuals suffering from mental disorders can be cured, or can at least acquire control over their actions, and leave the criminal justice system. Forensic mental health practitioners and scientists must establish a dialogue as psychiatrists and lawyers did in the nineteenth century, but this is not on the neuroscience agenda in today's France.

A critical discussion of criminal law concepts and criminal justice policy in the neuroscience era requires vision and caution. The defensive intellectual reflex of a French lawyer is to cling onto Descartes and to use the dual nature of the mind and body as a conceptual model for separating science and law. It is a comfortable position that is not without its flaws.

Bibliography

Aubert, A and Coudret, E, 'Prédictibilité du comportement: neuro-sciences et neuro-mythes' (2012) 2 *AJ Pénal* 80.

Barbier, G, Demontès, C, Lecerf, JR and Michel, JP, *Rapport d'information fait au nom de la Commission des affaires sociales et de la Commission des lois par le groupe de travail sur la prise en charge des personnes atteintes de troubles mentaux ayant commis des infractions* (Paris, Sénat—Commission des affaires sociales, 2010).

Burgelin, JF, *Santé, justice et dangerosité: pour une meilleure prévention de la récidive, commission Santé-Justice* (Paris, Ministère de la Justice, 2005).

Byk, C, 'Les neurosciences: une contribution à l'identité individuelle ou au contrôle social?' (2012) 5 *Revue de droit sanitaire et social* 800.

Byk, C, 'Responsabilité et dangerosité à l'aune des neurosciences' (2010) 133 *Revue pénitentiaire et de droit pénal* 325.

Canselier, S, 'Neurosciences' in *Dictionnaire permanent santé, bioéthique et biotechnologies* (Montrouge, Editions Législatives, 2013).

---

[96] Byk, 'Responsabilité et dangerosité à l'aune des neurosciences' (n 84) 341.

Casile-Hugues, G, 'La responsabilité pénale à la lumière des neurosciences' (2012) 1 *Revue pénitentiaire et de droit pénal* 9.

Chamak, B, 'Dynamique d'un mouvement scientifique et intellectuel aux contours flous: les sciences cognitives (United States, France)' (2011) 25 *Revue d'histoire des sciences humaines* 13.

Changeux, JP, *L'homme neuronal* (Paris, Fayard, 1983).

Chauvaud, F, *Les experts du crime. La médecine légale en France au XIXème siècle* (Paris, Aubier—Collection historique, 2000).

Chneiweiss, H, 'Les neurosciences et le droit: un dialogue difficile mais nécessaire ou comment identifier des causalités sans sombrer dans le déterminisme' (2013) 44 *La lettre des neurosciences* 28.

Clayes, A and Léonetti, J, *Rapport d'information fait au nom de la mission d'information sur la révision des lois de bioéthique* (Paris, Assemblée Nationale, 2010).

Claeys, A and Vialatte, JS on behalf of the Office parlementaire des choix scientifiques et technologiques, *Exploration du cerveau, neurosciences: avancées scientifiques, enjeux éthiques* [Minutes of the public hearing] (Paris, Assemblée Nationale—Sénat, 2008).

Claeys, A and Vialatte, JS on behalf of the Office parlementaire des choix scientifiques et technologiques, *L'impact et les enjeux des nouvelles technologies d'exploration et de thérapie du cerveau* (Paris, Assemblée Nationale—Sénat, 2012).

Claeys, A and Vialatte, JS on behalf of the Office parlementaire des choix scientifiques et technologiques, *Rapport sur l'évaluation de l'application de la loi n°2004-800 du 6 août 2004 relative à la bioéthique* (Paris, Assemblée Nationale—Sénat, 2008).

Coche, A, *La détermination de la dangerosité des délinquants en droit pénal, étude de droit français* (Aix-Marseille, Presses Universitaires d'Aix-Marseille, 2005).

Danet, J and Saas, C, 'De l'usage des notions de "délinquants anormaux" et "délinquants d'habitude" dans les législations allemande, belge, française et suisse', *Champ pénal/Penal field* [online] (2010) available at champpenal.revues.org/7955.

Danet, J and Saas, C, 'Le fou et sa "dangerosité", un risque spécifique pour la justice pénale' (2007) 4 *Revue de science criminelle et de droit pénal comparé* 779.

Devernois, P, *Les aliénés et l'expertise médico-légale* (Toulouse, Dirion, 1905).

Encinas de Muñagorri, R, 'Les techniques d'imagerie cérébrale dans le cadre d'expertises judiciaires' (2014) 113 *Experts* 8.

Fazel, S and Danesh, J, 'Serious Mental Disorder in 23,000 Prisoners: A Systematic Review of 62 Surveys' (2002) 359 *The Lancet* 545.

Fonteille, V, Cazala, F, Moulier, V and Stoleru, S, 'Corrélats cérébraux de la pédophilie: apports de la neurologie et de la neuro-imagerie' (2012) 38 *Encéphale* 496.

Foucault, M, *Les anormaux. Cours du collège de France, 1974–1975* (Paris, Gallimard-Seuil, 1999).

François, G, *La réception de la preuve biologique: étude comparative de droit civil et droit pénal* (PhD dissertation, University of Paris I, 2004).

Gaumont-Prat, M, 'La loi du 7 juillet 2011 relative à la bioéthique et l'encadrement des neurosciences' (2011) 231 *Les petites affiches* 10.

Goujon, P and Gautier C on behalf of the Commission of Laws, *Les délinquants dangereux atteints de troubles psychiatriques: comment concilier la protection de la société et une meilleure prise en charge médicale? Rapport d'information no. 420* (Paris, Assemblée Nationale—Sénat, 2005).

Haute Autorité de Santé, *Dangerosité psychiatrique: étude et évaluation des facteurs de risque de violence hétéro-agressive chez les personnes ayant des troubles schizophréniques ou des troubles de l'humeur. Recommandation de bonne pratique.* (Paris, Haute Autorité de Santé, 2011).

Herzog-Evans, M, 'Is the French Juge de l'application des peines a Problem-solving Court?' in M Herzog-Evans (ed), *Offender Release and Supervision: The Role of Courts and the Use of Discretion* (Nijmegen, Wolf Legal Publishers, 2015).

Hureau, J, Olié, JP and Archambault, JC, *Evaluation de la dangerosité psychiatrique et criminologique* (Paris, Académie Nationale de Médecine and Conseil National des compagnies d'experts en justice, 2012).

Jackson, J, 'Taking Comparative Evidence Seriously' in P Robert and M Redmayne (eds), *Innovations in Evidence and Proof* (Oxford, Hart Publishing, 2007).

Jonas, C, Senon, JL, Voyer, M and Delbreil, A, *Méthodologie de l'expertise en psychiatrie* (Paris, Dunod, 2013).

Kendell, RE, 'The Distinction between Personality Disorder and Mental Illness' (2002) 180 *British Journal of Psychiatry* 110.

Kerchove, M van de, 'Culpabilité et dangerosité—Réflexion sur la clôture des théories relatives à la criminalité' in C Debuyst and F Tulkens (eds), *Dangerosité et justice pénale* (Issy-les-Moulineaux, Masson, 1981).

Lagarde, X, 'Vérité et légitimité en droit de la preuve' (1996) 23 *Droits* 31.

Larrieu, P, 'La réception des neurosciences par le droit' (2011) 5 *AJ Pénal* 231.

Larrieu, P, 'Le droit à l'ère des neurosciences' (2012) 115 *Médecine & Droit* 106.

Larrieu, P, Roullet, B and Gavaghan C (eds) 'Neurolex sed ... dura lex? L'impact des neurosciences sur les disciplines juridiques et les autres sciences humaines: études comparées' (2013) Special Issue of the *Comparative Law Journal of the Pacific—Revue Juridique Polynésienne*.

Léonetti, J, *Rapport fait au nom de la commission spéciale chargée d'examiner le projet de loi relatif à la bioéthique* (Paris, Assemblée Nationale, 2011).

Nadel, L and Sinott-Armstrong, W (eds), *Conscious Will and Responsibility: A Tribute to Benjamin Libet* (Oxford, Oxford University Press, 2010).

Niboer, JF and Sprangers, WJJM (eds), *Harmonisation in Forensic Expertise. An Inquiry into the Desirability of and Opportunities for International Standards* (Amsterdam, Thela Thesis, 2000).

Oullier, O, (ed), *Le cerveau et la loi: analyse de l'émergence du neurodroit* (Paris, Centre d'analyse stratégique, 2012).

Oullier, O and Sauneron S (eds), *Actes du séminaire 'Perspectives scientifiques et légales sur l'utilisation des sciences du cerveau dans le cadre de procédures judiciaire'* (Paris, Centre d'analyse stratégique, 2009).

Pardo, MS and Patterson, D, *Minds, Brain and Law. The Conceptual Foundations of Law and Neuroscience* (Oxford, Oxford University Press, 2013).

Protais, C, 'Experts et expertises psychiatriques: la question de l'indépendance' in J Pelisse, C Protais et al (eds), *Des chiffres, des maux et des lettres. Une sociologie de l'expertise judiciaire en économie, psychiatrie et traduction* (Paris, Armand Colin, 2012).

Rachet-Darfeuille, V, *L'état mental de la personne: étude juridique* (PhD dissertation, University of Paris I, 2001).

Robert, JH, 'Punir dehors. Commentaire de la loi no 2014-896 du 15 août 2014' (2014) *Droit pénal*, étude 16.

Rödinger, C, 'The Obtainment and Use of Neuroscientific Knowledge in France' in TM Spranger (ed), *International Neurolaw. A Comparative Analysis* (Heidelberg, Springer, 2012).

Saas, C, 'Exceptional Laws in Europe, with Emphasis on "Enemies"' in M Caianiello and ML Corrado (eds), *Preventing Danger—New Paradigms in Criminal Justice* (Durham, NC, Carolina Academic Press, 2013) 33–59.

Saas, C, *L'ajournement du prononcé de la peine—Césure et recomposition du procès pénal* (Paris, Dalloz, 2004).

Senon, JL, 'Troubles psychiques et réponses pénales', *Champ pénal/Penal field* [online] (2005), available at https://champpenal.revues.org/77.

Senon, JL and Manzanera, C, 'L'expertise psychiatrique pénale: les données d'un débat' (2006) 2 *Actualité juridique Droit penal* 66.

Senon, JL and Voyer, M, 'Du concept de responsabilité et d'irresponsabilité en droit pénal français, comme fondement de l'expertise psychiatrique pénale' in O Oullier (ed), *Le cerveau et la loi: analyse de l'émergence du neurodroit* (Paris, Centre d'analyse stratégique, 2012).

Sordino, MC, 'Enjeux éthique des neurosciences et protection des données personnelles' (2011) 106 *Médecine & Droit* 47.

Sordino, MC, 'Le procès pénal confronté aux neurosciences: science sans conscience …?' (2014) 2 *AJ Pénal* 58.

Vidal, C, 'Vers une neurojustice?' (2011) 4 *Ravages* 17.

5

'Not Guilty by Reason of Insanity' in the Italian Jurisdiction. A Neuroscience Revolution?

BARBARA BOTTALICO AND AMEDEO SANTOSUOSSO

I. Introduction. Neuroscience and the Law

Judges in Europe and the United States have begun to take the most recent technological advancements in behavioural science into consideration in criminal proceedings. Only a few years ago, the law and neuroscience debate among legal scholars was mainly an anticipation of radically new, imminent developments, and an exhortation to judges and juries to prepare to face a new type of scientific evidence and to open the door to new scientific knowledge about the human brain.

The investigative field of cognitive neuroscience is having a great impact in this direction. Cognitive neuroscience brings together cognitive science, psychology and biology by focusing on the biological mechanisms underlying cognition, with a specific focus on the neural substrates of mental processes and their behavioural manifestations.[1] New technologies have greatly enhanced the ability of scientists to investigate the structure and function of the living brain. The principal technology employed by cognitive neuroscience for forensic use is functional Magnetic Resonance Imaging (fMRI), a brain imaging technique that provides high resolution, non-invasive reports of neural activity detected by a signal dependent on the blood oxygen level.[2] The possibilities opened up by neuroscientific research for the

---

[1] SK Erickson, 'Blaming the Brain' (2010) 11 *Minnesota Journal of Law, Science & Technologies* 27.

[2] For an introduction to fMRI see: SA Huettel, AW Song, G McCarthy, *Functional Magnetic Resonance Imaging* (Sunderland, Sinauer Associates, 2008). For a comprehensive scientific overview of the promises and perils of fMRI in a forensic setting, see E Rusconi and T Mitchener-Nissen, 'Prospects of Functional Magnetic Resonance Imaging as Lie Detector' (2013) 7 *Frontiers in Human Neuroscience* 594.

legal field are less blurred than they used to be a few years ago; neuroscientists and jurists have started to cooperate in various associations and initiatives.[3]

The past decade also saw crucial developments in forensic behavioural genetics, another relatively new scientific discipline seeking to understand the role of the genetic versus the environmental contribution to individual variations in human behaviour.[4]

Evidence based on neuroscience and behavioural genetics has mostly been presented to European and US criminal courts to support a plea of insanity or diminished responsibility,[5] but has only sporadically been accepted in court with that purpose.[6] There are indications that the situation has started to change.

Our contribution to this volume describes the most relevant features of the Italian legal system in relation to criminal responsibility assessments, with a focus on the insanity defence. We present recent Italian case law where neuroscience has had an impact on assessments of legal insanity. The first reported cases of admission of neuroscientific evidence in criminal trials took place in Italy and the United States. Most of the debate among legal scholars comes from these two jurisdictions. Therefore, for purposes of clarity, we discuss the similarities and differences between the two criminal justice systems.

The structure of this chapter is as follows. In Section II, we offer an introduction to the Italian regulation of criminal responsibility and the rules for the admission

---

[3] Some examples are the MacArthur Foundation Law and Neuroscience Project in the US and the European Association for Neuroscience and Law.

[4] In the early 1990s, a Dutch research team found some evidence of a correlation between violence and aggression and one identifiable genetic anomaly. Many of the male members of a large Dutch family exhibited a behavioural disorder characterised by mild cognitive impairments and antisocial behaviour. The researchers found that one nucleotide in the MAOA gene sequence was altered in these men. The alteration heavily impaired the production of the MAOA protein, a compound involved in degradation of the neurotransmitter serotonin and to a lesser extent of noradrenaline and dopamine. In earlier research dysregulation of the neurotransmitter serotonin had been associated with violent behaviour. See HG Brunner, M Nelen, XO Breakefield, XO, HH Ropers and BA van Oost, 'Abnormal Behavior Associated with a Point Mutation in the Structural Gene for Monoamine Oxidase A' (1993) 262 *Science* 578. A few years later, in 2002, the journal *Science* published the results of an experiment showing that men who had been abused in their childhood had a much greater risk of manifesting violent antisocial behaviour as adolescents and adults, if born with a particular allele of the MAOA gene. Various scholars began to forecast important applications of behavioural genetics in the legal field. A Caspi, J McClay, TE Moffitt, J Mill, J Martin, IW Craig, A Taylor and R Poulton, 'Role of Genotype in the Cycle of Violence in Maltreated Children' (2002) *Science* 851.

[5] The only known case in which the defendant underwent a neuroscientific test proposed by the prosecutor was in India in 2008. She was then sentenced to life imprisonment.

[6] fMRI scan results for the purpose of lie detection were rejected in 2010 by a court in Brooklyn, New York. In the same year in Illinois, Brian Dugan, defendant in a multi-homicide case, attempted to meet the requirement of the insanity defence by proving his psychopathy. The court admitted the expert testimony and the results of an fMRI scan, but the expert was not allowed to directly show the jury the images of the defendant's brain. He was eventually sentenced to death. On the case, see V Hughes, 'Science in Court: Head Case' (2010) 464 *Nature* 340. As to behavioural genetics, Deborah Denno surveyed in a recent article all the US criminal cases between 1994 and 2007 in which behavioural genetics was presented to judges as scientific evidence. Her conclusion was that 'the last 13 years have not revealed a legally irresponsible application of behavioural genetics factors in criminal cases. Rather, courts continue to regard behavioural genetics variably sceptically'. See D Denno, 'Revisiting the Legal Link between Genetics and Crime' in NA Farahany (ed), *The Impact Of Behavioral Sciences On Criminal Law* (Oxford, Oxford University Press, 2009).

of scientific evidence in criminal trials. Scientific evidence includes neuroscientific tests to support insanity pleas. Section III presents two Italian cases in which neuroscience played a crucial role in the assessment of the defendant's criminal responsibility and the decision on punishment. In Section IV we discuss the difficult relationship between law and psychiatry. We consider whether the introduction of a neuroscientific explanation of criminal behaviour is likely to bring profound changes into current evidentiary practice in court.

Section V presents the practical effects of a verdict of not guilty by reason of insanity or of diminished responsibility. We discuss the situation of criminal psychiatric facilities in Italy, soon to be replaced by community care-oriented facilities. The goal of the reform is to offer personalised treatment in a suitable psychiatric care-oriented setting, while current criminal psychiatric facilities are in practice detention establishments, providing little or no medical care to offenders.

Our conclusion (Section VI) is that neuroscience and behavioural genetics will not transform the current regulation of criminal responsibility and the legal standard of insanity. The assessment of responsibility, however, may be improved by advancement in our knowledge of the brain. In particular, in the near future, new neuroscientific technologies may be able to assist and integrate the methods of psychiatry into the assessment of mental illness and its impact on decision making, and enable experts to offer a more fine-graded and individualised evaluation of individual capacity and a more personalised form of punishment. This is consistent with the goals of the recent reform of criminal psychiatric facilities in Italy.

II. Regulation of Criminal Responsibility and Legal Criteria for the Admission of Neuroscientific Evidence

In this section we aim to offer an introduction to the regulation of criminal responsibility under Italian criminal law. We will also sketch the procedure for the admission of scientific evidence in criminal trials in Italy, focusing on the use of neuroscience-based tests to support the insanity defence.

Criminal Responsibility, Legal Insanity and Forensic Mental Health Expert Reports

Articles 88 and 89 of the Italian Penal Code (*Codice Penale*, or *CP*) set forth the requirements for criminal responsibility. The competency standard consists of both a cognitive and a volitional requirement. Article 88 provides that offenders who, at the time of committing a crime, because of mental illness, are not able to comprehend the unlawful nature of their act, or to act in accordance with that comprehension (*capacità di intendere e di volere*), shall not be criminally accountable (*imputabile*).[7] Article 89 provides that those who, because of mental illness, were in such a state of mind that their competency was severely diminished shall be partially accountable.[8] This regulation is representative of civil law systems with regard to criminal accountability.[9]

Scientific reports (*perizie*) are usually admitted by the courts as evidence of competency, or lack thereof, at the time of the crime. In the Italian criminal justice system, this type of evidence enters the criminal trial through expert witnesses (*periti*). Expert witnesses can be appointed by the judge, by the prosecution or by the counsel for the defendant. Article 220 of the Code of Criminal Procedure (*Codice di Procedura Penale*, or *CPP*) provides that expert reports can be admitted when they are necessary for the purposes of investigation or for the acquiring of data or assessments using specific technical expertise. Under Italian law the tendency to commit crime, the personality of the accused and more generally mental traits not dependent on pathological causes cannot be made central to expert reports. However, expert reports obtained during the enforcement phase of a sentence or as a preventive measure (*misura di sicurezza*), are not subjected to this prohibition.

Another provision relevant in the context of insanity pleas is Article 225 CPP; it provides that prosecutor and defendants have the right to appoint their own experts, in a number not exceeding, for each, that of the court-appointed experts.

The psychiatric report, aimed at detecting pathologies that may lead to a finding of incompetency, is currently the main tool available to the court to establish the criminal responsibility of the accused person.

Brain imaging techniques analyse the brain structurally and functionally. With respect to traditional techniques of psychiatric investigation, this could lead to

---

[7] Our translation. The original text of the provision reads as follows: 'Vizio totale di mente. Non è imputabile chi, nel momento in cui ha commesso il fatto, era, per infermità, in tale stato di mente da escludere la capacità di intendere o di volere'.

[8] Our translation. The original text of the provision reads as follows: 'Vizio parziale di mente. Chi, nel momento in cui ha commesso il fatto, era, per infermità, in tale stato di mente da scemare grandemente, senza escluderla, la capacità d'intendere o di volere, risponde del reato commesso; ma la pena è diminuita'.

[9] This definition is similar to the one provided in the Spanish Penal Code at Art 20. The first two paragraphs of the provision read as follows (our translation):

The following persons shall not be criminally accountable:

Those who, at the time of committing a crime, due to any mental anomaly or alteration, cannot comprehend the unlawful nature of the act, or to act in line with that comprehension.

A temporary mental disorder shall not result in exoneration from the punishment when provoked by the subject in order to commit the offence, or when he would or should have foreseen that it would be committed.

This regulation is also essentially coincidental to the one established in paragraph §20 of the German Criminal Code (Strafgesetzbuch—StGB), §11 of the Austrian Penal Code (StGB-Österreich), and the provisions in the French Penal Code, Art 122-1, among others, are also very similar. See also MI González-Tapia and I Obsuth 'Bad Genes & Criminal Responsibility' (2015) 39 *International Journal of Law & Psychiatry* 60.

a more accurate identification of the presence of brain damage. However, brain imaging could also lead to the identification of non-pathological deviations from the standard that could in principle explain criminal behaviour. Brain imaging could offer an explanation for behaviour without resorting to the diagnostic categories listed in medical nosography. In addition, behavioural genetics tests have been used to assess the character of the defendant and the propensity to crime and violence of individuals with particular allelic variants. There is evidence that a combination of genetic make-up and personal history could, at least in theory, make some individuals more inclined to aggressive behaviour. Can a proclivity to violence be considered pathology?

Before trying to answer this question, we will offer an analysis of the rationale of Article 220 CPP, which provides that the tendency to commit crime or the personality of the accused, and more generally mental traits not dependent on pathological causes, cannot be made central in expert reports. According to the majority of Italian legal scholars, and to Italian judges as detailed in case law, the provision aims to protect the privacy (*libertà morale*) of the defendant.[10] There is also widespread scepticism with regard to the reliability of the results of psychological and criminological investigations not related to the presence of disease and thus not of a 'medical' nature. Finally, it has been argued that there are major structural difficulties in expert reports when they are not aimed at identifying pathology.

Legal scholars have repeatedly expressed the idea that a scrutiny of the personality of the accused in the context of a criminal trial intrudes on personal dignity, constitutes a breach of the privilege against self-incrimination and could unduly influence the judge, who should instead make a decision based on proven facts alone.[11] Facts possibly include medical facts, but exclude mere intentions, propensities or non-pathological personality inclinations.[12]

---

[10] The phrase 'libertà morale' literally translates to 'moral freedom'. It encompasses several fundamental rights of the defendant in the criminal process, mainly personal dignity, privacy, self-determination and informed consent. It partially overlaps with the privilege against self-incrimination and the prohibition against unreasonable search and seizure.

[11] For a debate about the violation of the right to silence provided by the privilege against self-incrimination in the US legal system, see M Pardo, D Patterson and S Moratti, 'The Gathering of and Use of Neuroscientific Evidence in Criminal Trials in the United States. Compatibility with the 4th and 5th Amendments and with Due Process' (2014) 3 *Rivista Italiana di Filosofia del Diritto* 41; D Patterson and M Pardo, *Minds, Brains, and Law. The Conceptual Foundations of Law and Neuroscience* (Oxford, Oxford University Press, 2013); D Fox, 'Brain Imaging and the Bill of Rights. Memory Detection Technologies and American Criminal Justice' (2008) 8 *American Journal of Bioethics* 34.

[12] This prohibition is based on various factors, ranging from doubts surrounding the scientific reliability of this type of expert testimony, to issues concerning the protection of fundamental rights. There have been concerns that investigations having as their object the personality of the defendant may jeopardise the presumption of innocence. The ban on so-called psychological evidence is under criticism at the present time. Significant progress was made in the various fields of the psychological sciences. Critics also point out that under particular circumstances in the enforcement phase of the ruling it is in theory possible to partially circumvent the ban by relying on other provisions in the CCP, in particular on Arts 236 and 220 CPP.

With reference to examination and cross-examination, Article 64 CPP prohibits the use of 'methods or techniques' that may potentially affect the capacity to self-determine or the ability to remember and evaluate facts. The use of such techniques and methods remains prohibited, even when the person undergoing the examination consents to them. This provision is consistent with Article 188 CPP, which outlines a general limit to government authority in evidence gathering, to the exclusion of all evidence that restricts the individual's moral freedom. With this provision, the Italian legislator aimed to prohibit the use of tools such as hypnosis, 'narco-analysis' and the polygraph, regardless of their ability to produce reliable results; as we shall see, the courts have argued that this prohibition also extends to lie detection techniques, including techniques based on neuroscience.

However, expert reports that have personality or character as their object are in principle admissible during the sentencing phase of the trial. Article 133 provides that the court should take into account the severity of the crime and the likelihood of reoffending (*capacità a delinquere*) of the defendant in the sentencing phase, to decide on the severity of the sanction.

If taken in combination, the above-mentioned norms could give rise to some confusion. The legal system precludes the use of scientific evidence other than evidence aimed at ascertaining (the degree of) mental disorder. However, after this assessment has been made, the court may determine the punishment based on the offender's propensity to commit crimes.

The Constitutional Court (*Corte Costituzionale*) has ruled on the consistency of Article 220 CPP with Article 133 CP and constitutional provisions protecting the rights of the defendant.[13] In particular, with judgment no 124 of 1970, the Constitutional Court stated that the current regulation is not unconstitutional and added that 'it is not to be excluded that the [current] distrust for psychological assessments could become questionable in light of the development

---

[13] Two constitutional provisions are especially relevant here, Art 24, second paragraph and the first three paragraphs of Art 27. Article 24.2 reads as follows (our translation): 'Defence is an inviolable right at every stage and instance of legal proceedings'. The original text of the provision reads as follows: 'La difesa è diritto inviolabile in ogni stato e grado del procedimento'.
The first three paragraphs of Art 27 of the Italian Constitution read as follows (our translation):

Criminal responsibility is personal.

A defendant shall be considered not guilty until a final sentence has been passed.

Punishments may not be inhumane and shall aim to re-educate the convicted.

The original text of the provision reads as follows:

La responsabilità penale è personale.

L'imputato non è considerato colpevole sino alla condanna definitiva.

Le pene non possono consistere in trattamenti contrari al senso di umanità e devono tendere alla rieducazione del condannato.

of modern knowledge of the mind, and it is hoped that the legal standards will be updated'.[14]

In 2005, with the *Raso* judgment, the Italian Supreme Court (*Corte di Cassazione*) redesigned the ambit of the insanity defence. The Court stated that only mental disorders that contributed to causing the crime for which the defendant is being tried are relevant in the context of insanity pleas. Remarkably, the Court included personality disorders in the definition of legal insanity. The Court argued that Articles 88 and 89 CP refer to an infirmity of the mind resulting in a state of mind that would undermine or severely diminish competency, to the inclusion of psychopathy, and also of neuroses and affective disorders.[15]

The Italian criminal justice system has thus aligned with that of other European countries. Let us think of the German Penal Code, which mentions the 'disturbance of consciousness', and the French Penal Code, which makes reference to 'mental or neuro-psychic disorder'.[16] The ruling essentially embraced the suggestions that came from Italian legal scholars, who commented positively on the ruling, albeit with some caution about the possible uncertainties in its application.

Being no longer rigidly bound by psychiatric nosography, the judicial investigation of the character of the offender can now take into account all elements that may have led the person to commit the crime. Neuroscientific and genetic assessments can be used in court, also when not aimed at detecting brain damage. However, there are criminal-procedural controversies surrounding the admissibility of neuroscientific evidence to support the insanity defence. When admitted, neuroscientific tests are characterised as 'special evidence' (*prova atipica*), pursuant to Article 190 CPP.[17] Evidence labelled *prova atipica* is subject to a particularly strict admissibility test, comprising a relevance test and an assessment of its

---

[14] Corte Costituzionale, 24 June 1970, no 124, in *consultaonline*, available at www.giurcost.org/decisioni/1970/0124s-70.html.

[15] Corte di Cassazione, Joint Chambers, 25 January 2005, no 9163, Raso, in *Diritto Penale e Processo*, 2005, p 837; also available at CED Cassazione [Electronic Documentation Centre of the Court of Cassation], no 230317.

[16] For an introduction to forensic mental health assessment in the French legal system, see N Camalbert, A Andronikof, M Armand, C Robin and H Bazex, 'Forensic Mental Health Assessment in France: Recommendations for Quality Improvement' (2014) 6 *International Journal of Law & Psychiatry* 628.

[17] Our translation of Art 190 Italian Code of Criminal Procedure reads as follows.

> Evidence is allowed upon request of a party.

> The judge shall attend to the matter without delay and by ordinance, excluding evidence prohibited by the law or manifestly unnecessary or irrelevant.

Its original text reads as follows.

> Le prove sono ammesse a richiesta di parte.

> Il giudice provvede senza ritardo con ordinanza escludendo le prove vietate dalla legge e quelle che manifestamente sono superflue o irrilevanti.

potential to jeopardise individual self-determination and the capacity to remember and evaluate facts. The admissibility test is carried out by the court, and not by doctors or scientists; but there is no statutory regulation of the application of the methods and procedures for acquiring special evidence through an expert witness.

The cases reported in the following paragraphs will illustrate how expert reports have so far mainly relied on traditional, behavioural and neuro-psychological methods of investigation of the mind. Tests based on new neuroscientific and genetic techniques, when used on the defendant and described in the reports, had a secondary role; they supplemented behavioural and neuropsychological findings, adding support to the conclusions of the experts. The standard of admission of evidence has not been directly affected. However, judges are now faced with increasingly sophisticated defences, based on the use of new testing tools and techniques, whose scientific reliability, particularly for the assessment of mental capacity, is still uncertain and continues to be debated in the scientific community.

Proving the existence of a causal link between a mental condition and a particular behaviour has always been a major challenge to mental health forensic practitioners. There is no clear cause-and-effect relationship conforming to the criteria of causal continuity, consistency, and the temporal and phenomenological exclusion of other causes. Legal scholars have stressed that a linear causal chain running from the mental illness itself to criminal behaviour can never be found, mainly because of individual variability; the role played by basic personality; and the importance of emotional and environmental components. What type of contribution may neuroscience and genetics bring to this process?

A Comparative Introduction to Evidence Admission in Italian and US Criminal Procedure

The first reported cases of neuroscientific evidence admission took place in Italy and the United States. In this section we will offer a comparative introduction to the regulation of scientific evidence admission in the two jurisdictions.

Civil law and common law systems have different criminal procedures, particularly with regard to the admission of scientific evidence. Courts use a variety of devices to demonstrate insanity, but the principal is the expert's report. Understanding what evidence can be used by experts and introduced into a criminal trial is the first step when determining the impact of new technologies on assessments of responsibility.

In US criminal procedure, scientific testimony can be admitted in court if the method or the technique used by the expert complies either with the *Frye* or the *Daubert* standard, depending on the particular State. In cases judged by federal courts, the requirements laid down in Federal Rules of Evidence 403 (Exclusion of Relevant Evidence for Prejudice, Confusion, Waste of Time, or Other Reasons) and 702 (Testimony by Expert Witnesses) must be met.[18] Under the *Frye* test, scientific expert opinion is admissible when the relevant scientific community generally considers the technique reliable. The *Daubert* standard, today applied in most States, assigns to the judge the role of gatekeeper. The judge must verify whether (1) the theory or technique is falsifiable, refutable, testable and peer-reviewed, (2) the potential error rate is known, (3) standards and controls concerning its operation are established, and (4) the theory and technique is generally accepted in the relevant scientific community.

In the Italian legal system the admission of scientific evidence is regulated in the Code of Criminal Procedure, enacted in 1988. Under current procedural rules, the judge appoints an expert. In addition, both the prosecution and the defence can appoint their own experts who will proffer their own reports to the judge, possibly supporting or refuting the conclusions drawn by the court-appointed expert. In the sentencing phase of the trial, the judge (or panel of judges) evaluates the relevance and precision of all reports. The judge is 'the expert on the experts' (this concept is rendered with the Latin phrase *peritus peritorum*) and decides the case based on the scientific evidence he or she found most relevant, precise and reliable.

Both the Italian and US jurisdictions include a system of checks and balances regulating the impact of scientific evidence in the criminal process. In the US system the expert's testimony undergoes cross-examination to elicit favourable facts from the witness, or to impeach the credibility of the testifying witness and lessen the weight of unfavourable testimony. In the Italian legal system the report by the court-appointed expert is balanced by the parties' expert reports. At the end of the trial, all reports are reviewed and evaluated by the judge for the final decision.

Throughout the present chapter, we prefer to use the phrase 'expert report' when referring to the Italian criminal justice system and 'expert witness' with reference to the US criminal process, to reflect the fact that in civil law jurisdiction experts present the evidence in a written form. They draft a report, presented to and evaluated by the judge. In common law jurisdictions, experts present the result of their assessment orally, as non-expert witnesses do. They undergo examination and cross-examination in court and the content of their testimony is evaluated by the jury, based on the discussion in court.

---

[18] Federal Rule of Evidence 403 reads as follows: 'The court may exclude relevant evidence if its probative value is substantially outweighed by a danger of one or more of the following: unfair prejudice, confusing the issues, misleading the jury, undue delay, wasting time, or needlessly presenting cumulative evidence.' Federal Rule of Evidence 702 reads as follows: 'A witness who is qualified as an expert by knowledge, skill, experience, training, or education may testify in the form of an opinion or otherwise if: (a) the expert's scientific, technical, or other specialized knowledge will help the trier of fact to understand the evidence or to determine a fact in issue; (b) the testimony is based on sufficient facts or data; (c) the testimony is the product of reliable principles and methods; and (d) the expert has reliably applied the principles and methods to the facts of the case'.

III. The Use of Neuroscience to Support the Insanity Defence in Italian Case Law

Since 2009 the attention of the legal and scientific community has been focused on a few court cases in Italy, in which a forensic scientific expert presented the results of behavioural genetics and neuroscientific tests aimed at assessing the mental capacity of the accused.

We here present two cases that we deem essential to a discussion of the impact of neuroscience and behavioural genetics on the assessment of legal insanity. In the first case, known as *Albertani* from the surname of the defendant, the preliminary hearing judge (*Giudice delle Indagini Preliminari*, or GIP) at the Como court acknowledged the partial responsibility of the accused on the basis of results of psychiatric, neuroscientific and genetic tests.[19] In the second case, known as *Mattiello*, the Venetian court did not admit the neuroscientific tests proposed by the defence experts.[20]

What distinguishes these two cases from others is not only that experts conducted investigations using the techniques of neuroscience and behavioural genetics, but also the importance that the judges gave to the results of such tests. Indeed the judges made reference to the expert reports in the two rulings and, albeit with some caution, essentially trusted these new methods of scientific inquiry.

In general, judges assess the admitted evidence, the results obtained in tests administered by the experts and the criteria of interpretation that the experts adopted. The judge assesses the adequacy of the expert report, and particularly its consistency with facts. Subsequently, the judge must verify the validity of the scientific criteria, methods and tools that have been used by experts in their report; their adequacy in proving the facts; and the formal correctness and completeness of the report.

In its well-known judgment no 9163/2005, the Italian Supreme Court stated that

> in the presence of a variety of paradigms, the judge can only refer to scientific findings that, on the one hand, are the most up to date and, on the other hand, are the most generally accepted, and constitute a generalised application of the relevant scientific protocols.[21]

---

[19] Tribunale di Como, Gip, 20 May 2011, no 536, *Albertani* [2012] *Rivista Italiana di Medicina Legale* 246 ss.

[20] Tribunale di Venezia, Gip, 24 January 2013, no 296, *Mattiello* [2013] *Rivista Italiana di Medicina Legale* 1905 ss.

[21] Our translation. The original text of the relevant passage in the ruling reads as follows: 'pur in presenza di una varietà di paradigmi interpretativi, non può che fare riferimento alle acquisizioni scientifiche che, per un verso, siano quelle più aggiornate e, per altro verso, siano quelle più generalmente accolte, più condivise, finendo col costituire generalizzata (anche se non unica, unanime) prassi applicativa dei relativi protocolli scientifici'.

This does not mean that judges should make decisions based exclusively on established knowledge, without cognisance of the new science. Rather, the Court stressed that judges should keep an open-minded approach to investigations that have the potential to explain (for the insanity defence) what elements contributed to decrease or undermine competency. The balance between a general acceptance of the method, and therefore its scientific reliability, and the confidence in the ability of new techniques to explain human behaviour is precisely the focus of our analysis.

The *Albertani* Case

Stefania Albertani was arrested on 7 October 2009 for the attempted murder of both her parents. At that time, the defendant was already under investigation over her sister's disappearance. Her conversations were wiretapped. The judge asserted that Albertani's criminal behaviour was clearly illogical and not rationally tailored to the purpose of murder. Both the court and the defence appointed forensic mental health practitioners to assess her competency. The two reports came to opposite conclusions. The court-appointed expert held that the defendant was fully competent at the time of the crime, while the expert witness for the defence held that she was suffering from psychosis and not competent.

The court-appointed forensic mental health professional assessed the defendant's volitional and cognitive capacity and her mental condition by means of face-to-face interviews and the Rorschach inkblot test, both classical diagnostic tools in psychology and psychiatry.[22] He concluded that the defendant suffered from a type of 'hysteria', not specifically described in medical nosography. Her melodramatic and exaggerated demeanour was the symptom of a histrionic personality disorder, the expert witness argued. She appeared to suffer from a dissociative identity disorder, the expert contended; however, she did not suffer from a major mental illness that could justify the exclusion of her volitional and cognitive capacity at the time of the crime.

The defence eventually appointed a different expert and presented a new report. The new expert witness diagnosed a dissociative identity disorder and a genetically-based tendency towards aggressive behaviour. The assessment was based on a large number of tests. It consisted mainly of psychiatric assessment with traditional methods. However, it also included neuroimaging and neurophysiological investigations, and forensic behavioural genetics tests. The psychiatric assessment was based on long-established methods of mental health investigation, including face-to-face interviews, personality tests and

---

[22] The Rorschach inkblot test is used to detect thought organisation disorders, especially in cases where patients are reluctant to describe their thinking processes openly. The test is named after its creator, Swiss psychologist Hermann Rorschach (1884–1922).

neuropsychological tests. The experts also made use of a new test, developed by one of them; this is an adjusted version of the Implicit Association Test (IAT),[23] called the Autobiographical Implicit Association Test (aIAT).[24] The test requires the respondent to complete two blocks of categorisation trials, each of which pairs a different potentially autobiographical image (such as the image of the weapon used for the crime) with other images known to be autobiographical (such as an item of cloth owned by the defendant). The pattern of response times in the two blocks is assumed to be indicative of which autobiographical events are true. In their report for the court, the experts described this technique as 'the most reliable method to individually assess, with the greatest precision, autobiographical memories'. Its accuracy rate was estimated to be 92 per cent by the experts themselves.[25] But many doubts surround the scientific reliability of aIAT and the appropriateness of its use in court. There is very little literature on aIAT; what literature there is is mostly written by the inventor of the technique. The rest of the relevant literature consists of works by researchers not involved in the development of aIAT; they demonstrated experimentally the poor reliability of the test.[26] Respondents can easily cheat by deliberately slowing down or speeding up their response time!

As for the neuroimaging and neurophysiological investigations, the defendant underwent a neuroscientific test to detect the presence of a particular type of brain wave in particular regions of the brain.[27] The experts also tested a sample of women of the same age who had been diagnosed with antisocial personality disorder. Differences in the results showed that Albertani did *not* suffer from antisocial personality disorder, the experts argued. She also underwent Magnetic Resonance Imaging (MRI) to detect structural abnormalities of the central nervous system. The results were negative, but one other test based on MRI yielded interesting results.[28] The experts further tested a control group of 10 healthy women. They found statistically significant differences between Albertani and the controls, indicating, the experts argued, an incapacity to inhibit impulses, suggestibility and impaired decision-making capacities.[29]

---

[23] AG Greenwald, DE McGhee and JLK Schwartz, 'Measuring Individual Differences in Implicit Cognition: The Implicit Association Test' (1998) 74 *Journal of Personality and Social Psychology*, 1464.

[24] G Sartori, S Agosta, C Zogmaister, SD Ferrara and U Castiello, 'How to Accurately Detect Autobiographical Events' (2008) 19 *Psychological Science* 772.

[25] There is no additional confirmation of this figure. We are unable to find specialised literature supporting this estimate.

[26] B Verschuere, V Prati and JD Houwer, 'Cheating the Lie Detector. Faking in the Autobiographical Implicit Association Test' (2008) 20 *Psychological Science*, 410.

[27] The defendant underwent ElectroEncephalography (EEG) to detect Delta waves in her medial orbitofrontal regions. The forensic mental health practitioners who performed the test assumed the presence of Delta waves to be indicative of grey and white matter changes and ultimately of decreased brain activity in the area.

[28] The test was Voxel-Based Morphometry (VBM).

[29] The report stresses the differences between the grey matter of the defendant and that of controls, linked, the experts argued, with impairments in functions regulated by the anterior cingulate gyrus.

Finally, a molecular genetic analysis of the DNA of the defendant was conducted. The experts wrote that she was a carrier of alleles that, according to many published studies, are associated with a considerably increased risk of developing aggressive and impulsive behaviour.[30]

The Como court, represented by an individual professional magistrate, known as the pre-trial investigation judge (*Giudice per le Indagini Preliminari* or *GIP*), decided the case at the end of an abbreviated trial procedure (*Giudizio Abbreviato*), regulated by Articles 438 to 443 CPP. In the Italian criminal justice system, the pre-trial phase is conducted under the authority of the pre-trial investigation judge, who supervises the work of the public prosecutor and safeguards the rights of the person under investigation, when evidence is collected ahead of the trial phase. In particular situations narrowly defined in statutory law, the judge has the authority to order measures restricting the freedom of the person or people under investigation. The judge can also extend the duration of such measures, following a request by the public prosecutor. He or she can authorise the parties to collect evidence during the pre-trial phase, if they so request. The judge also has the authority to quash the indictment. In the case of an abbreviated trial, the same judge can rule on the case after the pre-trial investigation has been completed, if the defendant requests him or her to do so.

The abbreviated trial is a special, shortened type of criminal process. Upon the request of the defendant, criminal cases can be adjudicated solely on the evidence collected in the pre-trial investigation and possibly of additional evidence presented by the defence and admitted by the judge. In the abbreviated trial, if the judge finds the defendant guilty, he or she is to reduce the sentence by one-third and to convert a life sentence into 30 years' imprisonment.

Albertani was found guilty as charged. As the process was an abbreviated trial, the life sentence she would otherwise have received was converted into 30 years' imprisonment. Albertani was also found to have diminished capacity and the 30-year sentence was further cut to 20 years. The judge reasoned as follows:

> Considering the extreme difficulty and complexity of the case, the neuroscientific investigations carefully arranged by the experts for the defence and integrating the traditional psychiatric and neuropsychological investigations are welcome. Furthermore, the modifications which the scientific community is oriented to, as regard the revision of the fundamental categories of the psychiatric diagnosis in the DSM IV—Diagnostic and Statistical Manual of Mental Disorders—the most widespread and influential psychiatry book in the western world, are well-known; these modifications are moving in the

---

[30] The defence expert report reads as follows (p 86) (translation from Italian by medical geneticist Emiliano Giardina):

With reference to Albertani's genotype at MAOA-uVNTR locus, she is heterozygous 3/4 and the allele 3 is associated with a low efficiency form of the enzyme, notoriously related to aggressive and antisocial behaviour in men. In women these findings cannot be clearly interpreted: because of the epigenetic mechanism of X inactivation, heterozygous women show an intermediate phenotype. However, it's not possible to exclude the association. In addition, allele 4 is associated with criminal behaviour, especially associated with psychosocial adverse events. Miss Albertani carries both the adverse alleles at MAOA-uVNTR locus.

direction of an epistemological pluralism which will have to take account of the progress of neuroscience.[31]

The judge concluded that the defendant committed the crimes without having the 'full capacity to control her acts, or rather without preserving the full capacity to direct them, to feel their disvalue and to freely determine her actions'.

The *Mattiello* Case

Compared to *Albertani*, the court that judged the *Mattiello* case adopted a different approach to neuroscientific evidence. Dr Mattiello was a paediatrician accused of abusing six girls under the age of 10. The trial began before the Venetian Court in 2012.

Among the tests run by the defence experts to corroborate the insanity plea, Mattiello underwent an MRI test. He was found to suffer from a clivus chordoma, a rare brain tumour compressing the lower-middle part of the brain stem, with dislocation of the pituitary gland. The tumour was surgically removed.

The defence maintained that the tumour affected the functioning of certain parts of the brain and could have caused Mattiello's aberrant behaviour. A series of investigations followed, aiming to determine the possible influence of the cancer in the onset of the behavioural symptoms recently exhibited by the paediatrician, including his obsessive interest in photography, crying spells and attraction to his young patients, which Mattiello himself described as 'uncontrollable', as reported in the ruling.

The expert witnesses subjected the accused to neuropsychological and neuroscientific tests. In their report, they concluded that the defendant was not competent at the time of the crime. They argued that the tumour undoubtedly had affected his mental capacities. Both the impulses towards children and the onset of the disease dated back to about a year before his arrest. The experts argued that their conclusion was supported by the results of the aIAT test, the same test used in *Albertani*. The disease caused mental alterations in the defendant, making it impossible for him to 'do otherwise even if he had wanted to', the experts contended. He developed an irresistible attraction to children, which he had never felt before ('acquired paedophilia' was the label used by the forensic mental health experts appointed by the defence). His ability to inhibit sexual

[31] Our translation. The original text of the ruling reads as follows:
Ben vengano, dunque, nel presente processo, a fronte della estrema difficoltà e problematicità del caso che qui ci occupa, le indagini neuro scientifiche disposte con estremo rigore dai consulenti tecnici della difesa a completamente delle indagini psichiatriche e neuropsicologiche tradizionali. Tanto più che oggi sono note le modifiche verso cui è orientata la comunità scientifica internazionale in tema di revisione delle categorie fondamentali delle diagnosi psichiatriche del DSM IV—Diagnostic and Statistical Manual of Mental Disorders—, il più diffuso e influente testo di psichiatria nel mondo occidentale, modifiche che vanno verso un pluralismo epistemologico che non potrà non tener conto anche degli avanzamenti delle neuroscienze.

impulses was undermined by his incapacity to perceive the blameworthiness of sexual assault. According to the forensic mental health practitioners appointed by the defence, Mattiello was incompetent as a consequence of the combination of irresistible sexual urges and the inability to understand the reprehensible nature of acting on his impulses.

The judge-appointed experts were very critical of the report submitted by the experts appointed by the defence. They questioned the very existence of 'acquired paedophilia' as a psychiatric condition. The judge-appointed forensic mental health professionals argued that the behaviour of Mattiello should be regarded simply as sexual abuse, particularly severe because the victims were helpless minors. The tumour had no role in his behaviour, the experts concluded.

Their analysis of the defence experts' report made by the court-appointed experts is of special interest. In *Albertani*, the use of neuroscience tests in court was not commented on by any other qualified forensic mental health practitioners but its proponents.

In *Mattiello*, the court-appointed experts criticised the scientific reliability of the aIAT test. They emphasised that, while the IAT had undergone peer review and it could be considered validated based on the literature, it was not used in the same settings as the aIAT. The IAT was used for psychological investigations of prejudice. The aIAT had not yet been subjected to peer review, and the literature on the IAT could not be extended to the aIAT, the experts argued. The experts further argued that even if the aIAT was a scientifically validated method, it was, in essence, a lie detection method. Lie detectors cannot be admitted in Italian criminal trials, pursuant to Article 188 CPP. Under this norm, hypnosis, so-called 'truth serum' (ie drugs that can alter consciousness) and lie detectors have so far been considered illegal. The rule was originally introduced to prohibit the use of the polygraph, but it can be extended to the aIAT. The aIAT purportedly tests the truthfulness of statements by measuring the speed of response of the person undergoing the test. A fast response is taken to be a sign that the particular statement corresponds to the truth, while hesitation is interpreted as indicative of lying.

The Venetian court rejected the insanity plea. The doctor was convicted. The judge argued that the scientific thesis used by the experts for the defence was not scientifically reliable. The ruling was clear and appreciably informed. The judge emphasised that the systematic use of neuroscientific tests in competency assessments is in principle unnecessary. Their cost is prohibitive. It is not a responsible use of resources. More importantly, medical tests should be performed only when there is a specific medical indication and a disease is suspected. The variety of advanced techniques for investigating the brain and behaviour available today is such that extremely thorough testing will invariably lead to discovering deviations from the standard, the judge argued. However, abnormality is not synonymous with pathology, nor does the presence of an abnormality in itself prove incompetency, the judge contended. The judge also stated that the paedophilic conduct could not, in itself, be considered symptomatic of a mental illness. Paedophilia may be considered a 'personality disorder', and as such it could in principle be a ground for exclusion of criminal responsibility, based on the criteria outlined by the Italian Supreme Court and discussed above under Section II. However, the judge excluded that brain cancer had affected the behaviour of Mattiello, leading him to commit crimes that he would not otherwise have committed. The judge contended that the forensic mental health practitioners appointed by the defence had not demonstrated the existence of a link between the tumour and criminal behaviour. The scientific methods they used, the judge argued, were not sufficiently reliable. The judge agreed with the experts that the aIAT test was a lie detector, therefore not admissible as evidence in criminal proceedings.

Consistently with earlier decisions by the Italian Supreme Court on admissibility of scientific evidence, and particularly the *Cozzini* judgment,[32] the *Mattiello* ruling reaffirms that scientific proof can only be admitted in criminal trials if based on a scientific theory on which there is shared consensus in the scientific community.

The defendant was sentenced to five years' imprisonment and banned from holding public office and jobs at institutions frequented by minors.

IV. The Difficult Relationship Between Psychiatry and Law. Promises and Perils of a Science-Oriented Explanation of Human Behaviour

In *Albertani*, the defence experts presented the results of a burgeoning number of assessments, including personal interviews, neuropsychological and behavioural personality tests, memory tests, neuroimaging and behavioural genetics exams. By contrast, the court-appointed expert limited himself to interviewing the defendant, and to assessing her mental capacity through a traditional psychological test, the Rorschach inkblot test. This apparent gap in thoroughness between the two reports seems to have impressed the judge. The judge argued that the traditional psychiatric approach, based on behavioural assessment of the symptoms, 'can indisputably find completion in neuroscience'. The *Albertani* judge argued that no 'Copernican revolution' was underway with regard to the assessment, evaluation and diagnosis of mental pathology in forensic mental health reports. The assessment was still primarily carried out using traditional methods. The judge also argued that deciding a case based also on neuroscientific evidence did not mean the same as introducing 'deterministic criteria'. Relying on neuroscientific evidence does not mean inferring the existence of mental illness from the mere

---

[32] Corte di Cassazione, Fourth Criminal Chamber, 13 December 2010, no 43786, Cozzini, in *sicurlav*, available at www.sicurlav.it/pdf/sentenza%2043786_10.pdf.

presence of morphological alterations. Rather, the *Albertani* judge contended, our knowledge about cerebral morphology and human genetics allows us to find possible correlations between anomalies in particular brain areas and the risk of developing aggressive behaviour or a lack of capacity to control impulsiveness.

The problem of the usefulness and adequacy of mental health expertise in criminal trials is not new. The difficulties psychiatry and psychology encounter in creating a conceptual framework that judges or jurors can use to infer legal conclusions is a long-debated issue in European and US criminal justice systems. These questions have never been satisfactorily answered. Now they emerge again, with reference to neuroscience and behavioural genetics. Some contemporary legal scholars criticise traditional behavioural assessment methods of mental illness as inadequate, unreliable and perhaps impossible to prove through neuroscience. Others defend traditional assessment methods, which are tested and generally accepted, and view the use of neuroscience in forensics as potentially increasing diagnostic uncertainty. In 1984, eminent psychiatrist and criminologist Seymour L Halleck argued that, although the US Supreme Court in *Durham v United States* had reaffirmed the importance of not imposing punishment without culpability,[33] psychiatric knowledge in the process of excusing offenders had always been looked at with suspicion:

> As a rule, psychiatric testimony is viewed as a necessary part of the insanity defence proceedings but it may also be viewed as lacking in true value or authenticity. Sometimes psychiatric testimony is denounced as fraudulent. More often, it is tolerated as a necessary part of the insanity proceedings. The most common view is that psychiatry testimony is based on 'infant science' which has not yet developed sufficient maturity to assist society in resolving questions of fact or law.[34]

Halleck believes that the critiques of this discipline are mainly based on the idea that psychiatrists have little expertise to offer to the courts in decisions about a particular offender. Psychiatrists are believed to be unable to develop a conceptual framework that would assist judges and jurors. Halleck maintains that modern legal systems have not been developed with the intention of fine-tuning the punishment to the particular offender, but rather to the crime. The biological-sociological approach of Lombroso and his colleagues in Europe and the United States had little practical influence on the law, leaving little room for judges and jurors to take into account psychological differences between individual offenders.[35] The critique of psychiatry summarised by Halleck is not specifically directed to psychiatry as a science or as a branch of medicine, but rather to the difficulties in combining psychiatric expertise with the legal assessment

---

[33] Justice Bazelon, *Durham v United States*, 214, F 2nd 862, 876 (DC Cir 1954).

[34] S Halleck, 'The Assessment of Responsibility in Criminal Law and Psychiatric Practice' in DN Weisstub (ed), *Law and Mental Health, International Perspectives* (Oxford, Pergamon Press, 1984) 193–220.

[35] ibid, 198.

of insanity. Science is in constant evolution. It has different standards than law, particularly with regard to definitions. Scientists typically think probabilistically.[36] Conversely, the law strives to regulate behaviour. One of the goals of law is to draw a line between some situations and others, to make decisions about who should be held responsible and who should not with an acceptable degree of predictability.

The definition of criminal responsibility remains tied to moral and legal considerations, even though new scientific advances are raising new questions. As a matter of fact, the concept of responsibility does not seem to be challenged by any of the most recent scientific findings, nor by recent international case law. In essence, the courts have been very sceptical of the use of neuroscience in the context of assessments of responsibility. Where there might reasonably be an impact, in our view, is on the scale of punishment. New knowledge of the human brain and mental life gives judges and juries a broader range of information to better tailor their judgments to the particular offender. This may be the dawn of a transition towards a criminal justice system centred on mental health expertise, where the judgement on responsibility is based on the work of mental health practitioners as well as diagnostic technology. We shall explain.

The courts of law play a dual role. They assess responsibility and they choose the appropriate punishment. The criminal process runs through a four-pronged classification: *de facto* or analysis of the facts; *de jure* or assessment of whether the facts are a breach of the criminal law; responsibility and criminal liability evaluation; and the decision on punishment. The type and extent of punishment should be proportional to the offence and to the blameworthiness of the offender. An interesting aspect of the cases presented in this chapter is that criminal responsibility was not excluded. In *Albertani* the judge ruled that the defendant's capacity was *diminished*. The judge relied on neuroscientific assessments of mental impairment.

Can diminished capacity reflect 'partial' legal responsibility? In evaluating culpability, law and psychiatry (or neuroscience applied to psychiatry) both function with different fundamental assumptions. The law assumes that human beings generally act rationally and are free to choose from among different courses of action. When an insanity defence is raised, the criminal justice system seeks abnormalities that, in the individual case, may have hindered rational behaviour. From a scientific perspective, it is neither necessary nor useful to adopt that perspective. As Robert Sapolsky remarked:

> [G]ood scientists typically struggle to think in continua, a style that is a logical extension of thinking probabilistically. ... Of necessity, this cognitive style must butt heads with categorical demands in many settings ... This is particularly problematic in the realm of medicine that is intrinsically built on continua, namely psychiatry.[37]

---

[36] R Sapolsky, 'The Frontal Cortex and the Criminal Justice System' (2004) 359 *Philosphical Transactions of the Royal Society of London B* 1787.
[37] ibid.

The difficulties in the dialogue between law and psychiatry are, and have always been, the consequence of this fundamental difference of approach. Advances in behavioural sciences might contribute to building a bridge between the two domains of knowledge.

Neuroscience is based on statistical analysis. It can be a useful tool to assess brain damage and draw considerations on mental illness, but we maintain that it is not and it cannot be a type of comprehensive knowledge of a person, from her experience to her behaviour.

Further, as stressed by neuroscientists Cole Korponay and Michael Koenigs, and legal scholar Stephen Morse,[38] correlation does not mean causation; and causation does not mean compulsion. Law is a set of rules that guides human behaviour and actions. It has created an implicit set of concepts and assumptions (what Morse calls 'folk psychology') that considers persons to be rational agents. In the assessment of criminal responsibility, the two basic steps are the evaluation of the facts, and that of the mental state of the offender. Taking into account possible technical and scientific advancement in assessing the latter, the argument advanced by the judge in *Albertani*, who argued for the beneficial role of neuroscience and behavioural genetics, is theoretically appealing. The rapid and indisputable advancement of brain science may bolster our knowledge and understanding of human behaviour. Rejecting probable new scientific contributions out of concern for possible misuse is not a positive approach to a development that should be understood and regulated rather than rejected. As illustrated above, many doubts still surround the soundness of the results presented by defence experts in *Albertani*. However, in the future science may be able to give us more helpful insights into human behaviour.

The real issue now concerns law rather than science. The different dimensions in which science and law are connected are strongly affected by the increasing knowledge of the interaction between biological and environmental factors and their effect on behaviour. The nuances of science, when applied to legal thinking, seem in tension with established definitions of legal concepts and with traditional, widely accepted legal doctrines. Nonetheless, in 2016, the regulatory framework created by the legislator to allow science to enter the criminal trial is still tenable.

V. Consequences of a Successful Insanity Plea: Italian Criminal Psychiatric Facilities

According to the Italian Penal Code, a successful insanity plea should always lead to admission to a criminal psychiatric facility (*Ospedale Psichiatrico Giudiziario*, or *OPG*) for at least two years (Article 222). In the case of a felony conviction and

---

[38] See Chapters 2 and 9 in this volume.

of a ruling of diminished responsibility, the convict must be admitted to a facility that combines treatment and detention (*Casa di cura e di custodia*), for one year or more, depending on the gravity of the crime. The Penal Code uses two different phrases, '*Ospedale psichiatrico giudiziario*' and '*Casa di cura e custodia*'. However, there is only one type of criminal psychiatric facility in Italy. Both groups of defendants go to exactly the same type of facility. Nominally, it is primarily a facility aimed at treatment; in reality, its focus is exclusively on detention. In a joint report to the Italian Parliament in 2014, the Ministry of Health and the Ministry of Justice emphasised the profound inadequacy of current criminal psychiatric facilities.[39] The Italian government has recently decided to close down these facilities, which have a long and often controversial history. The first 'criminal asylum' (*Manicomio criminale*) in Italy was established in 1872 in Aversa, in the Southern Italian province of Caserta, for convicts who had 'gone mad in prison', so as to 'avoid the unpleasant consequences that they might have on law and order, discipline, hygiene, and safety in the penal houses of the Kingdom', as explained in a notice sent by the Italian Home Office in 1872.[40] As in most countries, in Italy there were also 'asylums' (*Manicomi*) for people diagnosed with mental illness; asylums were not part of the criminal justice system. Human rights abuses were known to be taking place in asylums. Asylums were closed with the Italian psychiatry reform law in 1978. Until 1978 the institutionalisation approach to the treatment of mental illness had strongly prevailed over the community care approach. The 1978 legislation overturned this and introduced a community care-based model.[41] However, in practice the actual transition happened gradually. The process was neither easy nor linear, and some 'asylums' remained open until the end of the 1990s, having changed only their names (*Ospedali psichiatrici*) and part of their most unacceptable patient management and treatment policies.

Until 2014 criminal psychiatric facilities in Italy were still regulated by a 1904 statute entitled 'Regulations regarding asylums and lunatics. Custody and care of lunatics' (*Disposizioni sui manicomi e sugli alienati. Custodia e cura degli alienati*).[42]

---

[39] Camera dei Deputati, Doc CCXVII, n 1, *Relazione sullo stato di attuazione delle iniziative per il superamento degli ospedali psichiatrici giudiziari* [Report on the state of implementation of the reform scheme of criminal psychiatric institution] (30 September 2014).

[40] U Fornari and S Ferracuti, 'Special Judicial Psychiatric Hospitals in Italy and the Shortcomings of the Mental Health Law' (1995) 6 *The Journal of Forensic Psychiatry* 381. Writing in the same year, Lombroso advocated the creation of criminal asylums for those who had become 'insane whilst awaiting trial or while in prison, and those driven to crime by habitual, evident illnesses, including pellagra; alcoholism; hysteria; puerperal disorders; epilepsy; most of the people whose relatives are insane or have epilepsy; and criminals suffering from a constitutional cranial abnormality' (our translation, from C Lombroso, 'Sull'istituzione dei manicomi criminali in Italia. Rendiconto del Regio Istituto Lombardo di Scienze' [On the establishment of criminal asylums in Italy. Report by the Royal Institute of Science of Lombardy] (1872) 11 *Rivista Discipline Carcerarie* 105).

[41] Parliamentary Statute no 80 of 1978. As to the problems encountered by mental hospitals in Italy, Michael Donnelly writes: 'The principal gatekeeper of mental hospitals, the psychiatric profession, had become a storm center of controversy. Not only were the abuses and overweening ambitious of psychiatric power challenged and criticized; even its traditional prerogatives were questioned as never before'. See M Donnelly, *The Politics of Mental Health in Italy* (Oxford, Routledge, 2003).

[42] Parliamentary Statute no 36 of 1904.

Article 1 of the Statute provides that mentally ill patients who 'are a danger to themselves or to others or who might excite public outcry, are to be kept and cared for in mental asylums'.[43] The provision made no reference to therapeutic intervention and it applied equally to regular and criminal asylums. The Italian Penal Code, enacted in 1930 and still in force, albeit with several amendments, required that the following people should be hosted in criminal psychiatric facilities: (i) incarcerated individuals whose sentence has been suspended because of supervening mental illness; (ii) offenders under psychiatric observation; (iii) offenders sentenced to a temporary stay in a criminal psychiatric facility; (iv) offenders acquitted on grounds of legal insanity, including minors; (v) offenders deemed only partially responsible, by reason of partial insanity.[44]

In Italy the treatment of the five groups of defendants listed above depends on the Ministry of Justice, not on the Ministry of Health, similarly to France, Spain, Portugal, Norway, Greece and Denmark, where the treatment centres are under the Ministry of Home Affairs, and unlike the United Kingdom and Sweden.[45]

With judgment no 253 of 2003, the Constitutional Court introduced the possibility for the court to administer a different security measure in place of psychiatric hospitalisation. The measure should 'ensure adequate care of the insane and contain their social dangerousness'. This ruling reaffirms the supremacy of community care over institutionalisation. One year later, with judgment no 367 of 2004, the Constitutional Court ruled that one particular type of preventive measure, known as 'provisional detention order' (of socially dangerous offenders in a criminal psychiatric facility), is unconstitutional in so far as the court cannot 'impose, in place of criminal psychiatric institutionalisation, a non-custodial security measure'. The Court stated that Article 206 of the Penal Code (regulating provisional detention orders) is unconstitutional insofar as it limits the choice of the criminal judge to imprisonment or institutionalisation, such as probation (*libertà vigilata*). The Court further argued that Article 206 violates the constitutionally protected right to health. The Court held that probation, regulated in Article 228 of the Penal Code, would in principle allow the implementation of more patient-focused therapeutic interventions, while adequately preventing socially dangerous offenders from reoffending.

Law no 81 of 2014 further reformed the system. In the case of a successful insanity or diminished responsibility plea, the judge can no longer sentence the offender to institutionalisation. Courts now have a legal obligation to administer a different

---

[43] Our translation. The original text of Art 1 reads as follows:

Debbono essere custodite e curate nei manicomi le persone affette per qualunque causa da alienazione mentale, quando siano pericolose a sé o agli altri e riescano di pubblico scandalo e non siano e non possano essere convenientemente custodite e curate fuorché nei manicomi.

[44] The relevant provisions for each of the five categories are, respectively, Art 148 CP; Art 99 Decree of the President of the Republic n 431/76; Art 206 CP and Art 312 CPP; Art 222 CP; Art 219 CP.

[45] Fornari and Ferracuti (n 40).

type of preventive measure (*misura di sicurezza*),[46] unless there are 'clear elements' suggesting that proper care can only be ensured through institutionalisation. The judicial psychiatric institutionalisation system is now regarded as anachronistic and obsolete, and its definitive demise is planned for the near future. At the end of 2014, seven judicial psychiatric hospitals were still open in Italy, hosting 857 offenders.[47]

The process of reform has been based on the principle of non-discrimination, and in particular of equal access to psychiatric care. The old system discriminated against psychiatric patients who were also criminal offenders.

A specially appointed Parliamentary Committee of Inquiry on the Efficiency of the Healthcare Service recently focused on criminal psychiatric facilities.[48] The Committee highlighted that these are in practice detention facilities, providing only scarce and very inadequate psychiatric care. The aim of the reform is to move from a legal concept of security centred on 'individual social dangerousness', meaning the probability of reoffending, to a new concept, better cognisant of the importance of the relation between individual behaviour and psychiatric treatment or detention setting. The provision of appropriate and adequate psychiatric treatment is becoming part of the very concept of security. With that goal, the Minister of Justice has announced the creation of a new type of criminal psychiatric residential facility (*Residenze per l'esecuzione della misura di sicurezza sanitaria* or *REMS*), operated by the local (regional) healthcare authorities, in collaboration with the Ministry of Justice. The new institutions should ensure the safety of patients, staff and public and provide a comfortable and safe environment for patients. The provision of adequate medical treatment aimed at effective rehabilitation and the preservation of security should not be in opposition. Furthermore, protecting privacy and dignity by providing a safe and secure environment for patients, staff and visitors should always be thought of as part of standard clinical care.

This approach may be seen as a step towards a more patient-oriented healthcare system. We believe that this is an ideal setting in which neuroscience and behavioural genetics could come to have a crucial role. For instance, various fMRI studies have demonstrated that 'neurogenesis', the growth and development of nerve tissue, can occur in more than one region of the adult mammalian brain, including the hippocampus, the olfactory bulb, the amygdala and the *substantia nigra*.[49]

---

[46] Security measures are taken to 're-socialise' the offender who has been considered socially dangerous by the court. They must be proportionate to the offence. The measures may be renewed at intervals of six months, following judicial reassessment (Arts 49 and 115 CP).

[47] The OPGs are located in Aversa, Barcellona Pozzo di Gotto, Castiglione delle Stiviere, Montelupo Fiorentino, Napoli, Salerno and Reggio Emilia.

[48] Senato della Repubblica, XVI legislatura—20 July 2011, Commissione Parlamentare di Inchiesta Sull'Effficacia e l'Efficienza del Servizio Sanitario Nazionale *Relazione sulle condizioni di vita e di cura all'interno degli ospedali psichiatrici giudiziari* [Report of living conditions and quality of care in criminal psychiatric facilities] (Rome, Tipografia del Senato, 2011).

[49] E Gould, 'How Widespread Is Adult Neurogenesis in Mammals?' (2007) 8 *Nature Reviews Neuroscience* 481.

Other studies have demonstrated that the amygdala plays a primary role in the development of empathy in humans, and empathy is precisely what seems to be lacking in a large number of mentally ill offenders.[50]

Neurogenesis in adult offenders can create the basis for rehabilitation and prevent recidivism. It can best be supported through the creation of an appropriate environment, where offenders can have the concrete opportunity to learn and to be treated in a way that makes them take responsibility for their actions and for their rehabilitation. This can be accomplished in various ways, including meetings with the victims if the victims give their consent, and programmes of interaction, to face the consequence of one's antisocial actions. This 'restorative justice' approach emphasises repairing the harm caused by criminal behaviour and ideally requires cooperative processes that include all stakeholders. Practices and programmes reflecting restorative purposes will respond to crime by identifying and taking steps to repair the harm done by offenders, involving all stakeholders, and transforming the traditional relationship between communities and their governments in their response to crime.[51]

The above example aims to show how discoveries on the human brain could also be usefully applied also in the post-conviction phase.

VI. Conclusions

The aim of this chapter was to explore whether neuroscientific technologies can influence insanity assessments in Italian courts. The strategy of our analysis was twofold. We described the most relevant features of the Italian legal system in relation to the assessment of criminal responsibility, focusing in particular on the legal insanity standards and on judicial verdicts of not guilty by reason of insanity. We analysed two recent cases, where neuroscience played a crucial role in expert reports and, in one case, in the eventual judicial decision to grant diminished responsibility. In each case, we discussed whether the new technologies supported and added to traditional methods in an insanity evaluation, and we presented the debate taking place in the legal and scientific community. We believe that current

---

[50] See especially J Decety, C Chen, C Harenski and KA Kiehl, 'An fMRI Study of Affective Perspective Taking In Individuals with Psychopathy: Imagining Another in Pain Does Not Evoke Empathy' (2013) 7 *Frontiers in Human Neuroscience* 489: 1 and BC Bernhardt and T Singer, 'The Neural Basis of Empathy' (2012) 35 *Annual Review of Neuroscience* 1.

[51] Among others, Daniel Reisel promotes this theory of justice. In 2013 Rosenberg and colleagues at Stanford showed that playing computer games that induce the user to behave in pro-social ways can lead users to engage in pro-social behaviour also in the real world. The results of their study also indicate that the attribution of 'superpowers' to one's avatar in the fictitious computer-generated setting leads to helpful behaviour in the real world, regardless of how participants used the 'superpowers' in the videogame. See RS Rosenberg, SL Baughman and JN Bailenson, 'Virtual Superheroes: Using Superpowers in Virtual Reality to Encourage Prosocial Behavior' (2013) 8 *PlosOne* e55003.

criminal-procedural rules that allow science to enter the criminal process are a reasonable method to defend society from criminal behaviour and to adequately take into account the social and biological individuality of the offender. The two goals need not be in opposition.

We then proceeded to critically examine a question that is often overlooked, if not completely ignored, in the literature: the treatment of convicted, mentally ill offenders in Italy, including its history and recent developments. We focused on the discrepancy between the goals of the legislator and the actual functioning of the Italian criminal justice system. We discussed the aim of the 2014 reform, designed to allow offenders who received a reduced sentence on grounds of insanity to receive adequate treatment in an appropriate environment.

In light of all this, we can draw three conclusions on the potential impact of neuroscience on the Italian criminal justice system.

Many of the problems posed now with reference to neuroscientific and behavioural genetic evidence are not new. They reflect the difficult relationship between law and psychiatry over the past centuries. We argued that the current regulatory framework is effective in preventing 'junk science' from entering the criminal trial.

We argued that the concept of criminal responsibility, as blameworthiness for committing an act prohibited by the law, will not be revolutionised by the admission and use of neuroscientific evidence in trials; unless science comes to prove that human beings are guided by the deterministic hand of biology and radically incapable of making free choices. By 'free' choices, we do not refer to 'free will' in a philosophical sense; we are not suggesting that individuals are not affected by the constraints of their biology and life history. Nevertheless, insanity assessment may be enriched by the advancement of neuroscience, integrating the investigation methods of psychiatry.

Finally, we believe that the main impact of neuroscience on the criminal justice system will be twofold. Punishment will better fit the individual, because of the increased understanding of the human brain and of the mind of the particular offender. Judges and juries will have a broader range of information on which to base their judgments. At the same time, psychiatry informed by neuroscience will offer better treatment of antisocial and mentally impaired offenders, to implement the principle provided for in Article 27, Paragraph 3 of the Italian Constitution: 'Punishment should not be inhumane and should aim for the re-education of the convict'.[52]

---

[52] Our translation. The original text in Italian reads as follows: 'Le pene non possono consistere in trattamenti contrari al senso di umanità e devono tendere alla rieducazione del condannato'.

Bibliography

Appelbaum, PS, 'Behavioral Genetics and the Punishment of Crime' (2005) 56 *Psychiatric Services* 25.

Baum, ML, 'The Monoamine Oxidase A (MAOA) Genetic Predisposition to Impulsive Violence: Is It Relevant to Criminal Trials?' (2013) 6 *Neuroethics* 287.

Bernhardt, BC and Singer, T, 'The Neural Basis of Empathy' (2012) 35 *Annual Review of Neuroscience* 1.

Brunner, HG, Nelen, M, Breakefield, XO, Ropers, HH and Oost, BA van, 'Abnormal Behavior Associated with a Point Mutation in the Structural Gene for Monoamine Oxidase A' (1993) 262 *Science* 578.

Buckholtz, JW and Meyer-Lindenberg, AM, 'MAOA and Bioprediction of Antisocial Behaviour: Science Fact and Science Fiction' in I Singh, W Sinnitt-Armstrong and J Savulscu (eds), *Bioprediction, Biomarkers and Bad Behaviour* (Oxford, Oxford University Press, 2014).

Camalbert, N, Andronikof, A, Armand, M, Robin, C and Bazex, H, 'Forensic Mental Health Assessment in France: Recommendations for Quality Improvement' (2014) 6 *International Journal of Law & Psychiatry* 628.

Caspi, A, McClay, J, Moffitt, TE, Mill, J, Martin, J, Craig, IW, Taylor, A and Poulton, R, 'Role of Genotype in the Cycle of Violence in Maltreated Children' (2002) *Science* 851.

Decety, J, Chen, C, Harenski, C and Kiehl, KA, 'An fMRI Study of Affective Perspective Taking in Individuals with Psychopathy: Imagining Another in Pain Does Not Evoke Empathy' (2013) 7 *Frontiers in Human Neuroscience* 489: 1.

Denno, D, 'Revisiting the Legal Link between Genetics and Crime' in NA Farahany (ed), *The Impact of Behavioral Sciences on Criminal Law* (Oxford, Oxford University Press, 2009).

Donnelly, M, *The Politics of Mental Health in Italy* (Oxford, Routledge, 1992).

Erickson, SK, 'Blaming the Brain' (2010) 11 *Minnesota Journal of Law, Science & Technology* 27.

Fornari, U and Ferracuti, S, 'Special Judicial Psychiatric Hospitals in Italy and the Shortcomings of the Mental Health Law' (1995) 6 *The Journal of Forensic Psychiatry* 381.

Forzano, F, Borry, P, Cambon-Thomsen, A, Hodgson, SV, Tibben, A, Vries, P de, El, C van and Cornel, M, 'Italian Appeal Court: a Genetic Predisposition to Commit Murder?' (2010) 18 *European Journal of Human Genetics* 519.

Fox, D, 'Brain Imaging and the Bill of Rights. Memory Detection Technologies and American Criminal Justice' (2008) 8 *American Journal of Bioethics* 34.

Gillham, NW, *Genes, Chromosomes and Disease* (Upper Saddle River, NJ, Financial Times Press, 2011).

González-Tapia, MI and Obsuth, I, 'Bad Genes & Criminal Responsibility' (2015) 39 *International Journal of Law & Psychiatry* 60.

Gould, E, 'How Widespread Is Adult Neurogenesis in Mammals?' (2007) 8 *Nature Reviews Neuroscience* 481.

Greenwald, AG, McGhee, DE and Schwartz, JLK, 'Measuring Individual Differences in Implicit Cognition: The Implicit Association Test' (1998) 74 *Journal of Personality and Social Psychology* 1464.

Halleck, S, 'The Assessment of Responsibility in Criminal Law and Psychiatric Practice' in DN Weisstub (ed), *Law and Mental Health, International Perspectives* (Oxford, Pergamon Press, 1984) 193–220.

Huettel, SA, Song, AW and McCarthy, G, *Functional Magnetic Resonance Imaging* (Sunderland, Sinauer Associates, 2008).

Hughes, V, 'Science in Court: Head Case' (2010) 464 *Nature* 340.

Lombroso, C, 'Sull'Istituzione dei manicomi criminali in Italia. Rendiconto del Regio Istituto Lombardo di Scienze' (1872) 11 *Rivista di Discipline Carcerarie* 105.

Pardo, M and Patterson, D, *Minds, Brains, and Law. The Conceptual Foundations of Law and Neuroscience* (Oxford, Oxford University Press, 2013).

Pardo, M, Patterson, D and Moratti, S, 'The Gathering of and Use of Neuroscientific Evidence in Criminal Trials in the United States. Compatibility with the 4th and 5th Amendments and with Due Process' (2014) 3 *Rivista Italiana di Filosofia del Diritto* 41.

Rosenberg, RS, Baughman, SL and Bailenson, JN, 'Virtual Superheroes: Using Superpowers in Virtual Reality to Encourage Prosocial Behavior' (2013) 8 *PlosOne* e55003.

Rusconi, E and Mitchener-Nissen, T, 'Prospects of Functional Magnetic Resonance Imaging as Lie Detector' (2013) 7 *Frontiers in Human Neuroscience* 594.

Sapolsky, RM, 'The Frontal Cortex and the Criminal Justice System' (2004) 359 *Philosophical Transactions of the Royal Society of London B* 1787.

Sartori, G, Agosta, S, Zogmaister, C, Ferrara, SD and Castiello, U, 'How to Accurately Detect Autobiographical Events' (2008) 19 *Psychological Science* 772.

Senato della Repubblica, XVI legislatura—20 July 2011, Commissione Parlamentare di Inchiesta Sull'Effficacia e l'Efficienza del Servizio Sanitario Nazionale *Relazione sulle condizioni di vita e di cura all'interno degli ospedali psichiatrici giudiziari* [Report of living conditions and quality of care in criminal psychiatric facilities] (Rome, Tipografia del Senato, 2011).

Tribunale di Como, Gip, 20 May 2011, no 536, *Albertani* [2012] *Rivista Italiana di Medicina Legale* 246.

Tribunale di Venezia, Gip, 24 January 2013, no 296, *Mattiello* [2013] *Rivista Italiana di Medicina Legale* 1905.

Verschuere, B, Prati, V and Houwer, JD, 'Cheating the Lie Detector. Faking in the Autobiographical Implicit Association Test' (2009) 20 *Psychological Science* 410.

6

Legal Insanity and Neurolaw in the Netherlands: Developments and Debates

GERBEN MEYNEN[*]

I. Introduction

The topic of this chapter is the regulation of and case law on legal insanity (*ontoerekeningsvatbaarheid*) in the Dutch criminal justice system. The first part of the chapter is a discussion of the characteristics of the insanity defence in the Dutch legal system. The second part is an analysis of the impact of neuroscience on the Dutch criminal justice system, and in particular on the assessment of criminal responsibility (*strafrechtelijke verantwoordelijkheid*) and legal insanity.

Two characteristics of the insanity defence in the Netherlands stand out. The insanity defence is available under Dutch law, but there is no legal standard specifying under what conditions a mental disorder present at the time of the crime can substantiate an insanity plea. In other legal systems the criteria are usually set down in statutory law or case law. For instance, the M'Naghten standard defines the criteria for legal insanity as follows:

> At the time of committing the act, the party accused was labouring under such a defect of reason, from disease of the mind, as not to know the nature and quality of the act he was doing; or if he did know it, that he did not know what he was doing was wrong.[1]

Another test or criterion for insanity is the Model Penal Code standard:

> A person is not responsible for criminal conduct if at the time of such conduct as a result of mental disease or defect he lacks substantial capacity either to appreciate the criminality of his conduct or to conform his conduct to the requirements of the law.[2]

[*] I am grateful to Tijs Kooijmans (Tilburg Law School) for his helpful comments.
[1] *M'Naghten's Case*, 10 Cl & Fin 200, 8 Eng Rep 718 (HL 1843).
[2] Model Penal Code. Official draft and explanatory notes: complete text as adopted 24 May 1962. (Philadelphia, PA, American Law Institute, 1985).

Some consequences of not having such a standard in the Dutch legal system will be considered. In the Netherlands five levels of criminal responsibility or insanity (*graden van toerekeningsvatbaarheid*) are used. Many jurisdictions rely on the dichotomy 'sane' versus 'insane', others also provide a 'diminished capacity' mitigating factor, leading to reduced sentences. I will discuss proposals for reform that have been advanced recently.

Neurolaw is certainly an area of strong scientific and legal interest in the Netherlands. A recent special issue of a renowned legal journal, the *Nederlands Juristenblad* or *NJB*, was devoted to neurolaw in Dutch law, forensic psychiatry and forensic psychology.[3] In the second part of this chapter, I will take this special issue as a starting point for sketching the debate about neuroscience and insanity in the Netherlands. I examine whether—and if so, how—neuroscience information contributes to insanity assessments in individual cases. Further, I discuss the use of medication and its possible implications for criminal responsibility. Then, I turn my attention to Deep Brain Stimulation (DBS). DBS is used as a medical treatment for a few conditions. It has been shown to cause major side-effects, sometimes profoundly affecting behaviour and decision-making capacity. What could be the implications regarding legal competency if someone were to commit a crime while on DBS? Next, I discuss some limitations intrinsic to current neuroscience techniques and their consequences for courtroom use. Finally, I will draw conclusions and identify a general challenge for neurolaw research, particularly relevant to small countries like the Netherlands.

II. The Insanity Defence in the Dutch Legal System

Until 1886 the Criminal Code in force in the Netherlands was the French *Code Pénal*. The Dutch Criminal Code came into force in 1886. The insanity clause was then Article 37 and it is now Article 39 of the Dutch Criminal Code (*Wetboek van Strafrecht*). Numbering aside, the content of the provision has hardly changed over almost 130 years.[4] The fundamental legal principle underlying the Dutch regulation of insanity is 'no punishment without guilt'.[5] Article 39 reads as

---

[3] Kogel, CH de, P van de Beek, F Leeuw, G Meynen and L Westgeest, 'Themanummer Neurolaw in Nederland' (2013) 88 *Nederlands Juristenblad* 3130.

[4] JB van der Leij, JL Jackson, M Malsch and JF Nijboer, 'Residential Mental Health Assessment within Dutch Criminal Cases: A Discussion' (2001) 19 *Behavioral Sciences and the Law* 691.

[5] T Kooijmans, *Op maat geregeld. Een onderzoek naar de grondslag en de normering van de strafrechtelijke maatregel* (Deventer, Kluwer, 2002). On legal insanity in the Netherlands, as discussed in this chapter, see also S Radovic, G Meynen and T Bennet, 'Introducing a Standard of Legal Insanity: The Case of Sweden Compared to the Netherlands' (2015) 40 *International Journal of Law and Psychiatry* 43.

follows: 'Anyone who commits an offence for which he cannot be held responsible by reason of a mental disorder or mental disease is not criminally liable'.[6] According to this provision, a defendant is not punishable when his criminal actions cannot be attributed to him, on account of deficient development or pathological perturbation of his mental faculties. But the provision does not list criteria for attributability. No legal standard like M'Naghten, the Model Penal Code standard, or the Irresistible Impulse test exist under Dutch law.[7] At the same time, the insanity defence is a highly relevant element in the Dutch criminal justice system. Approximately 4,000 adult defendants are evaluated by psychologists and psychiatrists each year and one of the questions in these assessments is the (level of) legal insanity.[8] In this section, some important characteristics of insanity evaluations in the Netherlands will be considered (see also Table 6.1 below at pp 153–54).

Who Performs the Evaluations and Under What Circumstances?

The Dutch legal system is 'moderately inquisitorial'.[9] The judge and the prosecution have the authority to order a psychiatric or a psychological assessment, or both. If the defence does not agree with the outcome it can request a 'second opinion' by a defence-appointed forensic mental health practitioner.[10] The decision to order the assessment may be based on the outcome of a short evaluation by a psychiatrist

---

[6] Translation of Article 39, based on PJP Tak, *The Dutch Criminal Justice System. Organization and Operation* (The Hague, WODC, 2003). An alternative translation, to be found in van der Leij et al (n 4), is: 'Not punishable is he who commits a criminal act for which he cannot be held responsible because of a defect or disorder of his mental capacities'. The original Dutch text reads: 'Niet strafbaar is hij die een feit begaat, dat hem wegens de gebrekkige ontwikkeling of ziekelijke stoornis van zijn geestvermogens niet kan worden toegerekend'.

[7] G Meynen, 'Een juridische standaard voor ontoerekeningsvatbaarheid?' (2013) 88 *Nederlands Juristenblad* 1384 and Tak (n 6).

[8] Nederlands Instituut voor Forensische Psychiatrie en Psychologie (NIFP), *Jaarbericht* (Utrecht, Ministry of Security and Justice, 2012).

[9] On the Dutch legal system, see C Brants, 'Justice Done and Seen to Be Done? The Institutionalized Relationship between the Press and the Criminal Justice System in the Netherlands' (1993) 3 *International Criminal Justice Review* 60:

Criminal proceedings are moderately inquisitorial, in that defence and prosecution are not completely opposed parties as in an adversarial system. The role of the prosecutor is, of course, to prosecute and to prove the defendant's guilt, but not at all costs; the prosecutor must also specifically safeguard the defendant's fundamental rights. On the other hand, the role of the defence is not so much to establish the defendant's innocence as to make sure that the prosecution does not unduly infringe upon his fundamental rights and to see that he gets a fair deal. The main purpose of a criminal trial in an inquisitorial setting is to establish the truth, and all parties (including the chairman of the court and other judges, who take an active part in questioning witnesses and generally directing the trial) work towards this end (p 65).

[10] On the Dutch legal system, also as related to forensic psychiatry, see P Bal and F Koenraadt, 'Dutch Criminal Law and Procedure: A Bird's Eye View' in F Koenraadt, AWM Mooij and JML van Mulbregt (eds), *The Mental Condition in Criminal Law* (Amsterdam, Dutch University Press, 2007) 13–35.

working for the Dutch Institute for Forensic Psychiatry and Psychology (NIFP).[11] The type of professional involved in the assessment depends, in part, on the condition of the person undergoing it. If a personality disorder or intellectual disability is suspected, the psychiatrist may advise that a psychological evaluation is performed, while in case of a suspected psychiatric disorder, such as psychosis, the choice will probably fall on a psychiatric evaluation.[12] The majority of assessments are performed by psychologists, rather than psychiatrists.[13] This used to be different. In the mid-1980s, psychologists started to perform evaluations of defendants as independent experts, and with a 1988 statute the government acknowledged this development and gave psychologists the authority to act as expert witnesses (*getuige-deskundige*) in the criminal process.[14] In some cases, the defendant is examined by both a psychologist and a psychiatrist in what is known as 'double evaluation' (*dubbelrapportage*). Usually, this is done when a combination of psychological and psychiatric pathologies is suspected, or when a particularly severe precautionary measure is considered, such as involuntary commitment to a high-security forensic psychiatric facility called TBS (*terbeschikkingstelling*). The term can be translated with some approximation as 'detention at the government's pleasure' and it is not a type of punishment, even though the particular defendant involved may experience it as such. It is a preventive measure. The Dutch legal system distinguishes between 'punishment' (*straf*) and 'measure' (*maatregel*), the latter can be imposed for purposes of prevention.[15] Defendants who suffered from a mental disorder at the time of the crime may be sentenced to TBS if they are still considered a threat to society. The risk assessment is made by forensic mental health practitioners, who often rely on structured risk assessment tools. Ultimately, the decision about TBS is up to the judge.[16] TBS is the most severe safety measure in the Dutch criminal justice system, in particular because of its potential duration. In the majority of cases, it is imposed for an indeterminate amount of time. The person sentenced to TBS must remain in the forensic psychiatric facility for as long as the risk of recidivism remains too high for release

---

[11] See also van der Leij et al (n 4).

[12] TS van der Veer and WJ Canton, 'Pro Justitia-rapportage' in H Groen, M Drost, and HLI Nijman (eds), *Handbook Forensische geestelijke gezondheidszorg* (Utrecht, De Tijdstroom, 2011).

[13] According to the 2012/2013 Yearly Report of the Dutch Institute of Forensic Psychiatry and Psychology, which is part of the Ministry of Justice, the total number of evaluations of adult defendants in criminal cases during that year was 4,526. Evaluations performed by psychologists only: 46.55%; evaluations performed by psychiatrists only: 18.12%; double reports (usually both psychiatrist and psychologist): 29.81%. See Nederlands Instituut voor Forensische Psychiatrie en Psychologie (NIFPP), *Het advies over het toerekenen* (Utrecht, Ministry of Security and Justice, 2014).

[14] WF van Kordelaar, 'Het psychologisch onderzoek pro Justitia' in BCM Raes and FAM Bakker (eds), *De psychiatrie in het Nederlandse recht* (Deventer, Kluwer, 2012).

[15] See Kooijmans (n 5); YAJM van Kuijck, 'Juridische kaders voor de geestelijke gezondheidszorg van de forensische patiënt' in H Groen, M Drost and HLI Nijman (eds), *Handboek Forensische geestelijke gezondheidszorg* (Utrecht, De Tijdstroom, 2011); and van der Leij et al (n 4).

[16] See GT Blok, E de Beurs, AG de Ranitz and T Rinne, [The current psychometric state of risk assessment scales for adults in the Netherlands] (2010) 52 *Tijdschr Psychiatr* 331.

into society.[17] Yearly or bi-yearly, the court, consisting of three professional judges, may repeat the assessment and decide for or against release from TBS, taking into account, among other factors, the reports made by the mental health professionals working in the facility where the person is interned. Every six years, independent behavioural experts perform an evaluation of the patient as well, and give advice to the court.[18]

In about 5 per cent of cases the assessment takes place by means of clinical observation, usually at the 'Pieter Baan forensic centre', located in Utrecht.[19] Defendants are placed under observation by a multidisciplinary team of behavioural experts for a period of seven weeks. This type of assessment is often performed when the defendant does not cooperate with a standard psychiatric or psychological evaluation. The clinical setting with continuous behavioural observation may give an adequate amount of information about the defendant's mental condition, even if he does not want to (fully) cooperate. Defendants suffering from multiple disorders and defendants in serious cases that attract media attention are also more likely to be evaluated at the Pieter Baan Centrum, which admits around 220 defendants per year.[20]

Questions to be Answered by Behavioural Experts

As mentioned, there is no statutory standard for insanity in the Dutch legal system. Still, there is a format of seven questions—asked by the prosecution or the judge—to be answered by psychiatrists and psychologists who perform the evaluation. This format is not codified in the law. It was originally proposed by psychiatrist Peter van Panhuis and it has remained in use with some modifications.[21]

0. Does the defendant cooperate and if not, what are your ideas/views about this lack of cooperation.

---

[17] See M Drost, 'Psychiatric Assessment After Every Six Years of the TBS Order in the Netherlands' (2006) 29 *International Journal of Law and Psychiatry* 257:
    Governments from outside the Netherlands have shown an increased interest in the Dutch TBS-system as an arrangement for continued detention of those perceived to be dangerous on completion of their sentence. In the UK, for example, the Home Affairs Committee in its First Report on 'Managing Dangerous People with Severe Personality Disorder' (DSPD) looked into the Dutch way of dealing with this particular group of mentally ill offenders.

[18] On the six-year evaluations see Drost (n 17):
    It is not the court, but the Ministry of Justice that assigns two independent expert witnesses (... one of them a psychiatrist) on behalf of the penal court. They will partly have to answer the same questions as at the pre-trial or regular extension stages: diagnosis at the time of the assessment and risk of recidivism related to the disorder. Of course the degree of accountability is no longer relevant at this stage, but the prognosis of the ongoing treatment is important. ... The difference with the recommendations at the regular extensions is that two professionals, not involved with the treatment itself, will not only have to form an opinion ... of the patient, but also of the treatment that has been offered and its results. (p 258).

[19] See van der Leij et al (n 4).

[20] See F Koenraadt, AWM Mooij and JML van Mulbregt (eds), *De persoon van de verdachte. De rapportage pro Justitia vanuit het Pieter Baan Centrum* (Utrecht, Kluwer, 2004).

[21] PJA van Panhuis, 'De vraagstelling in de Pro Justitia rapportage opnieuw bekeken' (2000) 7 *Proces* 103.

1. Is the defendant currently suffering from a mental disorder or defect? (Please add diagnosis.)
2. Was the defendant suffering from a disorder or defect at the time of committing the act?
3. Did the disorder influence the defendant's behavioural choices?
4. If so,
   (a) in what way did the disorder or defect influence the defendant's behavioural choices?
   (b) to what extent did the disorder or defect influence the defendant's behavioural choices?
   (c) what conclusion regarding legal insanity can be drawn?
5. What is the risk of recidivism (because of psychopathology-related problems)?
6. Which measures can be taken to reduce such risk?[22]

Over the past few years, the 'zero'-question has been gaining relevance. An increasing number of defendants are uncooperative. At least in part, this is assumed to be the consequence of fear of involuntary admittance to a TBS facility. The average duration of this measure has doubled in recent years, and it is now about nine years, with small variations that depend on the method of calculation.[23] It should be noted that in the Netherlands, defendants can be sentenced to a long prison term (eg 12 years) *plus* TBS, which will start after two-thirds of the prison term have been served.[24] Lawyers may advise their clients against cooperating with psychiatric evaluations, to avoid TBS.

Lack of cooperation causes considerable problems for psychiatrists and psychologists and for the courts. If a psychiatrist cannot reach a conclusion about the presence and impact of a mental disorder at the time of the crime, how can the court make a prudent and informed decision? This problem also emerges because, in the Netherlands, insanity is usually not raised by the defendant as an affirmative defence. Rather, insanity assessments are ordered by the court or prosecution.

---

[22] Translated and shortened for purposes of clarity. See also Meynen (n 7).

[23] See 'Toenemende verblijfsduur in de TBS. De ontwikkeling van de gemiddelde duur in de laatste 20 jaar.' [Increase in duration of TBS-custody. Changes of the average duration in the past 20 years]. Dienst Justitiele Inrichtingen, Ministerie van Justitie [Ministry of Justice] (2009).

[24] Some authors are critical of the practice of sentencing offenders to a (possibly long) prison term, followed by treatment in a TBS facility. See on this point H Nolet and V Verstappen, 'Behandeling tbs'er begint te laat' [Treatment of TBS-convicts starts too late] (2014) 37 *Medisch Contact* 1732. It has been argued that it is rather odd that after mental health professionals have confirmed that the offender suffers from a (possibly severe) mental disorder, the mentally ill offender is sentenced to prison instead of immediately being sent to TBS, a treatment setting. Yet, inverting the order would generate other problems. For instance, an important aspect of TBS is (intensive) reintegration into society: HJC Marle, 'The Dutch Entrustment Act (TBS): Its Principles and Innovations' (2002) 1 *International Journal of Forensic Mental Health* 83. A job is often part of this endeavour, among other aspects. If offenders serve a (long) prison sentence after a programme aimed at reintegrating them into society, the programme is to a large extent rendered ineffective.

This is a decision the defendant and his counsel may or may not agree with. In principle, the defendant can be sentenced to TBS even if mental health forensic practitioners cannot reach a conclusion about the presence of a mental disorder at the time of the crime due to lack of cooperation on the defendant's part.[25] However, the chance that the court may order TBS under that circumstance is considered to be lower.[26]

The six questions and the increasingly relevant 'zero'-question guide the forensic mental health professional; but they do not contribute to a definition of insanity, other than by articulating the question about the influence of the disorder on the behaviour of the defendant. A legal insanity test, such as the M'Naghten test or the Model Penal Code standard, defines the legally relevant type and degree of influence of a mental disorder on thought and actions: 'due to a mental disorder, the defendant did not know that what he was doing', or 'as a result of a mental disorder the defendant could not control his behaviour'. There is no similar standard in Dutch law. A parallel with Norway can usefully be drawn here. Article 44 of the Norwegian Penal Code reads as follows:

> A person who was psychotic or unconscious at the time of committing the act shall not be liable to a penalty. The same applies to a person who at the time of committing the act was mentally retarded to a high degree.[27]

The mere presence of a particular mental disorder—psychosis—at the time of the crime is sufficient to substantiate an insanity claim. There is no specification of the type of influence on the defendant's mind or criminal act that the pathology must have exerted. Norwegian law states that nothing more than the presence of a psychotic disorder at the time of the act is required to prove insanity. The phrasing of the six questions used by Dutch mental health forensic professionals strongly suggests that, unlike in Norway, some degree of influence of a mental disorder over the behaviour of the defendant is necessary to substantiate an insanity claim, but the nature of such influence is not specified. The Dutch format limits itself to providing a helpful structure for the behavioural expert's assessment. It defines the issues that should be addressed by psychiatrists and psychologists in their reports. Expert witnesses have to give an express answer to the question pertaining to the implications of the mental disorder or defect (and its influence on behaviour)

---

[25] AR Mackor, 'The Autonomy of Criminal Judges in Determining the Disorder and the Risk of Recidivism—Some Reflection on the Hoogerheide Case' in TI Oei and MS Groenhuijsen (eds), *Progression in Forensic Psychiatry. About Boundaries* (Deventer, Kluwer, 2012) 617–28.

[26] EMH van Dijk and M Brouwers, *Daling opleggingen tbs met dwangverpleging. Ontwikkelingen en achtergronden. Memorandum-1* (The Hague, WODC, 2011).

[27] Quotation taken from the translation of the Breivik Verdict in *Lovdata*, the law and case law database of the University of Oslo: TOSLO–2011–188627–24E. The section is interpreted as follows in the verdict: 'Being psychotic at the time of committing the act will unconditionally exempt the person from punishment, regardless of whether the offence is a result of the psychosis. This is often referred to as the medical principle'. See also I Melle, 'The Breivik Case and What Psychiatrists Can Learn from It' (2013) 12 *World Psychiatry* 16.

for the determination of legal insanity (question 4(c)). As a result, behavioural experts themselves have to formulate implicit or express legal insanity criteria in their individual assessment reports.[28] As van der Leij et al wrote, 'in general, courts follow the expert's advice, and in their sentences they frequently use the exact phrasing of the report'.[29] According to Tak:

> [I]n practice a person is not held responsible for his criminal conduct if at the time of such conduct, as a result of a mental disorder or disease, he lacks substantial capacity either to appreciate the wrongfulness of his conduct, or to bring his conduct into conformity with the requirements of law.

This phrasing resembles the Model Penal Code test for insanity. However, the Dutch criterion for legal insanity is less transparent and straightforward than this quote suggests. For instance, the psychiatrist or psychologist may reason that the defendant lacked 'free will' and that, therefore, the insanity defence should apply;[30] but it is not clear how exactly the lack of 'free will' relates to the M'Naghten or Model Penal Code insanity criteria.[31]

In one other case, the defendant's capacity to 'take stock of the situation and behavioural alternatives' was severely compromised and that had implications for the insanity judgment.[32] Prominent Dutch legal scholar de Hullu contended that a 'causal relationship between the disorder and the criminal act' is crucial.[33] This conception of insanity seems close to the 'product test' or 'Durham rule', according to which the criminal act should be the 'product of' the mental disease.[34] However, in the literature the product test is considered different from both the M'Naghten and the Model Penal Code standards, which do not require the crime to be the 'product' of the disorder.[35] In the United States, the product test has been considered a particularly problematic insanity standard.[36] In conclusion, Dutch case law does not define the legal insanity criteria.

---

[28] Meynen (n 7).

[29] Van der Leij et al (n 4) 700. The decision about the defendant's criminal responsibility is ultimately made by the judge.

[30] See for use of the phrase 'free will' Rechtbank Haarlem, 2 February 2006, ECLI:NL:RBHAA:2006:AV0882. See on free will and mental disorder G Meynen, 'Free Will and Mental Disorder: Exploring the Relationship' (2010) 31 *Theoretical Medicine and Bioethics* 429.

[31] On the notion of free will and criminal responsibility or legal insanity regarding the US legal context, see SJ Morse, 'The Non-Problem of Free Will in Forensic Psychiatry and Psychology' (2007) 25 *Behavioral Sciences and the Law* 203.

[32] Rechtbank Utrecht, 6 February 2012, ECLI:NL:RBUTR:2012:BV2995.

[33] J de Hullu, *Materieel strafrecht. Over algemene leerstukken van strafrechtelijke aansprakelijkheid naar Nederlands recht* (Deventer, Kluwer, 2012) 335.

[34] *Durham v United States*, 214 F 2d 862—United States Court of Appeals, District of Columbia Circuit 1954. On the product test, see also RF Becker, 'The Evolution of Insanity Standards' (2003) 18 *Journal of Police and Criminal Psychology* 41.

[35] C Elliott, *The Rules of Insanity: Moral Responsibility and the Mentally Ill Offender* (Albany, NY, State University of New York Press, 1996).

[36] Becker (n 34), RJ Gerber, 'Is the Insanity Test Insane?' (1975) *American Journal of Jurisprudence* 111.

Evaluation Before the Facts have been Established

A further characteristic of legal insanity in the Dutch legal system is that the behavioural expert should not assume that the defendant committed the crime. Usually, in the Netherlands, legal insanity is not an 'affirmative defence'. The forensic mental health evaluation takes place *before* the facts have been established by the court.[37] The defendant may choose not to plead guilty and deny the charges. The behavioural experts acknowledge this situation in their report, by using phrases such as '*if it is proven that the defendant committed the act*, then his responsibility should be considered diminished …'. The situation becomes particularly intricate if there is a relation between the criteria for a disorder and the crime, such as pyromania and arson. Unlike many other mental disorders, pyromania is closely related to performing criminal acts.

Forensic psychiatrists ascertain the presence and severity of a mental condition. This is different from establishing whether the crime was committed. The two questions should be considered independently. The Forensic Evaluation Guidelines by the Dutch Association for Psychiatry include the following practical rule for the forensic psychiatrist: 'Do not infer the existence of disorders from the criminal act'.[38] At the same time, not knowing whether the defendant committed the crime may constitute a considerable practical problem for expert witnesses, especially if the defendant is unwilling to cooperate or denies the charges.[39] In the Netherlands, the psychiatric evaluation takes place at an early phase of the criminal process. This has momentous consequences for the evaluation itself and for the type of conclusions that can or cannot be drawn.

Five Grades of Criminal Responsibility

In their advice to the court, behavioural experts can distinguish between as many as *five* levels of criminal responsibility or legal insanity. This is a typical characteristic of the Dutch legal system. Some defendants are considered criminally responsible (*toerekeningsvatbaar*) for their behaviour. Others are considered not responsible (*ontoerekeningsvatbaar*). Between the two extremes, there are three levels of diminished responsibility (*verminderde toerekeningsvatbaarheid*): slightly diminished; diminished; severely diminished. The five levels are not to be found

[37] In the standard situation, the evaluation of the defendant is initiated and ordered by the court or the prosecution. Yet, sometimes, insanity is raised by the defendant, as an affirmative defence.

[38] NVvP, *Richtlijn Psychiatrisch onderzoek en rapportage in strafzaken* (Utrecht, De Tijdstroom, 2012) 43.

[39] Van Marle notes that, in principle, denial may also be related to the presence of a mental disorder, like dissociative amnesia. See HJC Van Marle, 'Het strafrechtelijk psychiatrisch gedragskundigenonderzoek ("pro Justitia")' in BCM Raes and FAM Bakker (eds), *De psychiatrie in het Nederlandse recht* (Deventer, Kluwer, 2012).

in statutes. They evolved in case law and there is no formal definition of insanity and diminished responsibility. Dutch professor of forensic psychiatry Van Marle explains the five levels as follows:

> Undiminished responsibility means that the person concerned had complete access to his or her free will at the time of the crime with which he or she is charged and could therefore have chosen not to do it. Irresponsibility means that the person concerned had no free will at all with which to choose at the time of the crime with which he or she is charged. Important here is determining the moment when aspects of the disorder become manifest in the situation ('the scene of the crime') that will eventually lead to the perpetration. The earlier they play a role, the more inevitable will be the (disastrous) sequence of events, and the stronger will be the eventual limitation of free will.[40]

In legal practice, the judgement about the level of responsibility by the expert witness may have far-reaching consequences for the sentence. Legally insane defendants cannot be subject to punishment, in accordance with Article 39 of the Dutch Penal Code illustrated above. However, the defendant may be involuntarily admitted to a mental hospital for up to one year, or sentenced to TBS for an indeterminate period. In court practice, fully accountable defendants are not sentenced to TBS. A TBS sentence can only be issued if a number of requirements are met. The requirements concern the severity of the crime and the likelihood of reoffending and attacking persons or property.

III. Issues of Debate
and Proposals for Change

According to American legal scholar Firestone, 'probably no single issue in the annals of criminal law has stirred more controversy, debate, and comparison among laypersons, as well as jurists, than the insanity defence'.[41] The regulation of legal insanity is a controversial and debated question in the Netherlands as well.

Currently, there are several proposals to reform the insanity evaluation procedure. I will consider three questions. I will discuss whether it is justified to retain five levels of criminal responsibility. I will further consider whether it is prudent to expect forensic mental health practitioners to give their express opinion on criminal responsibility criteria, as they presently do. Finally, I argue that introducing a legal definition of insanity is to be recommended.

---

[40] HJC Van Marle, 'Forensic Psychiatric Services in the Netherlands' (2000) 23 *International Journal of Law and Psychiatry* 515, 527.

[41] MH Firestone, 'Psychiatric Patients and Forensic Psychiatry' in SS Sanbar (ed), *Legal Medicine*, 7th edn (Philadelphia, PA, Mosby Elsevier, 2007).

The Grades of Criminal Responsibility

It has been argued that the current number of levels of criminal responsibility—five—is too high. The recent Forensic Psychiatric Evaluation Guidelines recommend reducing the number of grades to three, by merging the various types of 'diminished responsibility' into one single category.[42] In the Guidelines, it is argued that the distinction between five levels of criminal responsibility is not based on state-of-the art psychiatric science, and the sub-division between three levels of diminished responsibility is considered particularly problematic.

The idea behind this simplification appears to be in line with Morse's view: 'Although responsibility is a continuum concept and an agent's level of responsibility depends on facts about the agent's capacity for rationality, we have only limited epistemic ability to make the fine-grained responsibility judgments that are theoretically possible'.[43] The proposal for simplification is not universally subscribed to. Mooij, professor emeritus of forensic psychiatry, argued that in forensic practice the existence of five levels helps judges to fine-tune the punishment and measure to the particular offender and crime. However, distinguishing between the five levels in practice may be a challenge. Van Marle wrote in 2007 (my translation): 'The differences between the five grades are not much elaborated upon in the literature ... It is in practice a question of whether everybody interprets the terms in the same way. An attempt to define them follows here'.[44] This passage illustrates the lack of clarity about the boundaries between the different levels. The fine-grained framework may be of help for determining the sentence, but qualms remain about the validity of expert advice based on that framework.

In its Guidelines, the psychiatric profession recommended abandoning the five-grade system. However, most legal insanity evaluations are performed by psychologists. Psychologists do not have a legal or professional obligation to follow the Guidelines for psychiatrists. Let us think of a practical example. Upon evaluating the same defendant, a psychiatrist and a psychologist could both feel that criminal responsibility is 'slightly' diminished. The psychologist is free to so advise the court, while the psychiatrist has to follow the Guidelines for psychiatrists and advise the court that criminal responsibility should be considered generically 'diminished'. The judge may infer that the two expert witnesses have a different opinion on the level of responsibility, which would be untrue. The psychiatrist is just following an assessment framework that does not include the category 'slightly diminished responsibility'.

There is an additional issue here, regarding the scope of professional expertise. It may not be appropriate to entrust forensic mental health professionals with the task of determining the number of levels of criminal responsibility or legal

---

[42] NVvP (n 38).

[43] SJ Morse, 'Rationality and Responsibility' (2000) 74 *Southern California Law Review* 251, 266.

[44] Van Marle (n 39) 127.

insanity. Legal insanity is a legal concept,[45] and it seems reasonable that legal experts and perhaps lawmakers should ultimately be in charge of determining the number of levels of legal insanity, after having consulted representatives from the psychiatric, psychology and other mental health professions.[46]

The five-level system has been and is being discussed by Dutch legal scholars. According to de Hullu, the Dutch legislator intended to introduce the dichotomy sanity versus insanity, rather than the current five grades structure.[47] None of the other legal grounds for justification or excuse (*strafuitsluitingsgronden*) in the Dutch Penal Code has a comparable five-level structure. Let us think of self-defence. There are not five grades of self-defence in the Dutch legal system. Either the ground of justification of self-defence applies, or it does not. The situation is different for insanity. Dutch courts have accepted and used five levels of legal insanity for decades.

In conclusion, the Dutch situation regarding the grades of legal insanity is untypical.[48] There is a lively debate about the appropriateness of retaining this framework; it could be abandoned in the near future.

The Psychiatrist Performing Legal Insanity Assessments

The format of questions guiding the legal insanity evaluation requires the expert witness to give express advice to the court about the level of criminal responsibility of the individual defendant. This has been subject to criticism.[49] Critics have argued that criminal responsibility and legal insanity are legal concepts, serving a legal purpose. Concepts such as 'symptom', 'disease', 'disorder', 'prevention' and 'treatment' are medical notions, but concepts such as 'criminal responsibility', 'intent' and 'insanity' lie in the legal domain, not in the realm of medicine.[50] The task of the forensic mental health professional should be to advise the court about issues and phenomena that form part of mental health professional expertise, rather than on the application of a legal notion. The tasks of the expert witnesses should not include the rendering of an opinion on whether the mental condition of the particular defendant meets the legal insanity threshold.[51]

---

[45] W Sinnott-Armstrong and K Levy, 'Insanity Defenses' in J Deigh and D Dolinko (eds), *The Oxford Handbook of Philosophy of Criminal Law* (New York, Oxford University Press, 2011).

[46] Meynen (n 7).

[47] De Hullu (n 33).

[48] At least this is true for Western legal systems.

[49] M Beukers, 'Gedragsdeskundige rapportage in strafzaken. Waar liggen de grenzen?' (2005) *Strafblad* 488 and JW Hummelen and DH de Jong, 'Toerekeningsvatbaarheid en toerekenen: de conclusie van de gedragsdeskundige versus het oordeel van de strafrechter' in HB Krans, AT Marseille, F Vellinga-Schootstra and PC Westerman (eds), *De deskundige in het recht* (Paris, Zutphen, 2011) 145–55 and Meynen (n 7).

[50] Meynen (n 7).

[51] ibid.

A similar debate exists in the United States, with some differences with respect to the Netherlands. Alec Buchanan writes that in the United States there is 'long-standing and widespread concern that psychiatric testimony is more likely than other evidence to intrude into the jury's realm'.[52] In the Netherlands, such a concern exists but it is far from being longstanding and widespread.

A further difference between the Dutch and the American jurisdiction concerns the absence of a legal standard defining the insanity criteria in the Netherlands.[53] Without a legal standard, it may be hard for judges to interpret the psychiatric and psychological findings. The psychiatrist may give a full argument, extending from the psychiatric findings to the very concept of legal insanity. By so doing, Dutch psychiatrists are not interpreting or applying a legal standard, as happens in the United States.[54] Dutch expert witnesses formulate their own argument, and possibly implicit legal insanity criteria, in their advice to the court. Hence, the incursion into the legal realm by the psychiatrist seems more substantial in the Dutch context than in the United States. Unlike American expert witnesses, Dutch forensic mental health practitioners render advice on how to understand the concept of legal insanity in the particular case, for example by phrasing their advice in terms of 'lack of free will' (*geen vrije wil*).

Introducing a Legal Insanity Standard

Recently, a proposal has been advanced to introduce a standard defining the criteria for insanity in the Dutch legal system.[55] The proposal relied on three main arguments, outlined below.

Introducing statutory insanity criteria will increase the clarity and transparency of insanity judgments in individual cases, it is argued. The various stakeholders in the trial, as well as the general public, will know in advance the criteria on which the legal decision is based. Incidentally, in jurisdictions in which insanity is an affirmative defence raised by the defendant, this appears to be an even more important issue because the defendant should be able to foresee whether he or she is likely to meet the insanity standard. This is not an attempt to confine the judge to the role of 'mouth of the law'. Even when express statutory criteria are present, their interpretation by the judge remains crucial.

The second argument concerns equality before the law. A statutory standard may help to ensure that similar cases are dealt with similarly. The fact that expert

---

[52] A Buchanan, 'Psychiatric Evidence on the Ultimate Issue' (2006) 34 *Journal of the American Academy of Psychiatry and the Law* 14.

[53] Tak (n 6) wrote: 'No statutory standards or case law standards are set for determining insanity'. See also Meynen (n 7) and Radovic, Meynen and Bennet (n 5).

[54] JL Knoll and PJ Resnick, 'Insanity Defense Evaluations: Toward a Model for Evidence-Based Practice' (2008) 8 *Brief Treatment and Crisis Intervention* 92.

[55] Meynen (n 7).

witnesses and the courts use different, and possibly implicit, criteria for insanity, may lead to unequal outcomes of the legal insanity decision-making process in individual cases.[56]

The last argument focuses on the role of the statutory insanity standard as an intermediary between medical findings and legal rules. Psychiatrists would not need to intrude on legal territory to explain their medical findings in terms of criminal responsibility. They could remain within their own domain of expertise and make reference to the statutory standard. Expert witnesses would not be expected to define the meaning of the notion of insanity by putting forward ad hoc insanity criteria in individual cases. Psychiatrists would basically limit themselves to doing what judges cannot do: performing a psychiatric evaluation.[57]

There are various possible legal strategies to introduce a statutory insanity standard into Dutch law. One approach could be importing a foreign standard such as the M'Naghten rule. One advantage of using such a standard is the availability of information about its strengths and weaknesses based on experiences in other legal systems. This knowledge may also be used to make sensible adaptations that reduce its weaknesses and increase its strengths. For instance, M'Naghten has been criticised because it ignores lack of control as an excusing factor. Therefore, one might want to add a control prong, or, alternatively, choose the Model Penal Code insanity standard discussed above.

In 'Een juridische standaard voor ontoerekeningsvatbaarheid?' I suggest a different approach.[58] Its rationale goes as follows. There is much debate about the criteria for legal insanity. In such debates, authors often make reference to moral philosophy to support their claims. Why not start with a philosophical theory about responsibility and *derive* the insanity criteria from the philosophical account? A choice needs to be made among the many ethical theories about responsibility. To provide an example of this line of reasoning, I explore the possibility of deriving criteria for legal insanity from Susan Wolf's account of responsibility.[59] Wolf takes the everyday notion that *in order to be responsible one has to be sane* as a crucial component of her framework of moral responsibility. In addition, she expressly refers to M'Naghten and even derives a conception of (in)sanity from that legal standard.[60] Wolf's theory is of a philosophical nature. If we analyse it from the perspective of (forensic) psychiatry, certain adaptations are required.[61] A revised version of Wolf's theory could result in the following tentative sketch of a legal insanity test.

---

[56] On the control element see S Penney, 'Impulse Control and Criminal Responsibility: Lessons from Neuroscience' (2012) 35 *International Journal of Law and Psychiatry* 99.

[57] Meynen (n 7).

[58] ibid.

[59] S Wolf, 'Sanity and the Metaphysics of Responsibility' in F Schoeman (ed), *Responsibility, Character and the Emotions* (Cambridge, Cambridge University Press, 1987) 46–62 and G Meynen, 'An Ethical Framework for Assessments of Criminal Responsibility: Applying Susan Wolf's Account of Sanity to Forensic Psychiatry' (2012) 35 *International Journal of Law and Psychiatry* 298.

[60] Meynen (n 59).

[61] ibid.

A defendant is legally insane if he suffers from a mental disorder, which resulted in one or more of the following:

1. The action was not under the control of the defendant's will.
2. The defendant's will was not stemming from himself; the will was forced upon him.
3. The defendant did not understand the action or its context, or did not appreciate the action for what it was.[62]

Below are some brief examples of disorders that may affect one or more of the three factors above.[63]

1. *The action was not under the control of the defendant's will.* A person with Tourette's syndrome, a neuropsychiatric disorder characterised by multiple motor tics, may hit and harm another person without any intention to do so.[64]

2. *The defendant's will was not stemming from himself; the will was forced upon him.* Some psychotic patients hear commanding voices (auditory hallucinations) they cannot but obey. This is a rare phenomenon, but it is known to occur.[65] Suppose a psychotic patient hears a voice commanding him to attack and seriously harm his neighbour with a stick. This may happen irrespective of the behaviour of the neighbour to the patient. The patient complies with the command, thus forming the will, at least in a generic sense, to attack his neighbour. When the attack actually happens, based on the facts, the judge could only conclude that the defendant's behaviour was intentional and his actions were willed. However, a forensic psychiatric evaluation may reveal that although the actions of the defendant were intentional in a legal sense, the formation of the intention was the consequence of a psychopathological phenomenon.[66] The action does not stem from the defendant's own desires, aspirations and values. Therefore, the defendant should be exculpated.[67]

3. *The defendant did not understand the action or its context, or did not appreciate the action for what it was.* Let us think of paranoid delusions.

---

[62] Meynen (n 7); see also Meynen (n 59).

[63] See also Meynen (n 7) and Meynen (n 59).

[64] Disorders in which 'control' in this sense is undermined are usually neurological rather than strictly psychiatric.

[65] LG Braham, P Trower and M Birchwood, 'Acting on Command Hallucinations and Dangerous Behavior: A Critique of the Major Findings in the Last Decade' (2004) 24 *Clinical Psychology Review* 513; S Bucci, M Birchwood, L Twist, N Tarrier, R Emsley and G Haddock, 'Predicting Compliance with Command Hallucinations: Anger, Impulsivity and Appraisals of Voices' Power and Intent' (2013) 147 *Schizophrenia Research* 163.

[66] See A Kalis and G Meynen, 'Mental Disorder and Legal Responsibility: The Relevance of Stages of Decision Making' (2014) 37 *International Journal of Law and Psychiatry* 601.

[67] Meynen (n 7).

One emblematic case was adjudicated in the Netherlands in 2010. A mother was convinced that she and her little daughter were persecuted by Satanists. She felt in danger of being killed by them, along with her daughter, and possibly in a terrible manner. The mother went up to the fourth floor of a department store and dropped her daughter, who was 18 months old. Immediately thereafter she jumped as well. The daughter died and the mother survived, severely wounded.[68] The behaviour of the mother cannot be characterised as automatism. It had clearly been intentional. It had not resulted from a command hallucination either, as no 'voice' had told her what to do. It had been her decision to act in that way, a decision based on a completely distorted view of reality, a delusional belief that Satanists were persecuting her and her daughter. Her actions had been a response to that perceived situation.

This tripartite preliminary framework for a new insanity standard, derived from ethical theory, offers a nuanced and not exceedingly complicated legal insanity test. It provides room for the cognitive element (M'Naghten) and for the control element. The framework distinguishes between two forms of 'loss of control', the 'automatism' type, meaning lack of intentional action, and the 'commanding voice' type, involving intentional action that is not rooted in the defendant's own desires, aspirations and values.[69]

In 'Een juridische standaard voor ontoerekeningsvatbaarheid?', I discuss two possible objections to introducing a standard for insanity in the Dutch legal system.[70] It could in theory be argued that we do not need a statutory insanity standard because forensic mental health professionals and judges involved in insanity assessments are already familiar with operationalising insanity in the Dutch jurisdiction. However, this position is untenable. Widespread knowledge of the practical working of insanity in the Dutch legal system is not an obstacle to codifying the definition and operationalisation of 'insanity' in statutory law, for purposes of transparency to all stakeholders in the criminal process and to the general public. The second possible objection is based on the opposite perception of current Dutch forensic practice. There is wide divergence of opinion on the definition and operationalisation of insanity, and it would be very difficult to reach the political and intra-professional consensus necessary to introduce a statutory standard. However, precisely for this reason it becomes critical to introduce an unambiguous definition of insanity, especially in view of the principle of equality before the law.

---

[68] A case in the Netherlands, Hof Amsterdam 17 September 2010, ECLI:NL:GHAMS:2010:BN7345. The example and comments are merely based on information from the published Court judgment.

[69] See also Wolf (n 59) on control and responsibility.

[70] Meynen (n 7).

Table 6.1: Characteristics of legal insanity in the Dutch legal system. The Netherlands has a moderately inquisitorial criminal justice system.

Characteristic	Remarks
Section 39 of the Dutch Criminal Code provides that a person who is not criminally responsible due to a mental disorder or defect cannot be punished.	— In the Netherlands, there is no legal insanity test such as, eg, M'Naghten or the Model Penal Code's test.
Psychiatric and psychological evaluations of defendants are ordered by the judge or prosecution.	— Most evaluations are ordered by the prosecutor. — Defendants increasingly refuse to cooperate, possibly to avoid a court-ordered compulsory admission to a psychiatric institution. This procedure is known as TBS and in most cases it is imposed for an indeterminate length of time. — Defendants may submit to the court a request for a 'second opinion' by a behavioural expert for the defence.
The facts in the case have not yet been established by the court when the legal insanity evaluation takes place.	— The behavioural expert, therefore, does not know whether the defendant has actually committed the crime. In their reports, behavioural experts have to use phrases such as 'If it is proven that the defendant committed the act, then ….'.
Evaluations are usually performed by psychologists or psychiatrists, or both.	— Approximately 4,000 adult defendants are evaluated per year (the Netherlands has a population of almost 17 million). — For TBS, which is the most far-reaching safety/ treatment measure, there must be two reports, one of which must be drafted by a psychiatrist. — As a rule, the experts have to be registered in the NRGD (Netherlands Register of Court Experts), but exceptions can be made, eg because of a particular expert's highly relevant expertise.
Behavioural experts specifically advise the court on (the degree of) the defendant's criminal responsibility.	— Some Dutch authors have criticised this practice, arguing that legal insanity is a legal concept, falling outside the scientific domain of medicine and psychology. This debate is close to the 'ultimate legal issue' discussion in the United States.

(continued)

Table 6.1: *(Continued)*

Characteristic	Remarks
There are five grades of criminal responsibility or insanity: 1. (Full) responsibility 2. Slightly diminished responsibility 3. Diminished responsibility 4. Strongly diminished responsibility 5. Legal insanity or lack of responsibility.	— The recent Guidelines for psychiatrists have replaced the five-level system with a three-level one, including only responsibility, diminished responsibility and insanity. However, there still is a lively debate surrounding this question. — Psychologists still use the five-level system, but the Dutch psychology profession is currently considering a reform. — Article 39 of the Dutch Criminal Code formally applies only to legally insane defendants (level 5). Levels 2, 3 and 4 have evolved in court practice. — Only a small percentage of behavioural experts' evaluations come to the conclusion that the defendant is legally insane (level 5).

IV. Neurolaw and Legal Insanity

Three Research Lines in Neurolaw

In just a few years, neurolaw has become a major field of interdisciplinary investigation. Three basic lines of research can be distinguished.[71]

The first is legal revision. The research question here is whether, and to what extent, neuroscience findings could or should lead to a revision of law and legal practices. An example is the question of free will in light of neuroscience findings. Some authors have argued that, based on neuroscientific studies on human volition, we should abandon the idea that people are 'uncaused causers' acting on their free will.[72] They refer to famous experiments, including Libet's Electroencephalography (EEG) study, which purportedly demonstrates that the conscious intention to act is preceded by characteristic brain activity, the so-called 'readiness potential'.[73] In the 1960s, Kornhuber and Deecke carried out an EEG study and observed that voluntary motor acts are preceded by a characteristic electrical signal in the brain, the *readiness potential* (RP). The RP is already visible at about

---

[71] G Meynen, 'Neurolaw: Neuroscience, Ethics, and Law. Review Essay' (2014) 17 *Ethical Theory and Moral Practice* 819 and G Meynen, 'Neurolaw: Recognizing Opportunities and Challenges for Psychiatry (Editorial)' (2016) 41(1) *Journal of Psychiatry and Neuroscience* 3.

[72] DM Wegner, *The Illusion of Conscious Will* (Cambridge, MA, MIT Press, 2002).

[73] B Libet, 'Do We Have Free Will?' (1999) 6 *Journal of Consciousness Studies* 47 and JA Radder and G Meynen, 'Does the Brain "Initiate" Freely Willed Processes? A Philosophy of Science Critique of Libet-type Experiments and Their Interpretation' (2013) 23 *Theory and Psychology* 3.

800 milliseconds before the motor act occurs.[74] This relatively long time span led neurophysiologist Benjamin Libet to hypothesise that the RP precedes the conscious intention to act.[75] In his now classic 1983 experiment, Libet found that the RP does precede the conscious urge or intention to act by several hundreds of milliseconds.[76] Libet et al concluded in their paper:

[T]he brain evidently 'decides' to initiate or, at the least, prepare to initiate the act at a time before there is any reportable subjective awareness that such a decision has taken place. It is concluded that cerebral initiation even of a spontaneous voluntary act, of the kind studied here, can and usually does begin unconsciously.[77]

Based on this study in combination with other neuroscientific and psychological data, it has been argued that free will is an illusion.[78] Davies emphasised that even though no single neuroscientific experiment univocally showed that human beings are not free agents, there is converging evidence from different disciplines supporting this assertion, and we should revise the law accordingly.[79] Others reject such claims, eg, Morse and, in the Netherlands, Mooij.[80]

The second area of research in neurolaw concerns the potential role of neuroscience in courtroom assessments of defendants, prisoners and perhaps prospective jurors.[81] Neuroscientific knowledge has the potential to inform psychiatric and psychological evaluations of defendants. In the future, neuroscientists may discover that certain psychopathological features in schizophrenia affect human decision making and actions in a way that is highly likely to lead to criminal behaviour. This could be very relevant in the evaluation of a defendant who suffers from schizophrenia. Furthermore, neuroimaging tools and techniques may be of help in evaluating individual defendants.[82] A fundamental question that has

---

[74] Radder and Meynen (n 73).

[75] B Libet, *Mind Time: The Temporal Factor in Consciousness* (Cambridge, MA, Harvard University Press, 2004).

[76] Libet (n 73) and B Libet, 'The Timing of Mental Events: Libet's Experimental Findings and Their Implications' (2002) 11 *Consciousness and Cognition* 291; discussion 304-333.

[77] B Libet, CA Gleason, EW Wright and DK Pearl, 'Time of Conscious Intention to Act in Relation to Onset of Cerebral Activity (Readiness-Potential). The Unconscious Initiation of a Freely Voluntary Act' (1983) 106 *Brain* 623, 640.

[78] S Spence, 'Free Will in the Light of Neuropsychiatry' (1996) 3 *Philosophy, Psychiatry, & Psychology* 75 and Wegner (n 72).

[79] PS Davies, 'Skepticism Concerning Human Agency: Sciences of the Self Versus "Voluntariness" in the Law' in NA Vincent (ed), *Neuroscience and Legal Responsibility* (Oxford, Oxford University Press, 2013) 113–34. See also J Greene and J Cohen, 'For the Law, Neuroscience Changes Nothing and Everything' (2004) 359 *Philosophical Transactions of the Royal Society B* 1775.

[80] See Morse (n 31) and AWM Mooij, 'De toerekeningsvatbaarheid: hoe verder?' (2012) 42 *Delikt en Delinkwent* 36.

[81] JW Buckholtz and DL Faigman 'Promises, Promises for Neuroscience and Law' (2014) 24 *Current Biology* R861; H Greely, 'Mind Reading, Neuroscience, and the Law' in SJ Morse and AL Roskies (eds), *A Primer on Criminal Law and Neuroscience. A Contribution to the Law and Neuroscience Project, Supported by the MacArthur Foundation* (New York, Oxford University Press, 2013).

[82] G Meynen, 'A Neurolaw Perspective on Psychiatric Assessments of Criminal Responsibility: Decision-making, Mental Disorder, and the Brain' (2013) 36 *International Journal of Law and Psychiatry* 93.

so far received relatively little attention is whether, or under what circumstances, neuroscientific tests can be compelled on the defendant.[83]

The third research line concerns neuroscience-based intervention. The most important type of intervention is treatment. Can neuroscience techniques, including Deep Brain Stimulation (DBS), be used to treat defendants who suffer from severe mental disorders and if so, under what conditions? This endeavour is not without its perils. Neuroscience could be used for purposes of behavioural manipulation, which has legal implications. Is it justified to assume that a person who was manipulated into breaking the law should not be held legally responsible? Let us think of a DBS device hacked by cyber criminals.[84] Bublitz and Merkel address such questions.[85]

The three neurolaw domains—legal revision, courtroom assessments and neuroscience-based intervention—are interrelated. For instance, the introduction of a new assessment technique or brain intervention may lead to legal reforms. In turn, legal reforms may lead to new neuroscience research lines and investments, and to the development of new strategies for neuroscientific assessment and intervention techniques.

Two of the three areas of neurolaw are directly relevant to assessments of criminal responsibility, and feature prominently in the Dutch debate on insanity: legal revision and neuroscience-based assessment.

The Neurolaw Debate in the Netherlands

The impact of neuroscience on the free will question is currently under discussion in Dutch forensic psychiatry. Like colleagues elsewhere, Dutch neuroscientists have argued that, based on what we know about the brain, human beings do not have free will.[86] Mooij wrote in 2012:

> It is clear that the theme of free will is of general interest, particularly given the flourishing of the neurosciences, and famous experiments purportedly disproving the existence of free will. This has had an impact on forensic psychiatry. Because diminished accountability—according to the commonly accepted legal view—implies lack of free

---

[83] See MS Pardo and D Patterson, *Minds, Brains, and Law. The Conceptual Foundations of Law and Neuroscience* (New York, Oxford University Press, 2013) and T Nadelhoffer, S Bibas, S Grafton, KA Kiehl, A Mansfield, W Sinnott-Armstrong and M Gazzaniga, 'Neuroprediction, Violence, and the Law: Setting the Stage' (2012) 5 *Neuroethics* 67.

[84] MN Gasson and B Koops, 'Attacking Human Implants: A New Generation of Cybercrime' (2013) 5 *Law, Innovation and Technology* 248.

[85] C Bublitz and R Merkel, 'Guilty Minds in Washed Brains? Manipulation Cases and the Limits of Neuroscientific Excuses in Liberal Legal Orders' in NA Vincent (ed), *Neuroscience and Legal Responsibility* (New York, Oxford University Press, 2013).

[86] V Lamme, *De vrije wil bestaat niet. Over wie er echt de baas is in het brein* (Amsterdam, Bert Bakker, 2010) and DF Swaab, *We Are Our Brains: A Neurobiography of the Brain, from the Womb to Alzheimer's* (New York, Spiegel and Grau, 2014).

will, and, therefore, implicitly presupposes the concept of free will, forensic psychiatrists find it increasingly difficult to make judgments regarding criminal responsibility.[87]

Recent developments in the free will debate changed the way some Dutch forensic psychiatrists perceive their advice to the court about criminal accountability. Different responses to this challenge have been formulated, but the law has not been revised so far.[88] It is my impression that, for a while, free will was 'the' neurolaw topic in the Netherlands. At present, free will seems to be merely one among other neurolaw questions under debate.

We will now discuss more neurolaw subjects, as presented in a recent special issue of a renowned Dutch legal journal, the *NJB*, entitled 'Neurolaw in the Netherlands'.[89] The publication of a special issue dedicated to neurolaw is indicative of strong and growing interest in neurolaw in the Netherlands. In his editorial, Dutch Supreme Court Justice Ybo Buruma writes that 'In the practice of the rule of law, neuroscience offers chances, but also risks that lawyers should not ignore'.[90] This phrase summarises the message of the special issue. Each of the three neurolaw domains listed above is discussed in it.

The first contribution to the special issue concerns the current role of neuroscience (and behavioural genetics) in criminal cases. De Kogel and Westgeest found and analysed 207 rulings from the years 2000 to 2012 in which neuroscientific data played a role, using the nationwide legal rulings database Rechspraak.nl.[91] Most such rulings were cases of serious violence or sexual offences.[92] In 72 of the 207 cases (34.8 per cent), neuroscience was used to assess insanity. This finding may be considered in line with the considerations made by Pardo and Patterson, who argued that legal insanity is 'one of the more plausible avenues by which neuroscience may contribute to the law'.[93] In several of the cases described, defendants were evaluated by a neurologist if neurodegenerative diseases and brain injuries were suspected. In one case, the defendant was an elderly man who had killed his spouse. The neurologist concluded that the defendant suffered from frontal lobe damage and dysfunction, resulting in impulse control problems. The cases in which neuroscience was used to answer the question about legal insanity are

---

[87] Mooij (n 80), my translation.

[88] See G Meynen, 'Vrije wil en forensisch psychiaters die zwijgen over toerekeningsvatbaarheid' (2011) 86 *Nederlands Juristenblad* 1951 and Mooij (n 80).

[89] De Kogel et al (n 3).

[90] Y Buruma, 'Recht en neurowetenschappen' (2013) 45 *Nederlands Juristenblad* 2611.

[91] The database does not include all court rulings, and therefore it may not include all cases in which neuroscientific evidence was admitted in court. As de Kogel and Westgeest state, the criterion for publication on the website www.rechtspraak.nl was 'mainly whether the court ruling was of importance for legal professionals or the wider public'. See also CH de Kogel and EJMC Westgeest, 'Neuroscientific and Behavioral Genetic Information in Criminal Cases in the Netherlands' (2015) *Journal of Law and the Biosciences* 1.

[92] CH de Kogel and L Westgeest, 'Neurobiologische informatie in Nederlandse strafzaken' (2013) 88 *Nederlands Juristenblad* 3132.

[93] Pardo and Patterson (n 83). On neurolaw and psychiatric evaluations of insanity see also Meynen (n 82) and with specific reference to the Dutch context see G Meynen, 'Neurolaw: de relevantie voor de forensische psychiatrie' (2014) 56 *Tijdschrift voor psychiatrie* 597.

different from the more common insanity cases that often involve (non-organic) psychosis. Neuroscience tends to be used to evaluate defendants who are thought to suffer from a 'neurological' disease rather than a 'psychiatric' disorder. De Kogel and colleagues argue for the involvement of more behavioural neurologists in evaluating defendants.[94] They propose establishing 'a (National) Centre for inter-disciplinary forensic evaluations in which behavioural neurologists, clinical neuropsychologists, and psychiatrists collaborate'. This is a valuable suggestion. The number of professions involved could even be extended beyond the three mentioned by including neuropharmacologists, neuroethicists and neurolaw scholars. The National Centre could also organise the training and education of forensic mental health practitioners.[95]

Roef and Verkes discuss the possible effects of medication, in particular antidepressants, on violent behaviour and criminal responsibility.[96] In several high-profile cases in the Netherlands, antidepressants were considered a factor in the genesis of the crime.[97] In one case, the defendant was a woman who killed her daughter and husband in their sleep with an axe. A few days before, she had restarted her treatment with the antidepressant paroxetine.[98] The court judged that her criminal responsibility was severely diminished. However, she was not considered insane. Roef and Verkes make several interesting remarks regarding the use of medication and criminal responsibility. First, the relationship between the use of medication and the commission of a violent crime is hard to prove in individual cases. There are usually more factors that may have contributed to the crime, perhaps in combination. It is difficult to determine the exact impact of medication use on behaviour. However, Roef and Verkes warn that the potential impact should 'not be underestimated, in particular in those cases where there is no history of violence', and when a sudden outburst of violence remains inexplicable based on the disorder alone. If a defendant took a particular type of medication, there most likely was a mental illness as well, for which the medication was prescribed. For instance, antidepressants are prescribed

---

[94] CH de Kogel, P Haselager, C Jonker, F Leone, and L Westgeest, 'Beperkingen van neurowetenschap en gedragsgenetica in de rechtspraktijk' (2013) 88 *Nederlands Juristenblad* 3157—3161.

[95] See also JA Silva, 'The Relevance of Neuroscience to Forensic Psychiatry' (2007) 35 *Journal of the American Academy of Psychiatry and the Law* 6 and JA Silva, 'Forensic Psychiatry, Neuroscience, and the Law' (2009) 37 *Journal of the American Academy of Psychiatry and the Law* 489. Silva emphasises the need to train and educate forensic psychiatrists with respect to neuroscience developments and their applicability in forensic psychiatry.

[96] D Roef and RJ Verkes, 'Medicijngebruik, agressie en strafrechtelijke verantwoordelijkheid' (2013) 45 *Nederlands Juristenblad* 3137.

[97] Bouvy and Liem studied 'the relationship between homicide, suicide and homicide-suicide rates and the rates of antidepressant use by gender and age group' in the Netherlands in the period 1994–2008. They conclude that their findings 'lend no support for an important role of antidepressant use in lethal violence'. See PF Bouvy and M Liem, 'Antidepressants and Lethal Violence in the Netherlands 1994–2008' (2012) 222 *Psychopharmacology (Berl)* 499. Critical remarks in response to this paper were made by D Healy and T Dehue, 'Antidepressants and Lethal Violence in the Netherlands' (2012) 222 *Psychopharmacology (Berl)* 543; author reply 545.

[98] Roef and Verkes (n 96).

following a diagnosis of depression. This may make it even more complicated to determine the exact contribution of each factor to the emergence of the criminal behaviour.[99] Roef and Verkes also make practical recommendations. There is often uncertainty as to whether defendants who claim to have been taking antidepressants actually did take them. Roef and Verkes suggest taking blood samples from defendants shortly after the crime in those cases when the defendant could be using medication.

Another topic discussed in the special journal issue on neurolaw is DBS. This promising technique is discussed from a neurolaw perspective by van de Beek, deputy chief prosecutor, and Denys, professor of psychiatry and one of the pioneers of the use of DBS for the treatment of severe obsessive-compulsive disorder.[100] DBS was first used as a last-resort treatment option for severe movement disorders, in particular Parkinson's disease. For this type of patient, DBS may bring about sudden and substantial improvement. The technique is now becoming available for an increasing number of disorders, albeit mostly in research contexts.[101] DBS has received attention not only for its impressive treatment results, but also for its severe side-effects. In the Netherlands, a patient receiving DBS because of Parkinson's disease developed a manic episode. During the episode he was severely deranged and legally incompetent to make decisions.[102] When the stimulation was turned off he regained his competency, but the Parkinson's symptoms returned with full force. The DBS was turned on again and the Parkinson's symptoms improved, but the manic symptoms returned. A hospital committee decided that the patient should make a choice about whether to receive further DBS treatment while off stimulation. However, when off DBS and competent the patient unequivocally chose to undergo DBS, 'even if this would lead to permanent admission to a psychiatric hospital'. Apparently, he found psychiatric symptoms more bearable than the symptoms of Parkinson's disease. The case has been described in detail by Leentjens and colleagues.[103] Van de Beek and Denys have argued that, in principle, a patient treated with DBS remains responsible for his or her actions, notwithstanding the known possible influence of DBS on behaviour. However, in their view, a psychiatric assessment may in some cases lead to a finding of diminished responsibility for the patient treated with DBS who has committed an offence.

---

[99] ibid.

[100] D Denys, M Mantione, M Figee, P van den Munckhof, F Koerselman, H Westenberg and R Schuurman, 'Deep Brain Stimulation of the Nucleus Accumbens for Treatment-refractory Obsessive-compulsive Disorder' (2010) 67 *Archives of General Psychiatry* 1061.

[101] XL Chen, YY Xiong, GL Xu, and XF Liu, 'Deep Brain Stimulation' (2013) 1 *Journal of Vascular and Interventional neurology* 200.

[102] A competency assessment was performed.

[103] AF Leentjens, V Visser-Vandewalle, Y Temel, FR Verhey, [Manipulation of mental competence: an ethical problem in case of electrical stimulation of the subthalamic nucleus for severe Parkinson's disease] (2004) 148 *Ned Tijdschr Geneeskd* 1394. See also comments on this case by W Glannon, 'Stimulating Brains, Altering Minds' (2009) 35 *Journal of Medical Ethics* 289.

The final contribution is entitled 'Limitations of Neuroscience and Behavioural Genetics in Legal Practice'.[104] The authors discuss the difficulties intrinsic to translating neuroscience findings into information that can help answer a legal question. Many 'inference steps' are required, each involving pitfalls and challenges. Neuroscience is complex, the authors argue, and at present we know very little that could be directly relevant for legal decisions. This picture does justice to the state of affairs. At the same time, the law and legal practice may be complicated as well. Like neuroscientific reasoning, legal verdicts rely on several 'inference steps'. It is critical to dispel the myth that the law and legal reasoning are always straightforward and conceptually accessible while, by contrast, neuroscience is intrinsically arcane and cryptic.[105] However, human intelligence is well able to handle intricate issues requiring several 'inference steps'. In my view, the challenge is to strike the Aristotelian golden mean between over-enthusiasm and excessive criticism regarding possible applications of neuroscience in legal practice, including the evaluation of criminal responsibility.[106]

Recently, in the *Tijdschrift voor psychiatrie* (Dutch Journal of Psychiatry) I discussed the influence of neurolaw developments on forensic psychiatry.[107] I argued that psychiatrists should actively take part in neurolaw research and debates. It will take effort on the part of the psychiatric profession to keep up to date with this rapidly developing field of research. Professor of forensic psychiatry and psychology Koenraadt considers it self-evident that neurolaw is relevant for forensic psychiatry and for the forensic psychiatric profession. He expresses concern that in the future, insufficient attention may be paid to ethical issues related to neuroscience and forensic psychiatry, and that neuroscientific findings may not be considered together with other relevant information.[108] Koenraadt warns against making decisions based solely on purportedly 'solid neuroscience data'. This caveat is very much in line with de Kogel and colleagues.[109]

V. Concluding Observations and Reflections

Two characteristics of legal insanity in the Dutch legal system stand out: the existence of five grades of criminal responsibility and the absence of a statutory

---

[104] De Kogel et al (n 94).

[105] See on this topic also G Meynen, 'Neuroethics of Criminal Responsibility. Mental Disorders Influencing Behavior' in M DeLisi and MG Vaughn (eds), *The Routledge International Handbook of Biosocial Criminology* (Abingdon, Routledge, 2015) 544–57.

[106] Meynen (n 93).

[107] G Meynen, 'Antwoord aan Goethals (Antwoord op Reactie op "Neurolaw: de relevantie voor de forensische psychiatrie" en "Forensisch psychiaters en forensisch psychologen: mind the gap")' (2014) 56 *Tijdschrift voor psychiatrie* 842 and Meynen (n 93).

[108] F Koenraadt, 'Forensisch psychiaters en forensisch psychologen: mind the gap' (2014) 56 *Tijdschr Psychiatr* 605.

[109] De Kogel et al (n 94).

standard defining the criteria for insanity. As in other countries, in the Netherlands there is considerable debate about the regulation of legal insanity and possible reforms. At the moment, the debate concerns primarily the number of grades. The five-level system is by now tried and tested, and it is known to generate practical problems regarding the determination of the exact level of responsibility. Recent professional guidelines for psychiatrists reduced the number of grades from five to three, a step later followed by the Dutch Institute for Forensic Psychiatry and Psychology.[110] Another topic of debate is the fact that Dutch forensic mental health professionals must render an express opinion about the (degree of) criminal responsibility in individual cases, without being able to rely on a statutory standard defining the criteria for insanity.[111]

Dutch legal scholars and the Dutch psychiatric profession consider new developments in neuroscience highly relevant to the determination of insanity in legal and forensic practice. A study showed that in one-third of all instances in which neuroscientific evidence was presented in criminal cases, it was used to purport or refute a claim of legal insanity.[112] In the Dutch context, the use of medication (particularly of antidepressants) and DBS have been discussed in connection with legal insanity. Dutch authors tend to acknowledge the significance of neuroscience for the law, but they also warn against pitfalls and hasty judgements. This approach is consistent with attitudes towards the impact of neuroscience on the law that have emerged in recent influential publications that discuss the question with reference to foreign legal systems.[113]

The involvement of the psychiatric profession in the new neurolaw developments is of paramount importance.[114] De Kogel and Westgeest have shown that legal insanity is the main domain of utilisation of neuroscientific tools in the Dutch criminal justice system.[115] This does not mean that psychiatrists should be expected to possess all the relevant knowledge and expertise. Given the variety and complexity of neurolaw topics, that would be impossible. Rather, collaboration between psychiatrists and neurologists and perhaps other neuro- and mental health experts, is a preferable route and it is already taking place in the Netherlands.[116] This requires that the psychiatrist knows when to consult and

---

[110] Nederlands Instituut voor Forensische Psychiatrie en Psychologie (NIFPP), *Het advies over het toerekenen* (Utrecht, Ministry of Security and Justice, 2014).

[111] G Meynen, 'Een juridische standaard voor ontoerekeningsvatbaarheid?' (2013) 88 *Nederlands Juristenblad* 1384.

[112] De Kogel and Westgeest (n 92).

[113] SJ Morse and AL Roskies (eds), *A Primer on Criminal Law and Neuroscience. A Contribution of the Law and Neuroscience Project, Supported by the MacArthur Foundation* (New York, Oxford University Press, 2013); Pardo and Patterson (n 83); TM Spranger (ed), *International Neurolaw. A Comparative Analysis.* (Heidelberg, Springer, 2012); NA Vincent (ed), *Neuroscience and Legal Responsibility* (New York, Oxford University Press, 2013).

[114] Meynen (n 93).

[115] De Kogel and Westgeest (n 92).

[116] Meynen, 'Antwoord aan Goethals' (n 107).

involve other experts, such as neurologists, neuropsychologists and possibly neuropsychopharmacologists. This is an ambitious venture for the psychiatric profession. Ideally, the psychiatrist should be able to connect and integrate different pieces of neuroscience information regarding a particular defendant. It is to be recommended that a national neurolaw centre be established, which does not currently exist in the Netherlands, for practical purposes and also for research and policy objectives. Neuroscientists, neuroethicists, and behavioural and legal experts could work side by side and confront the intriguing and intricate questions that are bound to emerge in the field of neurolaw.

The major challenge for neurolaw research concerns the fact that although the 'neuro' component in neurolaw, the human brain, is universal, the 'law' component is different across countries.[117] Neuroscience findings concerning memory, impulse control and planning are not bound to a particular jurisdiction or country. Results from a research group in Harvard could be used by a research group or by clinicians in Tokyo, Sydney or Paris.[118] The same is true for neuroscience-based intervention techniques. There is little difference between the DBS technique and its consequences for health in Amsterdam and in Dallas; however, the laws and rules related to the application and possible consequences of this technique may be very different. The admissibility of neuro-techniques in court as a means of evidence depends on rules and regulations of scientific proof in each particular criminal justice system. The *Daubert* and *Frye* standards of admission of scientific proof in the criminal process are highly relevant to neurolaw in the United States[119] but not in the Netherlands. The same is true with regard to the government's authority to compel brain scans in the criminal trial. While Dutch law acknowledges the right to remain silent, in the Dutch jurisdiction there is no equivalent to the elaborate general privilege against self-incrimination laid down in the Fifth Amendment to the US Constitution.

Future legal and policy solutions to vexed issues pertaining to the admission and use of neuroscientific evidence in the context of foreign jurisdictions are not necessarily relevant to the Dutch legal system. Ideally, the questions have to be addressed specifically to the Dutch jurisdiction. Most neurolaw research focuses on the Anglo-American legal context. This constitutes a major challenge for small civil law jurisdictions, including the Netherlands. Nevertheless, although the US and Dutch legal system are different, scholars in the Netherlands may benefit from the type of approach, analysis and argument used by US legal experts, as well as from research in other European countries with legal systems that are relatively similar to the Dutch jurisdiction.

---

[117] See also Meynen (n 93); Meynen, 'Neurolaw: Neuroscience, Ethics, and Law' (n 71).

[118] For similar considerations regarding the differences between jurisdictions and their relevance to scientific progress in forensic psychiatry, see also G Meynen and K Oei, 'Internationalizing Forensic Assessments of Criminal Responsibility' (2011) 30 *Medicine and Law* 529.

[119] Both are tests for admissibility of scientific evidence in US jurisdictions. See JW Parry, 'Expert Evidence and Testimony: Daubert versus Frye' (2004) 28(2) *Mental and Physical Disability Law Reporter* 136.

In conclusion, the regulation of legal insanity in the Netherlands and the role of neuroscientific evidence in court practice is highly debated, and in full development. Neurolaw has taken off, both in research and in legal practice. Authors generally warn against over-enthusiasm about neuroscience; at the same time, a sense of urgency emerges from many contributions.

Bibliography

Bal, P and Koenraadt, F, 'Dutch Criminal Law and Procedure: A Bird's Eye View' in F Koenraadt, AWM Mooij and JML van Mulbregt (eds), *The Mental Condition in Criminal Law* (Amsterdam, Dutch University Press, 2007) 13–35.

Becker, RF, 'The Evolution of Insanity Standards' (2003) 18 *Journal of Police and Criminal Psychology* 41.

Beukers, M, 'Gedragsdeskundige rapportage in strafzaken. Waar liggen de grenzen?' (2005) *Strafblad* 488.

Blok, GT, Beurs, E de, Ranitz, AG de and Rinne, T, [The current psychometric state of risk assessment scales for adults in the Netherlands] (2010) 52 *Tijdschr Psychiatr* 331.

Bouvy, PF and Liem, M, 'Antidepressants and Lethal Violence in the Netherlands 1994–2008' (2012) 222 *Psychopharmacology (Berl)* 499. doi: 10.1007/s00213-012-2668-2.

Braham, LG, Trower, P and Birchwood, M, 'Acting on Command Hallucinations and Dangerous Behavior: A Critique of the Major Findings in the Last Decade' (2004) 24 *Clinical Psychology Review* 513. doi: 10.1016/j.cpr.2004.04.002.

Brants, C, 'Justice Done and Seen to Be Done? The Institutionalized Relationship between the Press and the Criminal Justice System in the Netherlands' (1993) 3 *International Criminal Justice Review* 60.

Bublitz, C and Merkel, R, 'Guilty Minds in Washed Brains? Manipulation Cases and the Limits of Neuroscientific Excuses in Liberal Legal Orders' in NA Vincent (ed), *Neuroscience and Legal Responsibility* (New York, Oxford University Press, 2013).

Bucci, S, Birchwood, M, Twist, L, Tarrier, N, Emsley, R and Haddock, G, 'Predicting Compliance with Command Hallucinations: Anger, Impulsivity and Appraisals of Voices' Power and Intent' (2013) 147 *Schizophrenia Research* 163. doi: 10.1016/j.schres.2013.02.037.

Buchanan, A, 'Psychiatric Evidence on the Ultimate Issue' (2006) 34 *Journal of the American Academy of Psychiatry and the Law* 14.

Buckholtz, JW and Faigman, DL, 'Promises, Promises for Neuroscience and Law' (2014) 24 *Current Biology* R861–867. doi: 10.1016/j.cub.2014.07.057.

Buruma, Y, 'Recht en neurowetenschappen' (2013) 45 *Nederlands Juristenblad* 2611.

Chen, XL, Xiong, YY, Xu, GL and Liu, XF, 'Deep Brain Stimulation' (2013) 1 *Journal of Vascular and Interventional neurology* 200. doi: 10.1159/000353121.

Davies, PS, 'Skepticism Concerning Human Agency: Sciences of the Self Versus "Voluntariness" in the Law' in NA Vincent (ed), *Neuroscience and Legal Responsibility* (Oxford, Oxford University Press, 2013) 113–34.

Denys, D, Mantione, M, Figee, M, Munckhof, P van den, Koerselman, F, Westenberg H and Schuurman, R, 'Deep Brain Stimulation of the Nucleus Accumbens for Treatment-refractory Obsessive-compulsive Disorder' (2010) 67 *Archives of General Psychiatry* 1061. doi: 10.1001/archgenpsychiatry.2010.122.

Drost, M, 'Psychiatric Assessment after Every Six Years of the TBS Order in the Netherlands' (2006) 29 *International Journal of Law and Psychiatry* 257. doi: 10.1016/j.ijlp.2005.04.006

Elliott, C, *The Rules of Insanity: Moral Responsibility and the Mentally Ill Offender* (Albany, NY, State University of New York Press, 1996)

Firestone, MH, 'Psychiatric Patients and Forensic Psychiatry' in SS Sanbar (ed), *Legal Medicine*, 7th edn (Philadelphia, PA, Mosby Elsevier, 2007).

Gasson, MN and Koops, B, 'Attacking Human Implants: A New Generation of Cybercrime' (2013) 5 *Law, Innovation and Technology* 248.

Gerber, RJ, 'Is the Insanity Test Insane?' (1975) *American Journal of Jurisprudence* 111.

Glannon, W, 'Stimulating Brains, Altering Minds' (2009) 35 *Journal of Medical Ethics* 289. doi: 10.1136/jme.2008.027789.

Greely, H, 'Mind Reading, Neuroscience, and the Law' in SJ Morse and AL Roskies (eds), *A Primer on Criminal Law and Neuroscience. A Contribution to the Law and Neuroscience Project, Supported by the MacArthur Foundation* (New York, Oxford University Press, 2013).

Greene, J and Cohen, J, 'For the Law, Neuroscience Changes Nothing and Everything' (2004) 359 *Philosophical Transactions of the Royal Society B* 1775. doi: 10.1098/rstb.2004.1546.

Healy, D and Dehue, T, 'Antidepressants and Lethal Violence in the Netherlands' (2012) 222 *Psychopharmacology (Berl)* 543; author reply 545. doi: 10.1007/s00213-012-2764-3.

Hullu, J de, *Materieel strafrecht. Over algemene leerstukken van strafrechtelijke aansprakelijkheid naar Nederlands recht* (Deventer, Kluwer, 2012).

Hummelen, JW and Jong, DH de, 'Toerekeningsvatbaarheid en toerekenen: de conclusie van de gedragsdeskundige versus het oordeel van de strafrechter' in HB Krans, AT Marseille, F Vellinga-Schootstra and PC Westerman (eds), *De deskundige in het recht* (Paris, Zutphen, 2011) 145–55.

Kalis, A and Meynen, G, 'Mental Disorder and Legal Responsibility: The Relevance of Stages of Decision Making' (2014) 37 *International Journal of Law and Psychiatry* 601. doi: 10.1016/j.ijlp.2014.02.034.

Knoll, JL and Resnick, PJ, 'Insanity Defense Evaluations: Toward a Model for Evidence-Based Practice' (2008) 8 *Brief Treatment and Crisis Intervention* 92.

Koenraadt, F, 'Forensisch psychiaters en forensisch psychologen: mind the gap' (2014) 56 *Tijdschr Psychiatr* 605.

Koenraadt, F, Mooij, AWM and Van Mulbregt, JML (eds), *De persoon van de verdachte. De rapportage pro Justitia vanuit het Pieter Baan Centrum* (Utrecht, Kluwer, 2004).

Kogel, CH de, Beek, P van de, Leeuw, F, Meynen, G and Westgeest, L, 'Themanummer Neurolaw in Nederland' (2013) 88 *Nederlands Juristenblad* 3130.

Kogel, CH de, Haselager, P, Jonker, C, Leone, F and Westgeest, L, 'Beperkingen van neurowetenschap en gedragsgenetica in de rechtspraktijk' (2013) 88 *Nederlands Juristenblad* 3157.

Kogel CH de and Westgeest L, 'Neurobiologische informatie in Nederlandse strafzaken' (2013) 88 *Nederlands Juristenblad* 3132.

Kogel, CH de and Westgeest, EJMC, 'Neuroscientific and Behavioral Genetic Information in Criminal Cases in the Netherlands' (2015) *Journal of Law and the Biosciences* 1.

Kooijmans, K, *Op maat geregeld. Een onderzoek naar de grondslag en de normering van de strafrechtelijke maatregel* (Deventer, Kluwer, 2002).

Kordelaar, WF van, 'Het psychologisch onderzoek pro Justitia' in BCM Raes and FAM Bakker (eds), *De psychiatrie in het Nederlandse recht* (Deventer, Kluwer, 2012).

Kuijck, YAJM van, 'Juridische kaders voor de geestelijke gezondheidszorg van de forensische patient' in H Groen, M Drost and HLI Nijman (eds), *Handboek Forensische geestelijke gezondheidszorg.* (Utrecht, De Tijdstroom, 2011).

Lamme, V, *De vrije wil bestaat niet. Over wie er echt de baas is in het brein* (Amsterdam, Bert Bakker, 2010).

Leentjens, AF, Visser-Vandewalle, V, Temel, Y and Verhey, FR, [Manipulation of mental competence: an ethical problem in case of electrical stimulation of the subthalamic nucleus for severe Parkinson's disease] (2004) 148 *Ned Tijdschr Geneeskd* 1394.

Leij, JB van der, Jackson, JL, Malsch, M and Nijboer, JF, 'Residential Mental Health Assessment within Dutch Criminal Cases: A Discussion' (2001) 19 *Behavioral Sciences and the Law* 691.

Libet, B, 'Do We Have Free Will?' (1999) 6 *Journal of Consciousness Studies* 47.

Libet, B, 'The Timing of Mental Events: Libet's Experimental Findings and Their Implications' (2002) 11 *Consciousness and Cognition* 291; discussion 304–333.

Libet, B, *Mind Time: The Temporal Factor in Consciousness* (Cambridge, MA, Harvard University Press, 2004).

Libet, B, Gleason, CA, Wright EW and Pearl, DK, 'Time of Conscious Intention to Act in Relation to Onset of Cerebral Activity (Readiness-potential). The Unconscious Initiation of a Freely Voluntary Act' (1983) 106 *Brain* 623.

Mackor, AR, 'The Autonomy of Criminal Judges in Determining the Disorder and the Risk of Recidivism—Some Reflection on the Hoogerheide Case' in TI Oei and MS Groenhuijsen (eds), *Progression in Forensic Psychiatry. About Boundaries* (Deventer, Kluwer, 2012) 617–28.

Melle, I, 'The Breivik Case and What Psychiatrists Can Learn from It' (2013) 12 *World Psychiatry* 16. doi: 10.1002/wps.20002.

Meynen, G, 'Free Will and Mental Disorder: Exploring the Relationship' (2010) 31 *Theoretical Medicine and Bioethics* 429. doi: 10.1007/s11017-010-9158-5.

Meynen, G, 'Vrije wil en forensisch psychiaters die zwijgen over toerekeningsvatbaarheid' (2011) 86 *Nederlands Juristenblad* 1951.

Meynen, G, 'An Ethical Framework for Assessments of Criminal Responsibility: Applying Susan Wolf's Account of Sanity to Forensic Psychiatry' (2012) 35 *International Journal of Law and Psychiatry* 298. doi: 10.1016/j.ijlp.2012.04.011.

Meynen, G, 'A Neurolaw Perspective on Psychiatric Assessments of Criminal Responsibility: Decision-making, Mental Disorder, and the Brain' (2013) 36 *International Journal of Law and Psychiatry* 93. doi: 10.1016/j.ijlp.2013.01.001.

Meynen, G, 'Een juridische standaard voor ontoerekeningsvatbaarheid?' (2013) 88 *Nederlands Juristenblad* 1384.

Meynen, G, 'Antwoord aan Goethals (Antwoord op Reactie op "Neurolaw: de relevantie voor de forensische psychiatrie" en "Forensisch psychiaters en forensisch psychologen: mind the gap")' (2014) 56 *Tijdschrift voor psychiatrie* 842.

Meynen, G, 'Neurolaw: de relevantie voor de forensische psychiatrie' (2014) 56 *Tijdschrift voor psychiatrie* 597.

Meynen, G, 'Neurolaw: Neuroscience, Ethics, and Law. Review Essay' (2014) 17 *Ethical Theory and Moral Practice* 819. doi: 10.1007/s10677-014-9501-4.

Meynen, G, 'How Mental Disorders Can Compromise the Will' in W Glannon (ed), *Free Will and the Brain* (Cambridge, Cambridge University Press, 2015).

Meynen, G, 'Neuroethics of Criminal Responsibility. Mental Disorders Influencing Behavior' in M DeLisi and MG Vaughn (eds), *The Routledge International Handbook of Biosocial Criminology* (Abingdon, Routledge, 2015) 544–57.

Meynen, G, 'Neurolaw: Recognizing Opportunities and Challenges for Psychiatry (Editorial)' (2016) 41(1) *Journal of Psychiatry and Neuroscience* 3.

Meynen, G and Oei, K, 'Internationalizing Forensic Assessments of Criminal Responsibility' (2011) 30 *Medicine and Law* 529.

Mooij, AWM, 'De toerekeningsvatbaarheid: hoe verder?' (2012) 42 *Delikt en Delinkwent* 36.

Morse, SJ, 'Rationality and Responsibility' (2000) 74 *Southern California Law Review* 251.

Morse, SJ, 'The Non-Problem of Free Will in Forensic Psychiatry and Psychology' (2007) 25 Behavioral Sciences and the Law 203.

Morse SJ and Roskies, AL (eds), *A Primer on Criminal Law and Neuroscience. A Contribution of the Law and Neuroscience Project, Supported by the MacArthur Foundation* (New York, Oxford University Press, 2013).

Nadelhoffer, T, Bibas, S, Grafton, S, Kiehl, KA, Mansfield, A, Sinnott-Armstrong, W and Gazzaniga, M, 'Neuroprediction, Violence, and the Law: Setting the Stage' (2012) 5 *Neuroethics* 67.

Nederlands Instituut voor Forensische Psychiatrie en Psychologie (NIFPP), *Jaarbericht* (Utrecht, Ministry of Security and Justice, 2012).

Nederlands Instituut voor Forensische Psychiatrie en Psychologie (NIFPP), *Het advies over het toerekenen* (Utrecht, Ministry of Security and Justice, 2014).

Nolet, H and Verstappen, V, 'Behandeling tbs'er begint te laat' [Treatment of TBS-convicts starts too late] (2014) 37 *Medisch Contact* 1732.

NVvP, *Richtlijn Psychiatrisch onderzoek en rapportage in strafzaken* (Utrecht, De Tijdstroom, 2012).

Panhuis, PJA van, 'De vraagstelling in de Pro Justitia rapportage opnieuw bekeken' 7 (2000) *Proces* 103.

Pardo, MS and Patterson, D, *Minds, Brains, and Law. The Conceptual Foundations of Law and Neuroscience* (New York, Oxford University Press, 2013).

Parry, JW, 'Expert Evidence and Testimony: Daubert versus Frye' (2004) 28(2) *Mental and Physical Disability Law Reporter* 136.

Penney, S, 'Impulse Control and Criminal Responsibility: Lessons from Neuroscience' (2012) 35 *International Journal of Law and Psychiatry* 99. doi: 10.1016/j.ijlp.2011.12.004.

Radder, JA and Meynen, G, 'Does the Brain "Initiate" Freely Willed Processes? A Philosophy of Science Critique of Libet-type Experiments and Their Interpretation' (2013) 23 *Theory and Psychology* 3.

Radovic, S, Meynen G and Bennet, T, 'Introducing a Standard of Legal Insanity: The Case of Sweden Compared to the Netherlands' (2015) 40 *International Journal of Law and Psychiatry* 43.

Roef, D and Verkes, RJ, 'Medicijngebruik, agressie en strafrechtelijke verantwoordelijkheid' (2013) 45 *Nederlands Juristenblad* 3137.

Silva, JA, 'The Relevance of Neuroscience to Forensic Psychiatry' (2007) 35 *Journal of the American Academy of Psychiatry and the Law* 6.

Silva, JA, 'Forensic Psychiatry, Neuroscience, and the Law' (2009) 37 *Journal of the American Academy of Psychiatry and the Law* 489.

Sinnott-Armstrong, W and Levy, K, 'Insanity Defenses' in J Deigh and D Dolinko (eds), *The Oxford Handbook of Philosophy of Criminal Law* (New York, Oxford University Press, 2011).

Spence, S, 'Free Will in the Light of Neuropsychiatry' (1996) 3 *Philosophy, Psychiatry, & Psychology* 75.

Swaab, DF, *We Are Our Brains: A Neurobiography of the Brain, from the Womb to Alzheimer's* (New York, Spiegel and Grau, 2014).

Tak, PJP, *The Dutch Criminal Justice System. Organization and Operation* (The Hague, WODC, 2003).

Van Dijk, EMH and Brouwers, M, *Daling opleggingen tbs met dwangverpleging. Ontwikkelingen en achtergronden. Memorandum-1* (The Hague, WODC, 2011).

Van Marle, HJC, 'Forensic Psychiatric Services in the Netherlands' (2000) 23 *International Journal of Law and Psychiatry* 515.

Van Marle, HJC, 'The Dutch Entrustment Act (TBS): Its Principles and Innovations' (2002) 1 *International Journal of Forensic Mental Health* 83.

Van Marle, HJC, 'Het strafrechtelijk psychiatrisch gedragskundigenonderzoek ("pro Justitia")' in BCM Raes and FAM Bakker (eds), *De psychiatrie in het Nederlandse recht* (Deventer, Kluwer, 2012).

Veer, TS van der and Canton, WJ, 'Pro Justitia-rapportage' in H Groen, M Drost and HLI Nijman (eds), *Handboek Forensische geestelijke gezondheidszorg* (Utrecht, De Tijdstroom, 2011).

Vincent, VA (ed), *Neuroscience and Legal Responsibility* (New York, Oxford University Press, 2013).

Wegner, DM, *The Illusion of Conscious Will* (Cambridge, MA, MIT Press, 2002).

Wolf, S, 'Sanity and the Metaphysics of Responsibility' in F Schoeman (ed), *Responsibility, Character and the Emotions* (Cambridge, Cambridge University Press, 1987) 46–62.

7

On the Abolition and Reintroduction of Legal Insanity in Sweden[*]

TOVA BENNET AND SUSANNA RADOVIC

I. Introduction

Under Swedish criminal law, individuals are considered legally responsible and liable for their intentional unlawful actions, regardless of their mental state at the time of the crime. The current Penal Code drafted in 1962 came into force in 1965 and since then there has been no possibility of acquittal on the basis of legal insanity in the Swedish criminal justice system.[1] All defendants are treated as if sane, and are subjected to the same evaluation of intent (*mens rea*). If the requirements for intent are fulfilled, the defendant is convicted.

The above does not mean that mental state is of marginal relevance in Swedish law. The mental state of the defendant plays a critical role for the choice of sanction. The Penal Code prohibits the courts from sentencing an offender to imprisonment if the crime was committed under the influence of a 'severe mental disorder' (*allvarlig psykisk störning*). The sanction in that case is compulsory psychiatric care. The Swedish system is exceptional in this respect. Only Greenland,

[*] We would like to thank The Swedish National Board of Forensic Medicine for partly financing the empirical study described in this chapter, and Marianne Kristiansson, Peter Andiné and Olof Svensson for sharing their medical and psychological expertise.

[1] The Swedish Penal Code of 1864 employed the term 'tillräknelighet', which we have translated as 'accountability'. Other possible translations could be 'imputability', as in C Lernestedt, 'Insanity and the "Gap" in the Law: Swedish Criminal Law Rides Again' (2009) 54 *Scandinavian Studies in Law* 79. Another possible translation is 'capacity of liability' (SOU (Swedish Government Official Reports) 2002:3 *Psykisk störning, brott och ansvar* [Mental disorder, crime and responsibility]). To be held liable, the defendant had to be found accountable. Swedish law has never known a linguistic equivalent of the English phrase 'legal insanity', nor is the phrase used in the discussions of a possible new law. The reason may be that in the proposed legal regulation, legal insanity is not an excuse in the common law sense of the word. A forensic psychiatric evaluation is always ordered by the court, and the question of accountability can be raised by any party in the process. In every other aspect, a verdict of unaccountability in the Swedish legal context is equivalent to a legal insanity verdict in most other jurisdictions. Therefore, we use 'legally insane' and 'unaccountable' synonymously. A general discussion of the adequacy of the concept 'legal insanity' can be found in the concluding remarks.

and the States of Montana, Idaho, Utah and Kansas in the United States, have a similar regulation of legal responsibility.

The chapter starts with a presentation of the political, jurisprudential and scientific debate that preceded the formulation of the 1962 Penal Code. We then proceed to describe the debate that followed the legal change and to examine the many governmental reports that suggested a reintroduction of legal insanity or 'accountability' in Swedish criminal law. We will focus on the two most recent proposals for a new standard of accountability, presented in 2002 and 2012.

In subsequent sections, we present and discuss an empirical study that we conducted of forensic psychiatric court expert evaluations. The results of our study have ramifications for how the concept of legal insanity might be handled, if it were to be introduced into the Swedish criminal justice system.

II. Mental Disorder and Crime in Sweden

Care and Protection. The Introduction of the 1962 Penal Code

The Swedish Penal Code of 1864, which preceded the current penal code, distinguished between 'accountable' (*tillräkneliga*) and 'unaccountable' (*otillräkneliga*) defendants. A defendant who committed an unlawful act 'under the influence of insanity, mental deficiency or another mental abnormality of such a profound nature, that it must be considered on a par with insanity' was considered unaccountable and not liable for the act.[2]

The distinction between 'accountable' and 'unaccountable' defendants was subjected to extensive criticism, starting in the early twentieth century, coming primarily from the psychiatric profession. The dominating voice was that of Olof Kinberg (1873–1960), the first professor of forensic psychiatry in Sweden and a subscriber to the Positive School of criminology. According to Kinberg, medical science had shown that human actions are always the result of sufficient causes. He contended that the distinction between 'free agents' who should be held responsible for their actions and 'non-free agents' who should not, was based on metaphysical speculations rather than science. Kinberg argued that the concept of 'guilt' (*skuld*) should be discarded in a modern legal system, along with the idea that the function of punishment is retribution. Legal reactions to crime should aim to crime prevention and public protection and not be based on principles dependent on the metaphysical notion of free will.[3]

In the preparatory works of the 1962 Penal Code it was, however, argued that the concept of accountability should be discarded primarily for practical reasons.

---

[2] Penal Code, 1946, 5:5. Our translation. The original text of the provision reads as follows: 'under inflytande av sinnessjukdom, sinnesslöhet eller annan själslig abnormitet av så djupgående natur att den måste anses jämställd med sinnessjukdom.'
[3] O Kinberg, *Basic Problems of Criminology* (Copenhagen, Levin & Munksgaard, 1935) 71–72.

It was maintained that the most compelling argument against holding severely mentally disordered criminal offenders accountable was the belief that they should not be imprisoned. With the introduction of forensic psychiatric care as a penal sanction, the need for distinguishing between the accountable and the unaccountable was no longer pressing.[4] The considerations that led to the reform were later reported by Ivar Strahl (1899–1987), Professor of Criminal Law in Uppsala. He concluded that the legislator had chosen to take a humanitarian and practical perspective, rather than a philosophical one.[5]

Current Law

According to the current Penal Code (*Brottsbalken*, BrB) 1:2, unless otherwise stated in the law, an act shall be regarded as a crime only if committed intentionally. Liability for negligence and strict liability are specifically provided for in the law. The requirement for 'intent' is part of the mental element (*mens rea*). The *mens rea* and the 'unlawful act' (*actus reus*) constitute the two necessary elements of a crime. The requirements for intent are not specified in the law, they are instead defined in jurisprudence and case law. Different forms of intent have been described, all including a cognitive and a volitional criterion. The definition of the minimum requirement for intent, the 'indifference intent' (*likgiltighetsuppsåt*), was laid down in a 2004 Supreme Court ruling.[6] The defendant is required to have had an insight into, or an understanding of, the criminal act, including knowledge of its possible consequences. Additionally, the defendant must have been at least indifferent to the realisation of the consequences of the act. The cognitive criterion is often described as a requirement of a 'sufficient' degree of awareness of the circumstances and consequences of the act.[7]

The intent requirement is identical for all defendants. The criteria for the assessment remain the same, regardless of the mental state of the defendant at the time of the crime. This assessment can, however, be difficult if the defendant suffers from a severe mental disorder, such as psychotic delusions. The Supreme Court has discussed this issue in several cases. In a 2004 case,[8] the Court concluded that defendants suffering from a severe mental disorder are able to commit crimes intentionally if their mental capacities are sufficient to fulfil the criminal law requirements for intent. While the assessment may be more difficult to make in practice, the basic requirements should be interpreted in the same manner as

---

[4] An account of the discussion preceding the enactment of the Penal Code can be found in Lernestedt (n 1).

[5] I Strahl, *Allmän straffrätt i vad angår brotten* (Stockholm, Nordstedt, 1976) 77.

[6] Supreme Court of Sweden, 6 April 2004, Judgment in Case B 4189-03, reported in NJA 2004 p 176.

[7] See P Asp, M Ulväng and N Jareborg, *Kriminalrättens grunder* (Uppsala, Iustus, 2003) 275.

[8] Supreme Court of Sweden, 2 December 2004, Judgment in Case B 3454-04, reported in NJA 2004 p 702.

for any defendant. The Court held that 'there is no [criminal] intent if a normal person who had the same conception of the facts as the mentally disordered person would not have been regarded as having acted with intent'.[9]

The criterion is originally found in the commentaries to the 1962 Penal Code. The Court further argued that, in most cases, the application of this criterion would lead to the conclusion that the defendant acted with intent. This statement was commented on again in another case, where the Supreme Court pointed out that the criterion should not be understood as implying that intent assessments of defendants with a mental disorder should be performed less rigorously than for other defendants.[10]

Compulsory Psychiatric Care as a Sanction

The mental state of the defendant is of importance primarily when it comes to the choice of sanction. Chapters 30 and 31 of the Penal Code regulate sanctions in cases where the defendant is found to suffer from a mental disorder.

BrB 31:3 regulates sentencing to forensic psychiatric care:

> If a person who has committed a crime for which the sanction cannot be limited to a fine suffers from a severe mental disorder, the court may commit him to forensic psychiatric care if, with regard to his mental condition and other personal circumstances, admittance to an institution for psychiatric care combined with deprivation of liberty and other coercive measures, is called for.[11]

Until 2008, BrB 30:6 stated:[12]

> A person who commits a crime under the influence of a severe mental disorder may not be sentenced to imprisonment.
>
> If, in such a case, the court also considers that no other sanction should be imposed, the accused shall go free from sanction.[13]

The law is applicable to defendants who are found to suffer from a severe mental disorder, regardless of the crime committed, with the sole exception of

---

[9] Our translation. The original text of the provision reads as follows:
Principen brukar anses vara att uppsåt inte föreligger, om en normal människa, som hade samma föreställning om sakförhållandena som den psykiskt störde, inte skulle ha ansetts handla uppsåtligt, och det anses att prövningen av uppsåtsfrågan i de flesta fall torde ge till resultat att uppsåt föreligger.

[10] Supreme Court of Sweden, 7 March 2012, Judgment in Case B 4234-11, reported in NJA 2012 p 45.

[11] Our translation. The original text of the provision reads as follows:
Lider den som har begått ett brott, för vilket påföljden inte bedöms kunna stanna vid böter, av en allvarlig psykisk störning, får rätten överlämna honom till rättspsykiatrisk vård, om det med hänsyn till hans psykiska tillstånd och personliga förhållanden i övrigt är påkallat att han är intagen på en sjukvårdsinrättning för psykiatrisk vård, som är förenad med frihetsberövande och annat tvång.

[12] The 2008 amendment is presented separately below.

[13] Our translation. The original text of the provision reads as follows:
Den som har begått ett brott under påverkan av en allvarlig psykisk störning får inte dömas till fängelse. Om rätten i ett sådant fall finner att inte heller någon annan påföljd bör ådömas, skall den tilltalade vara fri från påföljd.

minor crimes sanctioned with a fine. The courts make their decisions on the basis of a forensic psychiatric expert opinion, issued by a team of experts at the National Board of Forensic Medicine. The Board is a state authority and a branch of the Ministry of Justice and provides expert opinions for the police, the prosecutors and the courts in the areas of forensic medicine, forensic psychiatry, forensic chemistry and forensic genetics.

The forensic psychiatric report is the result of a team forensic psychiatric investigation. The team includes a specialist in forensic psychiatry, a forensic psychologist, a forensic social worker and a representative of the psychiatric ward staff. The evaluation normally extends over a period of four to six weeks. Most defendants (75 per cent) are in custody and evaluated as inpatients. Approximately 500 evaluations are conducted each year and circa 300 individuals per year are sentenced to compulsory psychiatric care.[14] One task of the team is to render an opinion on whether the defendant committed the alleged offence under the influence of a severe mental disorder. The team also assesses whether the defendant suffers from a severe mental disorder at the time of the investigation and is thus in need of compulsory psychiatric care. The report is handed over to the court as a basis for the final judgement, which is made independently by the court.

'Severe mental disorder' is a medico-legal concept, and the basic requirement for compulsory psychiatric care, both in criminal and administrative law. The medical conditions representing severe mental disorders are primarily psychoses. However, in some cases severe dementia, depression with suicidal ideation and personality disorders with psychotic episodes can also constitute 'severe mental disorder' under Swedish law. Whether a mental disorder should be regarded as severe in the medico-legal sense depends on both its nature and degree. For example, schizophrenia is considered severe by nature but not always by degree, while depression is not severe by nature, but may be severe by degree.[15]

Problems, Criticism and the Beginnings of a Change

After the 1962 reform, the assessment of criminal intent for defendants found to suffer from a mental disorder proved to be difficult in practice. A particularly problematic situation occurs when the defendant suffers from a temporary state of insanity. The 1864 Penal Code stated that temporary insanity should exclude liability, and the preparatory documents of the 1962 Penal Code show that there was no intention to change this rule.[16] The objective of the abolition of legal

---

[14] Rättsmedicinalverket, *Årsredovisning* (Annual Report) 2014 (Stockholm, Rättsmedicinalverket, 2014).
[15] Prop (Government Legislative Bill) 1990/91:58. *Psykiatrisk tvångsvård* (Compulsory psychiatric care) p 85.
[16] See for example Prop 1962:10 p 576.

accountability in 1962 was to enable the courts to sentence mentally disordered offenders to psychiatric care. Offenders suffering from temporary insanity at the time of the crime were thought not to need that type of care. No specific regulation regarding the temporarily insane was introduced. It was instead taken for granted that temporarily insane offenders would not fulfil the requirement for intent and would thus be acquitted. However, this did not happen in court practice and the problems created by the lack of regulation of temporary insanity were pointed out early on.[17]

During the decades following the introduction of the Penal Code, several governmental committees were appointed to investigate the question of criminal liability for mentally disordered offenders. Governmental reports were presented in 1977, 1984, 1986, and 1988 discussing, among other matters, the legal definition of mental disorder and the principle of proportionality between crime and sanction. Under the 1962 regulation, a severe crime could result in nothing more than a few months of psychiatric care, while a minor offence could lead to several years of incarceration. It was also pointed out that the 1962 regulation resulted in systematic conflicts between the need for care of the offender and the exigency to ensure public protection; patients were at risk of being held within the forensic psychiatric system for a longer period of time than was justified by their need for mental health care.

Furthermore, pre-1962 conceptions of criminal responsibility and mental disorder, and of criminal sanctions as retribution, were still very much present in the discussion, albeit implicitly. One example will illustrate this. The 1984 committee suggested that, in line with the principle of proportionality, imprisonment should be made available as a sanction for severely mentally disordered offenders, but not for 'the small number of defendants who were so severely mentally disordered when they committed the crime, that it would be unreasonable, from an ideological point of view, to sentence them to imprisonment'.[18]

The 1988 committee expressly stated that a return to the rules in force before 1962 would be theoretically as well as practically appealing.[19] However, the Committee concluded that making detailed suggestions for legal change would not fall within the scope of its mandate. The Committee also put forward a proposal to introduce exemption from liability in cases of temporary insanity. The proposal did not become law, even though the legal and political consensus at the time was that it is in principle wrong to hold the temporarily insane criminally liable.

---

[17] N Jareborg, *Uppsåt och oaktsamhet* (Uppsala, Iustus, 1986) 38.
[18] SOU (Swedish Government Official Reports) 1984:64 *Psykiatrin, tvånget och rättssäkerheten* (Psychiatry, coercion and legal security) p 30. Our translation. The original text reads as follows: 'Det finns ett fåtal människor som är så allvarligt psykiskt störda när de begår brott att det ur straffrättsideologisk synpunkt skulle vara orimligt att döma dem till fängelse'.
[19] SOU (Swedish Government Official Reports) 1988:7 *Om legalitetsprincipen och om allmänna grunder för ansvarsfrihet* [About the principle of legality and about general grounds for exemption from liability] p 162.

It was considered unacceptable to have different rules regarding liability for crimes committed during a state of temporary insanity and crimes committed under the influence of a chronic or long-term mental condition.

In 1996 another governmental report was presented, entitled SOU 1996:185 *The limits of criminal liability (Straffansvarets gränser)*. The report includes a proposal to reintroduce the concept of accountability in Swedish criminal law. At the same time, the committee that drafted the report contended that the issue of legal accountability needed further consideration. The new legal accountability standard suggested in the 1996 report reads as follows:

> If an act is committed under the influence of a severe mental disorder or temporary insanity, the act does not constitute a crime, provided the defendant himself did not cause the [mental] condition and, as a consequence of the [mental] condition, lacked a basic capacity of judgement or the capacity to control his behaviour.[20]

The First Proposal for a Reform

In 1999 yet another committee was appointed to draft a reform of criminal liability rules for mentally disordered offenders. This resulted in the first comprehensive legislative proposal on legal insanity and was presented in 2002 and named SOU 2002:3 *Mental disorder, crime and responsibility (Psykisk störning, brott och ansvar)*. The report includes a standard for accountability, as well as a model system of criminal sanctions and public protective measures for mentally disordered offenders.

The Need for a Reform

The committee presents the arguments for reforming accountability, nicely summarising the legal and political debate that followed the enactment of the 1962 Penal Code. The Code had given rise to problems pertaining to psychiatric care, criminal law and public protection.

Regarding psychiatric care, the 2002 report includes a discussion of *special court supervision*.[21] The regulation of special court supervision can lead to offenders remaining in forensic psychiatric care when they no longer fulfil the medical requirements for compulsory psychiatric care. Other problems mentioned in the

---

[20] SOU (Swedish Government Official Reports) 1996:185 *Straffansvarets gränser* [The limits of criminal liability] p 581. Our translation. The original text reads as follows:
Begås en gärning under påverkan av en allvarlig psykisk störning eller en tillfällig sinnesförvirring utgör gärningen inte brott, om gärningsmannen inte själv vållat tillståndet och han till följd av detta har saknat omdömesförmåga eller förmåga att kontrollera sitt handlande.

[21] The court can impose special court supervision on offenders sentenced to compulsory psychiatric care if there is a perceived risk of relapse into serious criminality. Changes in safety measures including outpatient treatment, conditional release, as well as discharge, must be approved by an administrative court after consultation with the prosecutor.

report are the unsuitability of penal institutions to provide psychiatric care, as well as issues related to the principle of proportionality. For defendants found to have a severe mental disorder, even a minor offence can lead to an extensive time in institutional care, which also entails high societal costs. The committee questioned the ability of the current criminal justice apparatus to satisfy the need for care in an ethically appropriate way.

The criminal justice issues discussed in the report are of theoretical, ideological and practical nature. The attribution of criminal responsibility to defendants who had a completely distorted perception of reality at the time of the offence is characterised as 'unreasonable.' The lack of proportionality between crime and sentence is also mentioned, as well as problems concerning the assessment of intent when the defendant suffers from a severe mental disorder; the courts may 'far too readily' come to the conclusion that the defendant acted with intent.[22]

One problem is put forward as particularly grave. A person may commit a crime under the influence of a severe mental disorder, but no longer be in need of psychiatric care at the time of the court hearing and therefore not fulfil the requirements for compulsory psychiatric care. According to the imprisonment prohibition in BrB 30:6, that offender cannot be sentenced to imprisonment. The only sanction available would be a conditional sentence or probation. The committee considers this highly unsatisfactory, especially if the crime was very serious. This is not only a theoretical or scholarly question. In 1994 soldier Flink shot and killed seven people and injured three in a Swedish town named Falun. He was found to have committed the crime under the influence of a severe mental disorder; more specifically, an alcohol-induced psychotic state. However, by the time of the court hearing Flink had recovered. The Supreme Court ruled that the imprisonment prohibition did not apply to Flink, because his mental state at the time of the crime had been 'self-induced'. In essence, the Court applied the 'prior fault' doctrine or *actio libera in causa* principle, which was not explicitly stated in Swedish law regarding the imprisonment prohibition at the time. Flink was sentenced to life imprisonment. The rules on mentally disordered offenders in Swedish criminal law were heavily criticised after the *Flink* ruling.[23]

The Proposal

The proposal includes a reintroduction of the concept of accountability as 'a prerequisite for criminal liability'.[24] The standard is formulated as follows:

> An unlawful act should not entail liability for someone who due to severe mental disorder, temporary mental confusion, severe mental retardation or severe dementia,

---

[22] SOU (Swedish Government Official Reports) 2002:3 *Psykisk störning, brott och ansvar* [Mental disorder, crime and responsibility] p 26.
[23] Supreme Court of Sweden, 13 February 1995, Judgment in Case B 5718-94, reported in NJA 1995, p 48.
[24] SOU 2002:3, p 31.

lacked the capacity to understand the meaning of their act, or to adjust their actions according to such understanding.[25]

It was added that this rule should not apply, if the state of incapacity is 'self-induced' (prior fault doctrine).

The committee argued that the accountability rule is designed restrictively and is applicable to a smaller group of offenders than those targeted by the 1962 imprisonment prohibition. As a consequence of the reintroduction of a legal accountability rule, the special sanctions only applicable to mentally disordered offenders would be abolished. The regular sanctions, including imprisonment, conditional sentence and probation, would apply equally to all offenders. Psychiatric treatment for mentally disordered offenders found guilty would be provided by criminal justice institutions. Defendants found not guilty by reason of 'unaccountability' and in need of psychiatric care would be taken care of in ordinary psychiatric care institutions, in accordance with the health care legislation regulating compulsory psychiatric care.

The committee also put forward a suggestion of new public protective measures to be imposed when the defendant is acquitted on grounds of lack of accountability and the interest of public protection is 'particularly pressing'; or as an indefinite-term sanction, for very serious crimes against life or physical integrity, when the regular sanction is not considered sufficient to satisfy the interest of public protection. The public protective measures would include, among other measures, forensic psychiatric care and detention for an indeterminate amount of time.[26]

The committee concluded that the proposed reform would require rather extensive amendments to the criminal law. At the same time, it emphasised that legal change was necessary and urgent.[27] The committee estimated that the reform would be completed by 2004. However, it was not until 2008 that the extensive work of the 1999 committee resulted in legal change.

The Amendment of 2008

The 2008 reform consisted of an amendment to the imprisonment prohibition.[28] The amendment was the result of the works presented in 2002, but it was not the profound reform that the committee had suggested. It could, however, be seen

---

[25] SOU 2002:3, p 37. Our translation. The original text reads as follows:
En gärning skall inte medföra ansvar för den som till följd av en allvarlig psykisk störning, en tillfällig sinnesförvirring, en svår utvecklingsstörning eller ett allvarligt demenstillstånd har saknat förmåga att inse gärningens innebörd eller att anpassa sitt handlande efter en sådan insikt.

[26] SOU 2002:3, p 276.

[27] SOU 2002:3, p 341.

[28] BrB 30:6.

as a first step towards introducing the equivalent of a legal insanity standard in Swedish law.

Section 6 of chapter 30 of the Penal Code formerly prohibited imprisonment, for crimes committed under the influence of severe mental disorder. The provision was changed, to allow imprisonment on the basis of 'exceptional grounds':

> A person who commits a crime under the influence of severe mental disorder should preferably be sentenced to a sanction other than imprisonment. The court can sentence to imprisonment only on exceptional grounds. In the assessment of whether there are such grounds, the court should consider
>
> 1. the penal gravity of the crime,
> 2. whether the defendant has no need or limited need for psychiatric care,
> 3. if the defendant him- or herself caused the mental condition in connection with the crime, through intoxication or in other similar ways, and
> 4. other circumstances.[29]

The imprisonment prohibition was thus replaced by a presumption against imprisonment in cases where the defendant committed the crime under the influence of severe mental disorder. The presumption can be rebutted if the crime carries a statutory penalty of at least four years' imprisonment and if the defendant has only limited need for psychiatric care.[30] However, an express statutory exception was introduced, and it is phrased as follows:

> The court cannot sentence to imprisonment if the defendant, as a consequence of severe mental disorder, lacked the capacity to understand the meaning of the act, or to adjust their actions according to such understanding.[31]

By means of this exception, the imprisonment prohibition is now retained, but reserved for a smaller group of defendants described as 'the most severely mentally disordered'.[32] The exception does not apply when the state of incapacity was caused by the defendant himself or herself, eg, through intoxication (prior fault rule). With this amendment, the accountability standard suggested in the 2002 report was introduced, but in a different function than the one envisaged by the committee. Instead of delimiting criminal liability, the standard defines the group of offenders that qualify for the imprisonment exemption.

---

[29] Our translation. The original text of the provision reads as follows:
Den som har begått ett brott under påverkan av en allvarlig psykisk störning ska i första hand dömas till en annan påföljd än fängelse. Rätten får döma till fängelse endast om det finns synnerliga skäl. Vid bedömningen av om det finns sådana skäl ska rätten beakta 1. om brottet har ett högt straffvärde, 2. om den tilltalade saknar eller har ett begränsat behov av psykiatrisk vård, 3. om den tilltalade i anslutning till brottet själv har vållat sitt tillstånd genom rus eller på något annat liknande sätt, samt 4. omständigheterna i övrigt.
[30] Prop (Government Legislative Bill) 2007/08:97. *Påföljder för psykiskt störda lagöverträdare* (Sanctions for mentally disordered criminal offenders) p 18.
[31] Our translation. The original text of the provision reads as follows:
Rätten får inte döma till fängelse, om den tilltalade till följd av den allvarliga psykiska störningen har saknat förmåga att inse gärningens innebörd eller att anpassa sitt handlande efter en sådan insikt. Detta gäller dock inte om den tilltalade har vållat sin bristande förmåga på det sätt som anges i första stycket 3.
[32] Prop 2007/08:97, p 26.

The revised imprisonment prohibition has resulted in a new task for the National Board of Forensic Medicine. The courts may now request that the forensic psychiatric evaluation contain an assessment of whether at the time of the offence the defendant lacked the capacity to understand the meaning of the act, or to adjust his or her actions accordingly, by reason of a severe mental disorder. The Board carries out the assessment, while the court makes the final decision on whether the requirements for the imprisonment prohibition are met.

The government Bill introducing the amendment clarifies the meaning of the new rules with examples. The capacity to understand the meaning of the act is impaired 'when the defendant, as a consequence of psychosis or a similar mental state, had impaired reality testing, caused by delusions or confusion crucial to the defendant's understanding of the offence'. The capacity to adjust one's actions is considered impaired, for example, when the defendant suffers from schizophrenia with commanding voice-type auditory hallucinations.[33]

The legislative documents highlight the difference between the cognitive element of intent, and the defendant's capacity to understand the nature of the act. Both concern the defendant's understanding of the criminal act, but the former is relevant for determining liability, while the latter is of importance for the choice of sanction. The cognitive element of intent is described as the defendant's understanding of the circumstances and consequences of the criminal act, as defined by the law. The 'defendant's capacity to understand the nature of the act' designates the comprehension of the act 'in a broader sense'. The documents exemplify this, by describing a situation similar to the *Flink* case discussed above. A delusional man may think that he is a soldier at war, shooting enemy soldiers. He may understand that he is shooting and that other human beings will get hurt or killed, and thereby meet the requirements for the ascription of intentional killing. At the same time, the man may fail to understand that he is *not* at war, thereby failing to appreciate the meaning of the act in a wider sense.[34]

Unresolved Problems

The government Bill introducing the 2008 amendment shows that the government is cognisant of the need for a legal insanity reform. However, in the Bill it is stressed that, prior to a reform, certain issues should receive further consideration—mainly financial questions and problems pertaining to the allocation of competencies and responsibilities among the various authorities regarding the provision of psychiatric care and the enforcement of public protective measures. The government did nothing more than introduce minor legal changes, designed to not hamper the implementation of a possible later major reform.[35]

---

[33] Prop 2007/08:97, p 40.
[34] SOU 2002:3, p 367.
[35] Prop 2007/08:97, p 15.

III. A New Proposal for a Reintroduction of Legal Insanity

In the following section, we present the most recent proposal for the introduction of a legal insanity standard. The proposal is the result of the work of an inquiry chair appointed in 2008[36] and of a committee of legal and medical professionals and experts, hereafter referred to as 'the Committee'. It is to a large extent based on the 2002 proposal. The report is entitled *Psychiatry and the law—Compulsory care, criminal responsibility and public protection (Psykiatrin och lagen—tvångsvård, straffansvar och samhällsskydd)* and was presented in 2012.[37]

The report contains a comprehensive review of forensic psychiatric care and involuntary commitment law, and of other regulations pertaining to mental disorder and crime. Here, the focus will be on the discussion of and proposals regarding the regulation of criminal liability.

The Need for a Reform

'Dealing with offenders with mental deficiencies or deviations is one of the most difficult, fundamentally important and controversial problems in criminal policy', the Committee stated.[38] The stated ambition is to find 'flexible and yet robust' solutions, which as far as possible accommodate the demands for justice, humanity and protection against future violent acts.

The different arguments for a reintroduction of accountability are discussed in the report. Among them, the culpability principle, meaning that there should be no sanction without culpability, and the 'crime prevention argument', postulating that society members are not likely to comply with laws widely perceived as unjust. The 'internationalisation' argument is also mentioned. The regulation of insanity in the Swedish legal system is different from most jurisdictions, which could lead to various practical problems.[39]

The Committee further discusses the arguments against a reform, expressing appreciation for a legal system that prioritises crime prevention and treatment of mental illness; concern that a reform could lead to stigmatisation and discrimination of offenders with psychiatric conditions; and discomfort with the potential impact of deprivation of legal capacity on the psychiatric treatment of the offender.[40]

---

[36] Dir 2008:93.
[37] SOU (Swedish Government Official Reports) 2012:17 *Psykiatrin och lagen—tvångsvård, straffansvar och samhälsskydd* [Psychiatry and the law—Compulsory care, criminal responsibility and public protection].
[38] SOU 2012:17, p 521.
[39] SOU 2012:17, p 522.
[40] SOU 2012:17, p 531.

The Committee comes to the conclusion that a reform is necessary to implement the culpability principle and to tackle various problems, including the concept of intent being interpreted too extensively when the offender defendant is found to suffer from a psychiatric condition. The Committee emphasises that it would be ethically questionable to issue guilty verdicts for mentally ill defendants, just to give them access to the psychiatric treatment they need. Furthermore, the Committee stresses that accountability requirements formulated in relation to a specific act would protect mentally ill offenders from being regarded as incompetent in general.[41]

The Accountability Standard

The Committee proposes that unlawful acts committed by unaccountable defendants should not be considered crimes, nor expose the defendant to criminal liability. Accountability thus becomes one of the 'necessary elements' of a crime, consistently with contemporary continental European criminal law doctrine.[42]

The Committee expressly states that the accountability standard should be interpreted as in the 2002 proposal.[43] The final proposal is very close to the 2002 draft, with a slightly different wording, as detailed below:

An act does not constitute a crime if it is committed by someone who as a consequence of

1. severe mental disorder,
2. temporary mental confusion,
3. severe mental retardation or
4. severe dementia

lacked the capacity to understand the nature of the act in the situation in which they found themselves or to adjust their actions according to such understanding.

The above does not apply if the defendant themselves in connection to the act caused the lack of capacity by means of intoxication or in any other similar way.[44]

The accountability standard consists of two requirements. The defendant must have acted as a consequence of at least one of the four 'ground conditions' listed in the article; and the condition must have produced particular effects. This phrasing implies a causal relationship between the ground condition and the effects, as well

---

[41] SOU 2012:17, p 538.
[42] SOU 2012:17, p 539.
[43] SOU 2012:17, p 543.
[44] Our translation, The original text of the provision reads as follows:
En gärning utgör inte brott om den begås av någon som till följd av 1. en allvarlig psykisk störning, 2. en tillfällig sinnesförvirring, 3. en svår utvecklingsstörning eller 4. ett allvarligt demenstillstånd har saknat förmåga att förstå gärningens innebörd i den situation i vilken han eller hon befann sig eller att anpassa sitt handlande efter en sådan förståelse. Vad som nu har sagts gäller inte om gärningsmannen i anslutning till gärningen själv har vållat sin bristande förmåga genom rus eller på något annat sätt.

as between the effects and the unlawful act. It is the mental state of the defendant *at the time of the act* that should be evaluated for purposes of accountability.

The Ground Conditions

Exemption from liability can be granted if the defendant suffers 'from disrupted perception of reality, lack of self-control capacity, confusion, thought disturbance, hallucinations, or delusions'.[45] These can be symptoms of psychosis, which in turn is almost always considered a 'severe mental disorder' for legal purposes. Severe mental retardation and severe dementia are independent ground conditions. Temporary mental confusion impairs the capacity to understand or control one's actions, but it is not caused by a psychiatric disorder. Examples listed in the report include confusion caused by high fever, shock and physical trauma such as a blow to the head, hypoglycaemia, epilepsy, medication use, narcosis and hypnosis.[46]

The Effects

According to the Committee, the accountability test should assess 'the defendant's capacity to rationally understand the meaning of the act in the situation in which he or she found himself or herself'.[47] Defendants are unaccountable if delusional or mentally confused to an extent that renders them unable to relate their conduct to its '(f)actual context'.[48]

In the report it is emphasised that the lack of understanding does not necessarily have to concern the criminal act or its consequences. Defendants who 'found themselves in a different reality' and were unable to 'rationally understand the meaning of the act' are not accountable, even when their 'capacity to understand the criminal act' according to the criminal intent standard is intact.[49] The Committee illustrates the difference between evaluating intent and assessing accountability with the following example:

> The defendant attacks and tries to kill a person whom he believes is possessed by the devil. The defendant knows that he wants to kill the person and has the intent to do so. However, the defendant's actions are based on reasons that are so removed from factual reality that it can be argued that he lacks the capacity to understand the nature of the act in the particular context. Thus, the defendant is not accountable.[50]

The liability exemption also applies to defendants who possessed the capacity to understand the meaning of the act, but, because of mental illness, lacked the

---

[45] SOU 2012:17, p 545.
[46] SOU 2012:17, p 546.
[47] SOU 2012:17, p 542.
[48] SOU 2012:17, p 542.
[49] SOU 2012:17, p 542.
[50] SOU 2012:17, p 562.

capacity to behave in accordance with their understanding. Examples here are offenders suffering from strong imperative hallucinations or strong compulsions.[51]

The assessment is limited to accountability in relation to a specific unlawful act and at the time of that particular act.[52]

Judicial Proceedings and Legal Effects

The Committee designs a system in which the accountability question can be raised at any time of, and by any party in, the judicial process. The final decision is made by the court, based on a forensic psychiatric expert opinion.[53] The Committee clarifies that, before the question of accountability can be raised, the court must establish that an unlawful act has been committed. If the defendant is found accountable, the court proceeds to assess intent and the possible presence of grounds for excuse other than lack of accountability. A finding of lack of accountability will lead directly to acquittal.[54]

The burden of proof of accountability falls upon the prosecutor's office.[55] As a rule, the standard of proof is the 'beyond reasonable doubt' criterion. However, offenders are presumed to be accountable and the 'preponderance of the evidence' rule is applied, meaning that the prosecutor only has to prove that the evidence corroborating accountability outweighs the evidence against it. In Sweden, the preponderance of the evidence rule is also applied to the question of whether the defendant has a 'severe mental disorder'.[56]

Defendants found to be unaccountable are acquitted. The Committee suggests introducing a new type of declaratory judgment. The court should declare that the defendant did commit an unlawful act, but is not legally accountable.[57] The declaratory ruling should, in turn, produce legal effects, the most momentous of which are the public protective measures. In the 2002 report, it was suggested that the declaratory verdict should be equivalent to conviction. This means that acquittal on grounds of lack of accountability could result in a number of legal effects, including liability to pay damages, forfeiture of properties or deportation.[58] The new Committee did not present its own suggestion on this matter.

The public protective measures are applicable to acquitted unaccountable defendants and to offenders released from prison, under three conditions: the criminal act endangered or was aimed to endanger the life or health of the victim;

---

51 SOU 2012:17, p 543.
52 SOU 2012:17, p 542.
53 SOU 2012:17, p 563.
54 SOU 2012:17, p 706.
55 SOU 2012:17, p 567.
56 SOU 2012:17, p 571.
57 SOU 2012:17, p 706.
58 SOU 2012:17, p 708.

the crime is 'severe', meaning it carries a statutory penalty of at least six months' imprisonment; and there is a substantial risk of recidivism, taking into consideration the psychiatric condition of the defendant, previously committed crimes and other circumstances. It is also required that the unlawful act was committed under the influence of severe mental disorder, temporary mental confusion, severe mental retardation or severe dementia.[59] The latter requirement applies both to defendants acquitted on grounds of lack of accountability, and to offenders about to be released from prison.

Public protective measures include psychiatric care and treatment aimed to recidivism prevention. They consist of compulsory psychiatric treatment; restraint orders; residency, housing, education or work requirements; or prohibition of use of street drugs or alcohol.[60] Public protective measures can be imposed for a period of up to six months and can only be extended or revoked by an administrative court.[61] The measures can be carried out in dedicated forensic psychiatric facilities.

The Response to the Suggested Reform

The government report from 2002 and the new 2012 report were sent for formal consultation to a number of state authorities, institutions and associations, including universities, courts, patient organisations and medical societies. The reactions to the possible reintroduction of the concept of accountability were for the most part positive. However, the proposed regulation of public protective measures attracted strong criticism.[62] Concerns were also raised regarding the organisational and financial consequences of the reform, and the function and legal implications of the declaratory judgment. The proposal is under preparation but no further legislative steps have been taken. It is unclear whether or when the 2012 proposal will lead to new legislation.

IV. Testing the Proposed Legal Insanity Standard: An Empirical Study

Research on the implementation of the 2008 imprisonment prohibition could give insight into the possible consequences of the new legal insanity standard, should the proposal become law. We carried out a study of the manner in which Swedish

---

[59] SOU 2012:17, p 612.
[60] SOU 2012:17, p 649.
[61] SOU 2012:17, p 646.
[62] A more detailed account of the responses can be found in S Radovic, G Meynen and T Bennet, 'Introducing a Standard of Legal Insanity: The Case of Sweden Compared to the Netherlands' (2015) 40 *International Journal of Law and Psychiatry* 43.

forensic psychiatric teams and district courts have interpreted the two accountability criteria: the 'capacity to understand the meaning of the act' and the 'capacity to adjust one's actions accordingly'.[63] Current Swedish criminal and criminal
procedural law make no mention of legal insanity or accountability. Nevertheless,
in its report, the Committee explicitly stated that the phrasing of the imprisonment prohibition clause in the 2008 law has the same meaning as the accountability standard in the most recent legislative proposal. Therefore, our study may
serve as a predictor of the implementation and operationalisation of the insanity
regulation in the most recent legislative proposal, should it become law. The interest of the study extends beyond the Swedish context, since analogous definitions
of legal insanity are used in other jurisdictions.

The primary focus of the study is on mental health assessments in forensic
psychiatric expert opinions. We will also comment on how the assessments were
made by the courts.

Methods

The study included a total of 134 forensic psychiatric reports issued in 2010 at
the forensic psychiatric special units in Stockholm and Gothenburg, and the
corresponding district court rulings. A total of 460 forensic psychiatric reports
were issued in Sweden in 2010, of which 411 were in Stockholm and Gothenburg.

Two inclusion criteria were used. We included only cases where an assessment
had been specifically requested by the court, and cases in which the defendant had
been assessed as having committed the alleged offence under the influence of a
'severe mental disorder'.

The primary diagnosis for most of the defendants in our sample was psychotic
disorder (n=83). A substantial minority of offenders had been diagnosed with
a neuro-psychiatric disorder including ADHD (attention deficit hyperactivity
disorder) and autism spectrum disorder (n=20). The rest had other diagnoses.[64]
Most subjects had been charged with violent crimes.[65] The remaining 11 subjects
had been prosecuted for less serious offences, including trespass and property
damage. The content of the selected documents was systematised and interpreted
using a thematic analysis, as described by Braun and Clarke.[66]

---

[63] Mentally disordered criminal offenders comprise a vulnerable population. Therefore, ethical
considerations were especially important in this study. Data were recorded and handled with confi-
dentiality. Information concerning circumstances pertaining to individuals or individual offences is
reported anonymously, and only discussed to the extent that it was necessary for the purpose of the
study. The study was approved by the ethics committee at the University of Gothenburg (Dnr 469-12).

[64] Eight participants were diagnosed with a personality disorder, 6 with a substance abuse disorder,
5 had an affective disorder, 5 had a mental retardation and the remaining 7 had other diagnoses.

[65] In 68 cases the charge was assault, in 16 murder or manslaughter; 16 participants had been
charged with arson, 9 with sex offences, 8 with burglary, and 4 with unlawful deprivation of liberty.

[66] V Braun and V Clarke, 'Using thematic analysis in psychology' (2006) 3(2) *Qualitative Research
in Psychology* 77.

Results

Statements regarding the assessment of the capacity to 'understand' and 'control' (hereafter referred to as 'the capacities')[67] were found in 131 of the 134 reports. In 61% of the reports, the text mentions both 'understanding' and 'control'. In another 20%, only 'understanding' is mentioned, and in 5% only 'control'. For the remaining 14% of the reports, either there was no discussion of the capacities or we could not conclude whether the text referred to control, or understanding, or both.

Forty-four per cent of the reports take a clear position on the presence or absence of the capacities; nearly half of these (46%) conclude that the defendant completely lacked the capacities, 13% conclude that capacities were severely diminished and 39% that the capacities were diminished. Only in one case did the team come to the conclusion that both capacities were intact.

The Arguments Presented in the Forensic Psychiatric Reports

Ninety-two (69%) of the 134 reports include arguments corroborating and negating the defendant's capacity for understanding and control. We carried out a thematic analysis of the arguments, summarised here. Several arguments are sometimes put forward in the same report. Psychosis and symptoms of psychosis were the most frequently cited factors indicating a lack of capacity to 'understand' and 'control'. However, the defendant's behaviour before, after and especially during the act was also frequently referred to. Among the arguments contending that the defendant did possess the capacities, we found few references to psychiatric symptoms; the discussion focused instead on the purpose or motive of the act and on the defendant's behaviour.

Some of the arguments seem of direct psychiatric relevance, including confusion, poor impulse control and compulsive behaviour. Other factors mentioned as indicators of reduced capacity were not strictly psychiatric, and comprise the presence of personality traits including bad temper, poor judgement, self-centredness or impaired empathy. Some of the arguments pertain to the circumstances at the time of the act, such as stress and intoxication.

---

[67] In most reports, assessments of the 'understanding' and 'control' capacities were found under a dedicated heading. Comments pertaining to the same question and recorded in other parts of the reports were also included in the analysis. The selected material was translated into English us, and the meaning is as faithful to the original as possible. No attempts to correct grammatical idiosyncrasies were made. The two terms 'understanding' and 'control' frequently occur together in the material, and it is at times difficult to establish which capacity a particular argument is referring to. Nonetheless, we have as far as possible analysed factors affecting understanding and control separately.

Arguments based on purpose or motive, the defendant's understanding of right and wrong, and the defendant's behaviour, are used both to corroborate and to negate the capacities. The existence of an understandable motive behind the act is taken to indicate capacity; the lack of understandable motives or an apparently 'irrational' motive are taken to point towards incapacity. The ability to understand that the act was wrong in a legal or moral sense is often interpreted as denoting intact capacities. Factors revealing poor understanding of the wrongfulness of the action in a legal or moral sense are regarded as evidence of incapacity.

Statements describing the defendant's behaviour before, after, or during the act also occur in arguments for as well as against capacity. Wearing a disguise or expressly stating 'this is a robbery' are taken to imply that the defendant understood the nature of the act. So does behaviour after the act that suggests that the defendant was aware of the gravity of the act, including alerting the police or the emergency services. This also applies to precautions typically taken to escape prosecution, such as running away from the crime scene or disposing of a weapon. On the other hand, behaviour that seems confused, inexplicable, injudicious or simply ineffective to the outside observer is read as a sign that the person did not possess the capacity to 'understand'. The reports include situations where the behaviour of the defendant during the act was 'out of character', at odds with previous behaviour or with personality traits exhibited at the time of the investigation. A history of persistent violent behaviour is taken to indicate a proclivity to violence, interpreted as a personality trait rather than a pathological symptom. In one report, however, a history of violent behaviour is taken to demonstrate that the offender lacked the 'control' capacity.

The arguments used in the reports are presented in more detail below.

Arguments Set Forth as Indicating Intact Capacities

Below is a list of the arguments used in the reports as evidence that the defendant possessed the 'understand' and 'control' capacities, in order of prevalence. Examples are presented in footnotes.

1. **Purpose or motive** The presence of an explicit purpose or motive for the act is the argument most commonly mentioned as evidence of both capacities; most frequently, the intention to come into possession of money or street drugs, or to show one's will or opinion. In some cases, committing an unlawful act as a reaction to a perceived provocation is considered indicative of intact capacities.[68]

2. **Knowledge that the act was wrong** Nearly as frequently come arguments regarding the defendant's understanding that the act was legally or morally

---

[68] X has a personality disorder linked to somatic injury and is charged with aggravated arson. The following words are included in the report: 'A fact that indicates such understanding is that X describes a purpose for the fire setting: partly she was dissatisfied with the psychiatric care, and partly she saw a chance to escape if the ward was evacuated'.

wrong, including denial of charges, prevarication, denigration of others, remorse and the ascription of blame to others. Most reports making use of this argument include a description of the defendant's understanding of the act, or attitude towards the act, retrospectively, at the time of the evaluation.[69]

3. **Behaviour at the time of the act** Two aspects in particular are taken to indicate intact capacities: that the behaviour was adequate, intentional or purposeful; as well as factors suggesting that the defendant had control over his or her actions.[70]

4. **Behaviour after the act** Behaviour suggesting that the defendant is aware of the gravity and the consequences of the act is seen as a sign of an intact 'understand' capacity and, in some instances, also 'control' capacity. In the reports, this argument is used for defendants who alerted the police or emergency services after the act, or tried to avoid prosecution or punishment by fleeing the crime scene or disposing of the weapon. In one case, the fact that the defendant immediately surrendered and accepted hospitalisation is taken to indicate that he was able to understand what he had done, and aware that there would be consequences.[71]

5. **Past behaviour** In cases of arson, adaptation of the behaviour (for example, to avoid detection) is taken to suggest that the defendant possessed the capacity to control his or her actions. In one case, prior experience of emotional relief at fire setting is taken to indicate capacity. For violent crimes, a history of violent behaviour is interpreted as symptomatic of a behavioural pattern of violence or of an antisocial personality, indicating that the aggressive action is a deliberate response, for example a systematic way to handle conflict.[72]

6. **Nature of the act** This argument is used in two types of cases. It is used when the act in itself requires a particular ability, such as decisiveness or reflection. It is also used when the act typically has a definite goal or a purpose, indicating that the defendant must have been aware that the action was illegal: for example, financial gain for frauds.[73]

---

[69] X has autism spectrum disorder and is charged with assault. The following words are included in the report: 'He tries to explain away or smooth over his actions, and he expresses fear for not being allowed to stay, indicating that he is aware that the act was wrong'.

[70] X has schizophreniform disorder and is charged with robbery. The following words are included in the report: 'He behaved in an aggressive and threatening way and at the same time he stated that it was a robbery'.

[71] X has Asperger's syndrome and is charged with aggravated assault. 'X got rid of his weapon after the act, even though it had great sentimental value to him, which indicates that he was aware that it might be bad for him to be seen in possession of the weapon'.

[72] X has Asperger's syndrome and is charged with arson. The following words are included in the report: 'He has previously adjusted his fire setting behaviour in such a way that he started to light fires in secrecy in a fire pit in the woods, instead of in his house'.

[73] X has paranoid schizophrenia and is charged with attempted fraud. The following words are included in the report: 'The prosecuted attempted fraud is of such nature that it is difficult to imagine that one would not have understood that it was an illicit activity in some sense'.

7. **Planning of the act** Premeditation is taken to imply capacity. This also applies to plans for action conceived only a few minutes before acting. One report draws particular attention to planning as a sign of an adequate sense of reality and of consequential thinking skills.[74]

Arguments Set Forth as Indicating Compromised Capacities

This section presents the arguments put forward as evidence of incapacity in the reports, in order of prevalence. Examples are presented in footnotes.

1. **Delusions** The most frequently used argument taken to indicate incapacity is the presence of delusions at the time of the act. Delusions are deemed to affect capacity in different ways. In some cases, the unlawful behaviour is triggered by delusions, or the motive for acting could be characterised as delusional. In this type of case, delusions are taken to undermine the 'understand' capacity. In some cases, delusions are described as the driving force behind the act; in other cases, the behaviour is described as caused by delusions. The latter arguments refer to the 'control' capacity, as do statements describing the defendant as fully occupied or absorbed by delusions. Some reports use a more generic wording and state that the defendant was 'affected by delusions' or 'living in a delusional world'.[75]

2. **Behaviour at the time of the act** Apparently unplanned behaviour characterised by thoughtlessness, impulsivity or precipitance or ostensibly irrational, inexplicable, injudicious or ineffective, is considered indicative of incapacity. Seemingly odd behaviour, like attacking strangers, is taken to testify to a reduced 'understand' capacity. Lack of goal orientation, unstructured or random behaviour is interpreted as a sign of confusion, in turn a sign of impaired capacities. The same holds when, according to witnesses, the defendant was unresponsive, or his behaviour was precipitous, unexpected or unpredictable. Extreme violence and resistance against arrest are presented as arguments against the possession of the 'control' capacity.[76]

---

[74] X has a mild mental retardation and is charged with theft. The following words are included in the report: 'There is also an element of planning; he lingered at the workplace in order to be left alone before he tried to break into the locker'.

[75] X has a psychotic disorder and is charged with murder. The following words are included in the report: 'he interprets signals from the surroundings through a psychotic conceptual world, in which he attributes unreal and frightening properties to the victim. At the time of the act, she [the victim] has changed appearance from his mother to a beast and the violence is executed with the firm conviction that to refrain from acting would entail that he himself would be, if not killed, at least sexually abused'.

[76] X has schizophreniform disorder and is charged with robbery. The following words are included in the report. 'X behaved in a somewhat peculiar manner at the bank robbery. He was, among other things, dressed in an inappropriate outfit, he was smoking, eating an apple and played "hangman" with an employee at the bank'.

3. **Lack of consequential thinking** A limited ability to plan and to predict the consequences of one's own behaviour and of the behaviour of others are read as signs of incapacity.[77]

4. **Self-centredness and impaired empathy** Pathological egocentrism, inability to empathise and to understand how others think and feel are mentioned as signs that the defendant lacked the 'understand' capacity. Poor 'emotional imagination' lowering the incentive to consider other people's feelings attests to a poor 'understand' capacity.[78]

5. **Reality-testing deficiencies** Deficiencies in reality testing speak against the capacities. In the reports, they are often regarded as psychosis symptoms.[79]

6. **Hallucinations** The presence of delusional sensory experiences is discussed as an independent argument against the capacities, and occasionally also interpreted as a sign of psychosis.[80]

7. **Psychosis** In many reports, the fact that the defendant was suffering from psychosis or was in a psychotic state is interpreted as sufficient evidence of impaired capacities, and no other arguments against the capacities are put forward.[81]

8. **Confusion** A state of confusion, disorientation or disorganisation is considered indicative of incapacity. This is not limited to psychotic confusion.[82]

9. **Lack of knowledge that the act was wrong** Facts suggesting that the defendant has a poor comprehension of right and wrong, in a legal or moral sense, are taken to denote a deficient 'understand' capacity, and in one case also a 'control' deficit. In a few cases, lack of remorse is taken to speak against the possession of the 'understand' capacity. In one case, the defendant was visibly distressed when he learned that the victim had suffered psychological

---

[77] X has psychotic disorder and is charged with aggravated assault and other crimes. The following words are included in the report. '[T]he cognitive impairment that has been discovered presumably had a negative effect on his abilities to understand, plan and foresee the consequences of his actions'.

[78] X has schizoid personality disorder and is charged with arson. The following words are included in the report. 'On a cognitive level, X understands that his behaviour is criminal, but he lacks the capacity to create an emotional picture of the act, he is indifferent to other people's thoughts and feelings'.

[79] X has delusional disorder and is charged with assault and other charges. The following words are included in the report. 'X is believed to have been affected by psychosis, which entails that X, during the stress she experienced in connection with the acts, had a severely diminished capacity for adequate reality testing'.

[80] X has paranoid schizophrenia and is charged with aggravated damage to property and other charges. The following words are included in the report: 'Against ... understanding speaks the fact that X's behaviour is governed by voices'.

[81] X has schizophreniform disorder and is charged with a weapon offence and other charges. The following words are included in the report: 'What speaks against understanding is that X at the same time gradually developed psychotic symptoms'.

[82] X has catatonic schizophrenia and is charged with aggravated breach of domestic peace. The following words are included in the report, as evidence of incapacity to understand the meaning of the act: 'X was in state of acute confusion with disorientation in time and space'.

damage as a consequence of his aggression. This was taken to indicate a defective 'understand' capacity.[83]

10. **Stress** Poor stress tolerance is taken to be suggestive of compromised 'control' capacity. Stress is also mentioned along with mental problems as an accentuating or triggering factor. Some reports emphasise the presence of stressors in the living situation of the defendant. These are taken to have a general negative impact on the capacities.[84]

11. **Poor impulse control** Inadequate, limited or lacking impulse control is cited in the reports, as evidence of 'control' capacity impairment.[85]

12. **Distorted conception of reality** Poor appreciation of reality, lack of contact with reality and of sense of reality, and a compromised connection or relationship with reality are all considered relevant and are described as symptoms of psychosis.[86]

13. **Intoxication or addiction** Drugs- or alcohol-intoxication at the time of the act is taken to indicate incapacity. Abuse of, or addiction to, alcohol and street drugs is also regarded as a factor that amplifies the severity of other factors undermining the capacities.[87]

14. **Purpose or motive** Irrational or absurd purposes or motives behind the act are interpreted as symptomatic of incapacity. So is the absence of a motive, for example if there was no indication of tension or conflict between the defendant and the victim.[88]

15. **Compulsion** Ritualisation, obsessive-compulsive behaviour and lack of flexibility are mentioned as evidence of incapacity.[89]

---

[83] X has a mild mental retardation and is charged with false accusation. The following words are included in the report, as evidence of incapacity to understand the meaning of the act. The offender displayed 'lack of understanding of how society is constructed ... Any legal reasoning would be beyond her comprehension'.

[84] X has borderline personality disorder and is charged with robbery. The following words are included in the report: 'At the start the robbery, X's behaviour was characterised by impulsivity, and the lack of control intensified as the stress in the situation increased when he was denied money. The strong stress escalated to psychotic dissociations while the violence culminated'.

[85] X has borderline personality disorder and charged with arson and other charges. The following words are included in the report. 'It is deemed that X understood the meaning of her actions but had diminished control over her actions due to impaired impulse control'.

[86] X has schizophrenia and is charged with attempted aggravated theft and other offences. The following words are included in the report: 'His condition has been characterised by ... a psychotic conception of reality with an inability to differentiate between inner experiences and actual events'.

[87] X has schizoaffective disorder and is charged with assault and other crimes. The following words are included in the report: 'Finally, X was intoxicated at the time of the act, which further weakened his capacity for judgment and control'.

[88] X has paranoid schizophrenia and is charged with aggravated violation of a woman's integrity. The following words are included in the report. 'A fact that speaks against understanding is that X, in his state of psychotic deterioration, experienced himself as being invaded by the plaintiff's identity and emotions and felt he had become a part of her. He considered it necessary to use violence in order to help her to separate from him and become a stronger person'.

[89] X has pyromania and is charged with arson and other crimes. In the report, it is stated that the offender displayed 'compulsive surveillance of emergency alerts and of the rescue services' operations as well as difficulties being able to resist rushing off to accident scenes'.

16. **Delusional interpretation** Paranoid or delusional distorted interpretations of reality are cited as independent arguments against the capacities and as signs of psychosis, in combination with other psychotic symptoms.[90]
17. **Temper** In some reports, irritability and aggressiveness in the context of the act and general difficulties with emotion control are taken to be indicative of 'control' capacity impairment.[91]
18. **Impaired judgement** Impaired judgement is considered indicative of incapacity.[92]
19. **Behaviour after the act** Post-crime behaviour that is irrational or character-ised by high risk-taking is used as an argument against capacity.[93]
20. **Past behaviour** One defendant did not have a history of violent behaviour and did not appear to have an antisocial identification. This was interpreted as evidence of incapacity. However, in one other case, the fact that the defendant kept reiterating the same type of violent behaviour, influenced by the disorder, was considered a sign of incapacity.[94]

The Court Assessments

The study also includes an analysis of the corresponding court verdicts. The 'understand' and 'control' capacities are only relevant when the imprisonment prohibition is considered. Only in five of the 134 cases did the court *explicitly* consider the imprisonment prohibition. In all five cases, the court concluded that the imprisonment prohibition applied 'pursuant to' the forensic psychiatric report. The court did not reach its own independent conclusion on the content of the forensic psychiatric report, at least not explicitly, and no independent court evaluation of the report was written or presented.

---

[90] X has psychotic disorder and is charged with aggravated assault and other crimes. The following words are included in the report as evidence of lack of capacity to understand: 'long-standing men-tal deterioration, where he [the defendant] interpreted signals from the surroundings in an odd and unworldly manner'.

[91] X has mild mental retardation and is charged with theft and other crimes. The following words are included in the report: 'He had, during the time prior to the acts, experienced increased frustration at his workplace and, as a consequence of his state, has difficulties to handle emotions of anger and frustration'.

[92] X has autistic spectrum disorder and is charged with sexual exploitation of a minor and other crimes. The following words are included in the report: 'Regarding the capacity to understand the meaning of the actions … it can be concluded that X has an impaired judgement due to limited execu-tive functions'.

[93] X has schizophreniform disorder and is charged with robbery. The following words are included in the report: 'Even though he had obtained a lot of money through the robbery, he made a cash withdrawal of one thousand SEK from his account in the bank and identified himself by means of his driver's licence'.

[94] X has severe ADHD with behavioural impairments comparable to psychosis, and is charged with threat to a public servant and other crimes. The following words are included in the report: 'his capac-ity to adjust his actions according to his understanding is limited and his actions were controlled by misinterpretations of reality; and he has reacted the way he always does, i.e., by resorting to threats and violence'.

The courts' reasoning on the question of intent shows that the conclusions of forensic psychiatric expert reports were used not only for determining the sanction, but also in the assessment of criminal liability. In 67 cases (50 per cent), court rulings included a discussion of intent.[95] In 24 cases, the word 'understanding' (*insikt*) was used.[96] In 25 cases, the courts explicitly mentioned the forensic psychiatric expert opinion, and in 14 cases made specific reference to the 'capacity to understand the meaning of the act' or 'to adjust behaviour accordingly'.

Conclusions from the Study and Previous Research

The results of this study are fairly consistent with results of similar studies conducted in other countries. The study shows that the concepts of 'understanding' and 'control' in the Swedish Penal Code are interpreted by Swedish forensic psychiatric practitioners in a manner quite consistent with the interpretation given by their colleagues in other jurisdictions.

Most research in this area consists of statistical analyses of factors correlated with expert opinions on legal insanity and responsibility, to determine insanity acquittal predictors. Daniel and colleagues performed an extensive examination of 120 criminal defendants referred to a maximum-security unit in Missouri. Their goal was drafting recommendations for forensic psychiatrists on competency to stand trial and criminal responsibility. The authors found 30 variables correlating with criminal responsibility. The five variables with the strongest correlations were 'bizarre behaviour manifested at the time of the offence' that impaired understanding or volitional control (two separate variables), hallucinatory and/or delusional symptoms at the time of the crime, current diagnosis of a psychotic disorder, and schizophrenia. The variables also included impairments to memory, insight and orientation.[97] Lymburner and Roesch, as well as Rice and Harris, concluded that psychotic symptoms and the severity of the crime are the two main predictors of insanity acquittals.[98] A Canadian team investigated psychiatric and criminological characteristics in defendants found not guilty by reason of insanity and found that the most frequent main diagnosis in the sample was psychotic spectrum disorder.[99]

---

[95] This number is remarkably low, since all but one of the cases concern defendants that, according to the forensic psychiatric expert opinion, lacked or had a diminished capacity to understand their actions.

[96] In this case, the concept of understanding could also mean *insikt* as an element of intent.

[97] AE Daniel, NC Beck, A Herath and M Schmitz, 'Factors Correlated with Psychiatric Recommendations of Incompetency and Insanity' (1984) 12 *The Journal of Psychiatry & Law* 527.

[98] JA Lymburner and R Roesch 'The Insanity Defense: Five Years of Research (1993–1997)' (1999) 22(3) *International Journal of Law and Psychiatry* 213; ME Rice and GT Harris, 'The Predictors of Insanity Acquittal' (1990) 13(3) *International Journal of Law and Psychiatry* 217.

[99] AG Crocker, TL Nicholls, MC Seto, Y Charette, G Côté and M Caulet, 'The National Trajectory Project of Individuals Found Not Criminally Responsible on Account of Mental Disorder in Canada. Part 2: The People Behind the Label' (2015) 60(3) *Canadian Journal of Psychiatry. Revue Canadienne de Psychiatrie* 106.

Other recent studies of forensic psychiatric reports have found that the correlation between legal insanity and crime severity is often mediated by the diagnosis.[100] Barendregt, Muller, Nijman and de Beurs studied forensic mental health expert opinions on criminal responsibility in the Netherlands. They found that the evaluations were primarily focused on psychiatric symptoms, including personality disorders. They concluded that the cultural background of the offender and his or her crime-related personality characteristics also correlated with criminal responsibility. Further, they found that the context and characteristics of the criminal act, including the choice of weapon and the possible presence of an accomplice, were considered more relevant than the type of crime in the forensic expert opinions.[101]

A few studies have focused on the content of the forensic expert evaluations, rather than on factors correlating with the outcome of the assessments. Donohue and colleagues analysed 416 forensic mental health evaluations of defendants considered not criminally responsible in Maryland between 2002 and 2005. The study mainly focused on volition impairment. The factors most frequently cited by expert witnesses as proof of impaired volitional control were delusions; mania; crime planning; hallucinations; 'concerns for consequences of failing to act'; and disorganisation. Command hallucinations, the 'ability to defer acting for a period of time', consideration of alternative actions and 'hypothetical explorations' were also mentioned.[102] Spencer and Tie examined 40 reports provided by forensic psychiatrists from a high-security inpatient service. The reports concerned offenders acquitted on grounds of insanity by the Mental Health Court in Queensland, Australia, between 2004 and 2009. In all reports, the conclusion was that the defendant did not have the capacity to know the wrongfulness of the act. In one-third of these cases, the conclusion was based on the defendants' belief that they were under imminent threat and that they had acted to defend their lives. In almost half of the reports, it was stated that the defendant 'was unable to reason with a moderate degree of sense and composure' or 'unable to reason about the wrongfulness of their actions'. In 13 cases, only one psychiatric symptom was cited, mostly persecutory delusions generating the feeling of being threatened by the victim.[103]

---

[100] See for example R Cochrane, T Grisso and RI Frederick, 'The Relationship between Criminal Charges, Diagnoses, and Psycholegal Opinions among Federal Pretrial Defendants' (2001) 19(4) *Behavioral Sciences and the Law*, 565; JI Warren, DC Murrie, P Chauhan, PE Dietz and J Morris, 'Opinion Formation in Evaluating Sanity at the Time of the Offense: An Examination of 5175 Pre-trial Evaluations' (2004) 22(2) *Behavioral Sciences & the Law* 171.

[101] M Barendregt, E Muller, H Nijman and E De Beurs, 'Factors Associated with Experts' Opinions Regarding Criminal Responsibility in the Netherlands' (2008) 26(5) *Behavioral Sciences and the Law* 619.

[102] A Donohue, V Arya, L Fitch and D Hammen, 'Legal Insanity: Assessment of the Inability to Refrain' (2008) 5(3) *Psychiatry* 58.

[103] In a few cases, no other explanation was given but a mere reference to the fact that the offender suffered from an unspecified psychiatric disorder. J Spencer and A Tie, 'Psychiatric Symptoms Associated with the Mental Health Defence for Serious Violent Offences in Queensland' (2013) 21(2) *Australasian Psychiatry* 147.

Knoll and Resnick list a number of factors that they think should be taken into consideration in forensic mental health evaluations of the capacity to know the wrongfulness of the act. The list includes attempts to avoid detection; disposing of the evidence; efforts to avoid apprehension; express admissions of awareness that the act was wrong; rational or non-psychotic motives; notifying the police; and expressions of remorse and guilt. The authors also list factors that they suggest should be considered in volitional control assessments, including the ability to refrain from carrying out instructions (for example, orders from commanding voices); the ability to foresee consequences; the capacity to consider alternative courses of action; the deliberateness of the action; and decision-making abilities.[104]

Roberts, Golding and Fincham assigned undergraduate psychology students the task of evaluating vignette cases. The vignettes described the homicide of a mailman by a person suffering from mental illness. They were designed to include various examples and degrees of severity of mental disorders, bizarreness and elements of planning. The results showed that the participants perceived schizophrenia as strongly associated with legal insanity, especially when the content of the delusions was linked to the criminal act.[105]

In sum, previous international research indicates a strong link between the presence of psychotic disorders and assessments of lack of criminal responsibility. The literature also shows that non-psychiatric factors, including behaviour at the time of the act or planning, are considered relevant. The above-discussed study of forensic psychiatric expert reports carried out in Sweden by us shows that the most frequently used arguments against the 'understanding' and 'control' capacities are the presence of psychosis and of psychotic symptoms such as hallucinations and delusions. This is consistent with the findings of comparable studies discussed above, indicating a strong link between insanity and delusional systems linked to the motive of the crime.

The study also shows that descriptions of the defendant's behaviour before, during and after the act are rather recurrent in forensic mental health assessments (27 per cent). Spencer and Tie presented a similar finding. The behaviour mentioned in their study included: lack of attempts to escape; lack of planning; absence of attempts to conceal evidence; commission of the offence in the presence of witnesses; self-incriminating confessions to the police; and absence of non-psychotic motives. The same examples were also found in our material.

Many of the forensic psychiatric reports in our Swedish study mention the ability of the defendant to understand legal or moral wrong and the capacity to empathise. The ability to understand the wrongfulness of the act is mentioned in 25 per cent of the reports as a sign of intact capacity. The inability to understand

---

[104] JL Knoll IV and PJ Resnick, 'Insanity Defense Evaluations: Toward a Model for Evidence-based Practice' (2008) 8(1) *Brief Treatment and Crisis Intervention* 92.

[105] CF Roberts, SL Golding and FD Fincham, 'Implicit Theories of Criminal Responsibility: Decision Making and the Insanity Defense' (1987) 11(3) *Law and Human Behavior* 207.

the wrongfulness of the act is mentioned in 11 per cent of the reports as a sign of incapacity. However, Swedish law does not clarify whether knowing that the act was wrong in a legal or moral sense should be regarded as forming part of the 'understanding the nature of the act' requirement.

In our Swedish study we did not find any forensic psychiatric report indicating that the severity of the crime had been taken into consideration in the capacity assessment. More significant factors were, as found also by Barendregt and colleagues, the context of the crime and the manner in which the crime was committed.[106]

V. Concluding Discussion

The following section is a discussion of the general implications of the Swedish study presented above, as well as an evaluation of the proposal to introduce a legal insanity standard in Swedish law. The section begins with a discussion of forensic psychiatric expert evaluations of insanity and of the assessment of expert evidence in court.

Forensic Psychiatric Accountability Evaluations

How should accountability or insanity evaluations be performed in practice, and what should be assessed? The results of the empirical study presented above could provide an indication as to how forensic psychiatric assessments of 'understanding' and 'control' would be made and presented to the courts if a standard for accountability was introduced in Sweden. However, the results can also be discussed in relation to evaluations of legal insanity in other jurisdictions.

Most forensic psychiatric reports in our study include a relatively intelligible and accessible discussion of the 'understand' and 'control' capacities. The reports include a discussion of the relevance of psychiatric symptoms, along with other factors, and present arguments for and against the capacities. This type of report can form a good basis for the court's decision. In more than half of the reports, no explicit position is taken with regard to capacity. In our opinion, this need not necessarily be seen as problematic, considering that the final decision is left to the court.

However, even reports that exhaustively elucidate pro and contra arguments can prove difficult to interpret for the courts. Knoll and Resnick list a number of errors that they think should be avoided in insanity evaluations.[107] Some of the

---

[106] Barendregt et al (n 101).
[107] Knoll IV and Resnick (n 104).

errors occur in our material. One of them is grounding an unaccountability finding on no other consideration but the very presence of a particular mental disorder. Knoll and Resnick caution against this. In Sweden, as in most jurisdictions, the presence of a major mental disorder is not in itself proof that the defendant lacked the relevant capacities. Rather, the court needs to know how the mental disorder may have affected the defendant's cognition and volition at the time of the act.

The results point towards some other potential problems. Forensic mental health assessments tend to evaluate the ability to understand and the capacity to control one's actions in general, rather than in connection to the criminal act. One example can be made here. In the Swedish study we encountered many arguments focused on assessing the capacity to appreciate the wrongfulness of the act at the time of the forensic psychiatric evaluation, which may not correspond to the defendant's capacity to understand legal or moral right and wrong at the time of the act. This is a complicated issue; the law expressly requests an assessment of understanding and control in terms of *capacity*, and not of the actual control or understanding the defendant had over her actions at the time of the crime. The intention of the legislator seems to be that forensic mental health practitioners should focus on the impact of psychiatric conditions on general cognition and control abilities, this lying within the area of their expertise, but as pointed out above, a too generalised assessment may fail to answer the court's questions. In our view, the optimal psychiatric assessment should provide an evaluation of the capacity to understand and control but in *relation to* the criminal act.

Presentation and Evaluation of Forensic Psychiatric Expert Opinions in Court

The regulation of admission of forensic psychiatric expert opinions in criminal courts has been discussed extensively. In some common law jurisdictions, the 'Turner rule' applies. The rule states that expert opinions are not necessary, when, given the nature of the issue at hand, the judge and jury have the knowledge and experience to form their own conclusions. The 'Turner rule' has been used to exclude psychiatric testimony in numerous cases.[108] There has been extensive discussion of the role of the expertise of the judge (and the jurors) as opposed to that of forensic mental health practitioners. Sheldon and MacLeod interpret the 'Turner rule' as implying that forensic mental health practitioners can testify on mental pathologies, but not on personality traits.[109] Muzaffar maintains that this interpretation is too restrictive, mainly because it fails to acknowledge the

---

[108] RD Mackay and AM Colman, 'Excluding Expert Evidence: A Tale of the Ordinary Folk and Common Experience' (1991) 11 *Criminal Law Review* 800.

[109] DH Sheldon and MD MacLeod, 'From Normative to Positive Data: Expert Psychological Evidence Re-examined' (1991) 11 *Criminal Law Review* 811.

dimensional view of mental illness and it assumes a sharply defined dividing line between mental illness and 'normality'.[110] According to the United States Federal Rules of Evidence, the role of expert witnesses is rendering opinions on whether the defendant suffered from a serious mental disorder at the time of the offence. Expert witnesses are not allowed to directly address the question of whether the legal test for insanity has been met. They are not allowed to give testimony on the criminal elements of the case. Buchanan points out that the development of the rule reflects a long-standing concern that psychiatric testimony is more likely than other evidence to intrude into the jury's realm.[111] The core question is to what extent the courts should lean on forensic psychiatric expertise in their decisions.

The Swedish study carried out by us shows that the arguments used by forensic mental health professionals are heterogeneous. Some essentially coincide with psychiatric-diagnostic labels and focus on symptoms such as psychotic delusions or hallucinations. Others are related to the criminal act and focus on the defendant's behaviour and motives. The international debate on admission of psychiatric evidence in court is not directly applicable to the Swedish legal-procedural context. The Swedish jurisdiction allows 'free admission' and 'free evaluation' of evidence.[112] There are no legal rules that delimit the discretionary power of the court to assess evidence, by compelling the adjudicator to ascribe particular evidentiary implications to particular types of proof. The parties are free to introduce evidence they deem useful to their cause; the court can in principle exclude evidence only if superfluous or manifestly irrelevant, and can freely evaluate its evidentiary value. However, the issues under discussion are still pertinent as they concern the courts' appraisal of forensic expert opinions and of scientific evidence.

From the Swedish study material it is not clear to what extent the assessments of motives and crime-related behaviour are based on medical or psychological science. Some statements seem at least partially based on folk psychology and common sense. Incorporating folk psychology considerations into a forensic psychiatric expert report, along with assessments based on state-of-the-art medical science, is potentially problematic. The expert witness thus speaks as an expert consultant and as a layperson at the same time. In Sweden forensic psychiatric evaluations are conducted by psychiatrists and psychologists with a specialisation in forensics, and the assessments are thus based on psychiatric and psychological

---

[110] S Muzaffar, 'Psychiatric Evidence in Criminal Courts: The Need for Better Understanding' (2011) 51(3) *Medicine, Science and the Law* 141.

[111] A Buchanan, 'Psychiatric Evidence on the Ultimate Issue' (2006) 34(1) *The American Academy of Psychiatry and the Law* 14. The Federal Rule of Evidence 704(b) states:
No expert witness testifying with respect to the mental state or condition of a defendant in a criminal case may state an opinion or inference as to whether the defendant did or did not have the mental state or condition constituting an element of the crime charged or a defense thereto. Such ultimate issues are matters for the trier of fact alone.

[112] *Principen om fri bevisprövning*, laid down in chapter 35 section 1 of the Swedish Code of Judicial Procedure.

expertise, as well as on forensic medical expertise. Common sense assessments, concerning, among other questions, the defendant's motive, may be of value as criminal evidence if they are coming from a forensic expert. However, the courts ought to be able to distinguish this type of evidence from statements more clearly based on medical expertise, as the latter may be of higher evidentiary value.

The Proposed Criminal Responsibility Standard and its Implications

Should Sweden, after decades of legal and political debate, reform the law and reintroduce accountability as a prerequisite for criminal responsibility? If so, is the most recent legislative proposal satisfactory?

Consensus has gradually emerged in the Swedish debate that ascription of legal responsibility requires knowledge of the nature of one's actions, and capacity to act accordingly. We concur. This opinion is based on the intuition that blame requires guilt, and there can be no guilt without an element of understanding of and control over one's actions. This moral intuition is also enunciated in the fundamental principles of the Swedish criminal justice system.[113] We find several compelling reasons for introducing a standard for legal insanity in Sweden. The reintroduction of legal accountability would better reflect the culpability principle, a foundational rule in the Swedish jurisdiction. A reform would also protect defendants found to suffer from 'severe mental disorder' from being subjected to systematically inadequate intent assessments in criminal processes, as well as clarify the regulation of temporary insanity.

The current regulation of legal responsibility is incompatible with one other fundamental criminal law principle: the principle of proportionality. The amount of time served in forensic psychiatric care institutions is often not proportional to the gravity of the crime. Currently, the duration of the stay is not based on crime characteristics but rather on psychiatric treatment needs and estimated dangerousness. 'Forensic-psychiatric care with special court supervision' (*rättspsykiatrisk vård med särskild utskrivningsprövning*) is the most frequently applied sanction in Sweden to offenders who have committed violent crimes and are found to have a 'severe mental disorder'. Decisions to release from this type of care are made by administrative courts, based on the psychiatric condition of the patient and the estimated recidivism risks.[114] Offenders can thus be held for long periods of time in forensic psychiatric care institutions for less severe crimes. Furthermore,

---

[113] We acknowledge that the intuition itself as well as the principles it is based upon can be questioned on theoretical and empirical grounds. The principles may be unjust or subject to change, for example in the light of new neuro-scientific findings. These issues will not be further discussed here.

[114] Lag om rättspsykiatrisk vård (SFS 1991:1129) §§ 16–16 b.

the incarceration can continue solely based on a risk assessment, even when the offender no longer fulfils the requirement for severe mental disorder. We find this to be one of the more pressing problems in the current system.

The current Swedish system displays deficiencies in the legal treatment of offenders who suffer from mental disorder. In our view, these inadequacies are caused by the lack of distinct boundaries between divergent goals: the provision of mental health care, the sanctioning of crime, and crime prevention. In creating a distinction between these different interests, the introduction of a legal insanity standard equivalent in Swedish law is a possible step towards enforcing legal certainty, justice and fairness for offenders found to suffer from mental disorders.[115]

In conclusion, the introduction of an accountability standard is desirable. The next section is a discussion of how such a standard could be formulated and applied, as well as an examination of a number of critical issues in the most recent legislative proposal.

The Formulation of the Accountability Standard

The proposed standard consists of two requirements. The first requirement pertains to the presence of one or more ground conditions. The second requirement is that the ground conditions must have produced particular effects. It is expressly required that the effects are consequences of the ground conditions, and not of other causes. This structural choice is questionable. The purpose of the provision is providing an excuse to offenders who could not understand or control their behaviour. This purpose does not in itself motivate limiting the scope of application of the accountability clause in the suggested way. In its current phrasing, it only exculpates offenders found to suffer from one of the four ground conditions listed in the law. The Committee expressly stated that the incapacity to understand the meaning of one's behaviour and to act in accordance is not a sufficient ground for a verdict of lack of accountability; there is a requirement that the incapacity is the result of a ground condition. The Committee pointed out that the effects are in principle always caused by one of the 'ground conditions' listed in the provision, and argued that the 'ground condition' requirement functions in practice as a mere recommendation. The Committee also emphasised that not all offenders who meet the ground condition requirement will be considered unaccountable.[116]

---

[115] However, the authors would like to point out that such a standard would best be described as an 'accountability' or 'legal liability' standard. The phrase 'insanity defence' is not germane to the Swedish legal context, because the proposed standard would not constitute a 'defence' in the common law meaning of the word.

[116] SOU 2012:17, p 544.

The choice to limit the scope of application of the insanity standard to offenders who suffer from particular mental or medical conditions could in principle serve an important goal. Comparative criminal and criminal procedural law also shows that, internationally, most legal insanity standards have this same structure. Non-pathological emotions like anger, or repeated antisocial behaviour, would then not become sufficient grounds for excuse. The suggested ground conditions are four: severe mental disorder; temporary mental confusion; severe mental retardation; and severe dementia. 'Severe mental disorder' encompasses psychotic states, including delusions, hallucinations and pathological confusion.[117] The same concept is used in administrative law with regard to compulsory psychiatric care. The condition is thus defined in the same terms as the effects: a deranged ability to appreciate reality, which makes the statutory ground condition redundant. In case of a reform, we see no reason to keep the current connection between the concept of 'accountability' in criminal law and the notion of 'severe mental disorder' in administrative law.

In addition, the inclusion of dementia and mental retardation among the ground conditions seems arbitrary. The Swedish legislator may have felt the need to emphasise that the area of applicability of the accountability standard extends beyond psychiatric conditions. However, this goal could be achieved by using a phrase like 'recognised medical condition', a suggestion recently put forward by the Law Commission for England and Wales in 2013.[118] The regulation of exemption from liability should cover also temporary mental confusion, either by including it in the ground conditions listed in the clause, or by means of a separate provision.

The proposed accountability standard requires that the defendant lacked either the *capacity to understand the nature of the act* or the *capacity to adjust his or her behaviour accordingly*. The explanation of the meaning of these phrases in the report is quite laconic. The forensic psychiatric evaluations analysed in the study include a variety of arguments. In the arguments, 'understanding' and 'control' capacities are often referred to as one single entity. In most cases, it is not specified whether a particular argument is considered relevant for 'control', for 'understanding', or for both. One possible explanation is that Swedish forensic psychiatric and forensic psychological experts are not yet familiar with the new legal concepts, the law having been applied only for a few years, starting in 2008. However, after consulting forensic mental health practitioners, we have come to think that treating the 'control' and 'understanding' criteria as one single entity is in some instances intentional. The legal partition between 'understanding' and 'control' may not overlap with the psychiatric or psychological interpretation of what it means to be

---

[117] Prop 1990/91:58, p 86.
[118] The Law Commission for England and Wales, *Criminal Liability, Insanity and Automatism. A Discussion Paper* (2013).

able to understand or control one's actions. It may be argued that the two capacities cannot be examined separately in practice.

One could also question whether it is possible at all to identify and assess certain capacities in relation to a criminal act. The 'control' requirement, or 'volitional criterion', has been contested and discussed in depth.[119] In the United States, 'irresistible impulse' used to be a ground for insanity. It was abolished in many States, after John Hinckley was found not guilty by reason of insanity of the attempted assassination of Ronald Reagan.[120] This discussion is not addressed in the Swedish proposal.

A similar example can be drawn from a recent legislative discussion in Norway. The insanity standard in Norway is based exclusively on a medical criterion. The defendant must have been suffering from a psychotic disorder at the time of the crime, but there is no requisite for the lack of particular capacities defined in the law, nor is there a requirement of a causal relation between the psychotic disorder and the criminal act.[121] In a 2014 report, a Norwegian governmental committee discussed but rejected the option of revising the scope of application of the insanity standard by introducing a new requirement: the offender should suffer from a mental condition that produced particular cognitive and volitional effects.[122] The Norwegian committee wrote

> There are no empirical or scientific grounds for a conclusive assessment of whether the psychiatric condition exerted an influence over the defendant's act … It is also a matter of considerable uncertainty to take a position on the existence of a causal relationship between the mental state and the act, or on whether the defendant has understood the significance of the act. The psychiatrist is not in a position to give instructions for the assessment, and the lawyers are referred to unsubstantiated assumptions that lack solid foundations.[123]

On a theoretical level, we agree with the Swedish committee that both capacities are principally relevant for purposes of criminal liability. However, there are reasons to further examine how, or even if, capacity of understanding and control can be distinguished and assessed in practice, before suggesting legal formulations. This is an ongoing discussion of ancient origin, but it is also a topic of modern scientific research. Furthermore, there is a need for a greater consistency between the legal and the psychiatric interpretation of the concepts in question. Further scholarly and intra-professional reflection is needed to achieve a high degree of

---

[119] S Penney, 'Impulse Control and Criminal Responsibility: Lessons from Neuroscience' (2012) 35(2) *International Journal of Law and Psychiatry* 99.

[120] PW Low, JC Jeffries and RJ Bonnie. *Trial of John W Hinckley, Jr—A Case Study in the Insanity Defense* (New York, Foundation Press, 1986).

[121] I Melle, 'The Breivik Case and What Psychiatrists Can Learn from It' (2013) 12(1) *World Psychiatry* 16.

[122] For a comprehensive discussion of the works of the Norwegian committee, see L Gröning and GF Rieber-Mohn 'NOU 2014:10—Proposal for New Rules Regarding Criminal Insanity and Related Issues, Norway Post-22 July' (2015) 3(1) *Bergen Journal of Criminal Law and Criminal Justice* 109.

[123] NOU 2014:10, p 22. Our translation.

legal certainty and to better justify the use of forensic mental health expertise in court. Two questions are of particular concern. The first is the question of the prospect for mental health professionals to offer insight on the capacities. The second question involves the evaluation of forensic mental health reports in court and legal professionals' interpretation of medical statements.

The Declaratory Verdict and Its Legal Effects

A final topic of discussion with regard to the Swedish legislative proposal is the declaratory verdict of 'not guilty by reason of unaccountability' that would accompany the acquittal, and its legal effects. According to its proponents, the objective of the proposed reform is to exempt from criminal liability offenders unable to understand or control their actions because of a mental disorder. Inconsistently with this asserted goal, a suggestion is made that the declaratory judgment be equated with a conviction for all relevant legal implications, except the sanction. If this proposal is implemented, the only significant difference from the current regulation would be that under the new regulation, the defendant would not be given compulsory psychiatric care as an independent sanction within the criminal justice system.

The proposed reform also includes public protective measures, but exclusively for defendants who suffered from at least one of the four 'ground conditions' at the time of the unlawful act. This may lead to discrimination. Offenders who committed one single crime in their lifetime, coincidentally with the onset of their first psychotic episode, or while in a condition of temporary insanity, would be subjected to risk assessments prior to release. Conversely, recidivists with an extensive criminal record of violent crimes would in principle be released without any prior risk assessment. In the light of scientific research on risk factors for the reiteration of violent crimes,[124] the proposal can only been seen as discriminating against offenders with mental disorders.

Concluding Remarks

In conclusion, we find that a reintroduction of the concept of accountability could increase legal certainty, justice and fairness, and solve some of the conceptual and

---

[124] See HJ Steadman, EP Mulvey, J Monahan, PC Robbins, PS Appelbaum, T Grisso, LH Roth and E Silver, 'Violence by People Discharged from Acute Psychiatric Inpatient Facilities and by Others in the Same Neighborhoods' (1998) 55(5) *Archives of General Psychiatry* 393; J Bonta, M Law and K Hanson, 'The Prediction of Criminal and Violent Recidivism among Mentally Disordered Offenders: A Meta-analysis' (1998) 123(2) *Psychological Bulletin* 123; M Grann, J Danesh and S Fazel, 'The Association between Psychiatric Diagnosis and Violent Re-offending in Adult Offenders in the Community' (2008) 8(1) *BMC Psychiatry* 92; S Fazel, G Gulati, L Linsell, JR Geddes and M Grann, 'Schizophrenia and Violence: Systematic Review and Meta-analysis' (2009) 6 *PLoS Medicine* 8.

practical problems that systematically emerge under the current system. We do, however, find that a number of issues would benefit from further scholarly and intra-professional consideration, regarding both the formulation of the account- ability standard, and its legal effects. One particularly pressing issue is ensuring that the new law is consistent with human rights conventions and with the rights of persons with disabilities. The law should not under any circumstance discrimi- nate against persons who suffer from mental disorders.

The Swedish debate has, in our view, been too centred on the considerations that preceded the abolition of legal accountability in 1965. In order to advance, the discussion would greatly benefit from integrating the international and interdisciplinary debate on the subject and moving towards not only considering reintroducing, but also rethinking the 'insanity defence'.

Bibliography

Asp, P, Ulväng, M and Jareborg, N, *Kriminalrättens grunder* (Uppsala, Iustus, 2003).

Barendregt, M, Muller, E, Nijman, H and Beurs, E de, 'Factors Associated with Experts' Opinions Regarding Criminal Responsibility in the Netherlands' (2008) 26(5) *Behavioral Sciences and The Law* 619.

Bonta, J, Law, M and Hanson, K, 'The Prediction of Criminal and Violent Recidi- vism among Mentally Disordered Offenders: A Meta-analysis' (1998) 123(2) *Psychological Bulletin* 123.

Braun, V and Clarke, V, 'Using Thematic Analysis in Psychology' (2006) 3(2) *Qual- itative Research in Psychology* 77.

Buchanan, A, 'Psychiatric Evidence on the Ultimate Issue' (2006) 34(1) *The Ameri- can Academy of Psychiatry and the Law* 14.

Cochrane, R, Grisso, T and Frederick, RI, 'The Relationship between Criminal Charges, Diagnoses, and Psycholegal Opinions among Federal Pretrial Defend- ants' (2001) 19(4) *Behavioral Sciences and the Law* 565.

Crocker, AG, Nicholls, TL, Seto, MC, Charette, Y, Côté, G and Caulet, M, 'The National Trajectory Project of Individuals Found Not Criminally Responsible on Account of Mental Disorder in Canada. Part 2: The People Behind the Label' (2015) 60(3) *Canadian Journal of Psychiatry. Revue Canadienne de Psychiatrie* 106.

Daniel, AE, Beck, NC, Herath, A and Schmitz, M, 'Factors Correlated with Psychiatric Recommendations of Incompetency and Insanity' (1984) 12 *Journal of Psychiatry & Law* 527.

Donohue, A, Arya, V, Fitch, L and Hammen, D, 'Legal Insanity: Assessment of the Inability to Refrain' (2008) 5(3) *Psychiatry* 58.

Fazel, S, Gulati, G, Linsell, L, Geddes, JR and Grann, M, 'Schizophrenia and Violence: Systematic Review and Meta-analysis' (2009) 6 *PLoS Medicine* 8.

Grann, M, Danesh, J and Fazel, S, 'The Association between Psychiatric Diagnosis and Violent Re-offending in Adult Offenders in the Community' (2008) 8(1) *BMC Psychiatry* 92.

Gröning, L and Rieber-Mohn, GF, 'NOU 2014:10—Proposal for New Rules Regarding Criminal Insanity and Related Issues, Norway post-22 July' (2015) 3(1) *Bergen Journal of Criminal Law and Criminal Justice* 109.

Jareborg, N, *Uppsåt och oaktsamhet* (Uppsala, Iustus, 1986).

Kinberg, O, *Basic Problems of Criminology* (Copenhagen, Levin & Munksgaard, 1935).

Knoll IV JL and Resnick, PJ, 'Insanity Defense Evaluations: Toward a Model for Evidence-based Practice' (2008) 8(1) *Brief Treatment and Crisis Intervention* 92.

Lernestedt, C, 'Insanity and the "Gap" in the Law: Swedish Criminal Law Rides Again' (2009) 54 *Scandinavian Studies in Law* 79.

Low, PW, Jeffries, JC and Bonnie, RJ, *Trial of John W Hinckley, Jr—A Case Study in the Insanity Defense* (New York, Foundation Press, 1986).

Lymburner, JA and Roesch R, 'The Insanity Defense: Five Years of Research (1993–1997)' (1999) 22(3) *International Journal of Law and Psychiatry* 213.

Mackay, RD and Colman, AM, 'Excluding Expert Evidence: A Tale of the Ordinary Folk and Common Experience' (1991) 11 *Criminal Law Review* 800.

Melle, I, 'The Breivik Case and What Psychiatrists Can Learn from It' (2013) 12(1) *World Psychiatry* 16.

Muzaffar, S, 'Psychiatric Evidence in Criminal Courts: The Need for Better Understanding' (2011) 51(3) *Medicine, Science and the Law* 141.

NOU (Official Norwegian Reports) 2014:10 *Skyldevne, sakkyndighet og samfunnsvern* (Criminal capacity, expert knowledge, and the protection of society).

Penney, S, 'Impulse Control and Criminal Responsibility: Lessons from Neuroscience' (2012) 35(2) *International Journal of Law and Psychiatry* 99.

Radovic, S, Meynen, G and Bennet, T, 'Introducing a Standard of Legal Insanity: The Case of Sweden Compared to the Netherlands' (2015) 40 *International Journal of Law and Psychiatry* 43.

Rättsmedicinalverket, *Årsredovisning* (Annual Report) 2014 (Stockholm, Rättsmedicinalverket, 2014).

Rice, ME and Harris, GT, 'The Predictors of Insanity Acquittal' (1990) 13(3) *International Journal of Law and Psychiatry* 217.

Roberts, CF, Golding, SL and Fincham, FD, 'Implicit Theories of Criminal Responsibility: Decision Making and the Insanity Defense' (1987) 11(3) *Law and Human Behavior* 207.

Sheldon, DH and MacLeod, MD, 'From Normative to Positive Data: Expert Psychological Evidence Re-examined' (1991) 11 *Criminal Law Review* 811.

SOU (Swedish Government Official Reports) 1984:64 *Psykiatrin, tvånget och rättssäkerheten* (Psychiatry, coercion and legal security).

SOU (Swedish Government Official Reports) 1988:7 *Om legalitetsprincipen och om allmänna grunder för ansvarsfrihet* [About the principle of legality and about general grounds for exemption from liability].

SOU (Swedish Government Official Reports) 1996:185 *Straffansvarets gränser* [The limits of criminal liability].

SOU (Swedish Government Official Reports) 2002:3 *Psykisk störning, brott och ansvar* [Mental disorder, crime and responsibility].

SOU (Swedish Government Official Reports) 2012:17 *Psykiatrin och lagen— tvångsvård, straffansvar och samhälsskydd* [Psychiatry and the law—Compulsory care, criminal responsibility and public protection].

Spencer, J, and Tie, A, 'Psychiatric Symptoms Associated with the Mental Health Defence for Serious Violent Offences in Queensland' (2013) 21(2) *Australasian Psychiatry* 147.

Steadman, HJ, Mulvey, EP, Monahan, J, Robbins, PC, Appelbaum, PS, Grisso, T, Roth, LH and Silver, E, 'Violence by People Discharged from Acute Psychiatric Inpatient Facilities and by Others in the Same Neighborhoods' (1998) 55(5) *Archives of General Psychiatry* 393.

Strahl, I, *Allmän straffrätt i vad angår brotten* (Stockholm, Nordstedt, 1976).

The Law Commission for England and Wales, *Criminal Liability, Insanity and Automatism. A Discussion Paper* (2013) lawcommission.justice.gov.uk/areas/ insanity.htm.

Warren, JI, Murrie, DC, Chauhan, P, Dietz, PE and Morris, J, 'Opinion Formation in Evaluating Sanity at the Time of the Offense: An Examination of 5175 Pretrial Evaluations' (2004) 22(2) *Behavioral Sciences & the Law* 171.

8

Abolishing the Insanity Verdict in England and Wales: A Better Balance Between Legal Rules and Scientific Understanding?

LISA CLAYDON AND PAUL CATLEY

I. Introduction

One of the most problematic relationships between neuroscience and the law is the politicised area of claims of insanity. The relationship between medical science and the law has defined and shaped the insanity defence. The issue that reformers have had to grapple with since the inception of the modern defence of insanity is the public perception of the insanity plea. In 2012–13 the Law Commission for England and Wales, much to its credit, undertook a thorough review of the defences of insanity and automatism. This culminated in the publication of a Discussion Paper entitled *Criminal Liability: Insanity and Automatism*.[1] Preceding this document, a *Scoping Paper*[2] and supporting *Supplementary Material*[3] had been published. The law's effect is described in the *Supplementary Material* as attributing a label that is 'inaccurate, unfair and stigmatising'.[4] Perhaps another flaw identified is the most concerning:

> [T]he defence does not fairly identify those who ought not to be held criminally responsible as a result of their mental condition, and so some of those vulnerable people remain in the penal system, to their detriment, and to the detriment of society at large.[5]

---

[1] Law Commission for England and Wales, *Criminal Liability: Insanity and Automatism—A Discussion Paper*, published 23 July 2013.
[2] Law Commission for England and Wales, *Insanity and Automatism—A Scoping Paper*, published 18 July 2012.
[3] Law Commission for England and Wales, *Insanity and Automatism—Supplementary Material to the Scoping Paper*, published 18 July 2012.
[4] ibid para 1.32.
[5] ibid para 1.33.

In its discussion of how the criminal law with regard to the general defence of insanity should be reformed, the Law Commission identifies several issues which contribute to the underuse of the defence of insanity. One is the problematic distinction which was confirmed in *R v Quick* between sane and insane automatism.[6] This distinction is based upon the identified legal cause of the automatism claim. If the cause is identified as being external to the accused the appropriate plea is sane automatism whereas, if the legal cause is deemed to be internal, the plea is insane automatism. This distinction has both theoretical and practical flaws.[7] The distinction also creates real problems with the sentencing of those who are deemed insane automatons and yet may not suffer from a medically accepted mental disorder.[8] Another issue, a contributory factor in the underuse of the defence, is said to be the nature of the M'Naghten Rules themselves and how they are applied.

In reviewing the law and how it should be reformed the Law Commission only briefly touched upon the possible implications of growing scientific understanding of the brain for the reformed defence. The first part of this chapter will explore how the M'Naghten Rules have reached a point where they are viewed as complex and far removed from a modern medical perspective of mental disorder. It will also trace the difficult politico-legal environment in which the defence developed. The proposals put forward in the Law Commission's *Discussion Paper* will be reviewed. Finally, the chapter will consider whether the Law Commission has achieved in its conclusions and proposals the objective that it set out in the *Supplementary Material to the Scoping Paper*:

> We believe it is important as a matter of principle that criminal responsibility should be correctly ascribed. Doing so, through operation of the law, reflects society's judgment and attribution of blame. It is not just a matter of accurately communicating by means of a verdict what conclusion a court has reached about a person's culpability (what is described as 'fair labelling'), though that is important too.[9]

II. Historical Development of the Common Law of Insanity. The Trial of Daniel M'Naghten

The criticism that the defence 'does not fairly identify those who ought not to be held criminally responsible' leads to a question: how did this come about?

---

[6] *R v Quick* [1973] QB 910 (CA).

[7] For a discussion of these, see, for example, *Discussion Paper* (n 1) section headed 'Arbitrary classifications', paras 5.39–5.54.

[8] This leads to problems with the disposal/detention of such individuals who receive a 'not guilty by reason of insanity' verdict. Article 5 of the European Convention for the Protection of Human Rights and Fundamental Freedoms specifically through its interpretation by case law provides that those who are not of unsound mind should not be detained for 'treatment'. For a discussion of this see *Supplementary Material* (n 3) paras 5.5–5.41.

[9] ibid para 1.13.

The answer lies in the common law and its interpretation of the M'Naghten Rules. The rules were not set down in a legal case following legal argument. They are an explanation given in answer to questions put by the House of Lords, as the result of public and political disquiet at the acquittal[10] of Daniel M'Naghten, following what was possibly an attempt to assassinate the Prime Minister, Robert Peel. M'Naghten had shot and killed Edward Drummond, Peel's political secretary. Furthermore, the rules are set out in answer to questions regarding the instructions to be given to juries in particular circumstances—cases of partial insanity where there is evidence of a delusion that the criminal act will redress or avenge 'some supposed grievance or injury' or produce a public benefit.[11]

The political disapproval of the decision to acquit M'Naghten is palpable. It is clear from the report of what has become referred to as *M'Naghten's Case*. It is also clear from the discussion in the House of Lords following M'Naghten's acquittal as the result of his successful insanity plea. *Hansard* reports the Lord Chancellor as making the following statement at the opening of a House of Lords' debate upon the matter:

> A gentleman in the prime of life, of a most amiable character, incapable of giving offence or of injuring any individual, was murdered in the streets of this metropolis in open day. The assassin was secured; he was committed for trial; that trial has taken place, and he has escaped with impunity. Your Lordships will not be surprised that these circumstances should have created a deep feeling in the public mind, and that many persons should, upon the first impression, be disposed to think that there is some great defect in the laws of the country with reference to this subject which calls for a revision of those laws, in order that a repetition of such outrages may be prevented.[12]

The influence of public opinion on the discussion in the House of Lords is notable. The Lord Chancellor describes the subject matter of the debate as 'one in which the public take a deep interest. Everything, therefore, connected with it ought to be laid before the public, through your Lordships, with the upmost possible precision'.[13]

The outcome of this debate was that judges from the Queen's Bench were summoned to appear before the House of Lords to explain the law on insanity. Both the dissenting and the majority legal opinions show the animosity of the judges to the exercise by the legislature of this power.[14]

What Was the Purpose of the Interrogation of the Judges?

In answering this question it is necessary to look at some of the questions posed by the House of Lords and examine the answers given. The first question posed

---

[10] Daniel M'Naghten was found 'Not Guilty, on the ground of insanity': *M'Naghten's Case* [1843–60] All ER Rep 229, 230.
[11] ibid.
[12] HL Deb 13 March 1843, vol 713, col 2.
[13] ibid vol 715, col 2.
[14] *M'Naghten's Case* (n 10) Maule J 231D, Tindal LCJ 233B.

by the politicians was very focused with regard to the responsibility of those who suffered from a certain type of delusion and as a result of that delusion committed a criminal act. The question specifically focused on determining the criminal responsibility of someone who:

> at the time of the commission of the alleged crime … knew that he was acting contrary to law, but did the act complained of with a view, under the influence of insane delusion, of redressing or revenging some supposed grievance or injury, or of producing some supposed public benefit.[15]

This issue was also the central focus of the fourth and fifth questions posed by the House of Lords to the judges. The fourth question concerned the precise nature of what should excuse criminal responsibility and the fifth on the use of expert evidence to inform jury decisions. Their Lordships asked the judges: 'If a person under an insane delusion as to existing facts commits an offence in consequence thereof, is he thereby excused?'[16]

This question of what should excuse is central to the debate surrounding the defences of automatism and insanity to this day. Similarly issues surrounding expert evidence remain important. The final question put to the judges betrays scepticism of a certain type of expert evidence:

> Can a medical man conversant with the disease of insanity, who never saw the prisoner previously to the trial, but who was present during the whole trial and the examination of all the witnesses, be asked his opinion as to the state of the prisoner's mind at the time of the commission of the alleged crime, or his opinion whether the prisoner was conscious at the time of doing the act, that he was acting contrary to law, or whether he was labouring under any and what delusion at the time?[17]

The answers of the judges are not unanimous. Maule J dissents from the majority view given by Lord Chief Justice Tindal. Maule J's reasons for dissenting are interesting. He expresses concerns at giving insanity, a fixed, rule-bound, definition. Maule J is concerned at the specificity of the questions posed by the legislature. His particular concern is that he has not had the benefit of hearing adversarial legal argument on the issues raised by the questions. He is also concerned that, given the importance of the questions and the fact that the issue is 'of frequent use', the answers given will 'embarrass the administration of justice when they are cited in criminal trials'.[18] His concern here seems to be that the facts of such cases vary infinitely and therefore an inflexible statement of the law rather than a general principle will prove to be problematic. Underlying the reasoning, in his opinion, seems to be an implicit view that the House of Lords should never have entered into this dialogue with the judges as this is an unwarranted interference with the normal processes of the common law.

---

[15] ibid 230, I.
[16] ibid 231, B.
[17] ibid 231, C.
[18] ibid 231, E.

Maule J offers what he seems to consider an unsatisfactory answer to question one. He claims his answer cannot cover all the legal issues that arise: 'I am quite unable to do so, and, indeed, doubt whether it be possible to be done'.[19] He makes it clear that he has no sympathy with the question which he answers:

[O]nly so far as it comprehends the question whether a person circumstanced as stated in the question, is, for that reason only, to be found Not Guilty of a crime respecting which the question of his guilt has been duly raised in a criminal proceeding.[20]

His answer to the question is that such a person is responsible for his crime(s). According to Maule the test of insanity is based on the issue of knowing right from wrong. This test applies however deluded a belief system might be held by the defendant. On the issue of expert evidence Maule is of the view that this will entirely depend on a variety of issues, not just the facts of the case. He declines to give a firm answer to this question.

Maule's dissenting opinion seems, to say the least, sceptical of the political purpose behind the questions put to the judges. His opinion is interesting for what it has to say about an eminent Victorian judge's view of a politically based inquiry into the meaning and purpose of the common law plea of insanity. He emphasises the importance of the judge's role in advising the jury on how the law applies to the facts. He is clear that the reason he does not wish to see the law formalised is because he thinks it will interfere with this role:

[T]here are no terms which the judge is by law required to use. They should not be inconsistent with the law as above stated, but should be such as, in the discretion of the judge, are proper to assist the jury in coming to a right conclusion as to the guilt of the accused.[21]

On the subject of the use of expert evidence he is similarly clear. It should be admitted when it is required by the circumstances of the case:

[T]hough the person has never seen the person before the trial, and though he has merely been present and heard the witnesses. These circumstances, of his never having seen the person before, and of his having merely been present at the trial, are not necessarily sufficient, as it seems to me, to exclude the lawfulness of a question which is otherwise lawful,[22]

He draws authority from this statement from the actual trial of *R v Daniel M'Naughten*.[23] The tone of his dissenting opinion is that the common law is a flexible tool. It allows judges to work from principle and to advise juries in a flexible manner appropriate to doing justice in individual cases working from

---

[19] ibid 231, H.
[20] ibid 231, H–I.
[21] ibid 232, D.
[22] ibid 232, F.
[23] A report of the proceedings may be found in the Proceedings of the Old Bailey Reference Number: t18430227-874. In the report the spelling is M'Naughten whereas in the All England Reports it is M'Naghten.

accepted principles. Neither his opinion nor the opinion of the majority set out below suggests that the answering of the questions put by the politicians would alter the underlying law on insanity. Where the opinion of the majority differs is in suggesting an instruction that could be given to juries.

The M'Naghten Rules: The Presumption of Sanity

The opinion of the majority of the judges was given by Tindal LCJ. Like Maule J they object to being asked to give their opinion as to the application of the law. They also state that they would have preferred to hear legal arguments concerning the defence of insanity presented in an adversarial context. They conclude that it is their duty as judges to 'declare the law upon each particular case'. In view of this they state clearly that their answers do not alter the general law in terms of insanity but are specific to the law relating to those afflicted by insane delusions. More particularly their opinion as to the law focuses on those defendants who suffer from 'partial delusions only, and are not in other respects insane'.[24] The answer in this respect to the first question—regarding those acting 'under the influence of insane delusion, of redressing or revenging some supposed grievance or injury, or producing some supposed public benefit'[25] where the defendant knew that his acts were contrary to the law—is answered directly: 'he is nevertheless punishable according to the nature of the crime committed'.[26]

The answer given by Tindal LCJ to the question as to the proper instructions to be given to the jury and the questions to be submitted to the jury for their consideration when a defendant claimed to be 'afflicted by an insane delusion' has become known as the M'Naghten Rules. In giving this answer he specifically addresses the second and third questions posed by the House of Lords. The second was:

> What are the proper questions to be submitted to the jury when a person alleged to be afflicted with insane delusion respecting one or more particular subjects or persons is charged with the commission of a crime (murder, for example), and insanity is set up as a defence?[27]

The third question asked: 'In what terms ought the question to be left to the jury as to the prisoner's state of mind at the time when the act was committed?'[28] The answer to these questions was given as follows:

> jurors ought to be told in all cases that every man is presumed to be sane and to possess a sufficient degree of reason to be responsible for his crimes until the contrary be proved to their satisfaction, and that to establish a defence on the ground of insanity it must be clearly proved that, at the time of the committing of the act the party accused was labouring under such a defect of reason, from disease of the mind, as not to know the nature

---

[24] *M'Naghten's Case* (n 10) 233, E.
[25] ibid 233, E.
[26] ibid 233, F.
[27] ibid 233, G.
[28] ibid 233, H.

and quality of the act he was doing, or, if he did know it, that he did not know he was doing what was wrong.[29]

Clarification is given by Tindal LCJ to the interpretation and application of the jury instruction in particular circumstances and some of that clarification is noteworthy. First, he makes it clear that the requirement with regard to knowing that 'he was doing what was wrong' as employed by judges in such cases related to knowledge of the distinction between right and wrong. He comments that when put in this manner there was rarely any difficulty for juries. The relevant question for the jury was whether the accused 'was conscious that the act was one that he ought not to do, and if that act was at the same time contrary to the law of the land, he is punishable'.[30] Tindal LCJ remarks that the usual practice has been to frame the jury question in terms of whether 'the party accused had a sufficient degree of reason to know he was doing an act that was wrong'.[31] This question was to be put in relation to the criminal act with which the defendant is charged.

This response links to the majority's answer to the fourth question: 'If a person under an insane delusion commits an offence in consequence thereof, is he thereby excused?'[32] Their answer is that the accused must be treated as if the delusion were real. Tindal LCJ gives the following example:

> [I]f under the influence of his delusion he supposes another man to be in the act of attempting to take away his life, and he kills that man, as he supposes, in self-defence, he would be exempt from punishment. If his delusion was that the deceased had inflicted a serious injury to his character and fortune, and he killed him in revenge for such supposed injury, he would be liable to punishment.[33]

Finally, with regard to the provision of expert evidence; the majority of the judges are of the opinion that the scientific view is acceptable in such cases, but only where the expert is not answering issues raised on the facts which could and should be answered by the jury. The majority opinion is critical of the terms in which the question is posed suggesting that it would only be acceptable if the facts were not disputed. As in such a case: 'the question becomes substantially one of science only, it may be convenient to allow the question to be put in that general form, though the same cannot be insisted on as a matter of right'.[34]

What Was the Effect of *M'Naghten's Case*?

There is a strong implication that, following this statement of the law in relation to insanity, delusional beliefs would only found an insanity defence in prescribed circumstances. Where the delusional belief provided an explanation for why the

---

[29] ibid 233, I.
[30] ibid 234, B.
[31] ibid 234, B–C.
[32] ibid 234, C.
[33] ibid 234, E.
[34] ibid 234, H.

defendant felt her specific act was not wrong the plea might succeed. For example, where the delusion related to the need for self-defence the insanity plea might succeed. But, wrongness in this sense did not extend to her reasons for acting, in other circumstances, unless they were relevant to her understanding of the nature and quality of her physical act. Thus a delusional belief in the need for redress or revenge could not support a claim that the criminal act was not wrong. If this interpretation had been applied in *M'Naghten's Case* it seems likely that Daniel M'Naghten would have struggled to gain an acquittal. However, where insanity, unrelated to delusional beliefs of such a specific type and nature, was claimed, the assumption must be that the old law in relation to insanity held true.

The old law was based on the common law as set out in Hale's *History of the Pleas to the Crown*. Hale wrote of the difficulty of identifying insanity, and how the onus was upon the judge and jury to weigh the circumstances of the crime and the plea, 'lest on the one side there be a kind of inhumanity towards the defects of human nature, or on the other side too great an indulgence given to great crimes'. The most helpful measure, Hale concluded, was to ask the question whether the accused had 'ordinarily as great understanding, as ordinarily a child of fourteen years hath'. If he did, he was not insane.[35] There is a suggestion from the answers given by the judges in *M'Naghten's Case* that by the 1840s this definition of insanity had come to be interpreted by common law judges and explained to juries in terms of the ability of the accused to reason, or to be conscious that the act was one which he did not know he ought not to do.

The use of the defence of insanity and the application of the rules in the later part of the nineteenth century is variable. On occasion the defence was rejected, but the judge expressed concern about the outcome. Additionally, where public sentiment was engaged, then the judge's conduct of the trial was often heavily scrutinised. *Townley's Case* is a good illustration of both points.[36] Townley killed his fiancée when she asked to be released from their engagement so that she could marry someone else. Townley pleaded insanity but, following a direction in accordance with the M'Naghten Rules, the defence failed and he was convicted of murder by the jury. However, the judge then wrote to the Home Secretary drawing to his attention the fact that at the trial medical opinion had supported an insanity plea. The Home Secretary had the matter investigated by the Commissioners in Lunacy. The result was that Townley had his sentence commuted to penal servitude and thus avoided the hangman's noose.[37] As in *M'Naghten's Case*, there was public outcry at the perceived leniency of this revised sentence. The *Saturday Review* commented: 'What the defence seems to come to is this:—That the greater the rogue a man is, the more entirely is he free from responsibility'.[38]

---

[35] M Hale, *Historia Placitorum Coronæ* [The History of the Pleas of the Crown], Chapter IV, (1680) 30 (both quotations).
[36] *R v Townley* (1863) 3 F & F 839, (1863) 176 ER 384.
[37] R Smith, *Trial by Medicine* (Edinburgh, Edinburgh University Press, 1981) 132.
[38] *The Saturday Review* 16 (1863) 776–77.

The Developing Law

However, this does not mean that in all insanity cases the judges stuck rigidly to the M'Naghten Rules when advising juries. James Fitzjames Stephen[39] was responsible, later in his life, as the presiding judge in the trial of *R v Davis* for an extremely flexible interpretation of the M'Naghten Rules. He informed the jury that the test to be applied in this case to the plea of insanity was the M'Naghten Rules, but his direction to the jury was as follows:

> As I understand the law, any disease which so disturbs the mind that you cannot think calmly and rationally of all the different reasons to which we refer in considering the rightness and wrongness of an action ... may fairly be said to prevent a man from knowing that what he did was wrong ... Both the doctors agree that the prisoner was unable to control his conduct, and that nothing short of actual physical restraint would have deterred him ... If you think there was a distinct disease caused by drinking, but different from drunkenness, and that by reason thereof he did not know that the act was wrong, you will find a verdict of not guilty on the grounds of insanity.[40]

A stricter approach was adopted to the interpretation of the M'Naghten Rules in the first part of the twentieth century. *R v Codère*[41] considered the common law regarding the meaning of what became referred to as the first limb of the M'Naghten Rules. The Court of Appeal was asked to consider and refused to draw a distinction between 'nature' and 'quality' of a criminal act in the application of the rules. The argument which was put to the court was that 'quality' referred to the moral quality of the act. Lord Chief Justice Reading giving his opinion said 'that in using the language "nature and quality" the judges were only dealing with the physical character of the act, and were not intending to distinguish between the physical and moral aspects of the act'.[42]

Ruling Out Irresistible Impulse

In *R v True*[43] the Court of Appeal had reason to examine the status of the M'Naghten Rules again. The court considered what the legal approach should be where the only evidence put forward at trial was that at the time of the criminal offence True was 'certifiably insane'. It was argued on behalf of True that the

---

[39] Sir James Fitzjames Stephen was a distinguished judge and writer on criminal law: see in particular his books *A General View of the Criminal Law of England*, 1st edn (London, Macmillan & Co, 1863) 1863 and *A History of the Criminal Law of England* (three volumes), (London, Macmillan & Co, 1883). For assessments of his life and work see: KJM Smith, *James Fitzjames Stephen: Portrait of a Victorian Rationalist* (Cambridge, Cambridge University Press, 1988) and SJ Morse, 'Thoroughly Modern: Sir James Fitzjames Stephen on Criminal Responsibility' (2007) 5 *Ohio State Journal of Criminal Law* 505.

[40] *R v Davis* (1881) 14 Cox CC 563 (CrCt).

[41] *R v Codère* (1917) 12 Cr App R 21 (CCA).

[42] ibid 27.

[43] *R v True* (1922) 16 Cr App R 164 (CCA).

appropriate verdict after the trial should have been a special verdict under the Trial of Lunatics Act 1883. Evidence provided to the appeal court showed that all four medical witnesses were in agreement that the defendant was insane. The Crown had not called medical evidence to dispute these findings. A point at issue was the status of the M'Naghten Rules, it being claimed that medical science had made considerable advances since the rules were framed, nearly 80 years earlier.

A further point for consideration by the court was a reinterpretation of the rules which had appeared in the 1904 edition of *Stephen's Criminal Digest*.[44] The argument was made on behalf of the appellant that this gave recognition to a defence of irresistible impulse. The quotation submitted for consideration by the court was:

> No act is a crime if the person who does it is at the time when it is done prevented [either by defective mental power or] by any disease affecting his mind (a) from knowing the nature and quality of his act or (b) from knowing that the act is wrong; [or (c) from controlling his own conduct, unless the absence of the power of control has been produced by his own default].[45]

In the Court of Appeal, Lord Chief Justice Hewart refers to a note attached to the quotation that states that the words within the brackets are said to be 'doubtful'.[46] The appeal court heard evidence that the direction given in *Davis* by Stephens J reflected accepted law and had been followed in three subsequent cases.[47] The issue was also said by counsel for the appellant to have been reviewed by Lord Chief Justice Alverstone in *R v Jones (Victor)*,[48] where it was claimed that he recognised that 'loss of self-control, through mental disease, might be a possible ground of excuse; and left the question open for future consideration'.[49]

This was one of the issues that had to be decided on appeal in *True*. Hewart LCJ gave the judgment of the court. He reviewed the status of the medical evidence that the accused was insane at the time of the commission of the act. The argument on behalf of the appellant was that as this evidence was uncontested by the Crown the jury were bound to accept it. This argument was rejected by the Court of Appeal on the grounds that the jury was entitled to reach a decision based on the whole facts before them. Also rejected was the contention that there was a need to extend the ambit of the M'Naghten Rules to include cases where the accused was 'deprived of the power of controlling his actions'.[50]

---

[44] Stephen, JF, *Stephen's Criminal Digest*, 6th edn (London, Macmillan & Co, 1904).
[45] *True* (n 43) 165. The passage quoted being taken from p 21 of Stephen (n 44).
[46] *True* (n 43) 165.
[47] *R v Hay* (1911) 22 Cox CC 268, 75 JP 480 (CCC); *R v Fryer* (1915) 24 Cox CC 403 (Assizes); and *R v Jolly* (1919) 83 JP 296 (Assizes). In *R v True* the inclusion of *R v Hay* was disputed by the Crown as being an inaccurate report of the proceedings.
[48] *R v Jones (Victor)* (1910) 4 Cr App R 207 (CCA).
[49] *True* (n 43) 165–66.
[50] ibid 169–70.

Legally or Morally Wrong?

A further clarification with regard to the ambit of the rules came in *R v Windle*,[51] a case where the meaning of the second limb of the rules was considered. The appeal court confirmed that the limb of the rules which states 'if he did know it, that he did not know he was doing what was wrong'[52] should receive the following interpretation: the knowledge required was knowledge of legal not moral wrong.[53] This interpretation appears much more prescriptive and limiting than that origi-nally given by Tindal LCJ.[54] In 2007 the Court of Appeal were asked to revisit the issue of the applicability of the rules and in particular this limb of the rules in *R v Dean Johnson*.[55] What the court said about the rules is informative:

> It is to be remembered that the whole basis of what are described as the M'Naghten Rules in the answers given by the judges to a series of questions from the House of Lords which they dealt with without, it would appear, any argument by counsel. It has always been recognised that the M'Naghten Rules, accordingly, are rules which have to be approached with some caution.[56]

The court supported the interpretation of Lord Chief Justice Goddard in *Windle* that the knowledge of wrong referred to the issue of whether the defendant knew his criminal act was legally wrong. But they expressed strong reservations concerning the M'Naghten Rules. Johnson's appeal is dismissed but the appeal court states: 'This area, however, is a notorious area of debate and quite rightly so. There is room for reconsideration of rules and, in particular, rules which have their genesis in the early years of the 19th century'.[57]

A Place for Neuroscience?

This approach narrowed the question posed by the second limb of the rules. The defect of reason in relation to the rightness or wrongness of the act became a purely cognitive test. Did this defendant know the act was against the law? *Windle* also, by implication, confirmed the applicability of the rules to all cases of insanity. The judges, in answering the questions posed by the House of Lords following *M'Naghten's Case*, had been clear that their answers related only to par-tial delusions and did not extend to cases of insanity more generally. It is therefore

---

[51] *R v Windle* [1952] 2 QB 826 (CCA).
[52] *M'Naghten's Case* (nn 10 and 29) and accompanying text.
[53] Goddard LCJ giving the judgment of the Court of Appeal states: 'There is no doubt that the word "wrong" in the M'Naghten Rules means contrary to law and does not have some vague meaning which may vary according to the opinion of different persons whether a particular act might or might not be justified'. *R v Windle* (n 51) 3.
[54] See *M'Naghten's Case* (nn 10 and 23) and accompanying text.
[55] *R v Johnson (Dean)* [2007] EWCA Crim 1978, [2008] Crim LR 132.
[56] ibid [14] per Latham LJ (V-P).
[57] ibid [24] per Latham LJ (V-P).

not surprising that research into the use of neuroscientific evidence in court by defendants in criminal cases showed that no neuroscientific evidence had been adduced in support of this second limb.[58]

Given the mechanistic nature of the definition of the first limb of the rules it is surprising that little trace of expert evidence of a neurocognitive nature, explaining how action is experienced, has been recorded relating to this limb. This relationship was canvassed in *R v Burgess*.[59]

> Dr Fenwick, whose opinion was that this was not a sleepwalking episode at all. If it was a case where the appellant was unconscious of what he was doing, the most likely explanation was that he was in what is described as a hysterical dissociative state. That is a state in which, for psychological reasons, such as being overwhelmed by his emotions, the person's brain works in a different way. He carries out acts of which he has no knowledge and for which he has no memory.[60]

The Court of Appeal accepts this evidence in rejecting Burgess's appeal against the refusal of the trial judge to put non-insane automatism to the jury. The insanity verdict was upheld. The main ground for this was not the neurocognitive explanation of the behaviour but the law's distinction between external and internal causes of behaviour.

Further Problems in Interpreting the Rules: The Defence of Automatism

In the introduction, the problem of the distinction between insane and sane automatism was canvassed and is worthy of exploration in more detail. The first references to automatism occur in case law of about the turn of the nineteenth/ twentieth century. In the record of trials from the Old Bailey,[61] two trials contain reference to a plea of insane automatism based on medical evidence of epilepsy. These are two murder cases: Harry William Ball tried in 1910[62] and William Henry Philpot tried in 1912.[63] Ball succeeded in establishing a defence of insanity raising

---

[58] Catley, P and Claydon L, 'The Use of Neuroscientific Evidence in the Courtroom by Those Accused of Criminal Offences in England and Wales' (2015) 2 *Journal of Law and Biosciences* 1. This research focused on the use of neuroscientific evidence by defendants in reported criminal cases between 2005 and 2012. Although 204 cases were found in which those accused of criminal offences made use of neuroscientific evidence, none of those cases were cases where the insanity defence was pleaded.

[59] *R v Burgess* [1991] 2 AU ER 769.

[60] ibid 776.

[61] A report of the proceedings may be found at Proceedings of the Old Bailey Reference No: t19100718-27.

[62] Ball was tried on 20 July 1910 before Ridley J.

[63] Philpot was tried on 1 February 1912 before Ridley J. Philpot's claim that he was in an automatic state failed. He was found to have been sane at the time of the killing. Interestingly the jury found that Philpot acted in a fit of temper 'without intention of killing'. The judge pressed the jury on what they meant by 'without intention of killing'. The foreman of the jury explained that the jury 'unanimously

sufficient doubt in the mind of the jury to gain a guilty but insane verdict. The case report records much of the evidence given at trial and is remarkable because Ball's defence succeeds despite his actions in shooting the victim being witnessed: and, from the report given by the witnesses at trial and under cross-examination, seemingly being purposeful acts. There is a significant amount of medical evidence supporting the defence and prosecution cases and the eminence of one of the medical experts for the defence[64] may explain why the plea is successful.

The use of the automatism defence and its relationship with epilepsy was further considered in *Bratty v Attorney General for Northern Ireland*.[65] Bratty's defence team employed evidence relating to psychomotor epilepsy to argue a number of defences to a charge of murder. Three arguments were made at trial by the defence. The first was that Bratty was in a state of automatism at the time of the killing. The legal argument made to support this claim was that the Crown must prove beyond reasonable doubt that the 'acts constituting the crime charged were conscious and voluntary acts'.[66] Secondly, it was argued that Bratty was incapable of forming the relevant *mens rea* due to his impaired and confused state of mind. Thus the defence argued, in the alternative, that the appropriate verdict was guilty of manslaughter and not murder. Finally, if the first two were rejected, the jury should consider the insanity defence.[67] The judge put the defence of insanity to the jury but declined to ask the jury to consider a manslaughter verdict or the defence of automatism. Factually there was no dispute that he had strangled his victim with her own stocking but he claimed to have no memory of the events. Bratty was convicted of murder. Bratty appealed to the Court of Criminal Appeal in Northern Ireland regarding the judge's refusal to put the defence of automatism or the defence's legal argument regarding manslaughter to the jury. The Court of Criminal Appeal rejected this appeal. He then appealed to the House of Lords.

The House of Lords considered the relationship between insanity and automatism in some detail. The Lord Chancellor Viscount Kilmuir accepted that legal authority[68] required that the prosecution prove that the voluntary act of the

---

and emphatically' considered the accused 'did not realise the consequences of what he was doing'. The jury were asked to reconsider their verdict. The jury's reformulated verdict was: 'We find that the prisoner killed his wife, and very strongly recommend him to mercy'. Philpot was sentenced to death. A report of the proceedings may be found at Proceedings of the Old Bailey Reference No: t19120130-53.

[64] Theophilus Hyslop MD, senior physician Bethlem Royal Hospital, Lecturer on Mental Diseases St Mary's Hospital and London School of Medicine.

[65] *Bratty v Attorney General for Northern Ireland* [1963] AC 386 (HL).

[66] ibid 392.

[67] ibid.

[68] ibid 407 where Kilmuir refers to *Woolmington v DPP* [1935] AC 462. In *Woolmington* Lord Sankey states: 'the Crown must prove (a) death as a result of a voluntary act of the accused' (482). Earlier in his opinion Sankey says: 'All that is meant is that if it is proved that the conscious act of the prisoner killed a man and nothing else appears in the case, there is evidence upon which a jury may, not must, find him guilty of murder' (480).

accused killed the victim. The main issue considered in his opinion was how that argument should be made in court. Should the prosecution have to show that the act was voluntary once the accused asserted that the act was not voluntary? If evidence was required, what was the burden and where was it to be placed to establish the automatism defence? Should the burden be the same as in insanity cases where the burden rested on the defence? Furthermore how should the two defences be argued when the automatism defence rested on medical evidence that might also point towards an insanity verdict?[69]

Kilmuir answers the questions with regard to the overlap between evidence of insanity and evidence of automatism by saying that there needed to be sufficient evidence of confusion and lack of voluntariness to provide the evidential foundation for an automatism defence. He agreed with the trial judge that in Bratty's case there was no such evidence to place before the jury.[70] Kilmuir confirms that, in his view, the basis of the plea of automatism is to be found in common law principles regarding what must be established by the prosecution beyond reasonable doubt at trial. One of these principles was stated by Lord Sankey in *Woolmington* as requiring that the prosecution must establish that the criminal act resulted from 'a voluntary act of the accused'.[71] Kilmuir states that once there is sufficient evidence to raise the issue of automatism then, if

> the jury are left in real doubt whether or not the accused acted in a state of automatism, it seems to me that on principle they should acquit because the necessary mens rea—if indeed the actus reus—has not been proved beyond reasonable doubt.[72]

Lord Denning in his opinion gave a further gloss to these arguments attempting to define automatism in a manner which has been widely cited in subsequent case law:

> No act is punishable if it is done involuntarily: and an involuntary act in this context—some people nowadays prefer to speak of it as 'automatism'—means an act which is done by the muscles without any control by the mind, such as a spasm, a reflex action or a convulsion; or an act done by a person who is not conscious of what he is doing, such as an act done whilst suffering from concussion or whilst sleep-walking.[73]

In Denning's view there were two parts to the automatism defence: one which seemed confined to situations where the muscles brought about action but there

---

[69] The issue with regard to burden of proof will be considered later when examining the reform proposals.

[70] *Bratty* (n 65) 406. Kilmuir refers to Devlin LJ's statement in *Hill v Baxter* [1958] 1 QB, 277, 285: 'Unless there was evidence that his irrationality was due to some cause other than disease of the mind, the justices were not entitled simply to acquit'.

[71] *Woolmington v DPP* [1935] AC 462, 482 (HL).

[72] *Bratty* (n 65) 407.

[73] ibid 409. Lord Denning's definition of automatism in Bratty has been widely referred to in the case law of other jurisdictions. For example *R v Burr* [1969] NZLR 736; *State v Caddell* 215 SE 2d 348 (NC 1975); *Rabey v The Queen* [1980] 2 SCR 513; *Fulcher v State* 633 P 2d 142 (Wyo 1981); *Queen v Falconer* (1990) 171 CLR 30; *Ross v HM Advocate* 1991 SLT 564; *R v Parks* [1992] 2 SCR 871; *McClain v State* 678 NE 2d 104 (Ind 1997); *R v Stone* (1999) 134 CCC (3d) 353.

was no mental control of the resulting movement; and a second where the actor was not conscious of controlling the physical action. Both definitions were to prove problematic; the second even more problematic than the first. Regarding whether physical acts resulting from muscle movements may be differentiated and reported by an agent in the manner described by Lord Denning is to say the least contentious. It has led to considerable discussion of what it means to act voluntarily.

Neurocognitive Perspectives on Voluntariness

Neurocognitive research suggests that our ability to describe how we bring about basic actions when we are conscious is limited. The description of what distinguishes voluntary actions from stimulus-determined actions in a scientific sense is challenging. Haggard, in search of a scientifically satisfying description of voluntary action, attempts to refine what may be viewed as the dualistic descriptions of ordinary language and writes:

> A scientifically more satisfactory approach defines voluntary action by contrasting it with more stimulus-driven actions: voluntary action lies at one end of a continuum that has simple reflexes at the other end. Thus, whereas reflexes are immediate motor responses, the form of which is determined by the form of stimulation, the occurrence, timing and form of a voluntary action are not directly determined, or at best are only very indirectly determined, by any identifiable external stimulus.[74]

Complex Relationships

The relationship between automatism, insane automatism and insanity became increasingly complex after the cases of *R v Quick*[75] and *R v Sullivan*.[76] In *Quick* the distinction between sane and insane automatism was said to be dependent on the identified legal cause of the automatism being deemed to be external or internal. In *Quick* the cause was the failure to take food after an insulin injection to control diabetes. This cause was said to be external to the accused and therefore to be able to found a defence of sane automatism, whereas in *R v Hennessy*[77] the failure of a diabetic to take insulin meant that the underlying, legally relevant, cause of his behaviour was deemed to be internal, his diabetes. Thus despite some external factors, stress anxiety and depression being evidenced, the actual legal cause of the behaviour was a disease: diabetes.

The House of Lords in *R v Sullivan* considered the issue of the divide between insanity and automatism in greater detail. Sullivan committed an assault on a

---

[74] P Haggard, 'Human Volition: Towards a Neuroscience of Will' (2008) 9 *Nature Reviews Neuroscience* 934.
[75] *Quick* (n 6).
[76] *R v Sullivan* [1983] 2 All ER 673 (HL).
[77] *R v Hennessy* [1989] 1 WLR 287 (CA).

friend during the post-ictal phase of a seizure caused by psychomotor epilepsy. The issue on appeal was whether Viscount Kilmuir's definition of automatism in *Bratty* entitled a defendant such as Sullivan to an automatism defence—or was the only available defence insanity? Key to this distinction was the meaning of disease of the mind in the M'Naghten Rules. The House of Lords' opinions were unanimous. The main opinion being given by Lord Diplock, who reasoned that if the evidence before the court concerned what the law would view as a disease of the mind, any question with regard to the voluntariness of action should be considered as a plea of insanity.[78] Lord Diplock also affirmed the M'Naghten Rules as having general application in cases of insanity and not being restricted to cases of insane delusions.[79] The issue to be considered by the House of Lords was whether someone who 'whilst recovering from a seizure due to psychomotor epilepsy and who did not know what he was doing when he caused such harm and has no memory of what he did should be found not guilty by reason of insanity'.[80] Lord Diplock argued that even cases of 'temporary' insanity should fall within the rules.[81] He went on to state that to provide evidence of insanity the defence had to provide evidence to establish a disease of the mind which would demonstrate impairment of the following 'mental' faculties: reason, memory and understanding.[82]

This interpretation of insanity effectively meant that the insanity defence had become incredibly technical, difficult to argue and of limited attractiveness to a criminal defence team. The test had become a test of cognitive understanding and the legal definition of insanity as encompassed by the rules had removed many recognised mental disorders that relate to volitional impairment rather than cognitive impairment from the insanity defence. Thus a defendant who has sufficient understanding to recognise the physical nature and quality of the criminal act and has some comprehension that it was legally wrong, even if she believed it to be morally appropriate, on a strict application of the M'Naghten Rules cannot be legally insane.

Concerns Regarding the Underuse of the Defence

In reviewing the current law consideration has been given to the fact that little reference is made to neuroscientific evidence. In a sense as the law is based on old cases one cannot expect to find modern scientific understanding used in evidence to support or to disprove insanity or automatism pleas. Thus most comment in this chapter regarding neuroscientific findings is confined to the review of the reform proposals. The need for law reform in this area is pressing, not least because there is considerable evidence that the defence is underutilised.

---

[78] *Sullivan* (n 76) 677.
[79] ibid 676.
[80] ibid.
[81] ibid 678.
[82] ibid 677.

Research covering the period 1997–2001 put the number of successful insanity pleas in that four-year period at 72.[83] The Law Commission for England and Wales commissioned further research in preparation for the review of the insanity defence. This research revealed that there were 223 successful pleas of insanity in the period between 2002 and 2011.[84] The research found that the use of the defence fluctuated throughout this period. In the materials supporting the original *Scoping Paper* issued by the Law Commission an attempt was made to assess the number of defendants facing trial in the Crown Court who might be expected to be suffering from serious mental disorders at the time of the crime. Such a figure is hard to compute. However, the Commission sought to include within the *Insanity and Automatism Supplementary Material to the Scoping Paper* an informed guess as to the number of those suffering from a serious mental disorder who might be tried for a criminal offence(s) in the Crown Court. It was estimated that 10 per cent of the prison population suffered from serious mental illness.[85] Whilst it is accepted that the criminal law definition of insanity does not equate to medical ascriptions of serious medical illness, this 10 per cent figure still contrasts starkly with the fact that only 0.03 per cent of defendants[86] in any one year were able to mount a successful insanity defence. This would seem to contrast with the situation in 1843. Maule J refers to the fact that the questions posed by the House of Lords 'relate to matters of criminal law of great importance and frequent occurrence'. By this he is presumably meaning that claims of insanity were frequent.

A variety of reasons are suggested to be the cause of this. These include the diversion of offenders from trial by means of the fitness to plead provisions, or gaps in the data accessed for the research. Some of the possible reasons put forward for the failure to plead insanity are of concern. 'Some of those who plead guilty do so because of a mental disorder'.[87] Defendants who could raise the defence do not plead insanity.[88] Some who have a serious mental disorder at the time of the crime are unable to plead insanity because the legal definition of insanity means they simply cannot fit within the defence as defined at present.[89] Finally there is particular reference to defendants who suffer from a learning disability.[90] At present these defendants are not caught within the ambit of the insanity defence unless their IQ falls below 70.[91]

---

[83] RD Mackay, BJ Mitchell and L Howe, 'Yet More Facts about the Insanity Defence' (2006) *Criminal Law Review* 399, 400.

[84] RD Mackay, 'The Insanity Defence—Data on Verdicts of Not Guilty by Reason of Insanity from 2002 to 2011' in *Supplementary Material* (n 3) paras E.5 and E.6. of Appendix E.

[85] ibid 3.32.

[86] ibid.

[87] ibid (3).

[88] ibid (4).

[89] ibid (5).

[90] ibid (7).

[91] *R v Masih* [1986] *Crim LR* 395 (CA). The requirement that a defendant must have an IQ of under 70 to be classed as insane is much more stringent than the old approach set out by Hale (n 35) that a person was not insane if he had the understanding of a 14-year-old.

There are many good reasons why one might wish to see those who suffer from serious mental disorders identified. This should improve the manner in which they are treated by the criminal justice system. Implicitly the common law requires culpability to depend on proof of the ability of an individual to make their behaviour conform to the requirements of the criminal law. The present defences of insanity and automatism recognise that there are varying degrees of responsibility for actions. If someone is mentally disordered then their ability to adjust their behaviour may be severely compromised. Furthermore, if someone is seriously mentally disordered then the justice system may view them as less culpable but may wish to assess the risk of their problematic criminal behaviour recurring. Identifying before trial that a defendant may be seriously mentally disordered allows the justice system the opportunity to offer a fair hearing. If the law is formulated correctly then appropriate evidence may be called and a proper evaluation made by the jury of the guilt or innocence of the accused. These propositions are embraced by the Law Commission in the approach it takes in the *Discussion Paper* outlining how debate in the area should proceed.

III. The Law Commission's Proposals: The Proposed New Defence

It is interesting to note that the Law Commission has published its proposals in what is termed a 'Discussion Paper'.[92] Furthermore its conclusions and proposals are described as 'provisional'.[93]

The Law Commission proposes the abolition of the common law defence of insanity[94] and the creation of a new defence of not criminally responsible by reason of a recognised medical condition.[95] The new defence has obvious advantages in that it avoids the stigma of the term insanity and avoids the problem of inappropriately labelling those who are, for example, diabetic or sleepwalkers as insane.

---

[92] See n 1. Section 3A of the Law Commissions Act 1965, as amended by section 1 of the Law Commission Act 2009, places a duty on the Lord Chancellor to report to Parliament each year on the extent to which the Law Commission proposals have been implemented by the government. Where proposals are not implemented the report should identify any plans for dealing with the proposal (s 3A(1)(a)(i)) and where the proposals are not to be implemented must give reasons for that decision (s 3A(1)(a)(ii)). By labelling the document as a 'Discussion Paper', labelling their proposals as 'Provisional Proposals' and not including within the document a draft Bill the proposals would appear to fall outside the definition of a Law Commission proposal contained in s 3A(1)(6). Accordingly, no statement from the Lord Chancellor will be required if the government fails to implement the proposals set out in the *Discussion Paper*.

[93] See, for example, chapter 10 headed 'Our Provisional Conclusions and Proposals'. Although the 18 proposals contained in the chapter are identified as 'proposals', 15 of the 18 open with the words 'We provisionally conclude …'. Hereafter in this chapter reference will be made to Law Commission proposals, however it should be remembered that the proposals are 'provisional'.

[94] *Discussion Paper* (n 1) Proposal 1, paras 4.158 and 10.6.

[95] ibid Proposal 2, paras 4.159 and 10.7.

The proposed terminology also has the advantage that it avoids the focus on guilt evidenced in the phrase 'not guilty by reason of insanity' or the earlier phrase 'guilty, but insane'. To satisfy this new defence the defence:

> must adduce expert evidence that at the time of the alleged offence the defendant wholly lacked the capacity:
>
> (i)   rationally to form a judgment about the relevant conduct or circumstances;
> (ii)   to understand the wrongfulness of what he or she is charged with having done; or
> (iii)   to control his or her physical acts in relation to the relevant conduct or circumstances
>
> as a result of a qualifying recognised medical condition.[96]

Three Limbs, Not Two

The three limbs to the proposed new defence adopt a different approach from that advanced by the M'Naghten Rules as interpreted by subsequent case law.

The first limb focuses on rationality and the ability to form a judgement about relevant conduct or circumstances. This focus stems from the idea of having capacity for practical reasoning.[97] The reference to rationality in the first limb might be seen as mirroring the statement in the M'Naghten Rules that a man should be 'presumed to be sane and to possess a sufficient degree of reason to be responsible for his crimes until the contrary be proved to their [ie the jury's] satisfaction'.[98] However, the proposed new defence does not contain the additional requirements set out in the M'Naghten Rules and subsequent case law as to how the defence must be made out.[99] Under the new proposed defence a defendant would be able to satisfy the requirement if she 'wholly lacked the capacity … rationally to form a judgment about the relevant conduct or circumstances' even if she did know the physical nature and quality of her act or did know that what she was doing was wrong. She would satisfy this first limb so long as the reason that she wholly lacked the capacity was as a result of the recognised medical condition.

The second limb focuses on understanding the wrongfulness of the alleged criminal act. Again it may be seen as mirroring the M'Naghten Rules in that the rules refer to not knowing he 'was doing what was wrong'. As has been seen this has been interpreted narrowly by subsequent case law[100] as meaning what was legally

---

[96]   ibid Proposal 3, paras 4.160 and 10.8.

[97]   ibid Conclusion 3, para 10.3.

[98]   *M'Naghten's Case* (n 10) 233, I.

[99]   As discussed earlier the M'Naghten Rules additionally require for a successful plea of insanity that 'it must be clearly proved that, at the time of the committing of the act the party accused was labouring under such a defect of reason, from disease of the mind, as not to know the nature and quality of the act he was doing, or, if he did know it, that he did not know he was doing what was wrong', ibid.

[100]   *Windle* (n 51).

wrong. However, the Law Commission is seeking in its proposals an alternative interpretation.

> In Canadian case law, the accused need only appreciate that the act was something he or she ought not to do.[18] This approach leaves it open to show that the accused knew the act was against the law, which signals that it is generally thought of as wrong, but does not limit awareness of wrongfulness to awareness of illegality (as English case law does). We think this is an approach we should follow.[101]

This adoption of the Canadian approach can also be seen as a reversion to the earlier English approach.[102] This is an important distinction. By focusing on the appreciation of the defendant as to what she ought not to do, the new proposed defence is potentially much wider. A defendant suffering from a delusion could realise that what she was doing was legally wrong, but could nevertheless not consider it wrong in the sense that it was something that she ought not to do. There is nothing to suggest that Daniel M'Naghten, for example, did not know that it was legally wrong to kill. However, in his deluded state it is possible that he did not think it was wrong to fire the fatal shot, in the sense of appreciating that it was something that he ought not to have done.

The third limb relates to inability to control physical acts. This links less obviously to the M'Naghten Rules as initially set out in response to the questions of the House of Lords, but does link to the line of cases which have developed the idea of insane automatism. Those whose actions are involuntary from an internal cause and who are currently classed as insane would in many cases fall within the category of those whose inability to control their actions arose from a recognised medical condition.

The Law Commission explains the rationale behind the proposed reforms as follows:

> Our principal conclusion is that people should not be held criminally responsible for their conduct if they lack the capacity to conform their behaviour to meet the demands imposed by the criminal law regulating that conduct. This lack of capacity might consist in an inability to think rationally, or in an inability to control one's actions. The reason for that lack of capacity might lie in a mental disorder, or in a physical disorder.[103]

Whilst this rationale might seem particularly relevant to the first and third limbs of the proposed new defence, in reality an inability to think rationally would also cover the situation where a defendant was unable to understand the wrongfulness of the act.

All three limbs are built on a requirement that the defendant 'wholly lacked the capacity' to comply with the particular limb. This links to the proposed rationale behind the defence that 'people should not be held criminally responsible for

---

[101] *Discussion Paper* (n 1) para 4.22. The Law Commission also refer in the footnote (fn 18) to a similar approach being adopted by s 27 of the Criminal Code of Queensland.

[102] See for example *Davis* (n 40) and accompanying text.

[103] *Discussion Paper* (n 1) Appendix A. The question of criminal responsibility, para A.5.

their conduct if they lack the capacity to conform their behaviour to meet the demands imposed by the criminal law regulating that conduct'.[104] Substantial or partial impairment of capacity will not suffice. Whilst the rationale for this requirement is clear, it leaves the defendant who finds it exceptionally difficult to conform her behaviour to the criminal law's requirements without a defence. A defendant with greatly reduced impulse control because, for example, of damage to the pre-frontal cortex of the brain might find it very difficult to control her acts, but if she could not show that she 'wholly lacked the capacity … to control … her physical acts' she would be denied the defence. Arguably from a legal viewpoint this approach is correct. Those who have impaired capacity do, by definition, have some capacity even if that capacity is very substantially impaired. Such defendants, following conviction, may hope that their reduced blameworthiness will lead to a more lenient sentence. However, the converse could apply. If their reduced ability to conform their behaviour to the requirements of the law persists, this may lead a court to conclude that they are particularly dangerous and therefore lead to the imposition of a lengthier sentence.[105]

A Neurocognitive Case Study

Neuroscience is at the heart of Burns and Swerdlow's clinical case report[106] of an individual with a brain tumour and is illustrative of the difficulty of determining whether an individual has impaired capacity, substantially impaired capacity or wholly lacks capacity to control her actions. In this case a 40-year old school teacher, who had no history of criminal activity, began collecting pornographic magazines, visiting internet pornography sites, soliciting prostitutes and then made 'subtle sexual advances to his prepubescent stepdaughter'. He was convicted of child molestation and ordered to undertake an inpatient programme for sex addiction or go to jail. He attended the programme, but whilst on the programme he began seeking sexual favours from staff and other clients at the rehabilitation centre. He was expelled from the programme. The day before he was due to be sentenced to prison, he complained of a severe headache. By this stage he had additionally developed balance problems, walked awkwardly and was unconcerned when he urinated on himself. During a neurological examination, which followed the manifestation of this behaviour, he solicited female medical staff for sexual favours. MRI scans indicated that he had a large brain tumour 'displacing the right orbitofrontal cortex and distorting the dorsolateral prefrontal cortex'.

---

[104] ibid.

[105] DW Denno, 'The Myth of the Double-Edged Sword: An Empirical Study of Neuroscience Evidence in Criminal Cases' (2015) 56 *Boston College Law Review* 493. In this article Denno argues that the empirical evidence suggests that in the United States neuroscientific evidence is usually offered to mitigate punishment when sentencing. This is particularly true of death penalty trials.

[106] JM Burns and RH Swerdlow, 'Right Orbitofrontal Tumor With Pedophilia Symptom and Constructional Apraxia Sign' (2003) 60 *Archives of Neurology* 437–40.

The brain tumour was resected and his aberrant behaviour ceased. He walked normally, his balance returned, he no longer urinated on himself, no longer solicited sexual favours and no longer sought out pornography on the internet. He became able to complete various tests which, whilst the tumour was in place, he had been unable to undertake competently.[107] He successfully completed a Sexaholics programme and seven months later it was concluded that he no longer presented a threat to his stepdaughter and he was allowed to return to his home. Subsequently he developed a persistent headache and began secretly collecting pornography again. A further MRI scan was conducted, the tumour was found to have grown back again. The tumour was re-resected. Once again his behaviour ceased to be problematic.

Reading the report it is clear that the man's behaviour went through phases. Initially he would appear to have been a respected, law-abiding member of the community. He then began to behave in less socially acceptable ways, eventually culminating in criminal behaviour when he made sexual advances towards his stepdaughter. During this period he attempted to conceal his behaviour. This might suggest that he understood the wrongfulness of his actions. It does not, per se, mean that he could control his actions, though the fact that he was able to conceal his actions does suggest that he was able to control the timing of his actions so as to avoid detection. However, following conviction, whilst on the initial treatment programme it appears that he could not control his actions despite what is described in the report of his case as 'his strong desire to avoid prison'. Burns and Swerdlow report that 'our patient could not refrain from acting on his pedophilia despite the awareness that the behaviour was inappropriate'. Applying the proposed new test the man would seem, at this stage, to have retained the ability to 'understand the wrongfulness of what he did'[108] but it is arguable that he lacked the capacity to control his physical acts.[109]

Burdens and Standards of Proof

The new proposed defence places an elevated evidential burden of proof on the defence.[110] Generally the evidential burden[111] means that the defendant must provide evidence on which to base the defence. If the defence does this, it is then for the prosecution to prove beyond reasonable doubt that the defence does not apply. In the case of this proposed defence the evidential burden is elevated and

---

[107] Tests included his ability to write legibly, to draw a clock face and to copy various figures.
[108] The second limb of the proposed new test.
[109] The third limb of the proposed new test.
[110] *Discussion Paper* (n 1) para 4.135.
[111] 'It is a burden of raising, on the evidence in the case, an issue as to the matter in question fit for consideration by the tribunal of fact. If an issue is properly raised, it is for the prosecutor to prove, beyond reasonable doubt, that that ground of exoneration does not avail the defendant' per Lord Bingham in *Sheldrake v DPP* [2004] UKHL 43, [2005] 1 AC 264 [1].

it is proposed that the defence be required to provide evidence from two experts to support the claim.[112] The requirement for the defence to produce evidence from two experts exists in the current insanity defence; however there are two significant differences.

First, the present insanity defence involves a requirement that one of the experts should be a psychiatrist,[113] whereas the proposed new defence would simply require one of the two experts to be a registered medical practitioner.[114] This reflects the possibility explored in the *Discussion Paper* that the recognised medical condition might be a physical rather than a mental condition.[115] This seems eminently sensible. The current law's requirement that an expert on mental disorders should be called when the 'internal' cause is for example diabetes or sleepwalking is odd. Under the current law not only are individuals being stigmatised by the application of the inappropriate label of insane, but the experts being called to support the application of that label are perhaps not necessarily the most appropriately qualified.

The second difference relates to the standard of proof. Under the current law, the defence are required to prove insanity on the balance of probabilities. The Law Commission notes the potential anomaly that the jury or magistrates may think on the balance of probabilities that the defendant is not insane, but may have reasonable doubt as to whether the defendant is sane. In such a case the defence is not made out. Assuming that the prosecution have proved the elements of the offence then the defendant should be convicted, notwithstanding that the jury or magistrates have reasonable doubt as to the defendant's sanity.[116] The Law Commission cites approvingly the judgment of the Canadian Supreme Court in *Whyte*:

> The real concern is not whether the accused must disprove an element or prove an excuse, but that an accused may be convicted while a reasonable doubt exists. When that possibility exists, there is a breach of the presumption of innocence.[117]

The question of whether the current approach to the burden of proof in English insanity cases amounts to a breach of the presumption of innocence has been raised before the European Court of Human Rights. In *H v United Kingdom*[118] the Commission held that the insanity defence raised the presumption of sanity, not the presumption of innocence. Accordingly the Commission held that it did not breach the right to a fair trial under Article 6. Interestingly the Law Commission

---

[112] *Discussion Paper* (n 1) Conclusion 9, para 8.50.

[113] Technically the requirement is that one of the experts is 'approved for the purposes of section 12 of the 1983 Act by the Secretary of State as having special experience in the diagnosis or treatment of mental disorder'—see ibid para 7.36. In reality this generally means that the expert is a psychiatrist.

[114] Proposal 8, para 4.165.

[115] For discussion of this see for example *Discussion Paper* (n 1) paras 1.21, 3.18 and 4.36.

[116] This is discussed in ibid paras 1.63–1.64 and 8.4–8.45.

[117] *Whyte* (1988) 2 SCR 3, (1988) 51 DLR (4th) 481, 493 per Chief Justice Dickson quoted in *Discussion Paper* (n 1) para 8.12.

[118] *H v UK* App No 15023/89 (Commission decision) (unreported).

unequivocally finds 'the reasoning in this judgment to be unsound'[119] and that 'the better view is that the placing of the burden on the defendant is in breach of article 6(2)'.[120]

The proposed new defence approaches the burden of proof differently. When arguing that the defendant is not criminally responsible by reason of a recognised medical condition, the defence must satisfy the enhanced evidential burden outlined above. Once this has been done it is then for the prosecution to disprove the defence beyond reasonable doubt. In this way the proposed new defence better upholds the presumption of innocence than does the current insanity defence.

The 'Qualifying Recognised Medical Condition' Requirement

One interesting aspect of the proposed new defence is the focus on 'a qualifying recognised medical condition'. To avail herself of the proposed new defence a defendant must not simply show that she wholly lacked capacity:

(i)   rationally to form a judgment about the relevant conduct or circumstances;

(ii)   to understand the wrongfulness of what he or she is charged with having done; or

(iii) to control his or her physical acts in relation to the relevant conduct or circumstances

as a result of a qualifying recognised medical condition.[121]

There is therefore a need for the defence to satisfy the evidential burden by demonstrating a link between the medical condition and the lack of capacity. The mere existence of a 'recognised medical condition' will not suffice. The lack of capacity must 'result' from the medical condition.

The adjective 'qualifying' in the phrase 'qualifying recognised medical condition' is significant. Two types of recognised medical conditions are identified which it is proposed should not be 'qualifying' conditions. One exception is acute intoxication.[122] The Law Commission notes that acute intoxication is a recognised medical condition, but argue that the relevant prior fault case law on instances of self-induced intoxication should continue to apply in such cases.[123] Acute intoxication is differentiated from alcohol dependency syndrome, which it is suggested could be a qualifying condition.[124] The second exception covers anti-social personality disorders. The Law Commission proposes that these should be excluded on policy grounds.[125] In chapter 4 there is a lengthy discussion of

---

[119] *Discussion Paper* (n 1) para 8.20.

[120] ibid para 8.21.

[121] ibid Proposal 3, paras 4.160 and 10.8.

[122] ibid para 3.15 and paras 4.87–4.92.

[123] ibid para 4.91.

[124] ibid para 4.88.

[125] ibid para 4.93.

the nature of personality disorders and in particular of anti-social personality disorders.[126] The Law Commission notes how the classification of some disorders has changed over time. The Law Commission also notes that whilst many personality disorders are recognised medical conditions, the definitions of some personality disorders focus on the anti-social behaviour rather than on any clear underlying cause. The Commission concludes that the defence should not apply to 'any condition which is manifested solely or principally by abnormally aggressive or seriously irresponsible behaviour'.[127]

Notwithstanding these limitations, the phrase 'qualifying recognised medical condition' appears much wider than the reference to 'disease of the mind', which is at the heart of the current insanity defence. The term 'disease of the mind' belongs to an earlier age. In the twenty-first century it would be preferable to speak of medical conditions rather than diseases of the mind. Over the years the common law has stretched the meaning of 'disease of the mind' to include, for example, hyperglycaemia[128] and sleepwalking.[129] The term 'medical condition' applies much better to conditions such as sleep disorders[130] and diabetes.[131] It is also a better term to apply to conditions such as arteriosclerosis[132] and epilepsy,[133] which have been labelled as insanity. The Law Commission has been sensitive to leave the interpretation of the terms in the new defence open to advances in the understanding of medical conditions. Neuroscience itself may contribute to this understanding; indeed the accuracy of using brain—particularly FNC (functional network connectivity)—scans to classify cases of schizophrenia has been accepted.[134]

Removing the Internal/External Divide

One impact of the change from disease of the mind to recognised medical condition is that it dispenses with the problematic internal/external divide. This is to be welcomed. The current law has meant that hypoglycaemia caused by failing to eat after a dose of insulin has been deemed an external cause. Where the cause is deemed external the finding should be sane automatism. This would lead to the accused being acquitted and walking free from court, whereas a hyperglycaemic episode deemed to have an internal cause would lead to a finding of insanity. For example in *Hennessy* the accused failed to take a prescribed dose of insulin. Hennessy's loss of control was deemed to be caused internally. This distinction is

---

[126] ibid; see particularly paras 4.93–4.116.
[127] ibid Proposal 4, para 4.161.
[128] *R v Hennessy* [1989] 1 WLR 287, see n 75 and accompanying text.
[129] *Burgess* (n 59).
[130] Discussed in *Discussion Paper* (n 1) paras 1.101, 1.112 and 1.134.
[131] ibid para 1.112.
[132] *R v Kemp* [1957] 1 QB 399.
[133] *Bratty* (n 65) and surrounding text for discussion; *R v Sullivan* [1984] AC 156.
[134] MR Arbabshirani et al, 'Classification of Schizophrenia Patients Based on Resting-state Functional Network Connectivity' (2013) 7 *Frontiers in Neuroscience* 133:1.

difficult to defend logically or indeed scientifically.[135] The defendant who neglects to take insulin and the defendant who fails to take food having taken insulin can both be argued to be at fault. Both defendants' loss of control stems from their blood sugar level. Yet one defendant has the potential to claim sane automatism on the basis that the cause is viewed as external, whereas the other can only claim insanity as the cause is deemed internal or plead guilty to the offence and avoid the stigma of being found to be insane by the criminal courts. The new proposed defence would potentially apply to both defendants. If as a result of their recognised medical condition—in this case diabetes—the defendants wholly lacked capacity to control their physical acts as a result of the qualifying medical conditions then they would be entitled to the new special verdict of not criminally responsible.

The New Automatism Defence

This approach would mean that some defendants who are currently able to claim sane automatism would now fall within the 'not criminally responsible by reason of a recognised medical condition' defence. To prevent overlap the Law Commission proposes changes to the existing defence of sane automatism. The suggested reformed automatism defence would be 'restricted, broadly speaking, to cases of reflex and one-off causes of total loss of control'.[136] The current law on automatism is set out in chapter 5 of the *Discussion Paper*. The chapter concludes with two proposals: (1) that the current common law defence be abolished[137] and (2) that it be replaced by a recommendation that where

> the accused raises evidence that at the time of the alleged offence he or she wholly lacked the capacity to control his or her conduct, and the loss of capacity was not the result of a recognised medical condition (whether qualifying or non-qualifying), he or she shall be acquitted unless the prosecution disprove this plea to the criminal standard.[138]

The Law Commission identifies a limited number of hypothetical instances where its proposed new automatism defence would apply. These include a case where an individual is startled and has a reflex reaction,[139] a case where someone is hypnotised and commits offences whilst under hypnosis[140] and a case of a driver being

---

[135] The Law Commission quotes with approval in *Discussion Paper* (n 1) para 1.41 Peter Fenwick's comment that 'the line drawn between sane and insane automatism can never make medical sense': P Fenwick, 'Automatism, Medicine and the Law' (1990) 17 *Psychological Medicine—Monograph Supplement* 1.

[136] *Discussion Paper* (n 1) para 2.61.

[137] ibid para 5.123.

[138] ibid para 5.124.

[139] The example given is of an archer who is startled, and as result turns and looses an arrow which then unfortunately hits someone. *Discussion Paper* (n 1) para 5.106(1). Whether this description of a 'reflex' act is the same as that given by Haggard (n 74) is debatable.

[140] ibid para 5.106(2).

hit by a stone and temporarily losing control of her car.[141] In all these cases the Law Commission proposes that the defendant who wholly lacks capacity to control her conduct should be entitled to an acquittal, provided that the lack of capacity was not a result of the defendant's prior fault.[142]

Prior Fault

This exclusion of prior fault cases also applies to the proposed 'not criminally responsible by reason of a recognised medical condition' defence. A defendant who is at fault because she culpably caused herself to lose her capacity will not generally be able to rely on the proposed new defence.[143] However, applying the approach adopted in intoxication cases, it is proposed that if she is charged with a specific intent crime she should be acquitted.[144] Assessment as to whether a defendant was at fault for losing her capacity will take into account her medical condition if relevant. So, for example, a patient with Alzheimer's disease who forgets to take her prescription with the result that she loses capacity to control her behaviour may be deemed not blameworthy as her medical condition affects her memory and cognitive abilities.[145] Where an individual took a drug as prescribed and had no reason to believe that she would have an adverse reaction to the medicine which then caused her to wholly lose capacity she will be able to rely on the new defence.[146]

IV. Conclusion

The proposed new defence of 'not criminally responsible by reason of a recognised medical condition' should provide more scope for medical and scientific evidence, including neuroscientific evidence, than the current insanity defence. Both the current and the proposed defences require evidence from two expert witnesses. However, the limitation of the current defence in requiring not only evidence that the defendant suffered a defect of reason arising from a disease of the mind, but also evidence that as a result the defendant either did not know the nature or quality of her action or did not know it was legally wrong, means that as previously noted the number of cases in which it is successfully claimed each year is small. Notwithstanding the way 'disease of the mind' has been stretched to

---

[141] ibid para 5.104(1).
[142] ibid para 5.111.
[143] ibid para 4.124.
[144] ibid para 4.124. Such a defendant could be convicted of a basic intent crime.
[145] ibid para 6.80(2).
[146] ibid Proposal 14, para 10.19.

include conditions such as diabetes and sleepwalking, claims brought under the current law will fail if the defendant either did not know the nature and quality of her action or did not know it was legally wrong. The proposed new defence sensibly moves away from these three elements. 'Recognised medical condition' is both wider and more appropriate than 'disease of the mind'. The proposed new term should prove more comprehensible to jurors and more in line with scientific and medical understanding for expert witnesses. In many case neuroscientific evidence will be useful in determining whether a particular defendant does or does not suffer from a recognised medical condition.[147] It may also be relevant in determining whether the defendant wholly lacked capacity not in the sense of answering the question, but in the sense of providing evidence from which it might be inferred.

The reason expert evidence is likely to be required is that, as previously, the defendant's mental state at the time of the crime will have to be inferred. Robinson writes:

> Once it is appreciated that all evidence of mental states is inferential and that neither neurology nor psychiatry has any magic lantern to light up the concealed corners of the defendant's mind, the question for the courts becomes the more tractable one of determining the grounds of valid inference.[148]

Therefore the words used to filter the valid inferences are important ones: the expression 'wholly lacking capacity' will become central to both defences. In this sense 'capacity' is a word that will have a legal meaning not a scientific one.

The word has great utility as a filter to exclude unmeritorious claims. This defence would, after all, if successfully pleaded, declare someone not criminally responsible: a much clearer exculpation than the present 'not guilty by reason of insanity verdict'. It will only be applicable to the small number of defendants who fit within the narrow excuse provided by the defence. Capacity at the time of the crime will remain measurable only in retrospect and will be the province of the jury. The Law Commission is clearly of the view that this judgement is one for society and forms part of the framework of adjudication between the individual and the state.[149] This evidences the point made earlier regarding the political sensitivity of determinations that an individual is not criminally responsible.

---

[147] In *R v Sharif (Mohammed)* [2010] EWCA Crim 1709 brain scan evidence was used to show that Sharif had a neuro-degenerative condition. This strengthened the appellant's case that he had genuinely been unfit to stand trial rather than 'malingering' when his case was originally heard and led to his successful appeal against conviction. Similarly in a case such as that reported by Burns and Swerdlow (n 107), neuroscientific evidence will be valuable in showing not only that the defendant has a brain tumour, but also the likely impact of such a tumour on a person's ability to control her actions. In cases such as these neuroscientific evidence is unlikely to be used on its own, but, as the authors found in relation to other defences (see n 58), is likely to be used in conjunction with other evidence.

[148] DN Robinson, *Wild Beasts and Idle Humours: The Insanity Defense from Antiquity to the Present* (Cambridge, MA, Harvard University Press, 1996) 237.

[149] *Discussion Paper* (n 1) para 4.119.

The Law Commission's proposals, if enacted, would be a significant improvement to the current law. The clarification of the boundary between the revised automatism defence and the new verdict of 'not criminally responsible by reason of a recognised medical condition' is appropriately pragmatic. The new defences will allow the law to label more fairly and treat more justly those who are unable to make their behaviour conform to the requirements of the law. The abandonment of the stigmatising label of insanity has to be applauded. The whole approach brings a welcome clarity to this area of the law.

However, the new defence by the nature of its construction will be of limited applicability. This means that those who are found to have substantially impaired capacity to control their behaviour may remain within the prison system. The mental capacities of such prisoners may mean that they are vulnerable and this may be detrimental to them and possibly to society at large—an issue which the Law Commission originally focused upon when setting out its ambitions in reforming the current insanity defence.[150]

Bibliography

Literature

Arbabshirani, MR, Kiehl, KA, Pearlson, GD and Calhoun, VD, 'Classification of Schizophrenia Patients Based on Resting-state Functional Network Connectivity' (2013) 7 *Frontiers in Neuroscience* 133:1.

Burns, JM and Swerdlow, RH, 'Right Orbitofrontal Tumor With Pedophilia Symptom and Constructional Apraxia Sign' (2003) 60 *Archives of Neurology* 437.

Catley, P and Claydon, L, 'The Use of Neuroscientific Evidence in the Courtroom by Those Accused of Criminal Offences in England and Wales' (2015) 2 *Journal of Law and Biosciences* 1.

Denno, DW, 'The Myth of the Double-Edged Sword: An Empirical Study of Neuroscience Evidence in Criminal Cases' (2015) 56 *Boston College Law Review* 493.

Fenwick, P, 'Automatism, Medicine and the Law' (1990) 17 *Psychological Medicine—Monograph Supplement* 1.

Haggard, P, 'Human Volition: Towards a Neuroscience of Will' (2008) 9 *Nature Reviews Neuroscience* 934.

Hale, M, *Historia Placitorum Coronæ* [The History of the Pleas of the Crown] London (first published 1680, 1736).

House of Lords' *Hansard*, 13 March 1843.

---

[150] See n 5 and accompanying text.

Law Commission for England and Wales, *Criminal Liability: Insanity and Automatism—A Discussion Paper*, published 23 July 2013.

Law Commission for England and Wales, *Insanity and Automatism—A Scoping Paper*, published 18 July 2012.

Law Commission for England and Wales, *Insanity and Automatism—Supplementary Material to the Scoping Paper*, published 18 July 2012.

Mackay, RD, 'The Insanity Defence—Data on Verdicts of Not Guilty by Reason of Insanity from 2002 to 2011' in Law Commission for England and Wales, *Insanity and Automatism—Supplementary Material to the Scoping Paper*, published 18 July 2012.

Mackay, RD, Mitchell, BJ and Howe, L, 'Yet More Facts about the Insanity Defence' (2006) *Criminal Law Review* 399.

Morse, SJ, 'Thoroughly Modern: Sir James Fitzjames Stephen on Criminal Responsibility' (2007) 5 *Ohio State Journal of Criminal Law* 505.

Robinson, DN, *Wild Beasts and Idle Humours: The Insanity Defense from Antiquity to the Present* (Cambridge, MA, Harvard University Press, 1996).

Smith, KJM, *James Fitzjames Stephen: Portrait of a Victorian Rationalist* (Cambridge, Cambridge University Press, 1988).

Smith, R, *Trial by Medicine*, (Edinburgh, Edinburgh University Press, 1981).

Stephen, JF, *A General View of the Criminal Law of England*, 1st edn (London, Macmillan & Co, 1863).

Stephen, JF, *A History of the Criminal Law of England* (London, Macmillan & Co, 1883).

Stephen, JF, *Stephen's Criminal Digest*, 6th edn (London, Macmillan & Co, 1904).

The Saturday Review 16 (1863).

Cases

Bratty v Attorney General for Northern Ireland [1963] AC 386 (HL).

Fulcher v State 633 P 2d 142 (Wyo 1981) (Wyoming Supreme Court).

H v United Kingdom App No 15023/89 (Commission decision) (unreported).

Hill v Baxter [1958] 1 QB 277.

McClain v State 678 NE 2d 104 (Ind 1997) (Supreme Court of Indiana).

M'Naghten's Case [1843–60] All ER Rep 229.

Queen v Falconer [1990] HCA 49, (1990) 171 CLR 30 (High Court of Australia).

Rabey v The Queen [1980] 2 SCR 513 (Supreme Court of Canada).

R v Harry William Ball, Old Bailey Proceedings Online (www.oldbaileyonline. org, version 7.2, 25 January 2016), July 1910, trial of BALL, Harry William (22, barman) (t19100718-27).

R v Burgess [1991] 2 QB 92 (CA).

R v Burr [1969] NZLR 736 (New Zealand Court of Appeal).

R v Codère (1917) 12 Cr App R 21 (CCA).

R v Davis (1881) 14 Cox CC 563 (CrCt).

R v Fryer (1915) Cox CC 403 (Assizes).

R v Hay (1911) 75 JP 480, 22 Cox CC 268 (CCC).

R v Hennessy [1989] 1 WLR 287 (CA).

R v Johnson (Dean) [2007] EWCA Crim 1978, [2008] Crim LR 132.

R v Jolly (1919) 83 JP 296 (Assizes).

R v Jones (Victor) (1910) 4 Cr App R 207 (CCA).

R v Kemp [1957] 1 QB 399 (Assizes).

R v Masih [1986] *Crim LR* 395 (CA).

R v Daniel M'Naughten, *Old Bailey Proceedings Online* (www.oldbaileyonline.org, version 7.2, 25 January 2016), February 1843, trial of DANIEL M'NAUGHTEN (t18430227-874).

R v Parks [1992] 2 SCR 871 (Supreme Court of Canada).

R v William Henry Philpot, *Old Bailey Proceedings Online* (www.oldbaileyonline. org, version 7.2, 25 January 2016), January 1912, trial of PHILPOT, William Henry (33, tram conductor) (t19120130-53).

R v Quick (1973) QB 910 (CA).

R v Sharif (Mohammed) [2010] EWCA Crim 1709.

R v Stone (1999) 134 CCC (3d) 353, [1999] 2 SCR 290 (Supreme Court of Canada).

R v Sullivan [1984] AC 156 (HL).

R v Townley (1863) 176 ER 384, (1863) 3 F & F 839.

R v True (1922) 16 Cr App R 164 (CCA).

R v Whyte (1988) 2 SCR 3, (1988) 51 DLR (4th) 481 (Supreme Court of Canada).

R v Windle [1952] 2 QB 826 (CCA).

Ross v HM Advocate 1991 SLT 564 (High Court of Justiciary, Scotland).

Sheldrake v DPP [2004] UKHL 43, [2005] 1 AC 264.

State v Caddell 215 SE 2d 348 (NC 1975) (Supreme Court of North Carolina).

Woolmington v DPP [1935] AC 462 (HL).

Statutes

Criminal Code of Queensland.

Law Commissions Act 1965.

Law Commission Act 2009.

9

Legal Insanity in the Age of Neuroscience

STEPHEN J MORSE*

I. Introduction

Legal insanity is a legal and moral doctrine that seeks to identify those mentally abnormal criminal defendants who do not deserve to be blamed and punished for their criminal conduct. The thesis of this chapter may be simply stated. The insanity defence is morally required and the findings of neuroscience will not entail either its abolition or even extensive revision of it. As the chapter will make clear, the argument rests on moral, conceptual and scientific grounds.

I begin by explaining why an insanity defence is morally necessary and why the primary arguments for its abolition, including alternatives, fail conceptually and fail to do justice. Although a compelling case may be made that the US Constitution should require some form of insanity defence, the Supreme Court has never so held. Indeed, it has rejected hearing a case that squarely raised the issue. Consequently, the argument rests on a conception of justice that is not tied to any particular constitutional order. The chapter then turns to an analysis of the criteria for legal insanity, with special attention to whether an independent control test, in addition to a cognitive test, is conceptually coherent and practically workable. The chapter next considers the contribution neuroscience can at present make to adjudication of individual cases and to criminal law policy. It suggests that the current contribution is nil. Then it addresses whether in principle neuroscience poses any fundamental challenge to the validity of the doctrine of legal insanity and, more modestly, what revisions to the doctrine might arise from neuroscientific findings. A brief conclusion follows.

*I thank Ed Greenlee and Ben Meltzer for excellent, invaluable help. Parts II, IV, and V of this chapter are based on an article co-authored with Richard Bonnie: SJ Morse and RJ Bonnie, 'Abolition of the Insanity Defense Violates Due Process' (2013) 41 *Journal of the American Academy of Psychiatry and the Law* 488.

II. The Moral Basis of the Defence of Legal Insanity

Blame and punishment by the state are fundamentally unfair if an offender was not responsible for his crime. The affirmative defence of legal insanity applies this fundamental principle by excusing those mentally disordered offenders whose disorder deprived them of rational understanding of their conduct at the time of the crime.[1] This principle is simple but profound. Indeed, in recognition of this, the insanity defence has been a feature of ancient law and of English law since the fourteenth century.[2] It was universal in the United States until the last decades of the twentieth century and there is still almost near consensus among State and federal lawmakers that the defence must be retained.[3] It is a feature of almost every European criminal code, and even when there is no formal defence, severely mentally disordered defendants are treated differently from offenders with lesser or no mental disorder.

The concept of responsibility is intimately related to our most fundamental convictions about human nature and human dignity and our everyday experience of guilt and innocence and blame and punishment. It also explains our common aversion to the idea that we might simply be like machines responding to neural activities in the brain, and our resistance to thinking of all wrongdoing as sickness. Failing to provide an insanity defence confounds the meaning of what it is to be responsible for one's actions. It cheapens the idea of being a responsible person by classifying and holding responsible persons intuitively regarded as fundamentally non-responsible.

In both law and morals, the capacity for reason is the primary foundation for responsibility and competence. The precise cognitive deficit a person must exhibit can of course vary from context to context. In the criminal justice system, an offender who lacks the capacity to understand the wrongfulness of his actions as the result of severe mental disorder does not deserve full blame and punishment and must be excused in a sufficiently extreme case. Moreover, such offenders cannot be appropriately deterred because the rules of law and morality cannot adequately guide them. Failing to excuse some mentally disordered offenders is inconsistent with both retributive and deterrent theories of just punishment.

A similar baseline principle explains the many competence doctrines employed in the criminal justice process. At every stage, justice demands that some people

---

[1] M Moore, *Law and Psychiatry* (Cambridge, Cambridge University Press, 1984); H Fingarette and A Hasse, *Mental Disabilities and Criminal Responsibility* (Berkeley, CA, University of California Press, 1979); SJ Morse, 'Mental Disorder and Criminal Law' (2011) 101 *Journal of Criminal Law & Criminology* 885, 925.

[2] T Maeder, *Crime and Madness: The Origins and Evolution of the Insanity Defense* (New York, Harper & Row, 1985); N Walker, *Crime and Insanity in England*, vol 1 (Edinburgh, Edinburgh University Press, 1968); BE Elkins, 'Idaho's Repeal of the Insanity Defense: What Are We Trying to Prove?' (1994) 31 *Idaho Law Review* 151, 161.

[3] *Clark v Arizona* 548 US 735 (2006).

with severe mental abnormalities must be treated differently from those without substantial mental impairment because some impaired defendants are incapable of reason and understanding in a specific context. In the United States, for example, competence to stand trial,[4] competence to plead guilty and to waive counsel,[5] competence to represent oneself,[6] and competence to be executed,[7] are all examples in which the Constitution requires such special treatment. It is unfair to the defendant and offensive to the dignity of criminal justice to treat people without understanding as if their understanding was unimpaired. Evidence of mental disorder is routinely introduced in all these contexts to determine if the defendant must be accorded special treatment.

Legally insane offenders are not excused solely because they suffered from a severe mental disorder at the time of the crime. The mental disorder must also impair their ability to understand or appreciate that what they are doing is wrong or some other functional capacity that a jurisdiction believes is crucial to responsibility. The criminal acts of those found legally insane do not result from bad judgement, insufficient moral sense, bad attitudes or bad characters, none of which is an excusing condition. Rather, the crimes of legally insane offenders arise from a lack of understanding produced by severe mental abnormality and thus they do not reflect culpable personal qualities and actions. To convict such people offends the basic sense of justice.

The impact of mental disorder on an offender's responsibility and competence is recognised throughout the criminal law. Even the few US jurisdictions that have abolished the insanity defence recognise that mental disorder affects criminal responsibility because they permit the introduction of evidence of mental disorder to negate the *mens rea* for the crime charged.[8] As the Supreme Court has recognised, state infliction of stigmatisation and punishment is a severe infringement.[9] The insanity defence is grounded in long-recognised legal and moral principles and on routinely admissible evidence. Even if a defendant formed the charged *mens rea*, and most legally insane defendants do so, it is unfair to preclude a defendant from claiming and proving that he was not at fault as a result of lack of understanding arising from a severely disordered mind. Indeed, the defendant's severely disordered beliefs are typically the reason that *mens rea* is formed.

Historical practice, the near universal acceptance of the need for an independent affirmative defence of legal insanity, and the fundamental unfairness of blaming and punishing legally insane offenders provide the strongest reasons to conclude that fundamental fairness requires an insanity defence. Abolishing this narrowly defined and deeply rooted defence could plausibly be justified only if an

---

[4] *Drope v Missouri* 420 US 162 (1975).
[5] *Godinez v Moran* 509 US 389 (1993).
[6] *Indiana v Edwards* 534 US 164 (2008).
[7] *Ford v Wainright* 477 US 399 (1986); *Panetti v Quarterman* 551 US 930 (2007).
[8] *State v Beam* 710 P 2d 526, 531 (Idaho 1985); *State v Searcy* 798 P 2d 914, 917 (Idaho 1990).
[9] *In re Winship* 377 US 358, 363–64 (1970).

alternative legal approach could reach the same just result or if irremediably deep flaws preclude fair and accurate administration of the defence. After addressing the major counter-argument to the moral necessity of the insanity defence, the chapter will show that there are no such alternatives and, briefly, that the defence is no more vulnerable to risks of mistake and abuse than any other disputed issue in the penal law.

III. The Main Counter-Argument

The late Norval Morris presented the most recent, important, non-consequentialist argument for abolishing the insanity defence in his book, *Madness and the Criminal Law.* Professor Morris suggested numerous conse-quentialist arguments for rejecting the insanity defence, but, believing in desert as a limiting principle in criminal law, he confronted directly 'the question of fair-ness, the sense that it is unjust and unfair to stigmatize the mentally ill as crimi-nals and to punish them for their crimes'. In brief, Professor Morris argued that other causes, such as social disadvantage, are far more criminogenic than mental disorder (including severe disorder); yet, he pointed out, we do not excuse those who are poor or the products of broken homes. Professor Morris concludes, 'As a rational matter it is hard to see why one should be more responsible for what is done to one than for what one is'. This conclusion is surely correct. It does not follow from the argument presented for it, however, which makes a morally irrelevant comparison between socially disadvantaged persons and persons with severe mental disorders.

Professor Morris confuses causation with excuse, a confusion that has consist-ently bedevilled clear thinking about criminal responsibility. Causation is not per se an excusing condition in criminal law. All behaviour is caused, even if we are often ignorant of the causes. If causation were an excuse, no one would be held responsible for any behaviour, criminal or not. Moreover, causation is not the equivalent of the subspecies of the genuine excuse that we term compulsion. Compulsion exists when the person faces a regrettable hard choice that leaves one with no reasonable alternative to wrongdoing. We also sometimes say that people are compelled if they yield to an internal desire that they find it extremely difficult to resist. Again, if causation were the equivalent of compulsion, no one would be responsible because all behaviour would be compelled. Causation is not the issue; non-culpable lack of reason and compulsion are the genuine excusing conditions.

Consider the case of a person whose extreme irrationality stems from the unknowing ingestion of a powerful hallucinogen. Such a defendant, who is not responsible for the ingestion of the drug, is not held responsible for a conse-quent crime. How can we distinguish this case from that of a person who com-mits a crime in response to motivations produced by severe mental disorder, say, a sudden command hallucination buttressed by a consistent delusional belief that the action is necessary? Mentally disordered defendants who are not responsible for their impaired mental states should also be excused. In both cases the defendant is excused not because the behaviour was caused—all behaviour is caused—but because the defendant was sufficiently irrational and was not responsible for the irrationality.

The reason we do not excuse most disadvantaged criminals (or those whose criminal behaviour can be explained by other powerful causes) is not because we lack sympathy for their unfortunate background or because we fail to recognise that social disadvantage is a powerful cause of crime. Rather, most disadvantaged defendants are held responsible because they possess minimal reason and are not compelled to offend. A disadvantaged defendant whose stress causes him to be mentally disordered and thereby unable to distinguish right from wrong will be excused because that defendant is incapable of rational conduct in the context, not because the abnormal mental state is caused by disadvantage. Similarly, most mentally disordered persons are held responsible for acts influenced by their disorders because they retain sufficient reason to meet the low threshold standards for responsibility. In sum, the criteria for moral autonomy and responsibility are the capacity for reason and lack of compulsion, whereas the criteria for excuse are that the person is non-culpably lacking either the capacity for reason or is compelled.

IV. Why Alternatives are Morally Insufficient

This section first addresses the '*mens rea* alternative' and then considers sentencing.

The *Mens Rea* Alternative

The negation of *mens rea* and the affirmative defence of legal insanity are different claims that avoid liability by different means and trigger different outcomes. The former denies the prima facie case of the crime charged; the latter is an affirmative defence that avoids liability in those cases in which the prima facie case is established. The post-verdict consequences are also different. The former leads to outright acquittal; the latter results in some form of involuntary civil commitment. The two different claims are not substitutes for one another.

The primary reason that permitting a defendant to introduce evidence of mental disorder to negate *mens rea* cannot justly replace the affirmative defence of legal insanity is that the *mens rea* alternative is based on a mistaken view of how severe mental disorder affects human behaviour. In virtually all cases, mental disorder, even severe disorders marked by psychotic symptoms such as delusions and hallucinations, does not negate the required *mens rea* for the crime charged.[10] It is difficult to prove a negative, but cases, especially those involving serious crime, in which the *mens rea* for every offence charged is negated, are extremely rare. Rather, mental disorder affects a person's reasons for action. A mentally disordered defendant's irrationally distorted beliefs, perceptions or desires typically and paradoxically give him the motivation to form the *mens rea* required by the charged offence. They typically do not interfere with the instrumental ability to perform the necessary actions to achieve irrationally motivated aims.

Consider the following, typical examples, beginning with Daniel M'Naghten himself.[11] M'Naghten delusionally believed that the ruling Tory party was persecuting and intended to kill him.[12] As a result, he formed the belief that he needed to assassinate the Prime Minister, Peel, in order to end the threat. He therefore formed the intention to kill Peel. Thus M'Naghten would have been convicted of murder if a defence of legal insanity was not available. Indeed, his case has come to stand for one of the 'rules' enunciated by the House of Lords—that a defendant should be acquitted on grounds of insanity if he

> was labouring under such a defect of reason, from a disease of the mind, as not to know the nature and quality of the act he was doing, or if he did know it, that he did not know he was doing what was wrong.[13]

For a more contemporary example, consider the case of Ms Andrea Yates, the Texas woman who drowned her five children in a bathtub. She delusionally believed that she was corrupting her children and that unless she killed them when they were still innocent, they would be tortured in hell for all eternity.[14] She therefore formed the intention to kill them. Indeed, she planned the homicides carefully. Ms Yates was nonetheless acquitted by reason of insanity because she did not know that what she was doing was wrong. Even if she narrowly knew the law of Texas and her neighbours' mores, she thought the homicides were fully justified by the eternal good of the children under the circumstances. If only society knew what she 'knew', they would approve of her conduct as justified. For a final example, suppose an offender with aural hallucinations believes that he is hearing God's voice or delusionally believes that God is communicating with him and that God is commanding him to kill.[15] If the offender kills in response to this 'command hallucination' or delusion, he surely forms the intent to kill to obey the divine decree. Nonetheless, it would be unjust to punish this defendant because he, too, does not know right from wrong given his beliefs for which he is not responsible.

---

[10] SJ Morse, 'Undiminished Confusion in Diminished Capacity' (1984) 75 *Journal of Criminal Law & Criminology* 1; Morse (n 1) 933.

[11] *M'Naghten's Case* (1843) 8 ER 718.

[12] R Moran, *Knowing Right From Wrong: The Insanity Defense Of Daniel McNaughtan* (New York, Macmillan, 1981) 10.

[13] *M'Naghten's Case* (n 11) 722.

[14] DW Denno, 'Who is Andrea Yates? A Short Story about Insanity' (2003) 10 *Duke Journal of Gender Law & Policy* 1.

[15] eg, *People v Serravo* 823 P 2d 828, 830 (Colo 1992) (en banc).

In all three cases one could also claim that the defendant did not know what he or she was doing in a fundamental sense because the most material reason for action, what motivated the formation of *mens rea*, was based on a delusion or hallucination that was the irrational product of a disordered mind. Nevertheless, in all three cases the defendant's instrumental rationality, the ability rationally to achieve one's ends, was intact despite their severe disorders. They were able effectively to carry out their disordered plans.

In a recent case, *Delling v Idaho*[16] the US Supreme Court was asked to grant review to decide whether the Constitution requires some form of an insanity defence. The Court declined to grant review, so the issue is still undecided, but the facts are instructive. Delling's case is consistent with this most typical pattern of legal insanity claims in which the defendant clearly had the *mens rea* required by the definition of the crime but lacked capacity to understand or appreciate the wrongfulness of his conduct. Delling indisputably suffered from a major mental disorder, paranoid schizophrenia, and as a result, delusionally believed that his victims were stealing his brain and would thereby kill him. Delling therefore believed that he needed to kill the victims to save his own life. His grossly delusional belief was the cause of his formation of the intent to kill. It is also undisputed that Delling carefully planned his victims' deaths and learned from one failed attempt. Such evidence of his instrumental rationality is consistent with having such delusional beliefs. The trial judge explicitly found that Delling did not know right from wrong under the circumstances. Nonetheless, he was convicted of murder because legal insanity was unavailable as a defence.

Delling was not a morally responsible agent. He was completely out of touch with reality concerning his victims and the actions necessary to save his own life. He does not deserve blame and punishment for his murders. Delling is no more to blame than someone suffering from dementia, for example, who acts on the basis of similarly disordered beliefs. It is true, of course, that Delling poses a genuine threat to social safety as long as he remains deluded, but commitment after an insanity acquittal is more than sufficient to protect public safety, as all jurisdictions provide. Public safety is further enhanced if acquittees must prove their suitability for release and if tightly controlled programs of community supervision are in effect when they are released.

To further understand the injustice of the *mens rea* alternative, consider the facts in *Clark v Arizona*,[17] a US Supreme Court case in which *mens rea* may plausibly have been negated. Clark shot and killed a police officer who had pulled him over during a routine traffic stop. The officer was in full uniform and was driving his police cruiser. Clark undeniably suffered from paranoid schizophrenia and had the delusional belief that aliens were coming to earth and were threatening him. Charged with the intentional killing of a person knowing that person was a police officer—a form of aggravated homicide—Clark claimed that he believed that his

---

[16] *Delling v Idaho* 133 S. Ct. 504 (2012) (*cert.* denied).
[17] *Clark v Arizona* (n 3).

victim was a space alien disguised as a police officer. If Clark is believed, he did not intentionally kill a person and did not know the victim was a police officer. In a *mens rea* alternative jurisdiction, he could also not be convicted of recklessly killing a human being because his delusional beliefs negated this *mens rea* as well because he was not consciously aware of the risk that his victim was a person and a police officer. If Arizona had permitted Clark to introduce evidence of his disorder to negate *mens rea*, which it did not,[18] Clark would have been convicted of negligent homicide. The standard for negligence is objective reasonableness and the motivating belief was patently unreasonable.

Of course, convicting the severely disordered defendant of a crime based on a negligence standard is fundamentally unjust, as even Mr Justice Holmes recognised in his rightly famous essays on the common law.[19] Clark's unreasonable mistake was not an ordinary mistake caused by inattention, carelessness or the like. Defendants are responsible for the latter because we believe that they had the capacity to behave more reasonably by being more careful or attentive. In contrast, Clark's delusional 'mistake' was the product of a disordered mind and thus he had no insight and no ability to recognise the gross distortion of reality. He was a victim of his disorder, not someone who deserves blame and punishment as a careless perpetrator of involuntary manslaughter. He does not deserve any blame and punishment, and only the defence of legal insanity could achieve this appropriate result. Paradoxically, such a defendant's potential future dangerousness if he remains deluded would be better addressed by an insanity acquittal and indefinite involuntary commitment than by the comparatively short, determinate sentences for involuntary manslaughter.

Thus, the *mens rea* alternative is not an acceptable replacement or substitute for the insanity defence. Only in the exceedingly rare case in which mental disorder negates all *mens rea* would the equivalent justice of a full acquittal be achieved, albeit for a different reason. But again, this is the rarest of cases. Most legally insane offenders form the *mens rea* required by the definition of the charged offence and only the defence of legal insanity can respond justly to their blameworthiness. Finally, a defendant who negated all *mens rea* would be entitled to outright release and subject only to traditional involuntary civil commitment, which is far less protective of public safety than post-insanity acquittal commitment.

Sentencing

Consideration of mental disorder for purposes of assessing both mitigation and aggravation is a staple of both capital and non-capital sentencing, but it is no substitute for the affirmative defence of legal insanity. On moral grounds, it is unfair to blame and punish a defendant who deserves no blame and punishment

---

[18] A practice the Court held did not deny procedural due process.
[19] OW Holmes Jr, *The Common Law* (Boston, MA, Little, Brown & Co, 1945) 50–51.

at all, even if the offender's sentence is reduced. Blaming and punishing in such cases is unjust, full stop. Sentencing judges might also use mental disorder as an aggravating consideration, as occurred in Delling's case, because it might suggest that the defendant is especially dangerous as a result. Thus, sentences of severely mentally ill offenders might not be reduced or might even be enhanced. Again, injustice would result and public safety would not be protected as well as an indeterminate post-acquittal commitment would achieve. Third, unless a sentencing judge is required by law to consider mental disorder at sentencing, whether the judge does so will be entirely discretionary. Again, this is a potential source of profound injustice if the sentencing judge fails to consider severe mental disorder in an appropriate case. In short, only a required insanity defence would ensure that arguably blameless mentally disordered offenders have an opportunity to establish that state blame and punishment are not justified.

V. Practical Objections to the Insanity Defence are Inconsequential

A number of objections to the insanity defence have been raised by proponents of abolition, but they are insubstantial and provide not even a rational basis for abolishing a defence with such a profound historical, moral and legal basis. They certainly cannot survive a more searching analysis. In general, these objections relate to supposed difficulties of administering the insanity defence fairly and accurately. Specific objections include: (A) administering the defence requires an assessment of the defendant's past mental state using controversial psychiatric and psychological evidence, a task that is too difficult; (B) acquitting insane defendants endangers public safety; (C) the defence produces 'wrong' verdicts; and (D) defendants use it to 'beat the rap'.

Assessing Past Mental State Using Psychological and Psychiatric Evidence

It is often difficult to reconstruct past mental states and, as the US Supreme Court has repeatedly acknowledged, psychological and psychiatric evidence can be problematic.[20] Nevertheless, if all jurisdictions, including *mens rea* alternative jurisdictions, concede the necessity of proving *mens rea* (for all but strict liability crimes) before punishment may justly be imposed, then their argument against the insanity defence based on the difficulty of reconstructing past mental states must fail. They can succeed only if assessing past intent, knowledge and other

---

[20] *Clark v Arizona* (n 3) 740–41; *Kansas v Crane* 534 US 407, 413 (2002).

types of *mens rea* is easier than assessing whether the defendant was acting under the influence of severely abnormal mental states. After all, both *mens rea* and legal insanity refer to past mental states that must be inferred from the defendant's actions, including utterances.

The severe disorder that is necessary practically to support an insanity defence is in most cases easier to prove than ordinary *mens rea* because in most cases the former is obvious. And it is no harder to assess knowledge of right from wrong, for example, than to assess which *mens rea* was present. Despite the problems with mental health evidence, virtually all Western legal systems believe that assessing legal insanity at the time of the crime with mental health evidence is feasible. Indeed, it is routine. Moreover, the abolitionist jurisdictions permit introduction of such evidence to negate *mens rea*. Unless abolitionist jurisdictions are prepared to argue—and none has—that assessing *mens rea* with mental health evidence is uniquely reliable, the argument based on the deficiencies of mental health evidence lacks credibility. Finally, mental health evidence is routinely admitted in a vast array of civil and criminal contexts, including all the criminal competencies and sentencing.

Public Safety

As previously argued, the insanity defence poses no danger to public safety. Successful insanity defences are so rare that deterrence will not be undermined because few legally sane defendants will believe that they can avoid conviction by manipulatively and falsely raising the defence. More important, every jurisdiction provides for commitment to a secure mental facility after a defendant has been acquitted by reason of insanity. The US Supreme Court has approved the constitutionality of indefinite confinement (with periodic review) of such acquittees as long as they remain mentally disordered and dangerous.[21] Further, the Supreme Court has approved procedures for the commitments that are more onerous for acquittees than standard civil commitment.[22] It is of course true that acquittees might be released earlier than if they had been convicted and imprisoned, but there is no evidence that released acquittees pose a special danger to the community.[23]

---

[21] *Jones v United States* 463 US 354 (1983); *Foucha v Louisiana*, 504 US 71 (1992); Morse (n 1) 932.
[22] *Jones v United States* (n 21).
[23] MK Spodak, SB Silver and CU Wright, 'Criminality of Discharged Insanity Acquittees: Fifteen Year Experience in Maryland Reviewed' (1984) 12 *Bulletin of the American Academy of Psychiatry and Law* 373, 382; MR Wiederanders, DL Bromley and PA Choate, 'Forensic Conditional Release Programs and Outcomes in Three States' (1997) 20 *International Journal of Law and Psychiatry* 249, 249–57; LA Callahan and E Silver, 'Revocation of Conditional Release: A Comparison of Individual and Program Characteristics across Four States' (1998) 21 *International Journal of Law and Psychiatry* 177; GF Parker, 'Outcomes of Assertive Community Treatment in an NGRI Conditional Release Program' (2004) 32 *The Journal of the American Academy of Psychiatry and the Law* 291; HJ Steadman, L Keitner, J Braff and TM Arvanites, 'Factors Associated With a Successful Insanity Plea' (1983) 140 *American Journal of Psychiatry* 401, 402–03.

'Wrong' Verdicts

Another objection is that the insanity defence is especially prone to erroneous verdicts. This objection is unwarranted. There is no evidence that the factual determinations concerning whether a defendant has a severe mental disorder incapacitating him from understanding the wrongfulness of his conduct are especially prone to error. Expert evidence on these issues is routinely admitted and is subject to the usual rules of cross-examination.

The ultimate value judgements the insanity defence requires, such as the question whether the defendant is incapable of understanding the wrongfulness of his conduct, are no more intractable or unreliable than the many other value judgements that the criminal law asks finders of fact to make, such as whether the defendant grossly deviated from the standard of care to be expected of a reasonable person, or whether an intentional killer was reasonably provoked. In the United States it is entirely appropriate to leave to the jury considerable discretion to judge, in light of all the facts and circumstances of the particular case, whether the defendant's mental disorder undermined his criminal responsibility. Drawing the line between guilt and innocence is the task of the finder of fact as the legal and moral representative of the community.

Complaints about 'erroneous' insanity acquittals are factually exaggerated because the incidence of such acquittals is low and the complaints are speculative. There is no reason to believe that the insanity defence is particularly prone to error compared to other, equally indeterminate, value-laden criminal law doctrines. The wrong verdict argument does not provide a legitimate policy reason for abolishing the insanity defence.

Beating the Rap

Few defendants who are actually legally sane in some objective sense 'beat the rap' with the insanity defence. Experts using the proper diagnostic tools can reliably distinguish people who are faking major mental disorder.[24] The complaint that this defence allows large numbers of guilty criminals to avoid conviction and punishment is simply unfounded. Prosecutors and defence attorneys alike generally recognise that insanity is a defence of last resort that betokens an otherwise

---

[24] ML Perlin, '"The Borderline Which Separated You from Me": The Insanity Defense, the Authoritarian Spirit, the Fear of Faking, and the Culture of Punishment' (1997) 82 *Iowa Law Review* 1375, 1409. Further, it is best estimated that in the United States the insanity defence is raised in less than 1 per cent of federal and State trials and is rarely successful. National Mental Health Association, *Myths and Realities: A Report of the National Commission on the Insanity Defense* (Arlington, VA, The Association, 1983) 14–15; RA Pasewark, 'Insanity Pleas: A Review of the Research Literature' (1981) 9 *Journal of Psychiatry & Law* 357, 361–66; HJ Steadman, MA McGreevy, JP Morrissey, LA Callahan, PC Robbins and C Cirincione, *Before and after Hinckley: Evaluating Insanity Defense Reform* (New York, The Guilford Press, 1993).

weak defence and that seldom succeeds. Insanity acquittals are far too infrequent to communicate the message that the criminal justice system is 'soft' or fails to protect society. It is impossible to measure precisely the symbolic value of these acquittals, but it is also hard to believe that they have much impact on social or individual perceptions. So few insanity pleas succeed that neither aspiring criminals nor society assume that conviction and punishment will be averted by raising the defence.

If the defendant is genuinely legally insane and succeeds with the defence, he deserves to be acquitted and has not 'beaten the rap' at all. The 'tough on crime' justification that underlies this argument is based on a fundamental misconception about the meaning of an insanity acquittal. In cases of a successful insanity defence, the prima facie case for guilt has been established and the verdict thus announces that the defendant's conduct was wrong. Nonetheless, the defendant did not deserve blame and punishment and will be confined by commitment.

VI. Is Legal Insanity a 'Status' Excuse or a Context-Limited Functional Excuse?

In virtually all jurisdictions, legal insanity is established only if a mental disorder affected the offender's cognitive or control capacities as they bore on the specific instance of the crime charged. In contrast, in at least one much-discussed legal system, Norway, legal insanity is simply a status excuse *simpliciter*. That is, if at the time of the crime the offender was psychotic, that is all that is required to satisfy the test for legal insanity. At least in theory, the offender's psychotic symptomatology did not have to affect the practical reasoning that motivated the criminal conduct. This account must be distinguished from a causal test, which bears some resemblance to the Norwegian status test by requiring that mental disorder somehow must 'cause' the criminal behaviour.[25] I think that neither the status nor causal view is wise and neither is the best explanation of current doctrine and practice.

The status view can best be explored by considering the work of my esteemed friend and colleague, Professor Michael Moore, who claims that at least some people with severe mental disorder lack fundamental conditions for personhood and are not moral agents. Severe disorder is a status excuse and thus deprives people of responsibility *tout court*. In short, such people are not excused for specific actions, but instead are simply exempt from responsibility ascription. Moore lists nine criteria for moral personhood: (1) mental states; (2) consciousness$_1$; phenomenal experience: (3) consciousness$_2$; privileged access; (4) intentionality; (5) three parts to the soul (the platonic functional appetitive, rational and executory);

---

[25] *State v Pike* 49 New Hampshire 399 (1870); *Durham v United States* 214 F 2d 862 (DC Circuit 1954), overruled by *US v Brawner* 471 F 2 d 969 (DC Circuit 1972).

(6) practical rationality; (7) emotionality and the rationality of emotion; (8) character structure at a time and over time; and (9) autonomy. These criteria are an attractive account of agency, but I fear they will not do the work for moral responsibility that Moore wishes.

Many people who are clearly legally insane and most 10–13-year-olds meet these nine criteria, but Moore nonetheless denies their status as potential moral agents. He is of course correct that these people are not responsible, but this is inconsistent with his view of moral agency, which does not excuse them. Needed is a particular deficit that unites those we potentially excuse. Moore notes that practical rationality, his sixth criterion, must involve some degree of substantive and not simply instrumental rationality. I think that this is the key to understanding the excusing condition rather than severe 'madness' itself. We excuse when substantive irrationality impairs the agent's practical reasoning in the context in question.

People with severe mental disorder are not their disorders. They are persons with a disability, which is why the preferred locution at present is not to characterise people as their disorder, for example, as a 'schizophrenic', but as a 'person with' schizophrenia. This is cumbersome, but it is all too easy, in contrast to cases of physical disease, to think mistakenly that mental disorder is the entirety of a person. As DSM-5 recognises, all mental disorders, including the most severe, are heterogeneous in presentation.[26] Severe disorder heterogeneously affects the sufferer's life depending on a large number of factors, many of which are external. It need not affect every aspect of their lives. The category of 'Delusional Disorder' is an example. Sufferers are psychotic but their delusional beliefs operate only in those contexts in which the belief is motivating. People with psychotic disorders may be perfectly capable of substantive and instrumental rationality in most areas of their lives. Contra Bleuler, who Moore quotes approvingly, they are not 'stranger to us than the birds in our gardens', nor are they 'beyond good and evil' in the non-Nietzchean sense, as Moore claims. They are recognisably one of us.

Moore draws an analogy to children, but even with children the law does not uniformly treat infancy as an excuse and takes different views of their capacities depending on their age and what is at stake. Consider the common law excuse of infancy, which is often considered a status excuse: children 6 and younger are categorically exempt; children 7–13 are presumed non-responsible; and children 14 and older are presumed responsible. This is quite consistent with what we know about cognitive development. Although some outlier very young children might have the cognitive ability to be responsible, this would be such a rare case that individuation would be inefficient. For the intermediate group, cognitive development is generally incomplete, but the presumption of non-responsibility is rebuttable. Infancy is simply a proxy for lacking certain cognitive capacities and is not really a status excuse.

---

[26] American Psychiatric Association, *Diagnostic and Statistical Manual of Mental Disorders*, 5th edn (Arlington, VA, American Psychiatric Publishing, 2013) 20. For similar reasons, DSM-5 also cautions against thinking that any diagnostic category directly answers any legal question. Ibid 25.

The Supreme Court has held that minors categorically are insufficiently rational to deserve the death penalty or to be sentenced to mandatory life without parole for non-homicide crimes,[27] but there was a strong argument that the decisions should have permitted individuation, at least for older adolescents. I believe the Court drew a bright line for the sake of administrative convenience and to avoid the horrendous error of potentially wrongfully imposing these dreadful sentences. In *Miller v Alabama* the Court rejected mandatory life without parole for minors committed of homicide crimes, but permitted individuation in imposing this sentence.[28] In many jurisdictions minors are considered sufficiently rational to make an independent decision about whether to use birth control or to have an abortion. Even infancy is not clearly a 'status' for all purposes.

'Intellectual Disability' (ID) (formerly retardation or developmental disability) is a similar example. The Supreme Court categorically excluded people with ID from capital punishment because rationality defects mark this condition,[29] but conceded that such people could be criminally responsible and insisted on careful individuation about whether the convicted capital defendant did have ID.[30] The Court could have once again insisted on individuation even for those defendants concededly suffering from ID, which also presents heterogeneously, but for the same reasons as in *Roper* and *Graham*, opted for a categorical rule. Finally, in the civil context, whether people with ID should be treated as competent is a functional test that differs from context to context.

The same considerations are true of people with severe mental disorders. They may be competent or morally responsible for some conduct. Involuntary civil commitment, for example, no longer has the consequence of declaring the person committed civilly incompetent for all purposes, such as making contracts or voting. Moreover, those people who are omni-disabled are usually too disorganised to engage in criminal conduct other than simple assaultive or disorderly conduct, for which no sensible defendant raises an insanity defence. Those with severe disorders who commit crimes are usually quite instrumentally rational and mostly substantively rational as well. A specific cognitive deficit that irrationally and materially motivated the defendant is doing the work in most legal insanity cases. Consider M'Naghten, who delusionally believed the Tories were persecuting him and were a threat to his life,[31] or Andrea Yates, who delusionally believed that she was morally corrupting her children and thus they would be tortured for all eternity in hell unless she killed them when they were still 'innocent'.[32] Both carefully planned their conduct and executed it successfully (although M'Naghten's victim was Peel's private secretary, Drummond, who M'Naghten non-delusionally but mistakenly believed was Peel).

---

[27] *Roper v Simmons* 543 US 551 (2005); *Graham v Florida* 130 S Ct 2011 (2010).
[28] *Miller v Alabama* 132 S Ct 2455 (2012).
[29] *Atkins v Virginia* 536 US 304 (2002).
[30] *Hall v Florida* 134 S Ct 1986 (2014).
[31] Moran (n 12).
[32] Denno (n 14).

Moreover, the moral compass of those with severe disorders is often unimpaired. Suppose one believed what Andrea Yates believed. If these facts were true, as Ms Yates sincerely believed, then it would be morally permissible and perhaps even obligatory to kill one's children. To suggest that Ms Yates or other legally insane people lack all moral agency is contrary to the facts and I fear demeans them. It is preferable to say that she is not responsible for killing the children because she was psychotically motivated to do this particular crime, but she was responsible for much else in her life that had moral import.

It is useful to consider psychopathy to assess this issue. At the extreme, people with psychopathy, a personality disorder of unknown origin, completely or almost completely lack conscience, a sense of morality and the capacity for empathy.[33] They are incapable of recognising the normatively best moral reasons for respecting the rights of others. I believe that they are morally irrational, although they can be instrumentally rational and do understand criminal prohibitions and the potential costs of offending. I have argued elsewhere that severe psychopathy should be a predicate for excuse.[34] If the law permitted using psychopathy as a basis for legal insanity, it would best be explained by the lack of moral rational capacity, and not because psychopathy is a status.

Although plausible insanity defence cases are akin to mistakes of fact and law, the materially irrational motivation is the foundation of the excuse. Moore's views and mine are very similar, but I do not agree that a delusional person who engages in criminal behaviour unrelated to his delusion is not responsible because he is not a moral agent. If his conduct is rationally motivated although he is wildly out of touch with reality in other domains of his life, which is commonly the case, what good moral theory would exempt him from responsibility for rationally motivated actions?

Moore is correct that knowledge of right and wrong or knowledge of what one is doing is not precisely the issue because everything turns on how narrowly knowledge is interpreted. This is a normative question unanswered by adopting equally vague terms such as 'understand' or 'appreciate'. As an aside, most legally insane defendants did think their conduct was permissible or necessary, even according to conventional reality, if the facts were as the defendant believed. Consider Andrea Yates again.

If 'knowledge' is properly interpreted morally, most people who are legally insane do not know what they are doing in the sense that they are motivated by a non-culpable error about reality. The deific decree exception to a narrowly interpreted *M'Naghten* test does not prove that madness itself excuses. It confirms that material, irrational motivation about what one is doing is necessary for excuse. Contra Moore, we do need mental disorder plus some further non-culpable deficiency in practical rationality. Mental disorder must 'cause' the criminal conduct

---

[33] See RM Hare, *Without Conscience: The Disturbing World of the Psychopaths among Us* (New York, Pocket Books, 1999).

[34] SJ Morse, 'Psychopathy and Criminal Responsibility' (2008) 3 *Neuroethics* 205.

by severely impairing the person's practical rationality in the particular circumstances. We do not treat the further criterion for legal insanity, such as nonculpable lack of knowledge about what one is doing, independently because, as many have pointed out, mental disorder is used as an objective indicator that proves that the defendant's mistake about the motivating reality is not an 'ordinary' mistake.

The hardest case for my view is the person who is materially delusionally motivated, but who knows that what he is doing is wrong even if the facts were as he believed them to be. A commonly discussed example is the person who delusionally believes that his spouse is unfaithful, is wildly jealous, cannot be convinced by evidence or logic to the contrary, and indeed weaves counter-evidence and logic into the delusional belief system and thereby reinforces it. If he kills his spouse, should he be excused? He is clearly and severely mad. The DSM-5 diagnosis would be 'Delusional disorder, jealous type', a psychotic disorder, but note that the law virtually everywhere would not find him legally insane because he knew that what he was doing is wrong even if it were true that his spouse was unfaithful. Would Moore's status view excuse him? Perhaps so, because a psychotic belief motivated him, but is he a non-responsible agent generally? Seemingly not. If he committed theft, he should surely be responsible. For years I waffled on this issue, but now believe that the delusional spouse must be convicted, unless his moral compass is independently compromised by mental disorder. Even if all the facts and circumstances as he believes them to be were true, he would still be guilty of a crime. Faithlessness does not justify intentional homicide even if it reduces the degree of guilt in some circumstances. I would convict the delusional spouse of murder, but this well might be an appropriate case for my proposed 'guilty but partially responsible' verdict because he had a severe rationality defect in the context.[35] In that case, his degree of culpability and punishment would be reduced.

In conclusion, I do not think that the status account of legal insanity best explains current law. More important, I worry that if adopted, it would contribute, albeit marginally, to common misunderstandings and fear of mental disorder that continue to stigmatise and exclude people with such disorders.

The causal view is marginally more acceptable because it at least links the offender's irrational thinking specifically to the crime, but it confuses the nature of the defence. Moreover, as the influential US Court of Appeals for the District of Columbia, which had adopted the test, ultimately concluded, it is unworkable and it was abandoned.[36] The causal view implies that mental disorder is like a 'force' that moves, indeed compels, the agent's conduct. The true picture, however, is that mental disorder compromises the agent's practical reason, which motivates the agent to act. And irrational motivation is no more 'compelling' than rational motivation. Daniel M'Naghten's desire to save his own life is no stronger than the desire of the victim of a genuine, wrongful, deadly attack.

[35] SJ Morse, 'Diminished Rationality, Diminished Responsibility' (2003) 1 *Ohio State Journal of Criminal Law* 289.
[36] *US v Brawner* (n 25).

Most important, if mental disorder undoubtedly played a mentally causal role in a defendant's behaviour, non-responsibility does not follow. Consider the following case. Imagine a non-versatile career armed robber who suffers from diagnosable hypomania. He robs only during his episodes of hypomania because only then does he feel sufficiently energetic and confident enough to engage in his very active and dangerous pursuit. If our robber is caught and charged, it is not at all clear that he is sufficiently irrational enough to be excused, even though the mental disorder played a strong causal role in explaining his behaviour. A jurisdiction could try to avoid this difficulty by establishing that only severe mental disorder as a cause would excuse, but even severe mental disorders have heterogeneous presentations as we have seen. Finally, the jurisdiction could adopt a severe irrationality standard, but then it looks suspiciously akin to a straightforward cognitive test and indeed may collapse into one.

VII. The Tests for Legal Insanity

Legal insanity is a legal and moral issue, not a medical, psychiatric or psychological issue. The criteria for finding someone not criminally responsible—for deciding who is not a fit subject for blame and punishment—are thoroughly normative. With rare exception, this includes the mental disorder criterion, which for purposes of a legal rule is a legal test. Thus, the claim that a test is 'unscientific' is a category mistake. One may believe that certain types of mental states should excuse a criminal who possessed them at the time of the crime and may therefore criticise on moral grounds a test that does not include them, but that is a normative and not a scientific critique. A narrow test may be morally offensive, but it will not be scientifically erroneous.

The Mental Disorder Criterion

Except in the few jurisdictions discussed in the previous section, mental disorder alone, no matter how severe, is not an excusing condition even if it played a causal role in explaining the defendant's behaviour. Causation per se is not an excusing condition. The moral basis for the insanity defence is that in some cases mental disorder affects the defendant's capacity to act rationally[37] or to control his behaviour. These are the genuinely excusing conditions addressed by the criteria for legal insanity in addition to mental disorder. The issue is the defendant's impaired practical reasoning. Excuse is warranted only in those cases in which the impairment is sufficient, which is a moral and legal question. As a practical matter,

---

[37] H Fingarette, *The Meaning of Criminal Insanity* (Berkeley, CA, University of California Press, 1972) 179–215; Fingarette and Hasse (n 1) 218–39.

the defendant must have been out of touch with reality at the time of the crime to succeed with the insanity defence,[38] but many defendants who are concededly psychotic at the time of the crime may be convicted because their practical reasoning about the crime was nonetheless not sufficiently impaired. For example, Eric Clark, the defendant in the US Supreme Court case addressing the constitutionality of a very narrow insanity defence test, was incontrovertibly suffering from paranoid schizophrenia, but the trial court rejected the defence of legal insanity and convicted him because it concluded that Clark did know that what he was doing was wrong.[39]

The few jurisdictions that have a mental disorder criterion alone place great weight on mental disorder. The problem, as we have seen, is that there is great heterogeneity among people with the same diagnoses of major mental disorder and such heterogeneity is also apparent even within a descriptive category, such as 'psychosis'. Thus, even if a mental disorder criterion is met, it may blur what should be important moral differences in responsibility ascription.

In those jurisdictions that adopt the causal test without further criteria, the problem remains acute because the jurisdiction must decide which disorders that may play a causal role should qualify. It is obvious that personality disorders, disorders of impulse control and many others will scarcely create a non-responsibility condition, even if they are causally implicated in criminal conduct. The questions remain, however, which diagnostic categories should be required and how does one deal with the heterogeneity problems. The experience of the US Court of Appeals for the District of Columbia, which promulgated the famous *Durham* test in 1954, is instructive. As a practical matter, most of the expert witnesses in District of Columbia cases came from St Elizabeth's Hospital, a public hospital in the District. The difficulty was that the experts could not agree on which conditions qualified as disorders for the purposes of satisfying the test. In a famous case, the doctors changed their opinion on this matter over the course of one weekend. The Court's attempt to provide a generic definition proved equally unsuccessful. Finally, in the *Brawner* case in 1972, the same court reviewed the history of the difficulties and abandoned the *Durham* test as unworkable. It adopted the American law Institute (ALI) test instead, which includes a cognitive and control component in addition to the mental disorder and causation criteria.

Some commentators have proposed identifying properly qualifying disorders and some legislatures have specifically excluded some well-recognised disorders, but such interventions do not solve the problem. Even if one includes only major mental disorders, there is still clinical heterogeneity within them and not all sufferers may seem sufficiently irrational to qualify for an insanity defence, but this problem is largely ameliorated by the requirement that a sufficient cognitive or control defect results from the major mental disorder. The specifically excluded disorders, such as psychopathy, and addiction as common examples, lack a

---

[38] Steadman et al (n 24) 85.
[39] *Clark v Arizona* (n 3) 745–46.

principled basis for exclusion. They are recognised disorders and in severe cases can apparently cause serious cognitive and control problems. Thus, there seems no reason categorically to exclude them although successful cases may be rare. Fears of filling the courts with baseless claims seem overwrought and can be limited by motions *in limine*.

Cognitive Tests

Much scholarly ink has been spilled and many pixels illuminated about specific issues within *M'Naghten* and its variants, such as whether knowledge of right versus wrong means moral or legal wrong and whether an allegedly broader substitute for knowledge, such as appreciation or understanding, is preferable. I believe that such debates are beside the point. To begin, the test used does not seem to make much difference in the outcome,[40] a result I think is best explained by the jury's rough and ready conclusion that the defendant was or was not sufficiently irrational to deserve to be punished.

To the extent that an outcome might turn on moral versus legal wrong, the former should be preferred because it is more action guiding and provides a better fit with the underlying rationale for the defence. Note that all crimes for which an insanity defence is typically raised are acts that are also clearly immoral and illegal. The reason a legally insane offender typically commits the crime is primarily because he believes that he has a sufficient moral or legal justification for what he is doing. Consider Andrea Yates again, who delusionally believed that she needed to kill her children while they were still sufficiently pure or they would become corrupted and would be tormented in hell for eternity.[41] Yates knew it was legally wrong to kill her children and she might also have recognised that her neighbours might think it morally wrong to do so. Nonetheless, from her deluded, subjective point of view, she surely thought she was doing the right thing. If the facts and circumstances were as she believed them to be, the balance of evils was positive in this case. Ms Yates's knowledge of moral and legal wrong is beside the point, however. Although Ms Yates was instrumentally rational, she deserved to be excused because her actions were deeply irrationally motivated through no fault of her own.

Many critics of cognitive tests believe that the word 'know' is too narrow and that other, apparently broader terms should be used that encompass a somehow deeper understanding of what one is doing or that it is wrong.[42] Every lawyer

---

[40] SH Kadish, Schulhofer, SJ, Steiker, CS and RE Barkow, *Criminal Law and Its Processes: Cases and Materials*, 9th edn (New York, Wolters Kluwer Law and Business, 2012) 982.

[41] Denno (n 14) (providing a complete account of the case).

[42] See eg American Law Institute, *Model Penal Code and Commentaries*, vol 1 (Philadelphia, PA, The American Law Institute, 1985) § 4.01, 166, 169–70; D Mossman, '*United States v Lyons*: Toward a New Conception of Legal Insanity' (1988) 16 *Bulletin of the American Academy of Psychiatry and the Law* 49, 54–57.

knows, however, that almost any term used can be interpreted more or less broadly to reach the morally preferred result. Consider knowledge itself. Did Ms Yates know what she was doing? The answer depends on whether one takes a narrow or broad view of such knowledge. Ms Yates knew that she was killing her children, so she knew what she was doing in the narrow sense. On the other hand, her material motive for action—to save the children from eternal torment—was deluded, so she did not know what she was doing in a broader sense. She thought she was saving the children, but she was not. The same could be said of her knowledge of moral and legal wrong. Either result could be obtained by narrow or broad readings of 'understand', 'appreciate', or other contenders. Fine-grained parsing of small definitional differences will not be helpful to finders of fact. A legislature can certainly signal by using a term different from knowledge that it wishes to adopt a broader reading of its cognitive test, but juries will still make a rough and ready judgement and the word used has no influence on which expert and lay testimony will be admissible. In practice, the complete clinical picture will be brought to bear whichever word is used.

Control Tests

If a defendant was sufficiently irrational, no separate control test will be necessary to excuse him. Suppose, however, that the defendant was rational according to any ordinary definition, but claims that he could not control himself. Such claims are often associated with sexual disorders, substance disorders and impulse control disorders generally. These are the cases in which an independent control test is thought to be necessary. In the wake of John Hinckley's acquittal by reason of insanity for attempting to assassinate President Reagan and others, many State legislatures in the United States abolished a control test for legal insanity. The American Bar Association and the American Psychiatric Association also took positions rejecting the validity of control tests.[43] Although it may seem unfair to blame and punish an otherwise rational agent who cannot control himself, there was good reason to jettison control tests. The primary ground was the inability of either experts or jurors to differentiate the defendant who could not control himself from one who simply did not. The presence of mental disorder is of no help in this regard because criminal conduct is human action, even if it is the sign or symptom of a disease. Concluding that human action is not controllable because it is a sign or a symptom or because it has a neurophysiological basis is simply question-begging.[44] An independent, folk psychological demonstration that the conduct could not be controlled is required.

---

[43] American Bar Association, *ABA Criminal Justice Mental Health Standards* (Washington DC, American Bar Association, 1984) 330, 339–42; American Psychiatric Association, *American Psychiatric Association Statement on the Insanity Defense*, reprinted in (1983) 140 *American Journal of Psychiatry* 681.

[44] Fingarette and Hasse (n 1) 148–53.

I am an opponent of control tests because I have not encountered a convincing conceptual account of an independent lack of control and an operational definition of such an incapacity that would permit expert or lay testimony to resolve whether a defendant had such a problem.[45] I readily concede that lack of control may be an independent type of incapacity that should mitigate or excuse responsibility, but until a good conceptual and operational account of lack of control is provided, I prefer to limit the insanity defence to cognitive tests.

I believe that virtually all cases in which a control test seems attractive or necessary can be better explained as a cognitive problem. People who are out of touch with reality may have trouble controlling themselves in the sense that they cannot be guided by reason, but irrationality is the problem. For example, people with sexual or substance disorders may not appear irrational, but they do report intense craving and often engage in repetitive actions that can be ruinously costly to them. It seems natural to infer that they somehow cannot control themselves. I suggest that the lack of control arises from the intensity of desire that seems to drown out all the competing considerations that most of us use to control untoward desires. In other words, at times of peak arousal, people with these problems simply cannot be guided by the good reason not to yield to their desires.[46] Indeed, most attempts to explain lack of control arising from mental disorder in fact raise cognitive concerns. For examples, the first major, modern proponents of a control test were Sir James Fitzjames Stephen[47] and the Alabama Supreme Court, which adopted the 'irresistible impulse' test.[48] Both specified the folk psychological mechanism that caused the failure of control. Fitzjames believed that the problem was the failure to keep future consequences firmly in mind.[49] The *Parsons* decision spoke of the destruction of the power to choose between right and wrong, and, quoting an authority on medical jurisprudence, attributed this to reason losing its 'empire' over the passions.[50] In short, both proposed a rationality defect as the source of loss of control capacity.

Even if one accepts this theory of mitigation or excuse based on synchronic lack of rational capacity, in most cases the agent can still be held responsible. During those times when arousal is dormant or low, they do have intact rational capacity

[45] S Morse, 'Uncontrollable Urges and Irrational People' (2002) 88 *Virginia Law Review* 1025. SJ Morse, 'Against Control Tests' in PH Robinson et al (eds), *Criminal Law Conversations* (Oxford, Oxford University Press, 2009). The latter was a 'target' chapter that challenged proponents of control tests to provide the psychological process or mechanism that produced lack of control capacity and that could be the focus of testimony about it. Five critics responded to the chapter, but not one even remotely suggested a folk psychological mechanism or process.

[46] See SJ Morse, 'Addiction, Science and Criminal Responsibility' in N Farahany (ed), *The Impact of Behavioral Sciences on Criminal Law* (Oxford, Oxford University Press, 2009) (providing a fuller account).

[47] JF Stephen, *History of The Criminal Law of England*, vol II (Chesterland, OH, General Bookbinding Co, 1883) 120.

[48] *Parsons v State* 81 Alabama 854, 859 (1887).

[49] Stephen (n 47) 120.

[50] *Parsons v State* (n 48).

and recognise that they will yield in the future. It is therefore their duty to take whatever steps are necessary, such as entering treatment, to insure that they do not offend. If they do not take such steps, they are diachronously responsible for their later wrongful conduct by not avoiding the condition of their own excuse. In other words, even if sexual and substance disorders were to qualify as a sufficient mental abnormality for establishing legal insanity and even if people with these disorders were not rational at the time of the crime, a successful insanity defence might nonetheless be inappropriate in most cases.

Most recently, in his excellent chapter on the volitional excuse,[51] Professor Michael Moore accepts the challenge of defending a control test and providing a folk psychological account of loss of control. I will focus on his analysis of the 'incapacity' justification for a control excuse and not on the interesting things he writes about the 'fair opportunity' justification. Although I am willing in principle and mostly in fact to accept Moore's premises, I do not think that the conclusion he draws follows and his analysis of doctrine is better explained by different rationales.

A preliminary word on terminology is in order. Moore holds that volitions are independent executory intentions.[52] In virtually all cases that involve the excuse Moore defends, he recognises that volitions successfully execute the defendant's motivating intentions. Thus, it is somewhat strange for him to talk about a volitional excuse rather than a control or compulsion excuse. Consequently, I shall use the term 'control' because it more accurately describes what we care about. Moore and I agree that if there is independent control capacity, the can't/won't distinction is scalar, although the law treats it as binary, and counterfactual analysis will be necessary to draw the can't/won't line.

Moore's characterisation of cases requiring a control excuse are those in which the defendant did not do 'what he most wants to do', either because the agent is unable to form the 'right intention' or because the agent is able to form the 'right' intention, but is unable to execute it. Moore begins his analysis of the folk psychology of loss of control with a number of stipulations about 'desire, strongest desire, and intention', which he concedes are contested in the philosophy of mind and action. I accept his stipulations, but what is a poor country lawyer-scholar to do if others contest them? Moore then proposes and evaluates six models of the folk psychology of the lack of control, ranging from desire bypassing the will entirely to unstable preference shifts (described in terms of hyperbolic discounting by many addiction specialists). He is properly sceptical that most of the models he canvasses are the underlying, unitary foundation for a control excuse, but he does settle on one of them: motivation by 'ego-alien desires that refuse to be integrated into one's sense of the self', that 'seem alien to (rather than part of)

[51] MS Moore, 'The Neuroscience of Volitional Excuse' in D Patterson and M Pardo (eds), *Law and Neuroscience: State of the Art* (Oxford, Oxford University Press, forthcoming).

[52] MS Moore, *Act and Crime: The Philosophy of Action and its Implications for Criminal Law* (Oxford, Oxford University Press, 1993); Moore (n 51).

the reason-responsive … self'. I would analyse the folk psychology differently and paradoxically think that Moore underweights some of the models he rejects, but I will accept his psychology for the purpose of analysis.

I concede the psychology because all the models exemplify rationality defects properly understood. Moore's preferred model of ego-alien desires is a prime example. Generically, the 'ego-alienated' agent's desires are sealed off from the reason-responsive self. Moore quotes from many other thinkers who have reached similar conclusions about cases 'when a strong, emotion-laden, not-identified-with-self desire conflicts with a less strong, probably less emotion-laden but more identified-with-self desire, and wins'. The essence of all, I believe, is that the disjunct occurs because the agent is not fully rational, as Michael Smith, whom Moore cites approvingly, suggests.

All core criminal offences infringe on the rights of victims and communicate disrespect for the victim and for society. Everyone thus has supremely good reason not to commit core criminal law offences. I could quibble with how often genuinely ego-alien desires arise in criminal law cases and with Moore's account of them. Even if Moore's psychology is accepted, however, the problem that might excuse is a rationality defect best explained by the agent's inability to 'think straight', to access the good reasons not to offend, under circumstances that seem to disable those abilities, such as craving, intense emotion and the other variables Moore properly notes. I think this better explains the excusing and mitigating conditions in law that Moore addresses, such as provocation/passion, 'diminished capacity', involuntary intoxication and legal insanity. The other doctrines Moore adduces, such as necessity, duress and innocent aggressor, are better explained by a common sense, hard-choice situation the agent does not create and in which the agent on balance wholeheartedly harms another. No control excuse is necessary.

Even if a control test may be justified, Moore argues that it should only apply if the agent cannot, as opposed to will not, control himself. This is a scalar concept and probably every agent has this capacity to some degree, as demonstrated by the assumption that all those agents with a control problem would manage to resist offending if they were threatened with instant death. The ability of an agent to exercise control under such circumstances does not entail that he must be responsible. No just legal regime would be so unforgiving. It is sufficient to excuse if the agent lacks 'substantial' capacity, with that lack given varying normative content depending on the general stance of the legal system to the expansiveness of excuses.

Moore and I agree that counterfactual analysis is the primary way to evaluate an agent's control capacity. It is no surprise to learn that Moore metaphysically analyses capacity using David Lewis's possible worlds modal logic. The concept of capacity is contested within professional philosophy and Moore freely concedes some of the problems with his approach. More fundamentally for the law, how could the legal system ever practically use Lewis's methodology, even if it is metaphysically the most potent? Even Lewissians differ about how close the possible worlds must be. What is a country lawyer-scholar supposed to do?

I start, of course, by conceptualising control capacity in terms of cognitive deficits and then suggest a purely common sense, folk psychological, counterfactual methodology. Consider that refraining from most core criminal behaviour, such as not killing, not raping, not burning, not stealing and so on, is low-skill behaviour. If one has the general capacity to refrain as demonstrated by the agent's behaviour in other, similar circumstances—Does the agent always attempt to kill people who provoke him to anger? Does the paedophile always touch children when there is no witness?—then it is fair to infer that the agent probably had similar capacity at the time when the prohibited action occurred.[53] This conclusion is defeasible by showing that the specific circumstances of the instant case make it distinguishable from apparently similar circumstances, but the metaphysics of counterfactuals will not help with the practical determination that must be made. There will be no easy answers in many cases, but all one can do is attend to the relevant history and compare it to the present facts and circumstances.

Neuroscience and psychology simply cannot help solve these problems. What good research now exists is not remotely ecologically valid and there is serious question whether such research could be done at all, even if an institutional review board would allow the types of experimental interventions that would be necessary. We shall have to accept the necessity of behavioural evaluation.

In short, I welcome Moore to the ranks of those who understand control problems as rationality problems (anyone wants Moore as an ally) and hope that he will join me in challenging the proponents of control tests to provide a test independent of rationality defects.

The Problem of Psychopathy and Responsibility

An interesting and important issue that implicates the mental disorder criterion and both the cognitive and control tests is whether psychopathy should qualify as a mental disorder for purposes of legal insanity and whether at least some psychopaths seem to meet either a cognitive or a control test. Psychopathy is a well-validated mental disorder characterised by both conduct and psychological abnormalities.[54] For our purposes, the most important criteria are lack of conscience, lack of empathy and lack of concern for the rights and interests of other people. The issue is important because psychopathy is highly predisposing to

---

[53] See V McGeer and P Pettit, 'The Hard Problem of Responsibility' in D Shoemaker (ed), *Oxford Studies in Agency and Responsibility*, vol 3 (Oxford, Oxford University Press, 2015) 160.

[54] The 'gold standard' for measuring psychopathy is RD Hare's *The Hare Psychopathy Checklist-Revised*, 2nd edn (North Tonawanda, NY, Multi-Health Systems, 2003). An earlier, influential clinical description is H Cleckley's *The Mask of Sanity*, 5th edn (Augusta, GA, ES Cleckley, 1988). Although psychopathy is a well-validated diagnostic entity, it is not included in DSM-5. Psychopathic characteristics can be of greater or lesser severity. My discussion will assume that a potentially excusable defendant is severely psychopathic.

criminal behaviour, including heightened recidivism,[55] and is common among prisoners in maximum security prisons.[56] Psychopaths simply do not get the point of morality or the underlying moral basis of criminal law prohibitions. Criminal punishments are only prices to them. It may sound as if such people are simply callous and have an unfeeling character, but the dominant understanding today is that they are disordered for reasons not yet well understood.

The Model Penal Code's insanity provisions exclude from the defence a mental disorder 'manifested only by repeated criminal or otherwise anti-social conduct'.[57] Most courts have interpreted this provision to exclude psychopathy, but the words of the section do not entail this conclusion.[58] Repetitive antisocial and criminal behaviour is one factor that can increase psychopathy scores, but the diagnosis is not based on this factor alone. Thus, the language of the various tests for legal insanity permits a reasonable case for inclusion. In brief, the argument for excusing psychopaths, or at least some of them, is that they lack the strongest reasons for complying with the law, such as understanding that what they are doing is wrong and empathic understanding of their victims' plight.[59] They are likewise unmoved by considerations of how others would judge them morally or what others would morally expect of them. Most people can use empathy, conscience, understanding of the reason underlying a criminal law's prohibition, the viewpoint of others and prudential reasons to guide their behaviour. In contrast, as a result of their psychological deficits, psychopaths can be guided only by prudential, egoistic reasons not to be caught and punished. In other words, they cannot grasp or be guided by the normatively most desirable reasons not to offend, which could be expressed either as a cognitive or control defect. And according to the same argument, people with lesser but still substantial psychopathy should qualify for mitigation. In response, most advocates for continuing exclusion of psychopathy as a basis for the insanity defence argue that they are in touch with reality and know the rules and it is

---

[55] KS Douglas, GM Vincent and JF Edens, 'Risk for Criminal Recidivism: The Role of Psychopathy' in CJ Patrick (ed), *Handbook of Psychopathy* (New York, Guilford Press, 2006) 534 (urging caution on methodological grounds).

[56] See TA Widiger, 'Psychopathy and DSM-IV Psychopathology' in CJ Patrick (ed), *Handbook of Psychopathy* (New York, Guilford Press, 2006) 157–59 (noting that there is strong overlap between psychopathy and Antisocial Personality Disorder (APD), but the relation is asymmetric; APD is more prevalent among prisoners and virtually all prisoners who score high on psychopathy meet the criteria for APD, but not the reverse).

Psychopathy must be distinguished from APD, which is included in American Psychiatric Association, *Diagnostic and Statistical Manual of Mental Disorders*, 5th edn (Arlington, VA, American Psychiatric Publishing, 2013) 701–06. APD is diagnosed on the basis primarily of repetitive antisocial conduct. There are only two psychological criteria among the diagnostic criteria, lack of remorse and impulsivity, but neither need be present to make the diagnosis. Psychopathy, by contrast, always includes psychological criteria. As a result, psychopathy might plausibly be a candidate for a mental disorder that would support an insanity defence, but APD would clearly not qualify. Ibid.

[57] American Law Institute (n 42) § 4.01(2).

[58] Indeed, the Model Penal Code makes clear that its provision did not exclude a mental condition 'so long as the condition is manifested by indicia other than repeated antisocial behavior': ibid 164.

[59] See Morse (n 34) (providing a fuller account).

sufficient for criminal responsibility that psychopaths can reason prudentially about their own self-interest.[60]

Suppose one accepts on normative grounds, as so many do, that the capacity for prudential reasoning is sufficient for criminal responsibility. There remains one final argument for excusing at least extreme psychopaths based on their lack of even prudential reasoning ability. According to one plausible but controversial broad characterisation of psychopathy, most ably advanced by Paul Litton,[61] psychopaths are not rational at all because they lack any evaluative standards to assess and guide their conduct. They do not even possess evaluative standards related to the pursuit of excitement and pleasure. Litton concludes that 'it is not surprising that agents with a very weak capacity of internalizing standards act on unevaluated whims and impulses'.[62] Much of their conduct appears unintelligible because we cannot imagine what good reason would motivate it. In brief, psychopaths have a generally diminished capacity for rational self-governance that is not limited to the sphere of morality. They cannot even reason prudentially. Future research may convince legislatures or courts to accept such an understanding of some psychopaths and to extend the insanity defence to them, but this is not the current law, even for such extreme cases.

Finally, in the United States, there is a major practical objection to applying the insanity defence to psychopathic defendants. In all jurisdictions, a defendant acquitted by reason of insanity may be involuntarily committed to a secure hospital facility, a practice that the Supreme Court has held is constitutional.[63] The term of commitment varies, but the Supreme Court has upheld an indefinite term[64] as long as the acquitted inmate remains both mentally ill and dangerous.[65] It thus appears that this would be a secure form of incapacitation for dangerous psychopaths if psychopathy were accepted as a potentially excusing mental disorder. Despite the initial attractiveness of this solution to the danger psychopathy presents, it is unlikely to be successful. The insanity defence cannot be imposed on a competent defendant who does not wish to raise it,[66] and virtually no psychopath would raise the insanity defence because at present there is no effective treatment for adult psychopathy. Any psychopath acquitted by reason of insanity for any crime would potentially face a lifelong commitment to an essentially prison-like facility. In short, even if US law came to the conclusion that psychopaths should

---

[60] SH Pillsbury, 'The Meaning of Deserved Punishment: An Essay on Choice, Character, and Responsibility' (1992) 67 *Indiana Law Journal* 719, 746–47. For an intermediate position, see W Glannon, 'Moral Responsibility and the Psychopath' (2008) 1 *Neuroethics* 158 (arguing that psychopaths are capable of instrumental reasoning and are capable of being guided by moral considerations to some degree, but their cognitive and affective impairments warrant mitigation).

[61] PJ Litton, 'Responsibility Status of the Psychopath: On Moral Reasoning and Rational Self-Governance' (2008) 39 *Rutgers Law Journal* 349. The argument in the text follows Litton.

[62] ibid 382.

[63] *Jones v United States* (n 21).

[64] ibid.

[65] *Foucha v Louisiana* (n 21) 76.

[66] eg, *United States v Marble* 940 F 2d 1543 (DC Cir 1991).

be excused, few psychopaths would be willing to accept such 'lenient' treatment and society would still have to rely on a pure criminal justice response. Thus, the only potential solution would be some special form of involuntary civil commitment similar to sexual predator commitments. But there are major conceptual and constitutional problems with such commitments that render their extension even more problematic.[67]

VIII. The Contribution of Neuroscience

This chapter has suggested that despite the moral imperative of a jurisdiction adopting some form of insanity defence, it is a normatively based excuse that at present relies on quite inexact psychiatry and psychology. Although better science cannot resolve normative disputes such as how broad or narrow a test should be, it may resolve empirical questions, which would lead to better informed social policy and more accurate adjudication. The question is how much neuroscience can help.

The answer at present is that the contribution is virtually nil. The biological understanding of mental disorder is simply too sketchy and so few findings are well replicated that neurodata cannot be a sensible guide to legal policy making regarding legal insanity or the legal response to people with mental disorders in general. For example, neuroscience cannot demonstrate that people with some severe mental disorders have less behavioural control than people without such disorders. Claims that present neuroscience has considerably more to offer tend to cherry-pick the scientific studies and to draw broad and extensive inferences from them that the studies do not support.[68] Consequently, neuroscience furnishes no convincing evidence that an independent control test or a broad cognitive test for legal insanity seem morally indicated. And, with rare exceptions that are mostly limited to cases involving well-characterised neurological disorders with behavioural sequelae, such as epilepsy, neurotests are simply not sufficiently diagnostic of any of the criteria for legal insanity to be of much help in the adjudication of individual cases.

Before turning to a more specific discussion of the contribution of neuroscience, let us first make some general observations. In most cases in which legal insanity is raised, there is little dispute about whether the defendant suffers from a mental disorder. Rather, the dispute is about which mental disorder was present,

---

[67] S Morse, 'Uncontrollable Urges and Irrational People' (n 45).

[68] See eg TY Blumoff, 'Rationality, Insanity, and the Insanity Defense: Reflections on the Limits of Reason' (2014) 39 *Law & Psychology Review* 161, 193–97. I agree with this paper that a rational insanity defence should be far broader than an extremely narrow cognitive test, but I reach this conclusion on moral grounds and not because the neuroscience supports this conclusion. Professor Blumoff claims that some of the biological claims he made are 'brute facts'. They are not. The use of the papers cited in this article is a classic sign of Brain Overclaim Syndrome.

and about the content and severity of the signs and symptoms. For example, there may be questions about whether the defendant was delusional and the degree to which the defendant had some awareness of the mistakenness of his beliefs. The presence of severe mental disorder, especially including loss of touch with reality, is usually required as a practical matter[69] and sometimes it is required by statute.

There are a number of officially or quasi-officially recognised mental disorders about which we have gathered neuroscientific information. Some of them, such as schizophrenia or manic-depressive ('bipolar') disorder can be the basis for an insanity defence. If traumatic brain injury or brain disease causes an organic mental disorder, such as delirium or any other recognised mental abnormality, then it may uncontroversially be used to satisfy the mental disorder component of the insanity defence. Finally, a defendant who suffers from intellectual disability (formerly developmental disorder or mental retardation) may raise the defence.

Other disorders, such as addiction and psychopathy, are generally not considered sufficient or are specifically excluded as the basis for legal insanity by statute or case law. Nevertheless, there are two narrow situations in which people who have used alcohol or other substances may raise an insanity defence. First, if as a result of chronic intoxication a defendant has become severely mentally disordered in addition to being addicted, then such an addicted defendant may raise the insanity defence. These are called 'settled insanity' cases. In these cases, however, it is a rationality or control deficit independent of the symptoms of addiction that provides the basis for the excuse. Second, if the use of a substance triggers an underlying psychotic condition (that is, the defendant substantially loses touch with reality), and the disorder is independent of and outlasts the episode of drug use, the law treats these cases, too, as 'settled insanity'. The criteria for legal insanity are independent of the requirement of *mens rea*. Severe mental disorder seldom prevents a defendant from forming the *mens rea* required by the definition of the crime. Rather, it tends to explain why the defendant in fact did form the *mens rea*. For example, a person who kills because he delusionally believes he must do so to save his own life kills intentionally. In this case, legal insanity may be found because the defendant lacked rational understanding of his situation.

As we have seen, there is considerable interpretive controversy about the meaning of either cognitive or control tests of legal insanity, and especially about control tests. Interpretive questions about the meaning of legal insanity might hinder the valid use of neuroscience to aid specific legal insanity decision making. Moreover, the capacities for rationality and self-control are continua, but the law adopts a binary rule for legal insanity: either the defendant is or is not legally insane. The language of the legal insanity tests does not identify with specificity the amount of capacity that must be lacking. The jury or judge therefore has considerable discretion.

---

[69] Steadman et al (n 24).

At present, there is no biological diagnostic technique, including neuroscientific tests, to identify whether a person suffers from a mental disorder, and, if so, which one. In short, there are as yet no reliable 'biomarkers' for any mental disorder, although identifying such biomarkers is a paramount goal of current mental health research. As noted above, neuroscience has identified various neural differences between those suffering from mental disorders and normal controls, but none of the differences is sufficiently large and reliable to be diagnostic in individual cases. Abnormalities in the same region may be associated with more than one disorder. Moreover, there is evidence that there may well be a bias in reporting positive results of such differences.[70] At present, the diagnosis of mental disorder or intellectual disability must be based entirely on evaluation of mental states and actions.

The current lack of valid biological criteria for mental disorders occurs in part because the definitional criteria for most mental disorders, which are all mental states and actions, have not been well validated That is, it is not clear that the categories used by mental health professionals accurately reflect how 'nature is carved at the joints'. If these categories are artificial, then it is not surprising that the neuroscience related to them will not be terribly precise. Moreover, as repeatedly noted, there is great heterogeneity of behaviour that fits each diagnostic category,[71] again making it difficult to identify precise biological indicators. As the refinement of the diagnostic categories and the underlying neuroscience become ever more sophisticated, we can be reasonably sure that more precise diagnostic tools will become available. For now, however, neuroscientific evidence has little diagnostic utility in individual cases beyond what traditional clinical interviews and psychological tests provide.

We can be more optimistic about cases involving brain injury and neurological diseases because there tend to be more valid diagnostic tools for these conditions. Epilepsy, for example, can be diagnosed definitively using electrophysiological measurements, and the exact brain location giving rise to the epileptic activity can frequently be identified with some precision. For other neurological diseases such as Alzheimer's, however, behavioural assessment in the clinic continues to be the most reliable basis for diagnosis. Brain scans may be obtained on such patients, but primarily with the goal of ruling out other potential causes such as tumours. Excellent biomarkers do in fact exist for Alzheimer's (the famous fibrillary 'plaques' and 'tangles'), but at present these biomarkers can only be detected by microscopic examination of post mortem tissue, which is of little use to the law. Moreover, people with advanced Alzheimer's disease seldom commit serious crimes.

Tumours or focal brain injury are far more approachable with neuroscientific data. Anatomical brain scans can now identify tumours and injurious conditions such as stroke with great precision, and such data can be extremely useful in

---

[70] JPA Ioannidis, 'Excess Significance Bias in the Literature of Brain Volume Abnormalities' (2011) 68 *Archives of General Psychiatry* 773.
[71] American Psychiatric Association (n 26).

judging specific insanity defences. On post mortem examination, for example, it was found that Charles Whitman, the notorious mass murderer on the University of Texas campus in 1966, had a brain tumour that may have impinged on the amygdala, a structure that is involved in the regulation of emotion. Had Whitman survived the episode and been brought to trial today, structural imaging data not available then, together with his remarkable diaries, could certainly have been relevant to an insanity plea because it might have supported a claim that he lacked substantial rational or self-control capacity.

Perversely, our techniques for detecting abnormal structural conditions such as small tumours and strokes are now so good that a qualitatively different problem can arise: is the detected abnormality actually related to the criminal behaviour at issue? It is well recognised that many 'normal' people (judged by their behaviour) have abnormal growths in their brains, many of which are not considered dangerous or relevant to everyday life. In fact, a difficult problem for the growing field of neuroethics is whether otherwise healthy research subjects should be notified of small, abnormal brain conditions detected in scans conducted for research purposes completely unrelated to the health of the subject. The risk of a surgery to 'correct' such a condition can be far greater than the risk of simply living with it. Increasingly, therefore, courts will have to judge whether an abnormality detected on a structural scan and presented as evidence is actually relevant to the criminal behaviour at issue. Much will depend on how precisely the abnormality has been linked to legally relevant behavioural abnormalities.

More diffuse brain injuries such as those created by concussion or by transient loss of oxygen to the brain (anoxia) are much more difficult to assess, because even our most sophisticated imaging techniques do not have cellular-level resolution. Imagine a condition that leads to the loss of 5 per cent of all nerve cells in the brain, but the missing cells, rather than being clumped together focally, are randomly distributed throughout the brain. Such a condition might well lead to serious behavioural problems, but would be undetectable by modern imaging techniques. Currently, neuroscience can add little to behavioural criteria for diagnosing such conditions. Note, finally, how few insanity defence cases involve brain injuries of the type described. Most involve classic cases of delusions, hallucinations and the like that must be assessed purely behaviourally.

The more difficult question for neuroscience is whether it can provide directly probative evidence concerning the cognitive or control criteria of insanity defence tests. Even if a diagnosis is certain, the behaviour displayed by people with that diagnosis is extremely heterogeneous. Thus, the diagnosis alone will not reveal whether the further criteria are met. Of course, they are seldom met for people suffering from milder disorders and they are more often met with people suffering from more severe disorders, but even in the latter category, most people will not meet the criteria. Thus, evidence addressed specifically to cognitive and control problems as the law defines them will be necessary.

Neurotests cannot 'read' mental states, and there is as yet no neural marker for lack of self-control, although both of these areas are the subject of active experimental research. Thus, probative neuroevidence on these questions would have to be inferred from other neurodiagnostic findings with which the legal criteria might be associated. The most likely candidate is the congeries of abilities that neuropsychologists term 'executive function'. People with defects in executive control seem to have trouble inhibiting untoward impulses to action, but it is less clear that they are associated with defects of cognition, such as not knowing right from wrong or not knowing what one is doing. Further, such functions seem relatively reliably associated with that portion of the brain, the prefrontal cortex, which is evidently the brain substrate for much of our higher order, rational capacities. It is therefore conceivable that neurodata about structural or functional prefrontal cortex defects might become relevant to cognitive and control criteria. There is nonetheless room for caution. Impairments can produce completely opposite behaviour depending on the specific pathology involved. Further, the correlation is weak between performance on neuropsychological tests of executive function, which are the present 'gold standard', and real world behaviour.[72] The problem once again is how specific the information would be and to what degree it would permit inferences about the past, actual behaviour of individual defendants.

IX. The Neuroscientific Challenge to Legal Insanity and Criminal Responsibility

The criteria for ascribing criminal responsibility are mental states and actions. As long as the criminal law continues to ascribe responsibility and to apply punishments that are proportionate to desert, there will always be a role for legal insanity in a just moral order. We have always known that some people were crazy and that their craziness sometimes affected their practical reasoning when they committed crimes. Even the four American states that have abolished the insanity defence still permit defendants to introduce mental disorder evidence to negate *mens rea*. No amount of neuroscientific or any other type of scientific data could conceivably show that crazy behaviour does not exist. It would take a revolution in our moral concepts, not in our scientific understanding of mental disorder, to think that craziness should play no role in responsibility ascriptions. Thus, the new neuroscience poses no specific challenge to the insanity defence, although, as the next subsection will suggest, in the future it may support changes to the doctrine and more accurate adjudication.

Neuroscience allegedly poses wider challenges to the coherence and justifiability of the entire enterprise of criminal responsibility, however, namely the claims of neurodeterminism and the arguments that human beings are merely 'victims of

---

[72] RA Barkley and KR Murphy, 'Impairment in Occupational Functioning and Adult ADHD: The Predictive Utility of Executive Function (EF) Ratings versus EF Tests' (2010) 25 *Archives of Clinical Neuropsychology* 157.

neuronal circumstances' (VNCs). I have written extensively about both before,[73] so I shall be brief and conclusory. Interested readers can consult the previous publications to obtain the full arguments and evidence.

The assault on responsibility from neurodeterminism is the newest attempt to claim that hard deterministic incompatibilism is true. Neuroscience is the most recent science to allegedly fuel this claim, joining behavioural psychology, genetics, psychodynamic psychology, social structure, and a host of other sciences that were used to argue that the universe is deterministic (or something quite like it) and therefore no one can be really responsible for anything. Neuroscience does not prove the truth of determinism any more than any other science that has been used for this purpose. No science can prove the truth of determinism. It is simply a convenient working hypothesis that guides much scientific investigation. But if it is a metaphysical truth about how the world works, as many people believe, how can anyone be responsible? The short answer is that there is a group of metaphysical arguments known as compatibilism that assumes the truth of determinism but claims that robust responsibility is nonetheless possible. It is the position adopted by the vast majority of professional philosophers and it is consistent with the principles, doctrines and practices of criminal responsibility and with moral theories that we have good reason to endorse. In various forms, this answer to the hard determinist has been argued for about 400 years in the modern era. This issue simply cannot be resolved by science or philosophy, so the consistency of compatibilism with law, morality and the scientific world view provides ample reason to adopt it.

The VNC challenge is far more radical. It claims that we are not the type of creatures we think we are, namely, conscious agents who act for reasons and can be guided by reasons. This claim insists that our mental states do no causal work whatsoever above and beyond neural activity. Mental states are epiphenomenal according to this account and thus the standard picture, what philosophers of mind and action term the causal theory of action, is simply wrong. If this view is correct, compatibilism cannot save responsibility because compatibilism assumes agency based on mental causation, which is precisely what this view denies. Thus, responsibility principles and doctrines or any other action-guiding normative scheme rests on a mistake. Many proponents of this view believe that it entails adopting a consequential morality, but it entails nothing normative. Normativity is about reasons. If reasons play no role in our behaviour, then we have no reason to do anything, except, I suppose, to wait for determinism to happen.

As Jerry Fodor wisely counselled many years ago, however, do not worry. Everything is going to be alright.[74] Despite extravagant claims to the contrary, no neuroscientific or other scientific studies remotely prove that mental causation is false. The most seemingly probative experiments have proven either to contain

---

[73] See eg, SJ Morse, 'Lost in Translation? An Essay on Law and Neuroscience' in M Freeman (ed), *Law and Neuroscience* (Oxford, Oxford University Press, 2011).

[74] JA Fodor, *Psychosemantics: The Problem of Meaning in the Philosophy of Mind* (Cambridge, MA, MIT Press, 1987) xii.

artefacts or simply cannot be used to draw the inferences that VNC proponents adduce. At present, VNC is just a speculation that, in my view, echoing Fodor, is never going to be demonstrated convincingly simply because it is false.

X. The Potential Future Contributions of Neuroscience to Legal Insanity

Speculation about the future is simply that, speculation, but the following seems plausible. Neuroscience is likely to become a more important tool for adjudicating the mental disorder criterion and for understanding a defendant's mental capacities more generally. It is very unlikely to provide much help with the cognitive test that concerns mental content, but it may be more useful with control tests, which may not involve mental contents and are harder to assess behaviourally because doing so requires counterfactual analysis. Finally, it is possible that what we learn might support various reforms of the doctrine.

Although it would be possible to have a functional non-responsibility test based solely on the cognitive and control tests, for various reasons the mental disorder criterion will almost surely be retained. The most powerful argument for doing so is the claim that mental disorder provides an objective basis for believing that the cognitive and control tests are truly met. Whether or not this is true, mental disorder will remain. As noted, mental disorder must now be evaluated entirely behaviourally. There will be cases in which it is not clear how disordered the agent is. For example, there may be a question concerning whether the defendant was actually delusional or hallucinating at the time of the offence. At present, there is no external standard or test akin to a blood sample or a tissue sample to confirm whether the agent suffers from a particular mental disorder. We have only the behaviour itself to guide our conclusions. In the future, assuming that scans or other neurotests done weeks or months after the crime are diagnostic of the defendant's state at the time of the crime—a very large assumption—neuroscience may help to resolve such ambiguities.

This will be a hard task, however, as a result of what I term the 'clear-cut' problem. Cognitive and affective neuroscientists do not go on fishing expeditions. They have already identified a well-characterised behaviour or disorder that they wish to understand neurally. For example, if an investigator wishes to find a neural marker for delusional thinking, he must already have clearly identified by behavioural evaluation subjects who are delusional and comparison subjects who are clearly not. Even in such cases in which there is a clear behavioural cut between the two groups, there will tend to be overlap between the biomarker curves for each group. Neuroscience is not necessary in such cases because delusional subjects had already been clearly identified. It is the ambiguous cases that require more precise measures, but the biomarker is likely to be much less sensitive. Until the neuroimaging becomes vastly more precisely diagnostic, neuroscience will help least when it is needed most.

In the example of delusion, I am more optimistic than I am about biomarkers for the disorder categories. There is no doubt that some people are delusional or hallucinate, but whether, say, schizophrenia and major depression are accurate natural kinds is more open to question. Unless our current diagnostic categories are in fact ontologically valid, the potential to identify neural correlates of discrete signs and symptoms will be greater than the potential to identify the neural correlates of disorder categories.

Whether a cognitive test is met depends on the type of evaluation of other people's minds that we all do all the time and that makes successful social interaction possible. We simply need to determine what the defendant thought and believed at the time of the crime. Neuroscience is very unlikely to develop genuine, content-related biomarkers that will be fine-grained enough to answer questions about whether a defendant knew what he was doing or knew right from wrong. For example, even if a multivoxel pattern analysis can predict quite accurately whether a subject is adding or subtracting, it cannot identify which specific numbers are being added or subtracted. Understanding the defendant's general cognitive capacities might be indirectly relevant, but the same clear-cut problem arises. If the behaviour is clear enough, the neurodata is not needed; if the behaviour is not clear, neurodata will not help.

Neuroscience might conceivably help resolve questions about the need for an independent control test. That is, there may be cases in which the defendant appears relatively cognitively intact, but seems to have trouble controlling himself, which is not explained by cognitive deficiencies. Paedophiles who act on their desires, sufferers from impulse disorders and most addicts are familiar examples of such alleged cases. It is difficult to know how one would devise ecologically valid experiments testing control capacity that would be acceptable to an institutional review board and it seems that experimental work would be necessary. We cannot yet behaviourally identify clear cases of lack of control except in rare neurological conditions. Again, all we have is reverse inference speculation. For example, why does the paedophile keep assaulting children although he knows it is wrong, and doing so has caused him great legal, social and interpersonal costs. The thought is that it simply *must* be true that he cannot control himself even though he is firmly in touch with reality, knows and endorses the moral and legal rules, and dislikes himself for his conduct. But we do not know if this is true. And we cannot trust self-report, including allegations of strength of craving or desire.

Perhaps, however, future neuroscience might help to identify the brain mechanisms associated with folk psychological loss of control. If this were to occur, there would be strong moral reasons to adopt control tests for legal insanity, which are now properly disfavoured in Anglo-American law for the reasons given previously. This assumes again, however, that the problem arises independently of a cognitive problem. If the reason people seemingly cannot control themselves is a product of a cognitive defect, then no control test is necessary because cognitive defects are a well-accepted basis for claims of non-responsibility.

In conclusion, I am mildly optimistic about the ability of future neuroscience to help resolve certain adjudicative difficulties. In contrast, I suspect that it will not have much influence on insanity defence reform except, perhaps, to support the need for a control test as well as a cognitive test, but I am pessimistic about this possibility on conceptual and scientific grounds.

XI. Conclusion

There is a great deal of irrational neurolaw exuberance, fuelled by sufferers from Brain Overclaim Syndrome who have not had Cognitive Jurotherapy for it because they also have anosognosia and are in denial about their disorder. Neuroscience will not justifiably revolutionise legal insanity or criminal responsibility doctrines and practices in the short term and is unlikely to do so in the intermediate term. I hesitate to speculate about the long term because one should not underestimate scientific ingenuity, even when working on problems as hard as the brain–mind–action connection. It is possible that there will be large-scale changes based on confused thinking about the issues, but such changes will not be justifiable. As long as society takes people seriously as potential moral agents, some form of considering the influence of craziness on practical reasoning will be necessary for criminal justice to operate fairly. My cautious hope is that future neuroscience and other sciences might help make decisions about responsibility more accurate and fair by guiding the evaluation of empirical claims.

Bibliography

Literature

American Bar Association, *ABA Criminal Justice Mental Health Standards* (Washington DC, American Bar Association, 1984).

American Law Institute, *Model Penal Code and Commentaries* (Philadelphia, PA, The American Law Institute, 1985).

American Psychiatric Association, *American Psychiatric Association Statement on the Insanity Defense*, reprinted in (1983) 140 *American Journal of Psychiatry* 681.

American Psychiatric Association, *Diagnostic and Statistical Manual of Mental Disorders*, 5th edn (Arlington, VA, American Psychiatric Publishing, 2013).

Barkley, RA and Murphy, KR, 'Impairment in Occupational Functioning and Adult ADHD: The Predictive Utility of Executive Function (EF) Ratings versus EF Tests' (2010) 25 *Archives of Clinical Neuropsychology* 157.

Blumoff, TY, 'Rationality, Insanity, and the Insanity Defense: Reflections on the Limits of Reason' (2014) 39 *Law & Psychology Review* 161.

Callahan, LA and Silver, E, 'Revocation of Conditional Release: A Comparison of Individual and Program Characteristics across Four States' (1998) 21 *International Journal of Law and Psychiatry* 177.

Cleckley, H, *The Mask of Sanity*, 5th edn (Augusta, GA, ES Cleckley, 1988).

Denno, DW, 'Who Is Andrea Yates? A Short Story about Legal Insanity' (2003) 10 *Duke Journal of Gender Law and Policy* 1.

Douglas, KS, Vincent, GM and Edens, JF, 'Risk for Criminal Recidivism: The Role of Psychopathy' in CJ Patrick (ed), *Handbook of Psychopathy* (New York, Guilford Press, 2006).

Elkins, BE, 'Idaho's Repeal of the Insanity Defense: What Are We Trying to Prove?' (1994) 31 *Idaho Law Review* 151.

Fingarette, H, *The Meaning of Criminal Insanity* (Berkeley, CA, University of California Press, 1972).

Fingarette, H and Hasse, AF, *Mental Disabilities and Criminal Responsibility* (Berkeley, CA, University of California Press, 1979).

Fodor, JA, *Psychosemantics: The Problem of Meaning in the Philosophy of Mind* (Cambridge, MA, MIT Press, 1987).

Glannon, W, 'Moral Responsibility and the Psychopath' (2008) 1 *Neuroethics* 158.

Hare, RD, *The Hare Psychopathy Checklist-Revised*, 2nd edn (North Tonawanda, NY, Multi-Health Systems, 2003).

Hare, RM, *Without Conscience: The Disturbing World of the Psychopaths among Us* (New York, Pocket Books, 1999).

Holmes, OW Jr, *The Common Law* (Boston, MA, Little, Brown & Co, 1945).

Ioannidis, JPA, 'Excess Significance Bias in the Literature of Brain Volume Abnormalities' (2011) 68 *Archives of General Psychiatry* 773.

Kdish, SH, SJ Schulhofer CS Steiker and RE Barkow, *Criminal Law and Its Processes: Cases and Materials*, 9th edn (New York, Wolters Kluwer Law and Business, 2012).

Litton, PJ, 'Responsibility Status of the Psychopath: On Moral Reasoning and Rational Self-Governance' (2008) 39 *Rutgers Law Journal* 349.

Maeder, T, *Crime and Madness: The Origins and Evolution of the Insanity Defense* (New York, Harper & Row, 1985).

McGeer, V and Pettit, P, 'The Hard Problem of Responsibility' in D Shoemaker (ed), *Oxford Studies in Agency and Responsibility*, vol 3 (Oxford, Oxford University Press, 2015).

Moore, M, *Law and Psychiatry* (Cambridge, Cambridge University Press, 1984).

Moore, MS, *Act and Crime: The Philosophy of Action and its Implications for Criminal Law* (Oxford, Oxford University Press, 1993).

Moore, MS, 'The Neuroscience of Volitional Excuse' in D Patterson and M Pardo (eds), *Law and Neuroscience: State of the Art* (Oxford, Oxford University Press, forthcoming).

Moran, R, *Knowing Right from Wrong: The Insanity Defense of Daniel McNaughten* (New York, Macmillan, 1981).

Morse, SJ, 'Addiction, Science and Criminal Responsibility' in N Farahany (ed), *The Impact of Behavioral Sciences on Criminal Law* (Oxford, Oxford University Press, 2009).

Morse, SJ, 'Against Control Tests' in PH Robinson et al (eds), *Criminal Law Conversations* (Oxford, Oxford University Press, 2009).

Morse, SJ, 'Diminished Rationality, Diminished Responsibility' (2003) 1 *Ohio State Journal of Criminal Law* 289.

Morse, SJ, 'Lost in Translation? An Essay on Law and Neuroscience' in M Freeman (ed), *Law and Neuroscience* (Oxford, Oxford University Press, 2011).

Morse, SJ, 'Mental Disorder and Criminal Law' (2011) 101 *Journal of Criminal Law & Criminology* 885.

Morse, SJ, 'Psychopathy and Criminal Responsibility' (2008) 3 *Neuroethics* 205.

Morse, SJ, 'Uncontrollable Urges and Irrational People' (2002) 88 *Virginia Law Review* 1025.

Morse, SJ, 'Undiminished Confusion in Diminished Capacity' (1984) 75 *Journal of Criminal Law & Criminology* 1.

Mossman, D, '*United States v Lyons*: Toward a New Conception of Legal Insanity' (1988) 16 *Bulletin of the American Academy of Psychiatry and the Law* 49.

National Mental Health Association, *Myths and Realities: A Report of the National Commission on the Insanity Defense* (Arlington, VA, The Association, 1983).

Parker, GF, 'Outcomes of Assertive Community Treatment in an NGRI Conditional Release Program' (2004) 32 *The Journal of the American Academy of Psychiatry and the Law* 291.

Pasewark, RA, 'Insanity Pleas: A Review of the Research Literature' (1981) 9 *Journal of Psychiatry & Law* 357, 361.

Perlin, ML, '"The Borderline Which Separated You from Me": The Insanity Defense, the Authoritarian Spirit, the Fear of Faking, and the Culture of Punishment' (1997) 82 *Iowa Law Review* 1375, 1409.

Pillsbury, SH, 'The Meaning of Deserved Punishment: An Essay on Choice, Character, and Responsibility' (1992) 67 *Indiana Law Journal* 719.

Spodak, MK, Silver, SB and Wright, CU, 'Criminality of Discharged Insanity Acquittees: Fifteen Year Experience in Maryland Reviewed' (1984) 12 *Bulletin of the American Academy of Psychiatry and Law* 373.

Steadman, HJ, Keitner, L, Braff, J and Arvanites, TM, 'Factors Associated With a Successful Insanity Plea' (1983) 140 *American Journal of Psychiatry* 401.

Steadman, HJ, McGreevy, MA, Morrissey, JP, Callahan, LA, Robbins, PC and Cirincione, C, *Before and after Hinckley: Evaluating Insanity Defense Reform* (New York, The Guilford Press, 1993).

Stephen, JF, *History of The Criminal Law of England*, vol II (Chesterland, OH, General Bookbinding Co, 1883).

Walker, N, *Crime and Insanity in England*, vol 1(Edinburgh, Edinburgh University Press, 1968).

Widiger, TA, 'Psychopathy and DSM-IV Psychopathology' in CJ Patrick (ed), *Handbook of Psychopathy* (New York, Guilford Press, 2006).

Wiederanders, MR, Bromley, DL and Choate, PA, 'Forensic Conditional Release Programs and Outcomes in Three States' (1997) 20 *International Journal of Law and Psychiatry* 249.

Cases

Atkins v Virginia 536 US 304 (2002).
Clark v Arizona 548 US 735 (2006).
Delling v Idaho 133 S.Ct. 504 (2012).
Drope v Missouri 420 US 162 (1975).
Durham v United States 214 F 2d 862 (DC Circuit 1954).
Ford v Wainwright 477 US 399 (1986).
Foucha v Louisiana 504 US 71 (1992).
Godinez v Moran 509 US 389 (1993).
Graham v Florida 130 S Ct 2011 (2010).
Hall v Florida 134 S Ct 1986 (2014).
In re Winship 377 US 358, 363-64 (1970).
Indiana v Edwards 534 US 164 (2008).
Jones v United States 463 US 354 (1983).
Kansas v Crane 534 US 407, 413 (2002).
M'Naghten's Case (1843) 8 ER 718.
Miller v Alabama 132 S Ct 2455 (2012).
Panetti v Quarterman 551 US 930 (2007).
Parsons v State 81 Alabama 854, 859 (1887).
People v Serravo 823 P 2d 828, 830 (Colo. 1992) (en banc).
Roper v Simmons 543 US 551 (2005).
State v Beam 710 P 2d 526, 531 (Idaho 1985).
State v Pike 49 New Hampshire 399 (1870).
State v Searcy 798 P 2d 914, 917 (Idaho 1990).
United States v Marble 940 F 2d 1543 (D.C. Cir. 1991).
US v Brawner 471 F 2 d 969 (DC Circuit 1972).

INDEX

Lightning Source UK Ltd.
Milton Keynes UK
UKHW021039101222
413585UK00020B/262